Re-Thinking Economics

Once again, unfettered capitalism has failed. Promises for global prosperity and peace have given way to a world of deep recession, social upheaval and political instability. Once again, mainstream economics has proved its inadequacy. Despite its technical rigour and mathematical virtuosity, it failed dramatically to respond to the current crisis. Why is this so? Mainstream economics turns a blind eye to society. By assumption, it maims its analyses by wiping away what makes us what we are. There is pressing need for a critical discussion and new ideas.

We therefore turn to the insightful and stimulating work of Pierre Bourdieu. Arguably one of the major sociologists, he was also a major 'economist'. Yet his works on the economy have received only scant attention, especially from economists, be they 'mainstream' or 'heterodox'. Bourdieu helps to take a broader view and enrich our scientific imagination. By including dimensions of power, intuitive behaviour and social structures within the scope of his analysis, he provides for an alternative foundation of economics, based on an integrated, interdisciplinary theory. For the first time, this volume fills this gap in economics by featuring state-of-the-art research and experts from different social science disciplines. This book constitutes a first step, and hopes to become a milestone.

The book offers an innovative outlook and a unique source for social scientists of all fields, particularly economists and sociologists, who wish to engage in the study of Bourdieu and his economics with a view to developing a more pertinent theory. It will also constitute a useful reference for university students and administrators who would like to explore the economy from a Bourdieusian perspective.

Asimina Christoforou is Adjunct Professor, the Athens University of Economics and Business, Greece.

Michael Lainé is a PhD student in Economics, Bordeaux 4 University, France.

Routledge Advances in Heterodox Economics

Edited by Wolfram Elsner
University of Bremen
and
Peter Kriesler
University of New South Wales

Over the past two decades, the intellectual agendas of heterodox economists have taken a decidedly pluralist turn. Leading thinkers have begun to move beyond the established paradigms of Austrian, feminist, Institutional-evolutionary, Marxian, Post Keynesian, radical, social and Sraffian economics – opening up new lines of analysis, criticism, and dialogue among dissenting schools of thought. This cross-fertilization of ideas is creating a new generation of scholarship in which novel combinations of heterodox ideas are being brought to bear on important contemporary and historical problems.

Routledge Advances in Heterodox Economics aims to promote this new scholarship by publishing innovative books in heterodox economic theory, policy, philosophy, intellectual history, institutional history and pedagogy. Syntheses or critical engagement of two or more heterodox traditions are especially encouraged.

1 **Ontology and Economics**
Tony Lawson and his critics
Edited by Edward Fullbrook

2 **Currencies, Capital Flows and Crises**
A post Keynesian analysis of exchange rate determination
John T. Harvey

3 **Radical Economics and Labor**
Frederic Lee and Jon Bekken

4 **A History of Heterodox Economics**
Challenging the mainstream in the twentieth century
Frederic Lee

5 **Heterodox Macroeconomics**
Edited by Jonathan P. Goldstein and Michael G. Hillard

6 **The Marginal Productivity Theory of Distribution**
A critical history
John Pullen

7 **Informal Work in Developed Nations**
Edited by Enrico A. Marcelli, Colin C. Williams and Pascale Jossart

8 **The Foundations of Non-Equilibrium Economics**
The principle of circular and cumulative causation
Edited by Sebastian Berger

9 **The Handbook of Pluralist Economics Education**
Edited by Jack Reardon

10 **The Coming of Age of Information Technologies and the Path of Transformational Growth**
A long run perspective on the 2000s recession
Davide Gualerzi

11 **Cultural Economics and Theory**
The evolutionary economics of David Hamilton.
William M. Dugger, William Waller, David Hamilton, and Glen Atkinson

12 **The Cultural and Political Economy of Recovery**
Social learning in a post-disaster environment
Emily Chamlee-Wright

13 **The Foundations of Institutional Economics**
K. William Kapp
Edited by Sebastian Berger Rolf Steppacher

14 **Alternative Theories of Competition**
Edited by Jamee K. Moudud, Cyrus Bina and Patrick L. Mason

15 **In Defense of Post-Keynesian and Heterodox Economics**
Responses to their critics
Edited by Frederic S. Lee and Marc Lavoie

16 **The US Economy and Neoliberalism**
Alternative strategies and policies
Edited by Nikolaos Karagiannis, Zagros Madjd-Sadjadi and Swapan Sen

17 **Technological Change and Network Effects in Growth Regimes**
Exploring the microfoundations of economic growth
Torsten Heinrich

18 **The Foundations of Evolutionary Institutional Economics**
Generic institutionalism
Manuel Wäckerle

19 **Re-Thinking Economics**
Exploring the work of Pierre Bourdieu
Edited by Asimina Christoforou and Michael Lainé

This series was previously published by The University of Michigan Press and the following books are available (please contact UMP for more information):

Economics in Real Time
A theoretical reconstruction
John McDermott

Liberating Economics
Feminist perspectives on families, work, and globalization
Drucilla K. Barker and Susan F. Feiner

Socialism After Hayek
Theodore A. Burczak

Future Directions for Heterodox Economics
Edited by John T. Harvey and Robert F. Garnett, Jr.

Are Worker Rights Human Rights?
Richard P. McIntyre

Re-Thinking Economics

Exploring the work of Pierre Bourdieu

Edited by Asimina Christoforou and Michael Lainé

Routledge
Taylor & Francis Group
LONDON AND NEW YORK

First published 2014
by Routledge
2 Park Square, Milton Park, Abingdon, Oxon OX14 4RN

and by Routledge
711 Third Avenue, New York, NY 10017

Routledge is an imprint of the Taylor & Francis Group, an informa business

British Library Cataloguing in Publication Data
A catalogue record for this book is available from the British Library

Library of Congress Cataloging in Publication Data
Re-thinking economics: exploring the work of Pierre Bourdieu / edited by Asimina Christoforou and Michael Lainé.
pages cm
1. Bourdieu, Pierre, 1930–2002. 2. Economics–Sociological aspects.
I. Christoforou, Asimina. II. Lainé, Michael
HM479.B68R39 2014
330–dc23 2013047285

ISBN: 978-0-415-85892-2 (hbk)
ISBN: 978-0-203-79713-6 (ebk)

Typeset in Times New Roman
by Wearset Ltd, Boldon, Tyne and Wear

Printed and bound in the United States of America by Publishers Graphics, LLC on sustainably sourced paper.

To a Friend
for sharing wisdom, love and courage
A. C.

Contents

Figures

Tables

Contributors

Robert Boyer, Institute of the Americas (Paris), France.

Asimina Christoforou, Athens University of Economics and Business, Greece.

Fabien Eloire, University of Lille 1 and Clersé-CNRS laboratory, France.

Eric Gilles, University of Poitiers, France.

Michael Grenfell, Trinity College, University of Dublin, Ireland.

Doris Hanappi, University of California Berkeley, US and Swiss National Centre of Competence in Research LIVES, University of Lausanne, Switzerland.

Michael Lainé, Bordeaux 4 University, France.

Frédéric Lebaron, University of Versailles-Saint-Quentin-en-Yvelines (UMR 8085 Professions-Institutions-Temporalités, UVSQ-CNRS), France.

Gabriella Paolucci, University of Florence, Italy.

Franck Poupeau, CNRS, France and the International Joint Unit iGLOBES, CNRS/University of Arizona, US.

Part I

Introduction

1 Re-thinking economics – why Pierre Bourdieu?

Asimina Christoforou and Michael Lainé

Pierre Bourdieu (1930–2002), a philosopher turned sociologist bred by the very French tradition of *Grandes Écoles*, among the likes of Jacques Derrida, Michel Foucault, Jean Baudrillard and many other influential thinkers of the twentieth century, was a leading voice of social justice and path-breaking scientific analyses. In his research, his ambition was to devise a general theory which would demolish disciplinary borders across the social sciences and would be applicable to virtually all societies. In a scientific world marked by isolationism, with scholars locked in higher and higher ivory towers of tinier and tinier subject matters, Bourdieu's work is, to our knowledge, the most recent attempt in the social sciences at offering a general, grand perspective on society, on the ways people think and behave. The breadth and scope of his knowledge enabled him to blend philosophy, sociology, anthropology, linguistics, history and economics into an integrated, consistent theory of human behaviour and social reality. For him, the study of the economy was not a secondary theme. And it was all the less so as he endorsed and generalised many key economic notions such as capital, interest and strategy, by changing their meaning, which raised some confusion and misunderstanding – the common lot of pioneering thinkers. The basic objective of this volume is to implement a cross-fertilisation between Bourdieu's theories and that of economics so as to enrich our scientific imagination and our ability to think about globalisation and the erratic changes of modern society.

Bourdieu matters for the study of the economy. His research not only appeals to sociologists, but is of particular interest to economists. Indeed, Bourdieu was not only one of the major figures of sociology, with theories plunging deep into philosophical waters, his student training; he also devised a comprehensive set of novel analytical tools, the potency of which has virtually escaped notice outside sociology, especially that of the economist. This book is the first to try to remedy this loophole. His specific writings on the economy have been the subject of many articles. However, no book has been entirely devoted to the topic so far. This is a real puzzle since Bourdieu's most stimulating and insightful analytical tools were marred by economics. Of course, disciplinary borders have been very resilient, as most economists seldom take time to look beyond their field. Few economic studies, be they heterodox or not, have ever engaged in a critical discussion of Bourdieu's work. This book should be read as a plea for a unified theory of economic practice across the social sciences, without endorsing a hierarchy or dissolution of the specificity of economic analysis. Of course, the economy is subject to peculiar laws and motives, irreducible to those of other activities. Nonetheless, our main contention is that these laws are not fully apprehended by the current state of economics. It needs to be re-considered within the context of sociological analyses, chiefly that of Bourdieu's. Furthermore, the existence of specific laws does not preclude the existence of general ones. Put differently, the specificity of some economic laws can be subject to a systematic, general analysis.

In fact, it is time we abandon the sterile demarcation of disciplinary borders. Economics has already begun to open up to other sciences, namely psychology (the so-called strands of 'behavioural' and 'experimental economics'), biology ('evolutionary economics') and neuroscience. These borders are bound to fade away, since all these disciplines share the same subject matter, that is, decision-making writ large, as every economic phenomenon implies a human decision. Sociology on the other hand is not entirely absent, as in the works of institutional economics and Marxism, for instance. But so far it has been discarded from the mainstream. Why should economists shy away from considering what others have to say about the economy? Deep-rooted misconceptions have prevented a real dialogue from being implemented. Since Vilfredo Pareto, most economists believe that economics has to deal with rational behaviour, whereas sociology ought to be concerned with rule-based behaviour. We believe this interpretation to be biased and misleading. First, it can be rational to follow rules. Furthermore, the canonical subjective expected utility models, the most popular in economics, never define – and this is their *raison d'être* – what is concealed behind the smokescreen of 'utility'. It can be virtually anything, including social rules.

Thus the Paretian boundaries end up very much blurred. Actually, we observe that economics has influenced sociology via rational action theory. To take an example, the analyses of the economist Gary Becker and the sociologist James Coleman are broadly aligned. Yet sociological theory has rarely influenced economics and never really inspired Becker. We argue that there is no point in restricting ourselves to the principle of rational choice, since many economic phenomena obviously are not rational in the strict sense of a means–ends and cost–benefit analysis, yet they have a rationale, a reason or cause, which requires systematic analysis. Alternative interpretations of economic behaviour can be sought in the social sciences: so long as they share the same subject matter, the economy, they should unite. Moreover, they can provide for a more encompassing and stimulating explanation of individual action. But why are we so reluctant to go outside economics? As John Kenneth Galbraith noticed decades ago, such reluctance stems from a 'theological' viewpoint, derived from a normative belief, located beyond doubt, like faith, in the best of all worlds, one that consists of more or less rational people in more or less free, self-regulated markets. Since mainstream economics provides a theoretical framework that describes such a world, there is no need for alternative explanations. In our view, what is more interesting is to have a more complete and realistic account of the reasons and causes of economic behaviour, and mainstream economics usually fails to do so.

Of course, one might argue that our plea for re-thinking economics toward a unified theory must take account of the epistemological and methodological differences with sociology, and the possible inconsistencies that could emerge. Bourdieu was very much aware of these issues and his theoretical framework proves to be most appropriate in resolving them. He tried to overcome the traditional dichotomies that separate these areas of research, such as individual and structure, by developing an 'applied rationalism', a mid-way between rationalism and realism. In this manner, according to Bourdieu, we manage to avoid the pitfalls of adhering to either one of the two extremes. Rather than seeing them as opposing positions, we see them as complementary and unravel their 'hidden solidarity' to draw together theory and experiment. More importantly, as we discuss in detail below (see points 1 and 2 below), by overcoming the traditional opposition between rationalism and realism, Bourdieu devised a theoretical framework that is compatible with these philosophical tenets and the ways they are applied in economics, across its diverse strands: falsifiability à la Popper and positivism à la Friedman, which pertain to rationalism, and realism. By using this framework, economists are able to build stronger theories, which lead to testable predictions, can be falsified *and* are grounded on empirical studies. Hence they can produce theories that accommodate the progress made in economics and take it further by incorporating the social dimensions of economic behaviour, such as the interplay between agency and structure or the evolution of power relations (see points 3 and 6).

This book gathers the contributions of sociologists and economists alike, who try to use novel analytical tools in order to better account for economic phenomena. But why appeal to Bourdieu? How useful are his theories? Can his analytical tools be applied to economic analysis? It is up to the reader to judge, but we give at least seven reasons why Bourdieu should matter, to be expounded hereafter.

1. Any kind of social science faces a fundamental dilemma, owing to the fact that individuals bestow meaning on their actions and yet they do not necessarily realise the true reasons underlying their choices. Roughly speaking, two sorts of answers have been given to this dilemma. Scientists either *tend* to take at face value what people think and say of themselves, and thus society is comprised of the numerous interactions between them. Pragmatic sociology and ethnomethodology can be said to fall into this category. Or they *tend* to elaborate mathematical models and see whether they can predict behaviour: if anything, it would mean that people decided *as if* they used such models, without consciously endorsing them, as is the case in mainstream economics. What both answers have in common is that they do not delve into the determinants of decisions: the former adheres to what individuals consciously know and master, the latter does not want to probe (and indeed, this contributes to its appeal, since it can apparently accommodate the heterogeneity of human motives through the catch-all notion of 'utility'). In both cases, the human mind remains a black box.

Exploring the work of Bourdieu enables us to open such a box, and that's why his theories are so valuable. In fact, his whole theoretical enterprise stemmed from the will to avoid the illusions produced by these two approaches: the first reflects a kind of 'illusion of immediate knowledge', and the second is dubbed 'scholastic illusion'. A genuinely sound science should be built on an 'epistemological break' with what people spontaneously think of themselves, what seems 'natural', 'evident', or what is taken for granted. At the same time, it cannot turn a blind eye to their reflections and claims, *as if* they did not matter. This is *the* seminal tension that runs through Bourdieu's work. One cannot help but take heed of what people think, for it exerts some influence on their final decision, but one should also go beyond that in order to grasp the source of their motives and expectations. Each practice has a 'double truth' that is located both 'inside' and 'outside' of what individuals consciously expect. As we shall see, this 'double truth' provides a more accurate answer to the ongoing agency–structure debate.

2. First of all, Bourdieu purports that the 'laws' by which society works are to be concurrently uncovered and elaborated by the sociological discourse. He makes clear though that these sociological laws are of a statistical nature. People have more or less chances than others to think or behave in a certain way for a specific matter. But they are not irremediably compelled to do so. In a given social group or class, not every individual acts like others or thinks s/he should do so. Rather, a proportion of this group decides significantly differently from the average of the group as well as from the general population. That's all, but that is more than nothing. Incidentally, it implies that individuals can be said to be all alike and all different at the same time, for this is what statistics is about.

Second, there exists what Bourdieu called, following Popper, indeterminism. Causality is not a question of succession of events, that is, each event, the cause, being inevitably followed by another one, the effect. Causality is seen as success of events: sometimes the cause succeeds in being followed by the effect, sometimes it fails. Such a causality principle is of a probabilistic nature. Sociological laws make the effects more or less probable for certain groups of individuals than for the average population. Furthermore, even if some people decided to act in a specific way, there is no assurance that they will continue, since the cause can 'fail' (so to speak). This proposition has tremendous consequences. It means, for instance, that people are able to hold opposing views without being inconsistent, for this is what probability is about (a belief p that an event will occur implies a belief 1-p that it will not happen). We should also bear in mind a vital distinction: probability is so to speak mathematical as to society or social groups and metaphorical as to individuals.

Third, as a scientist very well versed in philosophy, Bourdieu endorsed Wittgenstein's criticism of the very notion of rule. According to the latter, a rule cannot be as precise as to provide an answer to each and every circumstance one can face. For all imaginable situations are virtually infinite: if a rule were to prescribe very precisely what to do, it would be tantamount to a network of infinite railways upon which our expectations would roll. But no one, of course, can ever install such railways since our time is finite and our abilities limited. Hence, a rule necessarily comprises vague and incomplete components. So, even when they obey sociological laws, individuals have a more or less significant margin of freedom. They improvise. Each time Bourdieu speaks of strategies, a key element of his theory, he accounts for the fact that there is an adjustment to specific laws, unnoticed by consciousness, as well as an improvisation, rendering the decision-maker's action non-mechanical, thus predictable *and* unpredictable at the same time.

3. This is a major departure from mainstream economics as well as rational action theories that are rife in other social sciences. Paradoxically enough, the proponents of such theories extol the virtues of individual freedom, as if they managed to account for every decision by reasons, thus viewed as uncaused causes. Bourdieu kept on scoffing at the actual determinism of these theoretical attempts: when individuals are said to maximise utility, they have *no choice* but to retain the option offering the highest payoff in terms of utility multiplied by probability! Even in behavioural economics, there is no room for genuine 'choice', since individuals are still modelled as maximising a mathematical function that distorts money or utility (called 'decision-values') and probability (called 'decision-weights'). Agency also seems to be desperately absent. In Bourdieu's theory, there is no maximisation; there is indeterminism and improvisation. Therefore, human agency has some role to play and, in spite of stringent sociological laws, there is leeway. Accordingly, Bourdieu also took distance from 'Marxism', which deterministically accounted for every phenomenon by the underlying economic infrastructure, expectations and thoughts thus being the mere reflection of class interests. Albeit Marx was indisputably one of his main sources of influence, he did not adhere to a Marxist theory.

4. Bourdieu was all the less a Marxist as he focused on the symbolic dimensions of economic activities. Such dimensions were never reduced to economic laws. They have a rationale of their own, even though they could be partly influenced by the economy. By extending the notion of capital to other non-economic domains such as culture, symbols and networks, he provided tools for grasping a more comprehensive picture of the heterogeneous motives and reasoning behind individual behaviour. Even in the economy, people do not always try to maximise economic capital (i.e. money). Their goals could be broader and include the accumulation of other types of capital, namely symbolic, cultural and social. Furthermore, their reasoning also depends on their social position guaranteed by the possession of all sorts of capital. It opens many avenues for further research. Forms of cultural and social capital are easier to assess by appealing to the educational qualifications and the nexus of social networks inherited by the family and the school and obtained through the individual's social trajectory. As to symbolic capital, or the capital that offers recognition and legitimacy to other types of capital and takes on the form of honour and status, it appears more elusive, in that it seems less susceptible to numerical measure, but nonetheless it is of paramount importance.

5. Possession (of capital) makes (social) position. And position entails (specific) reflection. By explaining expectations and decisions in relation to social

positions adequately defined, Bourdieu provides an alternative theory that departs from mainstream and rational action theories in three fundamental ways: it makes us look behind the smokescreen of 'utility' (the basis of preferences); it goes beyond probability in beliefs; and finally, it drops mathematical understandings of 'maximisation' in decision-making. It helps us look inside the black box of 'utility', which has been used by rational theorists to keep individual motives far from scientific scrutiny. *Noblesse oblige*: a specific social position implied by the possession of capital entices one to behave in a certain way or have certain expectations, even though probability calculus cannot be implemented by individuals. Instead, they rely on an analogical 'practical sense', aka 'habitus'. Moreover, Bourdieu's notion of habitus is predominantly qualitative, making it difficult to apply usual conceptions of maximisation. Yet at the same time we can say that *generally* it adapts rather well to the circumstances, or to the 'field', that is, to the objective social relations determined by the distribution of all kinds of capital and the social struggles between individuals.

6. There is a major blind spot in mainstream economics: power relations. Decisions and expectations are said to be the sole fruit of a pure reason, unsoiled by any social hierarchy. Or power is said to be encapsulated in the catch-all notion of 'utility'. Thus, we do not explain anything. We cover our ignorance with a word. No analysis of power is provided, and yet power prevails in everyday life. According to Bourdieu, power is a matter of inequality of capital. Behind each economic decision, technical and power issues can be very hard to disentangle. Power can give rise to symbolic violence, a vital concept that explains why people comply with hierarchy even though this might be against their interest, and why they do not dissent even though their objective situation of subordination and exploitation would seem to spur them to do so.

7. Notwithstanding the talk of bargaining 'power', in game theory the scientist focuses only on interactions. S/he assumes that players make a choice after carefully considering the choices of those with whom they interact while envisioning the problem from the same angle. There is no imagining the reactions of other people. This scope is too narrow, warns Bourdieu. According to him, individuals have more or less the whole structure of the field in mind while making decisions, and not only the persons with whom they interact. Undoubtedly, this view strongly challenges mainstream thinking, because, even outside game theory, explanations in, say, terms of 'networks' stick to the individuals we interact with. A field is more than a network, since it comprises *all* individuals engrossed in a specific activity, even though the decision-maker may *never* be in contact with them.

Finally, one possible cause for misunderstanding should be staved off. There is another seminal tension in Bourdieu's work, that with mainstream economics. Albeit he was very critical of rational choice theory, many of his analyses appear to have a flavour reminiscent of it. His methodology aspires to build scientific objects that do not necessarily exist in the everyday experience of individuals, to derive laws from them and then explain decisions and expectations with the clause 'everything happens *as if*' these individuals unconsciously followed such laws. Furthermore, individuals are said to 'maximise' symbolic capital. Besides, one critique (Caillé) castigated Bourdieu for confusing 'interest in' and 'interest to', which is alleged to be the main distinctive prejudice of both utilitarianism and mainstream approaches. When someone is interested in an activity, s/he does not necessarily act in an interested way. By disclosing the strategies behind apparently disinterested behaviour, Bourdieu is said to assume (some sort of) selfishness, like most mainstream models. Furthermore, because Bourdieu talks at length about capital, extending the notion to culture, symbols and networks, he is often accused of the kind of reductionism typical of mainstream economics. Finally, statistics and probability are widely used in his analyses.

Nonetheless, one should bear in mind that his theory and methodology rest on the 'double truth', which relies on field studies and realism and takes heed of individual *beliefs*, all features that many mainstream economists, proponents of Friedman (the famous 'as-if' methodology) and Popper (rejection of unfalsifiable theories), discard as irrelevant.[1] Moreover, the maximisation of symbolic capital has a metaphorical and not a numerical meaning, even when as scientists we apply Bourdieu's analytical tools to account for expectations and decisions. Also the alleged 'confusion' between the two meanings of the word 'interest' could produce a stimulating discussion that would help to dispel naïve oppositions between interestedness and disinterestedness. As regards capital, one should recall that Bourdieu had no essentialist definition of it: on the contrary, a given capital is always relational, that is, it depends on all other forms of capital and individual strategies at a given moment in time. Consequently, its very definition evolves through time, along with the struggles that take place in each and every field. And, finally, the widespread use of statistics and probability should appeal to economists and other social scientists, since it provides a sound basis for discussion and further research.

We do not encourage the uncritical application of Bourdieu's analytical tools, by treating them as petrified concepts or as dogmatic principles. We believe that future research should rejuvenate, supplement and deepen these concepts in order to incorporate and investigate current needs and contextual factors. Indeed, Bourdieu's respect to context across space and through time enabled him to formulate theories and methods that could be transferred to different places and historical eras, and, most importantly, that were open to new ideas. We respond to some of these innovations and develop them further in the chapters of the book.

The chapters featured in this volume undertake the task of exploring Bourdieu's analysis to form an alternative way of thinking in economics beyond the mainstream. Apart from the present introductory chapter (Part I), the book is divided into six parts. Part II asks '*Who is* Pierre Bourdieu?' and provides a *tour d'horizon* of Bourdieu's biography, writings on economics and key concepts, in order to enable the reader, particularly the less familiar economist, to delve into the specific topics of study discussed in subsequent chapters. In Part III, Bourdieu's concepts and ideas are analysed in relation to economic theories, including neoclassicism, neo-institutionalism, Keynesianism and Marxism. The objective is to trace the roots and fruits of Bourdieu's economic analysis and redefine our understanding of the economy, especially in light of the current global crisis.

Part IV develops on Bourdieu's conceptual tools, including the various types of economic, social, cultural and symbolic capital he introduces in his analysis. Two chapters re-open the issue of capital conversions and the social embeddedness of the economy, while the other two focus on Bourdieu's notion of social capital that has been largely misunderstood by economists and social scientists, and emphasises the role of social networks and power relations. In Part V, the objective is to stress the fact that Bourdieu's economic analysis is not a mere intellectual exercise, but can be crucial for applied economics and particularly for evaluating policy proposals in terms of normative considerations of fairness and security. Part VI contains an article written by Bourdieu that has never been translated and released in English before. We are proud to be able to offer the reader such a direct acquaintance with one of his major papers. In this article, the reader can discover a synthesis of his main economic topics, from his rejection of rational action theory to his specific conception of class and the agency–structure debate, cultural practices and education strategies. Finally, the conclusions of Part VII summarise the key points made in the volume and pose questions for further research with regard to Bourdieu's alternative approach.

In response to '*Who is* Pierre Bourdieu?', Gabriella Paolucci (Chapter 2) undertakes the rather challenging task of giving a short description of Bourdieu's biography and key concepts. In the first section, she delves into the life of Bourdieu: his early years in a remote agrarian region in France, his military service in Algeria during the war, his exchange with prominent academic institutions and writers of his time in Paris, and his active participation in national and international politics later in his life. His life-course is marred by the controversies and transformations which took place in the second half of the twentieth century and upon which he reflects throughout his work. As discussed in the second section of the chapter, Bourdieu's objective was to unify the social sciences under 'a general economy of social practices' and unravel the relational aspects of the economy and society. This led to the introduction of some of Bourdieu's main, and most controversial, concepts: the various forms of capital – economic, cultural, social and symbolic – and the novel notions of habitus, field and symbolic violence. The author describes these concepts in a brief and comprehensive way as a *lexicon* for the reader.

In the next chapter, Frédéric Lebaron (Chapter 3) studies Bourdieu's landmark contributions in relation to economics and the economy. The author begins by presenting the genesis of Bourdieu's sociology and its main concepts and how these contributed to the empirical knowledge of the economic field. Bourdieu draws from his experience and research in diverse societies and various areas of social exchange. His use of 'economic' concepts like 'capital', 'interest' and 'profit' aimed at unifying the conceptual apparatus of the social sciences without denying the specificity to any particular social universe, like the economy. According to Lebaron, this 'double constraint' led to a sense of the multiplicity of social spheres, beyond that of economic production, in which a diverse set of economic and non-economic assets can be defined and accumulated, thereby producing different sources of inequality. Bourdieu's theory of the economic field introduces a practical sense of economic behaviour that operates through the habitus and field, instead of the pure computations of an abstract mind, which classical rational action theory implies. Thus economic agents, as products of their social experiences, shape and are shaped, often in unconscious and embodied ways, by social structures and relations of concrete and symbolic domination.

In Part III, Frédéric Lebaron (Chapter 4) focuses on Bourdieu's conception of the economic field by presenting the 'symbolic foundations' of economic life that are incorporated in the notions of symbolic power and symbolic capital. As the author interestingly points out, Bourdieu continuously reflects upon and re-works these notions and applies them to divulge the power of symbolic domination, that is, the strength to impose meanings and make them appear legitimate by concealing the underlying power relations and the social inequalities they produce. This idea challenges conventional perceptions of the economy and rationality by bringing to the fore the issue of power and its symbolic effects in shaping economic practices, institutions and systems. Lebaron discusses the relevance of this perspective for the contemporary economic field, dominated by financial capitalism and the current global crisis. He focuses on the changes in institutional settings that emerge from economic struggles and their symbolic dimensions and determined relations in welfare-state capitalist economies. The novelty introduced here is the author's attempt to link this analysis to the neo-institutionalist tradition and enrich the ways this approach addresses the varieties of capitalism and the repercussions of neoliberal reforms in the context of the global crisis.

Then Gabriella Paolucci (Chapter 5) describes Bourdieu's theory on the relationship between the State and economics in modern capitalist societies. One of the most important contributions of Bourdieu's sociology is the analysis of the symbolic dimension of economic practices through a theory of 'symbolic capital', a form which all types of capital take when their possession is perceived as legitimate. Symbolic capital is closely related to the concept of 'symbolic violence': the violence exercised upon a social agent with his or her complicity. Here the State plays a leading role, since it appears to legitimately monopolise symbolic violence and act as the central bank of symbolic capital. For the author, Bourdieu's criticism of neoclassical economics and neoliberal politics can be placed in this theoretical perspective. Bourdieu sees neoliberalism as a belief system that mystifies interests and power by making them articles of faith. Thus, economic discourse becomes a symbolic order, which presents itself as universal and neutral, but increasingly becomes a tool to exercise power and produce symbolic violence, legitimated and distributed by the State.

Michael Lainé (Chapter 6) engages in an absolutely novel theme when he explores the possible links between Bourdieu and Keynes, not on a historical basis, but on a theoretical one, in order to open avenues for further common research between sociologists and economists. The chapter hinges around four headings: (1) the little use of probability calculus; (2) the end of body/soul and rational/irrational dichotomies, both offering a theory of intuitive, inductive, emotional thinking; (3) the sensibleness (rather than rationality) of expectations; (4) the possible deepening of animal spirits by habitus. Both leading scholars recognise that individuals are sometimes 'rational' by using probability calculus so as to maximise under constraints. Nonetheless, they contend forcefully that, for the great bulk of their everyday actions, individuals rely on spontaneous urges, intuitions or embodied principles, namely 'animal spirits' for Keynes, 'habitus' for Bourdieu. For the author, habitus could be viewed as the sociological underpinnings of animal spirits, since they are well attuned to one another. Thus he concludes that Bourdieu's work could enrich economists' conceptual tools by: (1) accounting for a power dimension between individuals; (2) letting the entire field and its structural, general laws come into play, apart from interactions between individuals; and (3) making preferences endogenous.

A topic that has raised great controversy regards Bourdieu's adherence – or not – to Marxist theory. Eric Gilles (Chapter 7) attempts to address this theme by distancing himself from standard forms of analysis that rely on commentators' personal, biased visions of these two scholars. Instead he takes what he describes as a 'materialist' approach to provide a meticulous inventory of Bourdieu's citations and quotations of Marx in order to identify, list and eventually analyse these statements. Thus, he is able to evade the deep-rooted prejudices and impassioned tones that often emerge in this debate. Gilles generally observes that Bourdieu cites Marx most frequently and favourably across his works, and acknowledges that Bourdieu's theories revolve around social classes and domination also addressed by Marx. Nonetheless, he concludes that Bourdieu's relation with Marx remains one of affiliation *and* rupture, so much that Bourdieu could not be labelled a 'Marxist'. This becomes particularly evident in the final sections where the author analyses the content of the quotations cited and provides a detailed exposition of the most striking differences between the two scholars on key concepts such as the value of labour, the labour/labour-power distinction, the abolition of alienation, the theory of social classes and the agency–structure debate.

We close this part by featuring a translated and updated version of a French article written by Robert Boyer and translated by Michael Lainé for the purposes of the book (Chapter 8). Boyer provides a critical overview of Bourdieu's economic anthropology and its relationship to régulation theory, which stresses the potentiality of social change. He tries to resolve the controversy raised by those who purport that Bourdieu has sunk into the economism and neoclassicism à la Becker which he so fervently distances himself from, and that his concepts of habitus and field can only contribute to an understanding of social reproduction, not transformation. In this chapter, the author argues that, despite the recurrent use of economic terminology, Bourdieu does not reduce social practice to a pure economic rationale that excludes social transformation. Quite the contrary: by re-contextualising terms like profit and capital in the habitus-field framework,

Bourdieu offers us a taxonomy of the conditions of change and an alternative socio-economics of the contemporary world. Boyer applies this innovative framework to expand his diachronic article and provide important insights into the recent history of the dominance of financiers and the emergence of the global crisis.

Part IV of this book begins with a chapter written by Michael Grenfell (Chapter 9). His objective is to re-open the issue of 'capital' and the different roles it plays in financial markets at a stage of late capitalism called 'post-modern economies'. The author begins by contrasting Bourdieu with classical Marxist and economic theory to briefly examine the underlying philosophy and epistemology of capital with relation to class reproduction, economic processes and social evolution. He then follows Bourdieu to investigate the symbolic, moral and social aspects of capital in a situation of rapid economic transformation by conducting a field analysis of financial sectors. His analysis shows how traditional structural relations with respect to time, honour and exchange values have been reconfigured and how forms of capital have now been (re-)converted in late-capitalist, post-modern economies, particularly in the wake of the global financial crisis: how debt became profit, how the future is now and now is the future, and how the virtual became real. By shedding light on the major actors and prevalent forms of rationality, such as rational action theory, this chapter articulates these inner tensions and contradictions and the ways they contributed to radical change and crisis.

Doris Hanappi (Chapter 10) wishes to take Bourdieu to envisioned futures by reconsidering 'embeddedness' from a Bourdieusian perspective. Social theorists and heterodox economists, who seek an alternative to rational choice theory, often draw on the embeddedness tradition whereby human agency is explained in terms of relational, institutional or cognitive forces. However, according to the author, standard applications to embed action in networks often consider the role of institutions and cognitions as secondary, or inscribe action into institutional settings and take social networks and cognitions for granted. To remedy the problems that emerge in these applications, the author turns to Bourdieu and his theory of field, which offers an alternative way to link human conduct and social structure by constructing a framework that accounts for the intertwinement of relations, institutions and cognitions, and how they may transform fields. Briefly, in this framework, individuals build images as a kind of representation of the other which allows them to locate themselves in the social structure and to identify other people's interests. These images are argued to be central in linking individual cognitions to social and institutional structures, and to help explain dynamics which make fields permissive to change.

The two final chapters of this part are dedicated to a now widely used, polysemous concept in the social sciences: social capital. Even though Bourdieu has dedicated relatively few pages to this form of capital, he considers it no less important. Fabien Eloire (Chapter 11) presents us with a rare, innovative outlook in the contemporary literature by returning to the original definition of social capital that was proposed in Bourdieu's 1980 article 'Notes Provisoires'. Here social capital is linked to a durable network, which gives its members access to capital resources and profits that are not their own, but are indirectly available through mutual friendship ties. Bourdieu goes beyond conventional *interactionist* conceptualisations à la Burt and Coleman by engaging in the analysis of the social field in conjunction with the ways agents benefit from their social connections. Thus, social capital is never independent of other forms of economic and cultural capital, since interactions actually emanate from objective structures, but also indirectly multiply the profitability of other forms of capital. Eloire empirically tests this definition by using data from the field and network of a group of restaurant owners in the metropolitan area of Lille, France. He observes that owners with equivalent cultural or economic capital, but higher social capital will also have higher symbolic capital: their establishments enjoy higher recognition and status in the market, and thus produce a 'symbolic profit' as 'gastronomic restaurants' with an accredited culinary style, which is different from monetary profits.

In the next chapter, Asimina Christoforou (Chapter 12) explains why Bourdieu's unique conception of social capital was finally discarded from the contemporary literature. As some critics purport, the dominance of rational choice that was explicated by Coleman, Putnam and Becker, and led by international organisations such as the World Bank, produced theories and methods that reduced social networks to a product of economic calculation and failed to incorporate their role in the reproduction of power relations, hierarchical structures and social inequalities. However, proponents and critics alike have given little attention to the transformative dimensions of Bourdieu's notion of capital. The author tries to remedy this loophole by reconstructing from a Bourdieusian perspective the basis for an alternative theoretical framework that would account for social capital as a source for social transformation. This would promote the study of social capital by incorporating the role of contextual factors, which are determined by the structure of the diverse forms of capital, and influence group formation, social struggles and change.

We come to Part V, which is dedicated to Bourdieu's politics and policies: what actions and measures must be taken to transform the world. Franck Poupeau examines this topic by suggesting ways to assess and build a sociology of domination from a Bourdieusian perspective (Chapter 13). The author asks why protest movements and social criticism against neoliberalism, such as the recent Indignados and Occupy movements in the wake of the financial crisis, have not been able to persuade governments and leaders for change in economic policies and institutions. He argues that left criticism restricts itself to condemning the misdeeds of capitalism and believing that this suffices to pursue a different world, when this only prevents us from unveiling and overcoming the sources of domination. He employs Bourdieu's concepts of habitus and symbolic violence to uncover how the dominated classes contribute to their own domination and the perpetuation of the arbitrary nature of the established order. He then stresses Bourdieu's notion of the 'collective intellectual': a group of scholars who use their knowledge to help develop more realistic and effective forms of social mobilisation and emancipation of these classes, rather than leaving them to their own devices or studying them as an intellectual curiosity.

The final part of the book, Part VI, features a most thought-provoking article written by Bourdieu and published in the mid-1970s. In this chapter (Chapter 14), we host a rare English translation, undertaken by Michael Grenfell for the purposes of the book. In this article, apart from Bourdieu's distinctive prose, the reader will virtually find a comprehensive overview of his basic ideas on: what science is; what is the nature of things and how they relate to one another; how statistical method can or cannot lead to sound theory; political beliefs; the formation of expectations; how and why social classes view one another; what their cultural and educational practices are; their specific relation to time; and why rational calculation that so prominently figures in economics cannot provide a complete and realistic account of human action. These ideas unfold as Bourdieu begins to develop his theory of social classes in the context of a theory of fields. Here the practices of a social class and its ability to forestall the future and calculate its chances for profit in terms of all types of capital are affected by social conditions. In particular, they depend on the distribution of the various forms of capital between agents and classes, as well as the reproduction strategies they implement, beyond economic ones, such as matrimonial, childbirth, educative and successor strategies. Bourdieu illustrates his point by focusing on how agents invest in education, and how their decisions are insufficiently explained by typical Beckerian-style theories of human capital accumulation and social mobility.

We close the volume with some concluding remarks in Chapter 15. We highlight the major points discussed in the book and develop some topics for further research, particularly in the empirical study of the economy from a Bourdieusian perspective. With this book, we hope to incentivise economists to re-think their theories and methods through the lens of Bourdieu's analytical framework, in order to confront mainstream approaches and provide a more realistic view of the economic world in which agents are treated as social and historical, as human, beings.

Note

1 For a complete exposition, please read Bourdieu's epistemological treaty – see the general bibliography at the end of the book.

Part II

Who is Pierre Bourdieu?

2 Biography – key concepts

Gabriella Paolucci[1]

The life of Pierre Bourdieu

The biographical illusion

Common sense, as well as "the typical illusion of the *lector*" (Bourdieu 1997a trans. Nice 2000: 2), treats the author's biography as a coherent whole, a continuous path, a meaningful unidirectional trajectory, as if it was "a sequence of successive states which are turned into steps of a necessary development" (1986b trans. Winkin and Leeds-Hurwitz 1987: 1). Bourdieu identifies this process as "the artificial creation of meaning" (ibid.). As Bourdieu argues in his essay, by paying homage to such "biographical illusion" one loses sight of the fact that a life presented in the form of a history is at once an artificial *post-hoc* and *ad-hoc* event, a logical exposition of chronologically ordered events in a manner meant to make sense both for the subject and for the object of the biography.

Against the narcissistic complacency and hence the biases and deceptions entailed by such "illusion", Bourdieu pinpoints that individual life is only understandable by reconstructing the network of relationships which characterised the field "with which and against which one has been formed" (2004 trans. Nice 2008: 4). Thus, within the short space of this chapter, Bourdieu's life shall not be treated as "the unitary expression of a subjective and objective 'intention' of a project" (Bourdieu 1986b trans. Winkin and Leeds-Hurwitz 1987: 1); its trajectory shall be placed within "the space of possibles" with and against which the philosopher's formation can be set. Only in this way can we understand his theoretical positions and access to the reasons for his numerous and radical breaks with the intellectual climate of the time, in particular with "the scholastic enclosure which … takes one of its most exemplary forms in the closed, separate world, set apart from the vicissitudes of the real world" (Bourdieu 2004 trans. Nice 2008: 8–9).

The French intellectual field

At the time, the French intellectual scene was dominated by the existentialist strand of phenomenology. In Bourdieu's opinion, however, Sartre embodied every negative aspect of the scholastic universe: "I can say that I constructed myself, as I left the scholastic universe, and in order to leave it, against everything that the Sartrian enterprise represented for me" (Bourdieu 2004 trans. Nice 2008: 23). He read Heidegger, Husserl and Merleau-Ponty:

> who was something special … he was interested in the human science and in biology and he gave you the idea of what thinking about immediate present day concerns can be like when it does not fall into the sectarian of over-simplifications of political discussion.
>
> (Ibid.: 5)

He also studied Marx's early writings.

Among pivotal figures in his formation were Henri Gouhier, with whom he wrote a *mémoire* (i.e. a Master's degree dissertation) about Leibniz, Martial Guéroult, Eric Weil, Alexandre Koyré, Jules Vuillemin and, most importantly, Gaston Bachelard and Georges Canguilhem. About them, he notes that:

> it is pretty much thanks to them and to what they represented – a tradition of the history of the sciences and of rigorous philosophy … that I tried, together with those people who, like me, were a little tired of existentialism, to go beyond merely reading the classical authors and to give some meaning to philosophy.
>
> (Ibid.: 4)

When Lévi-Strauss entered the scene and revolutionised the fields of both philosophy and social sciences, like many other thinkers of his generation, Bourdieu was aware that structuralism was an attractive pole difficult to resist; however, his relationship with Lévi-Strauss was rather one of contradiction.

Cleft habitus

When he died of cancer in 2002, Bourdieu held the Chair in Sociology at the *Collège de France*, the country's most prestigious academic institution. Whilst most of his colleagues came from Parisian bourgeois families belonging to the intellectual elite, his origins were much more modest. The family into which he was born on August 10, 1930 in Denguin – a small village in the heart of the geographically and culturally remote Béarn region (South-west France) – was an impoverished bourgeois family, where "every purchase … was a major discussion, discussed for days on end" (Bourdieu 2004 trans. Nice 2008: 85). Both his parents swam against the tide. His father – the son of a peasant share-cropper – worked as a postman before becoming a postal clerk: "voted far on the left … in that fairly conservative rural world" and taught his son "very simply, by his whole attitude, to respect 'humble folks', among whom he counted himself" (ibid.). Conversely, Bourdieu's mother "came from a 'great family' of peasants and had to defy her parents to make a marriage that was seen as far beneath her" (ibid.: 86). He thus recalls his native village childhood in his intellectual autobiography: "I think that my childhood experience as a 'renegade' who was the son of a renegade no doubt weighed heavily in the formation of my disposition towards the social world" (ibid.: 84–85). Throughout his whole life, Bourdieu was marred by this early ambivalence.

The way in which Bourdieu built his inaugural lecture at *Collège de France* – "to take as the object of my lecture the idea of delivering an inaugural lecture, of performing a rite of institution, thus setting up a distance from the role in the very exercise of the role" (Bourdieu 1982b trans. Adamson 1990: 109) – was exemplary of the ambivalence which characterised his position in relation to the intellectual world.

> Preparing my inaugural lecture brought home to me all my contradictions, in a concentrated form: the sense of being perfectly unworthy, of having nothing to say that was worth saying before such a court, probably the only one whose verdict I recognised.... Finally, I thought I saw a way out of the contradiction into which I was thrown by the very fact of a social consecration which assaulted my self-image...
>
> (Bourdieu 2004 trans. Nice 2008: 107–109)

Bourdieu had been well aware of his ambivalence towards the intellectual elite since the early 1940s, when he left home and started boarding school in the nearby city of Pau. He identified in these first institutional experiences the root of his own "cleft habitus", which was inhabited by tensions and contradictions:

> I understood recently that my very deep ambivalence towards the scholastic world was perhaps rooted in the discovery ... the contempt of the day pupils for the culture of the boarding school and of the boys from the small rural communes.... This dual experience could only compound the durable effect of a very strong discrepancy between high academic consecration and low social origin.
>
> (Ibid.: 99–100)

In 1951, Bourdieu was admitted to the *École Normale Supérieure* on Rue d'Ulm, where he studied for his *agrégation* in philosophy. He had Althusser as a "répétiteur" and Derrida as a student fellow. A prestigious institution which forged the academic and intellectual career of the French elite, for Bourdieu the ENS represented both a hard apprenticeship and an important step towards the academic and intellectual world. As a young provincial outsider, whose accent betrayed an "illegitimate" background, and as a result of direct contact with bourgeois culture and Paris intellectuals, Bourdieu soon developed the strong critical disposition towards closed, socially and culturally elitist educational milieu which would become a milestone of his intellectual position.

In Algeria

The call for military service in Algeria brusquely ended his teaching appointment in high school. For five years he lived in the French colony, where he fraternised with Jacques Derrida and Lucien Bianco, who were also serving in the French army. During the last months of his military service, he was appointed to the *Central Government Documentation and Information Unit*, which allowed him to become familiar with the Algerian society. He continued to work on his doctoral thesis on "The time structures of affective life" (which he never completed) whilst producing what he called "a little manual", which actually became a classic book (Bourdieu 1958 trans. Ross 1962). With this book, he wished:

> to tell the French, and especially people on the left, what was really going on in a country of which they often knew next to nothing – once again, in order to be of some use, and perhaps also to stave off the guilty conscience of the helpless witness of an abominable war.
>
> (Bourdieu 2004 trans. Nice 2008: 39–40)

During his stay in Algeria, Bourdieu experienced a "conversion of the gaze", which he has described at length in the many writings attesting his shifting outlook from philosopher to ethnologist and sociologist. He did not become immediately aware of such a shift and, whilst engaged in the first draft of *Sociologie de l'Algérie*, he still thought of himself as a philosopher:

> while telling myself that I was moving into ethnology and sociology, in the early stages, only provisionally, and that once I had finished this work of political pedagogy, I would return to philosophy ... I flung myself totally, oblivious to fatigue and danger, into an undertaking whose stake was not only intellectual.
>
> (Ibid.: 40)

In 1958, in order to pursue his research interests, he accepted an assistant's post in the *Arts Faculty* of Algiers, where he lectured on Durkheim and Saussure. He produced several major surveys, three books and many articles on the social structure and rituals of the Kabylia and highlighted the brutal impact of colonisation and war on the social fabric.

In most of Bourdieu's Algerian writings, political and scientific arguments appear to be inseparable, as one can gather by his many contemporary essays. Bourdieu constantly refers to the Algerian experience, which played a crucial role in the development of his scientific project. The findings of his Algerian fieldwork are published in two post-independence books (Bourdieu *et al.* 1963; Bourdieu and Sayad 1964). *Esquisse d'une théorie de la pratique* (Bourdieu 1972b trans. Nice 1977) is one of the first theoretical systematisations of the results of the ethnological research conducted in Algeria. In this book, he elaborated his conceptual apparatus, which enabled him to formulate the theory of practice as superseding the false objectivism–subjectivism dichotomy. The topics featured in his *Esquisse* were subsequently further investigated in *Le Sens pratique* (Bourdieu 1980g trans. Nice 1990), the true manifesto of Bourdieu's scientific project.

Academic and editorial achievements

Just before the generals' putsch in Algiers (1960) and in the face of life-threatening circumstances, Bourdieu managed to return to Paris, where Raymond Aron offered him an assistant's post at the Sorbonne. Aron also entrusted Bourdieu with the co-direction of the *Centre de Sociologie Européenne*, the research centre funded by the Ford Foundation, which Aron founded in 1959. Here Bourdieu ran a section devoted to educational and cultural sociology, which soon became a point of reference for both his students and other scholars. The young Bourdieu was appointed *maître de conference* at Lille University until 1964. In Lille he was reunited with Eric Weil, was introduced to historian Pierre Vidal-Naquet and, most importantly, he struck a friendship with philosopher and philologist Jean Bollack.

At the beginning of the 1960s, Bourdieu started intense publishing activity as editor of the book series *Le Sens commun* from Minuit and held the post until 1992. In the same year, thanks to the support of Aron, Braudel and Lévi-Strauss, he was appointed *directeur d'études* in section VI (social sciences) of the Parisian *École Pratique des Hautes Études*, which was run by Fernand Braudel. By working with Aron, he was able to grow as a researcher but a gap started to develop when Bourdieu published with Jean-Claude Passeron *Les Héritiers* (Bourdieu and Passeron 1964 trans. Nice 1979), his first work devoted to the schooling system, and he expressed an alternative view of the May 1968 events. Bourdieu distanced himself from Aron and created his own research unit, the *Centre de sociologie de l'éducation et de la culture.*

His studies on cultural practices, alongside his research into schooling institutions, dominated his intellectual production during the 1960s and resulted in two books on photography (Bourdieu *et al.* 1965 trans. Whiteside 1990) and on art galleries visitors (Bourdieu *et al.* 1966 trans. Beattie and Merriman 1990).

Bourdieu's intense empirical research was accompanied by epistemological reflections, as attested by *Le Métier de sociologue* (1968 trans. Nice 1991). At the end of the decade, Bourdieu published his second work on school, *La Reproduction* (1970 trans. Nice 1977), which became a classic of educational sociology. This book broadens the subject matter of *Les Héritiers* and engages in a critical analysis of scholastic institutions as entities that foster the reproduction of social inequality. This is where, for the first time, Bourdieu systematically introduced the notion of "symbolic violence". *La Reproduction* attracted much criticism and was perceived as being animated by determinism. His third book on the schooling system, where Bourdieu analyses the French "grandes écoles", would be published almost twenty years later (Bourdieu 1989b trans. Clough 1996)

In the 1970s, he was entirely committed to creating his own school of sociology and edited the journal *Actes de la recherche en sciences sociales*, which he had founded in 1975. In 1979, he published *La Distinction*, which epitomises his entire research on the cultural field over the previous fifteen years. This book was ranked amongst the ten most important sociological works of the twentieth-century by *The International Sociology Association* and is one of the most highly cited works in sociology today. Bourdieu became a well-known author and an esteemed international scholar in the broader field of humanities, beyond the sociological field. Throughout his career, he gave many lectures abroad, especially in Germany, Scandinavia, USA and Japan.

In the early 1980s, he was called at the *Collège de France*. His output over the decade includes: a collection of essays on language as a fundamental and executive tool of symbolic power (Bourdieu 1982b trans. Adamson 1990); a book where Bourdieu analysed his own academic milieu, testing the fulcrum of his epistemological proposal (1984a trans. Collier 1988); and an enquiry into the political implications of Heidegger's philosophical thought (1988 trans. Collier 1991).

Les Règles de l'art (Bourdieu 1992a trans. Emmanuel 1996) was published in 1992 and collected in a systematic way the results of a lengthy theoretical and empirical research into cultural production practices, with an emphasis on nineteenth-century French arts. In 1993, Le Seuil published a report on the monumental research featured in *La Misère du monde* (Bourdieu ed. 1993 trans. Ferguson 1999), which demonstrated the difficulties encountered by people of the dominated classes within contemporary society characterised by neoliberal economic regimes and Welfare State retrenchment. The success of the book both in France and abroad – it was translated in thirteen languages – is a testament of the influence exercised by Bourdieu at the international level. Bourdieu received a number of prizes and awards that attested the pivotal role he had achieved in the social sciences field not only in France but also abroad.

In 1993 Bourdieu was the first sociologist to be awarded the CNRS (*Centre National de la Recherche Scientifique*) Gold Medal, and later he received an honorary doctorate from the *Johann Wolfgang Goethe University* in Frankfurt and from the *Joensuu University* in Finland. In the same year, Bourdieu founded with success the *Liber-Raison d'agir* publishing house, whose first title was *Sur la télévision* (Bourdieu 1996a trans. Ferguson 1998). Two of Bourdieu's most significant works were published between 1997 and 1998: *Méditations pascaliennes* (1997a trans. Nice 2000) – an elaboration of his epistemology and philosophical anthropology – and *La Domination masculine* (1998b trans. Nice 2001), which draws on Bourdieu's previous ethnological research on Kabylia and interprets female submission as one of the most fitting examples of symbolic violence. This study received cold, if not openly hostile, reviews from feminists. In 1999, Bourdieu structured his course at the *Collège de France* on the work of Manet. These lectures were recently published in *Manet. Une révolution symbolique* (Bourdieu 2013).

Public political commitment

Whilst in previous years Bourdieu had rarely manifested his political leanings (in the 1950s, at *École Normale*, Bourdieu sat on a committee against PCF's [Parti communiste français; French Communist Party] Stalinism; in 1981 he supported Coluche's presidential candidacy and, alongside Michel Foucault, organised a petition against repression in Poland and the suppression of *Solidarnosc*; and later he wrote a report on education reform to President Mitterrand), the 1990s marked an even stronger engagement in national and international politics. In a way he tested the notion of "collective intellectual" posited in the final chapter of *Régles de l'art* ("For a Universal Corporatism").

In 1994, alongside Derrida and other intellectuals, he founded in Strasbourg the *European Writers' Parliament*. Also with Derrida, he campaigned for the rights of immigrants. In November–December 1995 he openly supported the railway workers' strike against the Juppé reform scheme for retirement pensions and even spoke at a rally staged at the Gare de Lyon against the government's neoliberal policies. In 1996 he was amongst the founders of the *États généraux du mouvement social* and in the winter of 1997/1998 supported the movement of the unemployed, which he perceived as a sort of "social miracle".

The main focus of his political engagement was his criticism of neoliberal politics and language, as well as the dismantlement of the Welfare State. In 1998, he supported the occupiers of the *École Normale Supérieure* and Algerian intellectuals that were forced into exile. In 1999 he was actively engaged against NATO's military attack on Serbia. In June 2000, Bourdieu participated in some ATTAC political initiatives (Association pour la Taxation des Transactions financière et l'Aide aux Citoyen; Association for the Taxation of financial Transactions and Aid to Citizens); he was in Millau and worked to organise a set of critical and progressive forces against economic globalisation. Furthermore, he wrote several analyses and articles on neoliberalism and imperialism and on the need for an international political organisation which could oppose them. Most of his political interventions are collected in two books published by *Raison d'agir* (Bourdieu 1998a trans. Nice 1998; 2001a) and in other eminent political publications (2000c; 2002a trans. Fernbach 2008).

Key concepts of Bourdieu's analysis

His scientific project

Bourdieu's sociological body of work attests an outstandingly broad intellectual background, which has produced one of the most significant attempts to combine classical social theory with a thorough analysis of contemporary society. The highly sophisticated theoretical framework that sustains the forty volumes and many papers written over a forty-plus year span should be ascribed with no doubt to the fact that Bourdieu, most unusually for a sociologist, was first of all a philosopher and all his theoretical framework is marked by philosophy.

Bourdieu tackled an increasingly diverse array of topics, including Algeria's economic structures during French colonisation, educational systems in contemporary society, masculine domination, aesthetic judgement, photography, housing issues and suburban marginalisation in contemporary metropolises. Despite this heterogeneity in his interests, his objective was to elaborate a "science of practices" that would allow for an original and rigorous critique of domination, the core of his scientific objectives, which brings unity to his wide-ranging sociological thinking and permeates each single inquiry.

At the core of Bourdieu's theoretical project stands his firm belief that the two apparently antithetical theoretical stances, objectivism and subjectivism, can and must be overcome, because "of all the oppositions that artificially divide social science [it is] the most fundamental" (Bourdieu 1980g trans. Nice 1990: 25). Whilst objectivism holds that social reality consists of sets of relations and forces that impose themselves upon individuals, subjectivism, on the contrary, takes individual representations as its basis, and asserts that social reality is but the sum total of the innumerable acts of interpretation whereby people jointly construct meaningful lines of (inter)action (Bourdieu 1980g trans. Nice 1990; Wacquant 2006: 6). Neither approach can singly capture the very nature of the social world, which is "intrinsically double", as the objectivist and subjectivist moments stand in a dialectical relation with each other.

According to Bourdieu, only a *relational* approach, which focuses on the mutual relationships between the entities of the social world rather than treating the properties of social agents as if they were substances, would allow us to overcome these theoretical difficulties. By reorienting and appropriating Hegel's statement, Bourdieu notes that "the real is relational" (Bourdieu 1994a trans. Johnson *et al.* 1998: 97).

This stance led Bourdieu to reformulate the very object of social science, which should no longer look at individuals, but rather consider the "double and obscure relation between habitus and field" (Bourdieu and Wacquant 1992 trans. Wacquant 1992: 126–127). *Habitus* and *field* are relational concepts whose interplay helps to explain their complex relations between the objective and subjective traits of the social world.

Habitus: the embodied history

The notion of habitus is one of Bourdieu's most important conceptual innovations. Yet it is one of the most misunderstood and contested of his concepts. Habitus is intended to resolve the central question of "how can behaviour be regulated without being the product of obedience to rules" (Bourdieu 1982b trans. Adamson 1990: 65).

Bourdieu defines habitus as a property of social agents that comprises a "structured and structuring structure" (ibid.). Being an internalisation of the structures of the social world, it is a "structured structure". In a very important sense, habitus is an "embodiment" of the entire social system. Such embodiment is the product of a slow, unconscious acquisition over time since childhood, through intimacy and tacit understanding, of the social regularities that are the mark of the social system. On the other hand, one's habitus generates perceptions, attitudes and practices. It is both the filter through which we interpret the social world and organise our perceptions of other people's practices, and the means through which we produce our own actions in the world. In this sense, it is a "structuring structure".

Notably, the habitus must not be conceptualised as a passive collection of knowledge, a set of rules we mechanically apply to social situations. It is an active, unconscious set of "dispositions" to act and to perceive. The notion of "disposition" is crucial to the theory of habitus: "It expresses first the result *of an organising action*...; it also designates a *way of being, a habitual state* (especially for the body) and, in particular, a *predisposition, tendency, propensity* or *inclination*" (Bourdieu 1972b trans. Nice 1977: 214). The dispositions are durable – they last over time – and transposable, that is, they are capable of being active within a wide variety of social situations. In this way, the habitus provides us with a practical mastery of social situations, one that derives from but does not coincide with the thoughtlessness of habit and the habituation that habitus produces.

Therefore, action is not driven by the calculative considerations of cost–benefit analysis, but by the set of dispositions comprised in the habitus. Bourdieu believes that the practices embodied, quite literally, in the habitus do not result from the agent's conscious rationality, will or agency. The practical skills acquired through and for action operate at a subconscious level. As an "embodied history", habitus is an operator of practical rationality which transcends individual conscience, whilst remaining open to subjective inventiveness and creativity.

Habitus does not determine our actions but guides them. It provides a "feel for the game", as Bourdieu states (1982b trans. Adamson 1990: 63). He uses the game metaphor to explain the generative nature of habitus and to stress how actors do possess a certain degree of autonomy within its boundaries: the social agent behaves as the good tennis player who, though completely governed by the play of the game, nonetheless completely governs it. When our habitus is correctly adjusted to the social game we are playing, we feel comfortable and "natural": we feel at home. When we move to another play – to another social setting – our habitus may be inappropriate to cope with the situation and we feel uneasy, not quite liking what is going on.

The habitus is not a state of consciousness but rather a "condition of the body". The durable dispositions which make the habitus a system are grounded in bodily attitudes. "The body is in the social world, but the social world is in the body (in the form of *hexis* and *eidos*)" (Bourdieu 1997a trans. Nice 2000: 152). The *hexis* includes all bodily automatisms, gestures, ways of talking, tastes, likes and dislikes into a symbolic universe in which physical and social geometries become interwoven. *Eidos* is "a specific mode of thought ... grounded in a prereflexive belief in the undisputed value of the instruments of the construction of reality" (ibid.: 99–100). Of course, to speak of the central role of the body does not mean that there is no cognition involved, since "appropriate practice (speaking a language or riding a bicycle) is knowledge and it even contains a particular form of reflection" (Bourdieu 1997a trans. Nice 2000: 80). It means that actions are automatic and spontaneous and that they often involve emotions like "shame, humiliation, timidity, anxiety, guilt" (Bourdieu 1998b trans. Nice 2001: 38).

Therefore, the definition of habitus as "embodied history" should be interpreted literally rather than metaphorically. Individual and social histories shape the habitus by permeating the bodies and by conditioning them according to class-specific (or gender-specific) values and traits. The role played by the body becomes increasingly central to the development of the theory of habitus and appears to be pivotal in the theory of symbolic violence. A striking example is Bourdieu's analysis of the subjection to the masculine order:

> The formative process ... which brings about this social construction of the body only very partially takes the form of explicit and express pedagogic action. It is to a large extent the automatic, agent-less effect of a physical and social order entirely organised in accordance with the androcentric principle (which explains the extreme strength of its hold).
>
> (Bourdieu 1998b trans. Nice 2001: 24)

The field: the objectified history

Whilst the notion of habitus pertains to the individual, the field pertains to a specific social game endowed with its own laws. The social world is composed of various fields (e.g. journalism, academia, politics, music, literature, school), which are characterised by different rules, interests and "capitals". Each field is comprised of many sub-fields. Although each field has its own laws, such laws obey a general functioning susceptible to a systematic analysis.

According to a comprehensive definition:

> The field is a network of objective relations (of domination and subordination, of complementarity or antagonism, etc.) between positions.... Each position is objectively defined by its objective relationship with other positions, or, in other terms, by the system of relevant (meaning efficient) properties which allow it to be situated in relation to all others in the structure of the global distribution of properties. All positions depend, in their very existence, and in the determination they impose on their occupants, on their actual and potential situation in the structure of the field – that is to say, in the structure and distribution of those kinds of capital (or of power) whose possession governs the obtaining of specific profits put into play in the field. To different positions ... correspond homologous *position-takings*.
>
> (Bourdieu 1992a trans. Emanuel 1996: 231)

The Bourdieusian concept of field is derived from physics; just as the magnetic field is a structured system of forces, the fields of the social world are networks of objective relations between gravity-specific positions. As a spatial metaphor consistent with the relational approach, the field exists only by virtue of the agents who trigger its governing rules and warrant its practical efficacy.

Regardless of their specific features, Bourdieu posits that there are structural and functional homologies between fields. A homology is a "resemblance within a difference" (Bourdieu and Wacquant 1992 trans. Wacquant 1992: 105–106). Fields are arenas characterised by struggles over the control of resources. There is an inequality in the distribution of these resources, so that each field is characterised by many shades of dominant and dominated positions. The type and content of the resource that is most valued (i.e. the stakes of a field) evolve through time as a result of such struggle. Most of the time, the aim of the game is the maximisation of symbolic capital (e.g. "honour" or "credit" for artists), but the very definition of symbolic capital is not immovable, since it is also the outcome of the struggles that take place in the field.

To illustrate how fields work, Bourdieu once again uses the game metaphor. Each field is like a game in which there are stakes that players fight for, and a form of investment made by players that Bourdieu refers to as *illusio*, i.e. the belief in the game. In particular, each field produces its specific form of illusio which

> pulls agents out of their indifference and inclines and predisposes them to put into operation the distinctions which are pertinent from the viewpoint of the logic of the field, to distinguish what is *important* ("what matters to me", is of interest, in contrast to "what is all the same to me", or *in-different*).
>
> (Ibid.: 227)

Illusio is then the immediate adhesion to the field's needs. As such:

> *illusio* does not belong to the order of explicit principles, theses that are put forward and defended, but of action, routine, things that are done, and that are done because they are things that one does and that have always been done that way.
>
> (Bourdieu 1997a trans. Nice 2000: 102)

The opponents who are "caught in the game" can struggle against one another only if they accept the game's and the stakes' legitimacy. This tacit agreement – "a collusion in the illusio", as Bourdieu puts it – is at the root of the competition between the players sharing the same positioning in a given field and constitutes the game itself.

The struggle entails that opponents agree on what is worth struggling for, which is something usually taken for granted, what Bourdieu refers to as *doxa*. As a result, the opponents help build common beliefs about the stakes' value:

> All those who are involved in the fields, whether champions of orthodoxy or heterodoxy, share a tacit adherence to the same doxa which makes their

> competition possible and assigns its limits.... It effectively forbids questioning of the principles of belief, which would threaten the very existence of the field.
>
> (Ibid.)

As the field defines the social position in which the agents' habitus operates, agents become endowed with a habitus, which allows them to acknowledge and recognise the rules and stakes of the game and to invest in the illusio. The outcome is the production of "reasonable" strategies, i.e. those in line with the game's logics within a given field, which are broader than "rational" strategies restricted to a calculative logic. Hence, beneath all conflicts lies a kind of objective complicity. Nonetheless, the interplay between habitus and field is always subject to change and set in motion by the agents' active involvement in the game. The habitus is not a mere reflection of the field, since there is leeway (straining as they are, social rules are not almighty) and hysteresis (a given field might have evolved since the time it helped shape an individual's habitus to the point that social rules are no longer the same).

Finally, by thinking in terms of field, one views the space of objective positions occupied by the agents as a factor which, ultimately, influences agents' position-takings, that is, "the 'choices' made by the social agents in the most diverse domains of practice" (Bourdieu 1994a trans. Johnson *et al.* 1998: 6). However, this relationship should not be understood by any means as a mechanistic one, since each position-taking is defined not only in relation to the whole array of position-takings, but also to the space of possibilities that is present in the field. The space of possibles is a system which, like grammar, "defines the space of what is possible but also allows for the invention of a diversity of acceptable solutions within the limits of grammaticality" (Bourdieu 1992a trans. Emanuel 1996: 236).

Capital and its forms

The structure of the field in a given moment is defined by the condition of "power relations" between agents, which depends on the specific form of capital that governs the agents' strategies within the field. Therefore, capital is meaningful and has value only in relation to a given field and within the limits of a field.

Bourdieu refers to the notion of *capital* as any resource that produces the "profits" which derive from participating in a field. He gives the term a broader meaning than that used in neoclassical economics: "it is in fact impossible to account for the structure and functioning of the social world unless one reintroduces capital in all its forms and not solely in the one form recognised by economic theory" (Bourdieu 1986a: 241).

The main forms of capital are: economic (i.e. money), social (i.e. the other individuals one knows), cultural (i.e. the legitimate cultural preferences and practices; the transmittable cultural goods; or the degrees and diplomas) and symbolic (a byword for the "honour", "credit" or "prestige" that is specific to a given field). Each form of capital can be converted into another form of capital through a conversion rate that differs in all fields. For example, cultural capital can be converted into economic capital by means of remuneration for services that require educational qualifications and training. Furthermore, the dominant or dominated position that one occupies in a field is a matter of the volume and type of capitals possessed. Thus, Bourdieu's vision offers a richer understanding of inequality and domination than a pyramidal perspective, since it depends on the possession of these diverse forms of capital.

The forms of capital which Bourdieu tends to analyse more in his research, both theoretically and empirically, are cultural capital and symbolic capital (social capital is analysed in Chapters 11 and 12 of the present volume). In fact, cultural capital may appear in three different states: the *embodied* state, i.e. in the form of long-lasting dispositions, such as expertise in a given cultural field or competence in legitimate language; the *objectified* state, i.e. in the form of cultural goods (books, instruments, machines, etc.); and the *institutionalised* state, i.e. in the form of educational certificates which objectify the recognition accorded by society to cultural competences. One of the main features of cultural capital in the embodied state is that it cannot be transmitted instantly (or at once) by bequest; indeed, social agents may acquire it only by means of a long-term work of apprenticeship and cultivation through which cultural capital becomes embodied, and, therefore, transforms every social being into the individual he/she actually is. In this respect, Bourdieu argues that embodied cultural capital is "external wealth converted into an integral part of the person, into a habitus" (1986a: 243). The notion of cultural capital is pivotal to the understanding of the apparatus operating in educational systems, in consumer behaviours, in the shaping of tastes and in the realm of cultural production.

Symbolic capital differs from other species of capital; in fact it is not a material entity but describes the effects produced by other forms of capital. In this respect, Bourdieu writes:

> I call symbolic capital any kind of capital (economic, cultural, academic, or social) when it is perceived according to the categories of perception, the principles of vision and division, the systems of classification, the classificatory schemes, the cognitive schemata, which are, at least in part, the product of the embodiment of objective structures of the field in consideration, that is, of the structure of the distribution of capital in the field being considered.... Symbolic capital is capital with a cognitive base, which rests on cognition and recognition.
>
> (Bourdieu 1994a trans. Johnson *et al.* 1998: 85)

This notion was used to examine symbolic productions of pre-capitalist Algeria, and later in the cultural field of modern capitalist societies, to explain agents' material and symbolic profits from rejecting the narrow logic of economic interest and displaying a kind of "disinterestedness" that values honour and loyalty, or artistic and scientific integrity.

All these forms of capital, along with the notions of *habitus* and *field*, belong to an integrated conceptual framework to provide a general theory of practice. To analyse these notions separately would be meaningless because "habitus, field and capital can be defined, but only within the theoretical system they constitute, not in isolation" (Bourdieu and Wacquant 1992 trans. Wacquant 1992: 96). Bourdieu clarifies the link between these three dimensions of practice through his well-known formula (1979 trans. Nice 1984):

$$[(\text{habitus})\ (\text{capital})] + \text{field} = \text{practice}$$

Whilst

> the field structures the habitus, which is the product of the embodiment of the immanent necessity of a field (or of a hierarchically interacting set of fields) ... the habitus contributes to constituting the field as a meaningful world, a world endowed with sense and value, in which it is worth investing one's practice.
>
> (Bourdieu and Wacquant 1992 trans. Wacquant 1992: 127)

Therefore, the three notions are so interconnected that the heuristic potentialities of each may unfold only through their reciprocal correlation.

Unveiling symbolic violence

Capital is power. Thus, those who possess more capital than others wield more power. In each field, there are more or less dominant and dominated positions. We might rashly think that the dominated should refuse such domination. In fact, they often consent to it, due to what Bourdieu dubbed *symbolic violence*, which lies at the very core of his sociology. This is a gentle, invisible, pervasive violence which is exercised through cognition and misrecognition, knowledge and sentiment: by endorsing the dominant point of views and symbolic representations, the dominated contribute to their domination. Although explicit reference to such violence is not present in all of Bourdieu's publications, the concept informs his entire body of work. Significantly, Bourdieu believes that sociology is a means by which symbolic violence is rendered visible as violence and encourages awareness of its arbitrary nature.

According to Bourdieu, contemporary social hierarchies and inequalities are produced and maintained less by physical force than by forms of symbolic power. Symbolic violence is "gentler" than physical violence, but it is no less real. It is the most efficient way through which domination is perpetuated. Such mode of domination substitutes "seduction for repression, public relations for policing, advertising for authority, the velvet glove for the iron fist [and] pursues the symbolic integration of the dominated classes by imposing needs rather than inculcating norms" (Bourdieu 1979 trans. Nice 1984: 153–154). In other words, open coercion is replaced by devices that are embodied in the habitus and justify the existing order. As such they secure the correspondence between individual cognitive structures and social structures, upon which lies the perpetuation or reproduction of power relations.

Symbolic violence consists of the recognition of legitimacy of domination by the dominated. It is not a free act of conscience; it is rooted in practices and dispositions which are usually understood as being "normal" and which, on the contrary, are "politically constructed" alongside the categories of perception which support them. In Bourdieu's mind symbolic systems are not geared exclusively towards communication and social integration, but they also act as powerful domination tools insofar as they are veritable constitutive agents of reality. The correspondence between social and cognitive structures may be therefore regarded as "one of the most solid props of social domination" (Bourdieu and Wacquant 1992 trans. Wacquant 1992: 14). As they elaborate their relation with the dominant, the dominated possess only the cognitive structures they share with them, and given that such structures are "the embodied form of the relation of domination, [this] causes that relation to appear as natural" (Bourdieu 1998b trans. Nice 2001: 35). Such misrecognition bestows on symbolic violence its specific efficacy and ensures that "the arbitrary power which makes imposition possible is never seen in its full truth" (Bourdieu and Passeron 1970 trans. Nice 1977: 11). It should then come as no surprise that such violence rests on the *doxa*, the unquestioned set of fundamental beliefs, as we have seen above.

One of the fields in which symbolic violence is mostly exercised is the modern bureaucratic field, i.e. the State. Bourdieu defines the State as "the holder of the monopoly of legitimate symbolic violence" (1989b trans. Clough 1996: 22; 2012: passim). The State is heavily responsible for the production and reproduction of the ways in which social reality is perceived. Bourdieu highlights that "one of the major powers of the State is to produce and impose (especially through the school system) categories of thought that we spontaneously apply to all things of the social world – including the State itself" (1993b trans. Wacquant and Farage 1994: 1). Thus, the State guarantees and legitimates the relations of domination. It is also "the source of the symbolic efficacy of all the rites of institution, those which are at the basis of the family, for example, and also those which are performed through the functioning of the educational system" (Bourdieu 1997a trans. Nice 2000: 175). As the core of symbolic violence, the State acts as "the central bank of symbolic capital" and guarantees all acts of "legitimate imposture" and "constitution" which are required to ground the authority of who actually holds the power; such acts include the mysterious "power of nomination", the "juridical verdict" and the power to create "natural" realities such as the family, which Bourdieu deems to be "a fiction, a social artefact, an illusion" (1994a trans. Johnson *et al.* 1998: 25).

Given that school is the State institution where symbolic violence is most successfully exercised, a massive portion of Bourdieu's writings on symbolic violence deals with educational systems (Bourdieu and Passeron 1964, 1970; Bourdieu 1989b). By the inculcation of what he called the "cultural arbitrary", school reproduces social order, providing cognitive and moral bases to maintain it. From such a point of view, the "titles" (diplomas and qualifications) provided by the educational system represent veritable means of symbolic violence: they legitimise and reproduce a social system founded on injustice and inequality, preventing the dominated from questioning domination.

Bourdieu also discloses the mechanism of symbolic violence in other fields, such as consumption and gender relationships (Paolucci 2011). In his most influential work on consumerism, Bourdieu argues that class distinctions and hierarchies are maintained through consumption practices (Bourdieu 1979). In his essay on gender, he analyses masculine domination as "a paradigmatic form of symbolic violence". In order to understand this form of domination, one must analyse both its invariant features and the historical work of dehistoricisation through which social institutions – family, school, church, State – "eternalise the arbitrary at the root of men's power" (Bourdieu 1998b trans. Nice 2001).

Note

1 Gabriella Paolucci is Associate Professor of Sociology at the University of Florence, Italy. Her main research areas are: temporal structures of contemporary societies, urban policies, European welfare models and sociological theories. She is a member of several editorial boards for scholarly journals of social sciences. She has directed many research projects linked to a variety of issues, at both national and international level. On Bourdieu's sociology, she has published several articles and two books (*Bourdieu dopo Bourdieu*, Torino, 2010; *Introduzione a Bourdieu*, Bari, 2011.)

3 Bourdieu's writings on economics and the economy

Frédéric Lebaron[1]

Introduction

Since the beginning of his scholarly endeavours, Bourdieu's conception of society has integrated 'the economic dimension' as a central element. The 'economic order' was for him an object of empirical study, but it was also a permanent source of theoretical reflection, which could be transferred to other domains, such as education and culture. Even though his work is closely connected to, sometimes directly inspired by, economics, he develops a separate and autonomous set of analytical tools, which in return may be used to renew the analysis of economic realities, provided they are applied with a clear awareness of contexts and historical conditions. We begin by presenting the genesis of Bourdieu's sociology and its main concepts to show how Bourdieu contributed to the empirical knowledge of the economic field. Then we present its basic theoretical points as regards the economic field.

The genesis of Bourdieu's sociology and his conceptual apparatus

Trained as a French philosopher, Bourdieu became a sociologist in Algeria (at that time part of France) during the second half of the 1950s. There he worked as a university assistant, in Algiers, right after his military service during the 'Algerian war'. In 1958, on the basis of intensive readings of French and British anthropologists and a first set of ethnographic observations, Bourdieu wrote his first book, an erudite synthesis, *Sociologie de l'Algérie*, which was soon translated into English under the title *The Algerians* (Bourdieu 1958 trans. Ross 1962).

In this book, we observe that, early on, Bourdieu develops an interdisciplinary perspective on society and the economy. This novel outlook is strongly influenced by the work of Max Weber on capitalism, as indicated by the basic use of the concept of 'ethos', defined as the system of economic concrete values of a group. For Bourdieu, 'economic rationality' is not a 'natural' characteristic of individuals but the arbitrary historical result of their socialisation inside a social group and an economic system. In particular, he analyses the contradictions between capitalist rationality, which is imposed by colonial institutions and various (state and non-state) actors, and traditional norms, which are reproduced through informal socialisation and founded on the logic of honour-based reciprocity and the refusal of any individual accumulation. Traditional norms tend to prevail, but are put under growing pressure in light of overpowering capitalist forces introduced by formal colonial and state institutions. For example, watching the fields and the way plants grow, though unproductive in capitalist terms, was traditionally conccived as an activity, as a contribution. However, with the introduction of a productive and profit-oriented mind, this activity begins to be perceived as 'unemployment' (for a recent discussion, see Martin-Criado 2008: 63).

This analysis was developed and refined in the following years through in-depth empirical work, with his former Algerian student Abdelmalek Sayad (Bourdieu and Sayad 1964), and also in collaboration with young official statisticians working on the French labour-force survey (Bourdieu *et al.* 1963). In these works, Bourdieu developed a critical analysis of official statistics, like the notion of 'unemployment', which appear inadequate when they are mechanically transferred from one society to another. In a traditional society, unemployment is kept invisible, as there is no clear-cut distinction between activity and non-activity, productive and non-productive tasks. In surveys about employment, people tend to respond that they are employed even when their level of real activity is close to zero. On the other hand, the more traditional a region is, the less it is inclined to define non-active situations in terms of 'unemployment' (see Bourdieu *et al.* 1963).

In the 1960s, Bourdieu returned to France and deployed his (intensively trained) ethnological eye in the context of his own birth region, the Béarn (in the deep south-west of France, close to Spain). By studying the evolution of marriages (and the growing number of bachelors) among poor peasants, he tried to explain the devaluation of masculine assets in matrimonial exchanges and strategies, in a period of intense social change: urbanisation, economic growth, growing access to education. The most traditionally socialised men, who work on the farm, are losing their value in the eyes of young women, in favour of more 'urbanised' and 'modern' dispositions. This is made obvious with the ethnographic analysis of the 'bachelor's party' ('le bal des célibataires') where 'traditionally minded' men are unable to cope with new dancing and acting codes (for a synthesis, see Bourdieu 2002b; Bourdieu 2002b trans. Nice 2008).

Through his teaching in Lille and Paris, and his leading role in the collective work undertaken at the *Centre de sociologie européenne* (Centre for European Sociology at the *École Pratique des Hautes Etudes* then *École des Hautes Etudes en Sciences Sociales*), directed by Raymond Aron, in the 1960s, Bourdieu participated in various important empirical studies. They were centred on the reproduction of class inequalities through culture and school. *Les Héritiers* (*The Inheritors*) (1964) and *La Reproduction (Reproduction)* (1970), written with Jean-Claude Passeron, are the most famous books of this period and gave birth to a strong impetus for the sociology of art, the sociology of culture and of course the sociology of education, in France and many other countries (see

Sapiro 2012). The study of class inequalities directly relates these fields to the study of the 'productive system' and the global economy, which can also be seen as a stratified social space. Bringing symbols, culture and education back in the study of social class is then a way to develop a more comprehensive understanding of the way social divisions structure the entire society, including the 'productive sphere'.

In all these works, a close connection was realised between economics and sociology through the use of concepts like 'exchange', 'heritage', 'capital' (especially 'cultural capital'), 'profit', 'market' and 'interest'. Bourdieu's objective was to unify the conceptual apparatus of the social sciences without denying specificity to any particular social universe, like the economy itself. This double intellectual constraint led him to a sense of the multiplicity of social spheres, beyond that of economic production, in which a diverse set of economic and non-economic assets can be defined and accumulated. In a multidimensional conception of society, there are different sources of inequality, which need to be systematically analysed. Bourdieu would use Geometric Data Analysis, a set of statistical tools developed in France under the influence of Jean-Paul Benzécri, to grasp this multidimensionality of social structures (see Benzécri 1973). In this statistical framework based on abstract linear algebra, statistical observations are described as clouds of points in Euclidean spaces, a technique which allows us to have a more visual appraisal of statistical regularities (Lebaron 2010).

From the second half of the 1960s, Bourdieu developed his own theoretical apparatus, based on a reflexive re-reading of his previous empirical works. This conceptual apparatus is summarised in the 'tryptic' capital–habitus–field. In the following, we briefly describe this tryptic in relation to economics and the economy, along with his conception of symbolic violence.

Capital

The concept of 'cultural capital' (first 'cultural heritage') was initially developed as a metaphor coming from economics, transferred into the realm of culture, allowing the analysis of particular inequalities and their familial process of transmission. Using economic models and concepts against economism (Lebaron 2003), Bourdieu attempted to unify economics, and the analysis of cultural spheres ('cultural goods', 'cultural markets'...) around a 'materialistic' system of concepts, without reducing cultural practices to economic determinants.

Rapidly, other forms of capital helped Bourdieu to better assess the complexity of social structures and the always particularly shaped distribution of social resources: symbolic capital (referring to the accumulation of prestige on names, families, etc.) and social capital (defined as a system of relational interactional resources, which are accumulated by individuals and families). These two types were especially relevant to understand the logic of the familial strategies of peasants in Béarn ('reproduction strategies'), but they can be seen as a universal aspect of social life in any society or organisation, including the most modern capitalist companies. Maintaining its 'image' (through the use of various labels, for example) and connecting to other key-actors in a field (through various informal and formal networks) appear major stakes for any large company.

Capital in this sense is related to a set of 'economic' concepts: 'accumulation', 'conversion', 'investment', 'profit' and also 'exchange'. The systematic use of these concepts extends the realm of economic categories substantially and has therefore been criticised (for example, by Caillé or Favereau). But this 'Bourdieuconomics' (Svendsen and Svendsen 2003) can also be seen as an attempt to unify the social sciences without reducing all social behaviours to economic interests. This is possible provided they are used in connection with a theory of practice (associated to the concept of habitus) and a theory of multidimensional social interests and structures (associated to the concept of field).

Habitus

Around 1966, while writing about Panofsky's analysis of Gothic architecture (Bourdieu 1967), Bourdieu shifted from the Weberian notion of ethos (enlarged to social classes) to the concept of habitus, used in order to interpret individual's practices without losing their collective inscription. Habitus is the central concept which allows Bourdieu to propose an alternative to rational action theory (RAT). It is a system of dispositions, which are socially produced and reproduced and which tend (in a probabilistic and not deterministic way) to structure the representations, the actions, the 'tastes', etc., of individuals according to their various social experiences. Habitus is also the key to understanding the stability of social inequalities. Inequalities not only rely on economic assets, but also on the distribution of the diverse forms of non-economic capital. Through the habitus, these assets are deeply 'internalised', 'embodied', hence they are largely made unconscious and 'naturalised'.

Class habitus, that is, the dispositions developed by belonging to a certain social class, are related to 'culture' and 'education', not only to material living conditions, and to the global economic system, which favours particular dispositions, like ascetism or consumerism. In a capitalist society, habitus tends to be oriented toward economic rationality.

But as Bourdieu will first develop in *Esquisse d'une théorie de la pratique* (*Outline of a Theory of Practice*) (Bourdieu 1972b; Bourdieu 1972b trans. Nice 1977) and in subsequent books about rationality (especially, Bourdieu 2000b; Bourdieu 2000b trans. Turner 2005), RAT is an imaginary anthropological construction, which confuses the logic of things and the things of logic, in a classical scholastic biased conception. In other words, for Bourdieu, by defining action in abstract terms, RAT is actually typical of the way scholars tend to project their specific social and epistemic condition (they are 'cut' from action and practice, have time and can develop abstract reasoning) over their analysis of concrete reality, and thereby forget the real conditions of any concrete 'practice'. Practice is a fuzzy mobilisation of dispositions to their external environment. They imply a largely unconscious and physical adaptation, at the opposite of the pure computations of an abstract mind.

Field

Around the same time, while working on the social history of intellectuals and writers in a dialogue with Sartre, Bourdieu also felt the need for an 'intermediary' structure (or a 'social sub-system'), between individual agents and the global society, first in order to avoid all the oversimplifications based on a mechanical analysis of an author's or creator's class determinations. This gave birth to the concept of field, defined as a particular social space inside the global social space, where particular interests (what he calls 'illusio', or sense of the game) are at stake and particular assets are valued. This leads Bourdieu to a new conception of 'interest', embedded in the more comprehensive notion of 'belief in a game', that is related to a kind of psycho-sociological investment, which has specific features according to the fields.

The intellectual field provided a first example: the activity of creation cannot be reduced to the effects of class memberships as sometimes done in Marxist tradition, or seen through the lenses of economic imperialism as a quest for monetary profit. His reflections on the notion of field will rapidly extend to the field of power that is the central place where the relative value of economic and non-economic assets is put into question and becomes the stakes of struggles between fractions of the dominant class. Then, it will be extended to the political and the economic fields.

This conception stresses the multidimensionality of the assets which are at stake inside a complex society, including the economic field itself, much more diverse and complex than usually thought, always embedded in some symbolic dimension. Far from game theory, interactions between actors are symbolic in nature. They depend on this multidimensional set of resources and they are not the product of totally conscious strategies, even at top decision levels or in the most rationalised sectors like finance. And in opposition with Marxist class struggle, each field generates very specific kinds of stakes which oppose actors, particularly competitors and rivals, and not only social classes, around particular symbolic stakes.

Symbolic violence

Since his Algerian work, Bourdieu has tried to develop a conception of domination by the use of a general conception of symbolic life, based on Weber, Durkheim and Marx. The notion of 'symbolic violence' allows us to think about domination as a reality which is far beyond the direct use of physical violence and relies on the acceptation of the dominant – his status, words and representations – as 'naturally dominant'.

This analysis directly applies to the internalisation of managerial legitimacy or to the acceptance of public policy measures, by workers and citizens, even if they contradict their apparent interest. Symbolic violence relates to the importance of language and discourse also in economic life. Through communication and the media, dominants tend to impose a set of representations and processes as natural and universal. By speaking, for example, in terms of 'management' and 'governance' instead of 'chiefs', hierarchical commandment and exploitation, this dominant economic-corporate discourse creates a pacified and cooperative representation of the economic world and denies any conflicting interests.

Bourdieu and the economic field: a set of empirical contributions

Bourdieu's first studies in Algeria provided him a consciousness of the historicity of economic structures, especially modern, post-World War II capitalism. As a historical long-term invention, modern capitalism depends on the systematic production and reproduction of economic dispositions (a particular ethos and habitus), especially as regards rationality, time and money. Agents must be oriented towards a rational 'calculable' future and must become able to actualise their income and profit, through more and more explicit and formal operations, etc. They tend to 'accumulate' economic capital, using rational instruments in that goal. But these dispositions vary according to their primary socialisation, their trajectory and more generally their social condition. Dimensions of 'traditional' societies (reciprocity, gift, etc.) remain important and always mixed with a more 'modern' economic rationality, which is rooted in practical routines and unconscious bases. This is obvious through the analysis of gift as a remaining feature in contemporary social life, and also through the notion of the particular non-economic illusio of certain fields (like the religious, bureaucratic, artistic or scientific fields), where being 'interested' is a matter of disqualification.

In 1963, Bourdieu coordinated a monograph realised by young scholars (Luc Boltanski and Jean-Claude Chamboredon) at the *Centre de sociologie européenne* (Centre for European Sociology). This work initiated an original analysis of 'credit' as a central social relationship in contemporary economies, which would be systematised in *Les Structures sociales de l'économie* (*The Social Structures of the Economy*) (Bourdieu 2000b; Bourdieu 2000b trans. Turner 2005), years later. The study showed that relations of an agent or a household to banks and credits depend strongly on agents' and households' social characteristics, embodied as an economic ethos. Moreover, it analysed the interactions between bank employees and credit customers as an unequal social relation, based on unequal linguistic and economic competence. It insisted on the social precondition for an alleged 'natural' kind of exchange on the market for credit. By analysing the concrete interactions between sellers and buyers in a marketplace (an exhibition hall), Bourdieu puts into light all the social dimensions involved in this apparently 'natural' transaction. He described the way buyers are engrossed into a set of new issues where they may be more or less at ease and 'competent' (from a linguistic and technical point of view, and also because they are less conscious of what is at stake in this interaction).

The surveys and publications on 'tastes' that Bourdieu produced from the 1960s (beginning with a survey on photography) and were of paramount interest for the study of consumption practices culminated in the *magnum opus La Distinction* (*Distinction*) in 1979 (see Coulangeon and Duval 2013). Among many other issues, this book can also be seen as a major contribution to a sociology of consumption and lifestyles, which relates the individual's systems of tastes to their habitus that is perceived as a coherent matrix for any 'individual' or 'collective' choice, operating in a dialectical move between diffusion and distinction. *La Distinction* makes a concrete move towards an operational sociological analysis of (economic) 'choice', assuming that 'tastes' strongly matter in the economic field, and that 'practices' do not depend on the explicit consciousness of an objective and adequate means to fulfil it. Following this line, the analysis of the market for houses in *Les Structures sociales de l'économie* begins with an analysis of the social construction of the demand for houses, which varies across the social space, and of course across time and space. Tastes depend on social conditions, including cultural characteristics, and are the complex product of social trajectories, in a multidimensional social space. Here again, this conception is rather far from the RAT conception of a universal consumer, making rational decisions on the basis of prices and qualities, under a budget constraint, without mobilising her/his entire life trajectory into any economic choice (as is the case in Bourdieu's view).

From the late 1960s, Bourdieu and his group were developing empirical research about leading groups, especially economic groups. In 1978, this led to an article, with Monique de Saint-Martin, about 'Le patronat' (the 'company leaders'), which developed an in-depth analysis of the various types of managers one found at the head of large French companies in the first half of the 1970s and the consequences as regards types of management. Among the main results was the persistence of an opposition between state-related company leaders, especially in finance, and familial traditional capitalism, but also the beginning ascension of business-school trained managers inside the field. This trend would become obvious ten years later when the book *La Noblesse d'État* (*State Nobility*) was published (Bourdieu 1989b; Bourdieu 1989b trans. Clough 1996). Such changes would also be described in his work that was published in the late 1990s and dealt with the ascension of a new economic elite in the field of French literary publishers (Bourdieu 1999).

In his work on 'housing', Bourdieu insisted on the complex relations of homology between the space of consumers and the space of producers in this particular field, as in any other economic field. Actors deploy strategies to 'produce' (construct) the demand and, also, simultaneously, to adapt and react to it. He also showed the centrality of public actors in the dynamics of the field. The field of public policy makers is then seen as always part of the study of any kind of market or sector.

Rather far from the use of a simplified model of economic action – for example, inspired by game theory – Bourdieu prefers to stress the complex web of interdependences which fundamentally (and unconsciously) organise a field and its concrete historical dynamics. One therefore first needs to describe the concrete characteristics of 'efficient agents' and their relationships before studying the concrete way they adapt to changing structural conditions.

A theory of the economic field

If one tries to sum up Bourdieu's theoretical contribution in economics without losing too much of the richness of his empirical analyses, which ran over 40 years of various empirical investigations, several elements can be mentioned:

- Economic individual actors are the product of their social experiences, largely unconscious and embodied: they structure their tastes, but also their strategies and orientations in the economic field, including at the top of companies or in the political and bureaucratic fields. This is the way Bourdieu challenges classical rational action theory with an original sociological theory of practice, opening to a set of systematic observations (and possibly, today, to a dialogue with neuroeconomics and experimental economics).
- Economic structures appear as strong constraining frames for individual and collective actions: they cannot be reduced to the networks of interrelations between various nodes, since they more deeply consist in multidimensional social spaces, fundamentally structured by the distribution of various assets (symbolic, cultural and social capital as well as economic).
- Domination is a central aspect of Bourdieu's conception of the economy: either in the global social space or in any specific economic field, the polarisation between dominant groups and the others strongly structures any concrete interaction between them. This domination is both concrete (material, physical...) and symbolic, varies across time and space, and does not reduce to 'class struggle' in the Marxist sense.
- Capitalism is a historical construction, rooted in long-term changes in social dispositions as well as the invention of specific institutions, especially credit and bank, but also the State.
- The economic *illusio* – that is, the fundamental belief which is at the basis of the economic field as an autonomous 'game' ('business is business') – is a complex historical product, in which economics has played a major role, in providing a sophisticated representation of individual actors and markets.
- Markets are always connected to the political sphere, and their dynamics depend on the bureaucratic field as well as changes in the economic field itself.

Bourdieu's sociology has proven being very flexible and adaptable to a large amount of empirical objects, including realities situated at the heart of modern capitalism, like finance and decisions of investment. It can therefore highly contribute to the contemporary reflection on an 'alternative economic thinking' which takes seriously the need for pluralistic methodologies and for various exchanges between intellectual traditions and scientific methodologies.

Note

1 Frédéric Lebaron is Professor of Sociology at the University of Versailles-Saint-Quentin-en-Yvelines (UMR 8085 Professions-Institutions-Temporalités, UVSQ-CNRS). He has been Professor at the UVSQ since September 2013, after 16 years at the University of Picardie-Jules Verne in Amiens, where he directed the Centre universitaire de recherches sur l'action publique et le politique – épistémologie et sciences sociales (CURAPP, UMR 7319 UPJV-CNRS). He specialises in social sciences methodology, economic sociology, political sociology and social inequality. He has written and edited several books, including: *Lectures de Pierre Bourdieu* (Ellipses, 2012, with G. Mauger); *Les Indicateurs sociaux au XXIème siècle* (Dunod, 2011); *La Crise de la croyance économique* (Croquant, 2010); *Le Savant, le politique et la mondialisation* (Croquant, 2003). He has also published around 70 articles and chapters of books in various journals and collective books.

Part III

Roots and fruits of Bourdieu's economic analysis

4 The symbolic basis of economic life

Frédéric Lebaron

Introduction

In this chapter, we will present Bourdieu's conception of the 'economic field' through a discussion of what we call the 'symbolic foundations of economic life' (Lebaron 2002). Indeed, Bourdieu's work on the economy, which covers his entire intellectual trajectory, systematically re-evaluates the symbolic dimension of economic practices, institutions and systems. It is especially important in comparison with the scientific representations of the economic field which are provided by (various types of) economics.

In the first section of this chapter, we present the way Bourdieu integrates symbolic elements at the core of his sociological theory. In the second section, we show that it leads him to an analysis which challenges usual conceptions of the economy. We discuss the relevance of this perspective for the contemporary economic field, dominated by financial capitalism and its global crisis since 2007. We will particularly insist on the symbolic dimensions of economic struggles and the creation of institutions which represent groups and collective interests, as they are determinant components of economies and industrial relations in welfare-state capitalist societies. We will also discuss some of the questions raised by this re-evaluation, especially as regards its possible articulation with neo-institutionalist economics, particularly around the various types of capitalism and neoliberal reforms in the context of the global crisis.

Bourdieu and the symbolic aspects of social life

Bourdieu's sociological theory is associated with a set of concepts referring to *symbolism* and the *symbolic* function[1]: he makes use of the concepts of 'symbolic sanction', 'symbolic violence', 'symbolic power', 'symbolic capital', 'symbolic profit', 'symbolic goods', 'symbolic struggle'. We will rapidly present the general conception behind the use of the most central of these concepts.

A conception of symbolic power[2]

The 'power of symbolic domination', as Bourdieu and Passeron state in the first proposition of *La Reproduction* in 1970, is 'every power which manages to impose meanings and to impose them as legitimate by concealing the power relations which are the basis of its force' (Bourdieu and Passeron 1970: xv). They explain that this power 'adds its own specifically symbolic force to those power relations' (ibid.). This central proposition in sociological theory can easily be decomposed into three sub-propositions:

1 At the foundation of the relations between agents and groups, there is a relation of 'inequality-asymmetry' (in French 'rapport de force' or 'power relation').
2 This 'inequality-asymmetry' is hidden by meanings and discourses, which tend to make it legitimate.
3 This symbolic dissimulation adds its specific force to the inequality-asymmetry, which is thus doubled by the symbolic force.

Comments by Bourdieu and Passeron ('scolie 1' and 'scolie 2' of *La Reproduction*) insist on the fact that this proposition paves the way for sociological theory, by leaving room to the relative autonomy and the interdependence of symbolic relations and power relations. Their proposition is contrary to two standard sociological propositions (in a classical dialectical move): for the first one, symbols are purely created by free individuals, whereas for the second one, pure power relations, seen as mechanical, leave no autonomy to symbolic relations. The first one can be associated with subjectivist philosophy; the second one with materialist or economic objectivism.

Bourdieu and Passeron explicitly associate three authors to different solutions in order to articulate the three propositions. Durkheim tends to leave aside the inequality-asymmetry of power relations (especially class divides). Weber tends to reduce any social relation between agents to a general legitimacy relationship (by forgetting the power relations in which legitimacy is imposed to a particular group by another). Marx tends to underestimate the efficacy of symbolic action and gives excessive importance to material power relations, i.e. class struggles.

Bourdieu would develop the articulation between these three authors in an article about symbolic power (Bourdieu 1977e). Durkheim, Marx and Weber correct each other and this provides for a more *balanced* theory of symbolic power. This original construction is inspired by a general anthropological perspective deriving from Durkheim, Mauss and Lévi-Strauss. Nonetheless, it aims at describing power relations and divisions between groups, which derive from the respective sociological legacies of Weber and Marx.

Symbolic capital[3]

In Bourdieu's empirical work, his general theoretical framework is related to a more specific use of symbolic notions. This culminates in the creation and the use of the concept of *symbolic capital* on the basis of an ethnological fieldwork in Kabylia.[4]

The concept of symbolic capital is the fourth general type ('specie') of capital dealt with in Bourdieu's sociological theory, together with cultural, economic and social capital. As symbolic capital is not exactly situated on the same plane as the other species, it emphasises the symbolic dimensions of social life, which gives it a particular role in the reinforcement of other species, in coherence with the theory of symbolic power expounded above. Bourdieu even discusses its existence as a genuine sort of capital and sometimes seems to hesitate between the use of this concept and more indirect formulations, like 'the symbolic effects of (all sorts of) capital' (Bourdieu 1997a: 285).

In one of the definitions proposed by Bourdieu during the 1980s, symbolic capital is, precisely, defined by any other sort of capital when it comes to its recognition or its perception according to particular schemes. As Bourdieu puts it:

> symbolic capital is nothing but economic or cultural capital as soon as they are known and recognised when they are known according to the perception categories they impose, the symbolic power relations tend to reproduce and reinforce the power relations which constitute the structure of the social space.
>
> (Bourdieu 1997a: 285)

In a text written in 1960 about 'the sense of honour' among Kabyle peasants, Bourdieu also uses the notion of 'symbolic profit' to analyse the 'embeddedness' (and the 'dissimulation') of economic logics into considerations of prestige and honour (Bourdieu 1972b: 29–60). The conceptual mix between pure symbolic processes and economic mechanisms is then made possible, and it will remain a central feature of Bourdieu's sociological theory: economic dimensions and symbolic structures are always 'thought together'. For example, work is not an autonomous reality, defined by a monetary value, for Kabyle peasants: it is a social activity, embedded in a set of reciprocity and honour mechanisms.

Bourdieu's analysis of marriages in Béarn during the turn of the 1960s is centred on the reproduction of economic and symbolic capital among peasant families (Bourdieu 1962). The analysis goes on during the 1960s, and nourishes Bourdieu's theoretical reflection. The formula 'maximisation of economic and symbolic capital' is used in an article of 1972 (Bourdieu 1972a) in order to describe strategies aiming at maintaining both the level of patrimony and some more 'perceptual' and even 'undefined', 'fuzzy' though highly relevant, aspects of their social identity, like the honour surrounding the name of the family, which objectifies its relative position in the social structure of the peasant world. In the context of a marriage arrangement, avoiding a decline from the family of the potential bride as a result of misalliance is an obvious example of such a strategy, which aims at preventing a blow to the honour of the proposing family and maintaining its symbolic value.

There is a link between the concept of symbolic capital and the systematic introduction of *strategies* in Bourdieu's analysis. Strategies are not purely economic, but they are also largely symbolic, in the sense that their aim is maintaining a certain reputation and honourability, and not only to increase wealth or material profits, even if this second dimension is always present to some extent. Among the synonyms then used by Bourdieu to define symbolic capital is the notion of 'collectively recognised credit' (Bourdieu 1972b: 121), which is first the expression of the importance attributed to a person by symbolic construction processes, and which also shows the way Bourdieu tries to think out the symbolic embeddedness of economic notions, and to connect them to more fundamental social processes.

In *Méditations pascaliennes* (translated into English as *Pascalian Meditations*), Bourdieu generalises the notion of symbolic capital to an 'existential sociological' theory inspired by Pascal: being *important* for others, then for oneself is related to the fact of 'being occupied, projected towards aims', etc. Symbolic capital, defined as recognition and consideration, appears as the basis of social existence, as an existence 'for the others'. 'Of the most unequal distributions, and probably, in any case, the most cruel, is the distribution of symbolic capital, that is, of social importance and reasons of living' (Bourdieu 1997a trans. Nice 2000: 241). Institution rituals, inside the family and more generally (nomination, ordination, etc.), are interpreted as ways to organise this distribution, and reproduce and transfer symbolic capital.

The symbolic dimensions of economic life[5]

In Bourdieu's view, too strong a distinction between material and symbolic dimensions of social reality can lead to fallacies. The most common one, present in Marxist theory, is the opposition between the *economic infrastructure* and the intellectual (legal, political…) *superstructure*, which causes a disastrous division of work between economists (interested in wealth, money, production, wages, profits, etc.) and other social scientists (more devoted to cultural, psychological or purely intellectual issues).

In line with Durkheim (see Steiner 2005), Bourdieu thinks there is no ontological heterogeneity between the sphere of representations, beliefs, etc. and the sphere of economic interests, institutions and actions. He even uses the notion of 'total social fact' created by Mauss to refuse the idea that economic life should escape from sociological understanding because of its autonomy as a particular sphere of reality (Bourdieu 2000b). One therefore needs:

> to abandon the economic/non-economic dichotomy which makes it impossible to see the science of 'economic' practices – including those that are experienced as disinterested or gratuitous, and therefore freed from the economy – as economic practices aimed at maximising material or symbolic profit.
>
> (Bourdieu 1980g trans. Nice 1990: 122)

The expansion of the economic sphere and the growing role of economic criteria

Bourdieu considers the global economic order as a symbolic order. We can speak of an economic order because a specific kind of social belief and interest, called *illusio*, has been made 'autonomous' from the rest of social reality, leading social agents to refer more and more to economic criteria and stakes (in the narrow sense of material profit or utility maximisation) and to leave aside other social criteria, at least in some of their practices.

The invention of a particular *illusio* (*investment in a game* and also *libido*; Bourdieu 1994a) is hence at the origin of this autonomous economic order. The economic field is anything but a particular case of field. '[The] fundamental laws [of the fields] are often tautologies. That of the economic field, which has been elaborated by utilitarian philosophers, [is] 'business is business' (Bourdieu 1994a trans. Johnson *et al.* 1998: 83). The history of this field is the history of an autonomisation process and also of an expansion process, because the law of this field has tended to determine the entire social life although it is limited by the existence of other fields – in particular, the religious field, the bureaucratic field and fields of cultural production.

In this spirit, Bourdieu analyses the expansion of economic criteria of evaluation in contemporary societies, especially during the neoliberal period, which begins in the 1970s in Western countries. During this period, the religious field, the bureaucratic field and the various fields of cultural production (e.g. art, literature, science) are put under stronger pressures and are made partially more dependent from the economic field. This process is larger than the effects of monetisation or financialisation, as they are described in economic history. It is a transformation of collective beliefs, which gives birth to new types of behavioural patterns and new institutions.

The way a society defines and measures (or not) its objectives and its performances gives a good idea of its prevailing beliefs and norms, the hierarchies of the social functions which structure it. In particular, the growing importance of *financial criteria of evaluation* of firms therefore expresses the imposition of a certain definition of social value, which is correlated to the growing power of financial actors in the global society. One cannot isolate one process from the other, since 'financial power' expresses itself in terms of 'financial criteria' at various levels of the economic field. The 'financialisation' of capitalism is hence a particular symbolic evolution of the economic field.

This symbolic imposition is not achieved without strong struggles and resistance, but it is the expression of a general shift in the balance of powers between social groups, which is denied and not perceived as such. It creates a strong shift in *ideologies*, in the sense that it contributes to the centrality of the economic field, and especially finance – financial discourse and criteria – as the core legitimacy principle in contemporary society.

With the success of benchmarking methods in public policies as well as inside large companies, the generalisation of evaluation is largely based on economic criteria and legitimised by economic discourses. The example of the 'economy of knowledge' and the measure of 'productivity' inside the scientific field illustrates a process by which external forces try to impose their criteria to fields which are relatively autonomous, and which contributes to modify the global balances between social fields and field-specific ideological representations. In

These aspects of economic domination are, of course, present in the neo-institutionalist literature (see, for example, in sociology, Powell and DiMaggio 1991; Fligstein and McAdam 2012). The originality of Bourdieu is probably to link them systematically with discursive and representational (psychological) elements, which are consubstantial to the creation of new institutions regulating the relations between social groups. In Fligstein and McAdam's conception of 'strategic action fields', the competition between dominants and incumbants is not only material but has also cultural and intellectual, and even 'existential', dimensions (see in particular chapter 2).

For Bourdieu, international domination, as it is described in-depth in the political economy literature (for example, in the work of Strange 1994), is also a process of symbolic domination. One classically describes the military domination of the US, its political hegemony and its economic power, especially obvious after the fall of its twentieth-century challenger, the Soviet Union. In these three domains (military, political and economic powers), symbolic domination is fundamental but, as Bourdieu's theory predicts, it is also less perceived, precisely because US domination is largely accepted and seen as normal or natural, or taken for granted.

The domination of the dollar as a fundamental asymmetry inside the international monetary system illustrates this point: the value of the dollar is the expression of the expected value of the economy of the United States, but it is also a currency which is given an international status because of the belief in its long-term value, even in the case of strong commercial imbalances. The discrepancy between the objective imbalances and the still central monetary function of the dollar is, precisely, the expression of the symbolic domination of the United States. In the same line, one can analyse the attraction of Treasury bonds in a context of very important US budget deficit and public debt: it is based on a similar symbolic attraction, which compensates the growing statistical objective imbalances. Objective structural relations seem less and less in favour of the position of the US economy, especially in comparison with China. But its dominant position is doubled by a strong symbolic domination, which hides at least partially the changing objective positions.

Symbolic dimensions involve of course 'non-rational' aspects of social life, but this conception also refuses to distinguish on an abstract basis between 'rational' and 'non-rational' aspects of human behaviour. The symbolic order is composed of various sorts of beliefs, including the belief in 'rationality', especially as regards economic criteria.

A second aspect of the symbolic domination of the US is the domination of American ideology, under the traits of the domination of American scientific discourse about institutions and social reality, especially, through the domination of US economics, management and legal conceptions. The domination of economics in the training of political and bureaucratic elite (like the leaders of central banks) is also a domination of US-based education programmes, like PhDs in economics, which is the symbolic basis of the reproduction of US broader US domination. In periods of crisis, like the 2007–2009 financial and economic crisis, the arbitrariness of this symbolic domination appears more visibly, which may accelerate the decline of the objective domination inside various social spheres.

Bourdieu also transposed his theory of class domination to masculine domination, which has become for him a paradigm of symbolic domination, in the sense that this domination is internalised by the dominated group and requires its complicity, because it is based on unconscious processes and recognition at the same time (elements which are all present in the 1977 definition of symbolic power). Masculine domination does not reduce to material inequalities, which are fundamental, but it adds the relatively autonomous strength of the symbolic division between a masculine pole, seen as superior, and a feminine one, seen as inferior (what anthropologists call the 'unequal valence' of genders inside symbolic structures).

This theory is centred on the stabilising and reproducing forces of domination, without denying the existence of struggles and changes, especially through political action. The dialectical and complex interactions between symbolic changes and objective inequalities (that is, inequalities in the distribution of various sorts of capital) are a challenge: how can one explain at the same time changes in the symbolic expression on one side (for example, symbolic victories of the feminist movement in the 1970s) *and* the various paths of changes in gender inequalities?

The answers relate to the issue of struggles and resistance.

Economic struggles, the working class and social movements

Economic struggles, in this general framework, cannot be reduced to the 'distribution or repartition conflicts' in the sharing of added value as it is usually understood from a strict macroeconomic or 'national accounting' point of view. The stake of economic struggles is to legitimate or contest an always socially arbitrary quantitative distribution of objects, money, etc. In line with Durkheim and his followers, Bourdieu's economic sociology does not reduce 'value' to a 'substantial' objective reality but relates it to a partially arbitrary power relation (see Orléan 2011 for a close analysis). This distribution process depends on the perception of what is 'normal' and 'acceptable' by social agents and the interaction between them. Conflicting norms relate to economic dominant representations, especially the ones provided by management and economics, in order to justify an (at least partially) arbitrary 'state of the world', and against which other representations may be used. Resistance and contestation are based on the possibility of a limit to symbolic domination. In the case of colonial societies, once the established order is denounced as unequal and unfair by organised political and military forces, a revolutionary change becomes possible (Bourdieu 1958 trans. Ross 1962). This is what Bourdieu calls 'symbolic revolution' – that is, an inversion of traditional order and social hierarchies. In periods of turmoil like the Chinese 'cultural revolution', this process of inversion may be of a great magnitude and produce total reversal of traditional hierarchies.

The existence of a 'social class' is the product of a process of symbolic unification taking place on the basis of similar existence conditions inside larger social spaces (Bourdieu 1979; 1979 trans. Nice 1984). The creation of institutions (unions, professional organisations, parties, etc.), which *represent* groups, is a way for these groups to exist in the public sphere, not only through claims, but also symbolic representations, discourses, strategies and actions. 'Spokespersons' have a major role in this process. They personify the group and give it a concrete aspect. They also produce the discourses which structure the public existence of the group. This process of *representation* (in various senses) of collective interests is a central component of economies where 'industrial relations' have been institutionalised. Institutions like collective bargaining systems, social security systems, social policy agencies and schemes appear as the stabilised results of symbolic struggles; they result in establishing a temporary 'consensus', which can also be broken at any time, as it is the case, for many of them, with neoliberal policies (see below the role of the State in the transformation of the housing market).

In this sense, Bourdieu appears rather close to neo-institutionalist analyses, especially when they stress the central role of institutions inside the economy, like the labour market and industrial relations: an economic system or field is first defined, usually at a national level, by a set of institutions through which production, distribution and exchanges are organised, and they may vary strongly across time and space. In this intellectual tradition, industrial relations are a major component of various sorts of capitalist (or 'socialist' in the case of the Soviet Union, China, etc.) institutional settings. Types of 'compromise' between the labour movement and company leaders are institutionalised in various norms, for example, as regards wages and power decisions inside companies. This is obvious in 'regulationist' analyses of Fordism as a particular setting organising the distribution of productivity gains among social groups (Boyer and Saillard 1995).

For Bourdieu, the existence of 'varieties of capitalism' and also of different neoliberal dynamics, which has been stressed by neo-institutionalists (Hall and Soskice 2001; Boyer *et al.* 2011; Amable 2005) is obvious: each national space has its own particular symbolic social history, whereby a diverse set of working class, a particular sort of socialist movement and social state institutions emerge. A comparative history of these processes is hence necessary to understand the various ways a society can achieve economic objectives, and to understand the dynamics of accumulation and crises (see Bourdieu 2012).

Companies, entrepreneurs and consumers as symbolic actors

Companies, corporate leaders and economic actors in general are not only motivated by economic remunerations (profits or monetary gains, utility), but also by what Bourdieu names 'symbolic profits'. Entrepreneurs, for example, accumulate symbolic capital of a specific kind, which is defined in the global economic field, and in particular sub-fields within it. They try not only to get richer through their activity, but also to get recognition for their 'innovative' or particularly 'efficient' action.

A first aspect of this analysis is to integrate into economic analysis the role of cultural – and in particular educational – characteristics of economic actors. This is obvious in Bourdieu and de Saint-Martin's study of 'Le patronat', which distinguishes cultures of French economic leaders depending on their membership to familial dynasties and their training in prominent business schools or administrative institutions like the *École nationale d'administration* (Bourdieu and de Saint-Martin 1978). In France, a traditional opposition exists between a financial-state oligarchy, which controls state capitalism, and a more familial capitalism, which is still relevant today.

A second aspect developed by Bourdieu, especially in his article 'Le champ économique' (Bourdieu 1997d), is to stress the importance of symbolic dimensions in daily economic competition between firms in the market. This dimension is obvious in sectors which are directly connected to the cultural world, like publishing companies. In this case, the value of books obviously refers to both economic and symbolic criteria. A publisher needs to accumulate symbolic capital of a certain kind. But it is also present in any sector where economic strategies aim at imposing a certain symbolic definition of products or services, through marketing, advertisement and the construction of particular needs among customers. The core of economic daily life itself is, hence, symbolic. Creating 'names' and 'brands' (for companies or leaders) is a major stake of distinction in the economic field. It imposes a reference to markets and consumers in order to become a part of the daily universe of cultural references of customers. This is even the case in the financial sphere, where objects, like complex financial products, are of a symbolic nature and their success depends on actor's systems of perception, even without any attempt to produce a 'brand image' or any conscious strategy of the firm. This symbolic dimension does not reduce to 'brand image', since what is at stake is more generally the way any 'economic good or service' is perceived by consumers, competitors, etc., especially through 'evaluation schemes'. These stakes are obvious in the case of cultural goods, wine or gastronomy, which are permanent subjects of symbolic struggles (see Garcia-Parpet 2009): the value of a particular wine, for example, relates to the construction of its quality and its singularity (Karpik 2007), and the imposition of particular ways of perceiving it. The process of symbolic definition of a good or a service involves a set of conflicting actors, which compete in order to impose their own representation of this definition. This conception enlarges the perspective in the sense that it imports in the economic analysis all the scientific tools which have been developed to study the literary or the intellectual fields: symbolic conflicts are present at any stage of economic action, from the investment decisions to the company strategies.

Thus, the analysis of markets does not rely solely upon the collection of data about economic profits and, more generally, the objective material conditions of production (which is of course necessary). It further demands an investigation into the various ways in which companies and their leaders are constructed as public references through communication and media, and into the ways they try to construct their own identity through discourse (storytelling, etc.) and representations. Also customers are symbolic actors, whose consumption patterns are embedded into their lifestyles, depending on their class, and more generally on a set of social conditions (Bourdieu 1979).

In this conception of the market, Bourdieu appears close to analyses centred on the notion of 'organisational field' developed in the classical texts regrouped by Powell and DiMaggio (1991), or, more recently, the theory of 'strategic action fields' by Fligstein and McAdam (2012). This conception insists on the importance of 'meso-level' social universes, characterised by particular sets of organisational rules and power stakes, where symbolic relations are important. But whereas these authors stress the organisational dimension of fields, and the way actors create coalitions and strategic alliances, Bourdieu would insist more on the centrality of symbolic stakes among all participating agents in each particular field, which would include struggles for the production of corporate strategies.

State, politics and the economy

The close link between economics and politics is a characteristic of economics, which grew close to political powers in order to help them accumulate wealth and power inside the economic world system (see Fourquet 1980). The two dominant traditions in post-World War II economics – neoliberal and Keynesian economics – have been produced and diffused in close relation with specific elite groups (bureaucratic, political and economic). This has been described through studies about the spread of economic ideas (Colander and Coats 1993).

Economics, while describing itself as 'pure' and 'autonomous', never ceased being very close to decision-makers. Breaking with the normative tendency of economics which is hidden behind a positivist rhetoric, Bourdieu suggests stressing the political dimension of economic objects and to consider political struggles as constitutive of economic reality, hence arguing for a synthesis between political science, sociology and economics. This synthesis has also been promoted by a group of scholars that study social capital.

One of the important empirical results of Bourdieu's research in the field of personal housing stresses the role of the State in the process of the social construction of markets. The birth of a policy which, in the 1970s, favoured the development of personal credit in order to give people greater access to private housing property was a way to integrate popular and middle classes into the economic system through access to property.

No market can exist without a complex set of laws and regulations, which do not only 'regulate' it from the outside but also 'frame' it from the inside. The bureaucratic field is a relatively autonomous social space where different actors compete to impose, among other stakes, a universal definition of economic reality. This universal, as well as a particular kind of 'interest to disinterestedness', was invented through a complex historical process which presupposed the concentration of symbolic capital in the hands of certain dominant actors (particular fractions of the nobility), able to call themselves 'the King', and later 'the State'. 'Thus was progressively established a specific economic logic, founded on levies without counterpart and redistribution functioning as the basis for the conversion of economic capital into symbolic capital' (Bourdieu 1994a trans. Johnson *et al.* 1998: 43). For Bourdieu, this specific economic logic plays an important role in the social construction of the economy. It is divided between contradictory forces. Since the building of what has been called a welfare state, one has to distinguish between the *little State nobility*, defining the 'left hand' of the State (teachers, social workers, nurses, agents of public services, etc.), and the *grand State nobility*, which constitutes the 'right hand' of the State. According to interviews published in *La Misère du Monde*, Bourdieu argues that shifts to neoliberalism and the transformation of European states have intensified the contradiction between these two forces. This is even more obvious in times of crisis and austerity policies, typically imposed by the right hand on the left hand.

Bourdieu's texts grouped in 'Language and symbolic power' (from 'Ce que parler veut dire', Bourdieu 1982a trans. Raymond and Adamson 1991) contain theoretical articles and applications of this theory to different fields and questions: the State and the *political field*, with analyses about official vocabulary and classifications (the State tends to have a 'monopoly of symbolic violence'), analyses about delegation, representation, spokesmen, etc. The application of this theory to the question of political power is based on the articulation of three analytical strategies:

1. the analysis of the use of political discourse as a denial of domination and, for the State or the judicial discourse, as a way to impose a neutral legitimate order denying the existence of power relations;
2. the analysis of the objective structural and statistical relations (the space of social classes or in some occurrences the space of class struggles) *behind* the words and linguistic exchanges, which are at the foundation of authority, domination and power; and
3. the study of the symbolic power of discourse as a power of creation in itself ('performativity' in a larger meaning than Austin's).[6]

One has here again the three theoretical components which were underlined above. In particular, as an illustration of the third element, one can mention the classical example of the 'theory effect', with the category of 'working class' (and 'exploitation') produced and reproduced by Marxist and socialist doctrines, allowing these doctrines to be part of the reality of the social world (as it is obvious in 'socialist' states). It shows that Bourdieu integrates symbolic struggles and actions as a way to try and change social reality, but on the basis of strong invariant structural mechanisms and reproducing forces. In *Distinction*, he also sees symbolic struggles as a key to understanding consumption practices and permanent behaviour changes inside a stable structural pattern. This pattern is a social space, defined by relations between different assets. To be different and to distinguish oneself from others – to manifest 'finer' tastes, like playing golf and going to the opera, characteristic of the upper classes, or to defend the 'authenticity' of playing a 'man's' game like rugby or listening to ghetto rap music, characteristic of the lower classes – is a permanent stake of a large number of cultural and consumption attitudes. Empirical results in a large set of countries tend to show that the space of lifestyle is still strongly structured by social class membership, provided it is defined in relational terms as Bourdieu tries to do (see Coulangeon and Duval 2013).

Conclusion

On many occasions, Bourdieu extends his sociological analysis to the apparently mechanical reproduction of 'economic domination' and accumulation of 'economic capital'. The examples of the devaluation of Béarn peasants' symbolic capital, 'paternalism' in traditional economy or the modern case of 'new management' methods show the importance of symbolic domination processes inside the economic field, where the objective hierarchies of power, income and prestige are euphemised, redefined, and transfigured by discursive processes. Symbolic capital appears to be central in the economic field as a resource related to all other resources, a kind of asset that doubles all the other assets. Bourdieu re-thinks the economy on the basis of this general posture. Through the stress he puts on the role of social properties of economic actors, the centrality of language and symbols in the economy, and the multidimensionality of any economic field, Bourdieu may help neo-institutionalists to renew the analysis of concrete realities.

Notes

1 This preoccupation was already present at the very beginning of his intellectual trajectory, when he described the importance of family *names* as central symbols in the traditional logic of honour in Algeria (Bourdieu 1958).
2 This paragraph is based on a communication presented at the 'Beyond Bourdieu' conference in Copenhagen in 2008.
3 For more detailed developments, see Lebaron (2014).
4 Not surprisingly, the notion of symbolic capital itself (defined as 'prestige, honour, in brief *hurma*' in 1972) really emerged as such in anthropological texts about Algeria, especially Kabylia. In *Esquisse d'une théorie de la pratique* published in 1972 (and translated into English as *Outline of a Theory of Practice*), one finds one of the first occurrences of the well-known representation of social resources which is based on the four species of capital, and an asymmetric role ascribed to symbolic capital that provides others with their values, but also dissimulates the origin of this value (which creates a logical circle). '[S]ymbolic capital [...] has a particular effect provided and only provided it dissimulates the fact that "material" species of capital are at its origin, and, finally, at the origin of its effects' (Bourdieu 1972b: 376).
5 This paragraph is based on a rewriting and expansion of our article 'Toward a new critique of economic discourse', originally published in English in *Theory, Culture and Society* (Lebaron 2001).
6 For Bourdieu, 'performativity' is directly related to the inequality of symbolic capital, and depends on social conditions, which enlarges the notion of performativity.

5 The State and economics

A Bourdieusian critique

Gabriella Paolucci

Introduction

One of the most important contributions of Bourdieu's sociology is the analysis of the symbolic dimension of economic practices. Since his early ethnographic studies on traditional Algerian society, Bourdieu has shown interest in the ways mythical and ethical representations contribute to the reproduction of the economic and social order that produce them. This becomes his starting point in developing a theory of 'symbolic capital', a form which all types of capital take when their possession is perceived as legitimate. Produced by the transfiguration of power relations into meaning relations, symbolic capital is closely related to the concept of 'symbolic violence': the violence exercised upon a social agent with his or her complicity. In this context, the State plays a leading role, since it appears to legitimately monopolise symbolic violence and act as the central bank of symbolic capital. Bourdieu's criticism of neoclassical economics and neoliberal politics can be placed in this theoretical perspective. Bourdieu analyses neoliberalism as a belief system that mystifies interests and power by making them articles of faith. Neoliberal discourse is a symbolic order which presents itself as universal and neutral, but increasingly becomes a tool to exercise power. Bourdieu stresses that the economic discourse contains the effect both of naturalisation and of universalisation, which produce symbolic violence, legitimated and distributed by the State.

This chapter focuses on Bourdieu's theory of the relationship between the State and economics in modern capitalist societies. In particular, it addresses the domination effect of neoliberal discourse as a discourse controlled, selected, distributed and legitimated by the State.

The symbolic dimension of economic practices

As is well known, Bourdieu's initial research in Algeria played a pivotal role in his intellectual trajectory. It is in Algeria that the issues, the topics and the concepts which constitute the body of Bourdieu's sociology began to take shape. Whilst in the country, alongside sociological surveys, Bourdieu conducted anthropological research into the archaic Kabyle society. These studies were published between the late 1960s and the early 1970s, and were further systematised within two books: *Esquisse d'une théorie de la pratique* (Bourdieu 1972b) and *Le Sens pratique* (Bourdieu 1980g). The issue addressed by Bourdieu in these works is central to our argument. In fact, one needs to understand what is 'the determinative contribution that ethical and mythical representations can bring to the reproduction of the economic order of which they are the product' (Bourdieu 1980g trans. Nice 1990: 129). His answer to such a question constitutes the very ground for the formulation of his theories on symbolic domination and on the State.

Bourdieu observed that in the Kabyle society within some reproduction strategies (common to all archaic societies) the 'relations of force' (*rapports de force*) between individuals are transmuted into relations of meaning. Institutional void calls for 'elementary forms of domination', an expression which Bourdieu borrowed from Durkheim's terminology. The exercise of domination can be fully enacted only in a direct form, i.e. from person to person, given that the individuals are mutually dependent in terms of survival. As a result of the ties that bind all social actors, the economic relations – and, broadly speaking, the relations of force – cannot be recognised as such and must be concealed. In other words, as Bourdieu noted in his paper on the forms of domination later included in *Le Sens pratique*: 'domination [...] takes place overtly and has to be disguised under the veil of enchanted relationships; [...] in short, to be socially recognised, it must be misrecognised' (ibid.: 126).

Such process of misrecognition can be easily detected in the honour-bound strategies. By analysing the *khammessat*, exchange of gifts and dowry, Bourdieu discovered that the economic nature of social relations is dissimulated and, as we shall see, the dissimulation constitutes one of the cornerstones of symbolic domination. As much as they are presented and perceived as being 'disinterested' and irrelevant to the economic field, in reality such practices are basically interested, that is, oriented, by economic interests. The ostensible disinterest hides material interest which is symbolically transfigured (Paolucci 2010).

In the *khammessat* system – which is a verbal contract similar to the metayage (a system of farming on halves) – those who cultivate the land (*khammès*) are completely submitted to the landlord, who alone is entitled to dictate the contract's terms. The *khammès* abdicates freedom and initiative and receives only a small share of the harvest. The essential characteristic of such a contract is that, although based on relations of force, it is purported as a friendly agreement between two persons and guaranteed only by the loyalty demanded by honour. The asymmetry of the relationship is tempered with the influence exerted by the community, which is inclined to censure any abuse by the landlords. Such 'interested fictions' see to it that 'far from seeing himself as a slave or alienated proletarian, the *khammès* shares in the integral life of the family or tribal group, sharing its concerns and sufferings, and its sporadic misery' (ibid.: 76). In short, the *khammessat* consists in an economic tie based on the exploitation between two social agents but neither of them perceives it as being exploitative because the nature of the economic relationship is disguised under the veil of ethical relationships. Private and particular interests are 'transmute[d] into disinterested, collective, publicly avowable, legitimate interests' (Bourdieu 1972b trans. Nice 1977: 40). As Bourdieu argues '[their] essence remains implicit because unquestioned and unquestionable' (ibid.: 199).

Gift exchanges and marriage strategies, i.e. the dowry, also follow the same logic. The gift appears to be a machine which transforms the economic nature of the exchange into a symbolic relation and which, more generally, dresses up arbitrary inequalities as legitimate differences. Thus, as a 'commerce of honour', dowries are but another form through which the exchange of gifts and counter-gifts takes place. Such a collectively sustained lie – both to oneself and to others – is at the heart of the functioning of symbolic exchange, which Bourdieu defines as 'a fake circulation of fake coin' (ibid.: 6).

The symbolic capital

In order to describe the euphemisation of economic interest, Bourdieu introduced the concept of 'symbolic capital', a key notion in his work. By referring to the Kabyle society, Bourdieu provides a definition of symbolic capital in *Le Sens pratique*:

> In an economy which is defined by the refusal to recognise the 'objective' truth of economic practices, that is, the law of 'naked self-interest' and 'egoistic calculation', even 'economic' capital cannot act unless it succeeds in being recognised through a conversion that can render unrecognisable the true principle of its efficacy. Symbolic capital is this denied capital, recognised as legitimate, that is, misrecognised as capital (recognition, acknowledgement in the sense of gratitude aroused by benefits can be one of the foundations of this recognition) which, along with religious capital, is perhaps the only possible form of accumulation when economic capital is not recognised.
>
> (Bourdieu 1980g trans. Nice 1990: 118)

As mentioned in the previous chapter, symbolic capital bears a different status from other forms of capital which constitute Bourdieu's conceptual apparatus, and rests on a different analytical plain. As the product of the transmutation of relations of force into relations of meaning, symbolic capital refers to and complements the notion of symbolic violence. Moreover, symbolic capital makes it possible for the social order – alongside its hierarchies and the deriving relations of domination – to appear as being seemingly natural and as taken for granted. As Bourdieu remarks in his *Méditations Pascaliennes*:

> every kind of capital (economic, cultural, social) tends (to different degrees) to function as symbolic capital ... when it obtains an explicit or practical recognition, that of a habitus structured according to the very structures of the space in which it has been engendered.
>
> (Bourdieu 1997a trans. Nice 2000: 242)

Symbolic capital was deployed to illustrate the specific forms assumed by the misrecognition of economic interests at the basis of symbolic productions in Kabyle society, which Bourdieu treated as a sort of laboratory for studying the strategies of accumulation, reproduction and transmission of symbolic capital. It was then applied to analyse the ways in which symbolic domination functions within contemporary societies. We return to this topic in the next section.

There is a clear gap between the 'objectivist' perspectives – held by Marx, Polanyi, Sahlins and Lévi-Strauss – on pre-capitalist social forms, and the view held by Bourdieu, who, whilst recognising the role played by material (i.e. economic) coercion, sees in the symbolic forms in which coercion is transfigured a further energy that supports it and contributes to reproducing it. In fact, according to Bourdieu, symbolic productions[1] possess the ability to exercise another kind of power. Their 'almost magical power' enables them to obtain the equivalent of what is obtained through coercion by virtue of the specific effect of mobilisation which can be implemented only if such power is recognised, that is, misrecognised as arbitrary. In this respect, Bourdieu argues that symbolic power is the 'power to constitute the given by stating it, to act on the world by acting upon the representations of the world' (Bourdieu and Wacquant 1992 trans. Wacquant 1992: 148). As he remarked in his 'Sur le pouvoir symbolique' (Bourdieu 1977e trans. Adamson 1991), symbolic power is 'a transformed, i.e. misrecognisable, transfigured and legitimated form of the other forms of power' (Ibid.: 170).[2] Such a theoretical perspective – which Bourdieu refers to as 'the economy of symbolic exchanges' (Ibid.) – overcomes the classical dichotomy between culturalism and economicism, object and subject. This is 'the most constant and important intention' (Bourdieu and Wacquant 1992: 43) in Bourdieu's work – as noted in Chapter 2 of the present volume.

According to Bourdieu, the relationship between the structuring and structured aspects of symbolic productions is at the very core of their ability to exercise power in the social world: 'as instruments of knowledge and communication "symbolic systems" can exercise a structuring power only because they themselves are structured' (Bourdieu 1977e trans. Adamson 1991: 166). By virtue of their dual property, symbolic productions can act as instruments of domination:

> It is as structured and structuring instruments of communication and knowledge that 'symbolic systems' fulfil their political function, as instruments which help to ensure that one class dominates another (symbolic violence) by bringing their own distinctive power to bear on the relations of power which underlie them and thus by contributing, in Weber's terms, to the 'domestication of the dominated'.
>
> (Bourdieu 1977e trans. Adamson 1991: 167)

The 'materialist theory of the economy of symbolic goods', which Bourdieu tried to build throughout his whole career, puts at the centre of the enquiry 'the objectivity of the subjective experience of relations of domination' (Bourdieu 1998b trans. Nice 2001: 34) and is located at the intersection of three distinct classical theories on the foundation of power: Weber's legitimacy theory (i.e. domination as 'the probability that a command with a specific given content will be obeyed by a given group of persons'), Durkheim's consensus theory (i.e. the internalisation of 'primitive forms of classification', which constitutes the foundation of the immediate and pre-reflexive consensus on the meaning of the world) and the Marxian perspective, with specific reference to its view on dominant ideology.[3]

As far as an analysis of symbolic power is concerned, none of these approaches is in itself comprehensive, given that, as Bourdieu and Passeron argue, 'the conditions which enable each of them to be constituted exclude the possibility of the object-construction carried out by the other two' (Bourdieu and Passeron 1970 trans. Nice 1977: 4).

The State as 'the central bank of symbolic capital'

The approach developed by Bourdieu on the collective euphemisation process of the material interests within the Kabyle system is echoed in his analysis of the symbolic power within modern societies. Here the presence of institutions exempts individuals from exercising domination directly and violence is – so to speak – built into the very core of such institutions. The State is the modern institution which is mostly responsible for ensuring the conservation and the legitimation of relations of domination, as it masterminds the *doxic* submission to social order and the credence to the legitimacy of domination.

Bourdieu's state theory, which first appeared in texts published in the 1980s and the 1990s (Bourdieu 1984a trans. Collier 1988; 1989b trans. Clough 1996; 1993b trans. Wacquant and Farage 1994) and which spans across his work, is fully articulated in *Sur l'État* (Bourdieu 2012), the posthumous text featuring his 1989–1991 lectures at the Collège de France. We could think about, for instance, Bourdieu's works between the 1960s and the 1970s on dominant ideology, political representation and reproduction strategies, which all address the structures and the functions of modern States. Moreover, we could mention Bourdieu's writings on the emergence of the juridical field, on the genesis and the structure of the bureaucratic field, on the science of government; these are all works in which Bourdieu begins to fully and explicitly address the issue of the State as being one of the centres that are mostly responsible for symbolic domination (Bourdieu 1993b trans. Wacquant and Farage 1994). We also need to remind the reader of two of Bourdieu's crucial works: *Homo Academicus* (Bourdieu 1984a trans. Collier 1988), in which we find the first definition of the State as being 'recognised as legitimate, that is [...] the holder of the monopoly of legitimate symbolic violence' (ibid.: 27); and *La Noblesse d'État* (Bourdieu 1989b trans. Clough 1996), which features one of the most rigorous analyses of symbolic violence exercised by the State through one of its agencies, i.e. the educational system. Furthermore, the most comprehensive guide to Bourdieu's thinking on the State is now available, i.e. his 1989–1992 Collège de France lectures (Bourdieu 2012).

In Bourdieu's view, the State heavily contributes to the production and reproduction of the instruments that build social reality. It organises and regulates practices and exercises a formative action of durable dispositions by imposing on social agents constraints and obligations. The State also imposes – both in reality and in people's minds – all the fundamental principles of social classification produced by the application of cognitive categories, which are thus reified and naturalised, that is, the State has the ability to impose and inculcate in a universal manner a *nomos*, a shared principle of vision and division, identical or similar cognitive and evaluative structures. Consequently the State is the foundation of a 'logic conformism' and of a 'moral conformism', 'of a tacit, prereflexive agreement over the meaning of the world which itself lies at the basis of the experience of the world as "common world"' (Bourdieu 1993b trans. Wacquant and Farage 1994: 13).

Moreover, the State is:

> the source of the symbolic efficacy of all the rites of institution, those which are at the basis of the family, for example, and also those which are performed through the functioning of the educational system, which, between those it selects and those it eliminates, sets up durable and often definitive symbolic differences, universally recognised within the area of its authority.
> (Bourdieu 1993b trans. Wacquant and Farage 1994)

Thus, by recalling Durkheim's definition of religion and by underscoring the analogies between State and religion, Bourdieu claims that the State fulfils 'fundamental functions such as social conservation, i.e. preserving the conditions that enable the accumulation of capital *in that* it is a principle of orthodoxy, a collective fiction, a well-founded illusion' (Bourdieu 2012: 19). In short, the State is the institution *par excellence* entrusted with exercising symbolic violence.

Following Weber, Bourdieu argues that the State is characterised by the monopoly of the violence exercised over a given territory and over its inhabitants; however, he broadens the definition of violence by adding a symbolic dimension: 'the State is an X (to be determined) which claims the monopoly of the legitimate use of the physical and *symbolic* violence over a definite territory and over the totality of the corresponding populations' (Bourdieu 1993b. trans. Wacquant and Farage 1994: 3). In a way, Bourdieu's definition substantiates Weber's definition of the State, as 'the most brutal relations of force are always simultaneously symbolic relations' (Bourdieu 2012: 260).

Clearly Bourdieu's formulation does not oppose theories held by Weber, Marx (though differently) and mainstream Western political philosophy, which regarded repressive forces as a common feature of State action. Bourdieu widens the State's scope so that the physical dimension of violence goes hand in hand with the symbolic one. He criticises the way in which those thinkers have thematised State action in exclusively political terms and have failed to address the development of devices of legitimacy which incarnate themselves 'simultaneously in objectivity, in the form of specific organisational structures and mechanisms, and in subjectivity, in the form of mental structures and categories of thought and perception' (Bourdieu 1993b trans. Wacquant and Farage 1994: 40). Ultimately, such theories failed 'to rupture with the State-thought' (ibid.: 37) even when, as in Marx, they radically questioned its action. In other words, they failed to move towards what Bourdieu referred to as an 'epistemological questioning' of the logical conformism relentlessly produced and reproduced by the State. The exercise of such epistemological surveillance is the only antidote against the risk of being 'thought by a State that we believe we are thinking' (ibid.: 35).

Bourdieu engages in the 'genetic' reconstruction of the State, which he considers as 'the most effective weapon against State-thought' (Bourdieu 2012: 183). The State emerges – as in Weber – in parallel with the development of specialised units which exercise violence; the concentration of physical capital in the hands of a few is paralleled by the concentration of economic capital through taxation and the establishment of a legitimate language. According to Bourdieu's model of the emergence of the State, it is the culmination of a process of concentration of different species of capital: capital of physical force or instruments of coercion, economic capital, cultural or informational capital, and symbolic capital. As Bourdieu argues, 'it is this concentration as such which constitutes the State as the holder of a sort of meta-capital granting power over other species of capital and over their holders' (ibid.: 4). This meta-capital is the *symbolic capital* here.

The concentration of the different species of capital proceeds hand in hand with the construction of the corresponding fields, leading indeed to the emergence of a specific 'statist' capital (i.e. capital over the State), which enables the State to exercise power over different fields and over the different particular species of capital and especially the rate of conversion between them (ibid.: 4). Consequently the construction of the State proceeds with the construction of a field of power, which Bourdieu defines as 'the space of play within which the holders of capital struggle in particular for power over the State, i.e. over the statist capital granting power over the different species of capital and over their reproduction' (ibid.: 5). Therefore, Bourdieu integrates Weber's perspective with a reconstruction of the concentration of *symbolic capital* and this is what makes this theoretical construct original.

As the place which concentrates most of the symbolic capital and the deriving power – 'objectified [...] codified, delegated and guaranteed by the State, in a world bureaucratised' (Bourdieu 1993b trans. Wacquant and Farage 1994: 8) – the State acts as a *central bank of symbolic capital* and grants every act of 'legitimate imposture' and 'constitution' that is necessary to uphold the authority of State power. Such acts include, amongst others, the mysterious 'power of nomination', which is a very mysterious act whose logic is similar to the magical practices described by Mauss, 'which mobilises the capital of belief accumulated by the functioning of the magical universe' (ibid.: 11).[4] Nomination belongs to the category of *official* acts or discourses 'symbolically effective only because they are accomplished in a situation of authority by authorised characters, "officials" who are acting *ex officio*, as holders of an *officium*, that is, of a function or position assigned by the State' (ibid.: 13). Bourdieu ranks among these acts also the 'juridical verdict', 'a legitimate exercise of the power to say what it is and to make exist what it states', and the construction of 'natural' realities such as the family, which is indeed:

> a fiction, a social artefact, an illusion in the most ordinary sense of the word, but a 'well-founded illusion', because, being produced and reproduced by the guarantee of the State, it receives from the State at every moment the means to exist and persist.
>
> (Bourdieu 1996b: 25)

These brief remarks clearly show that the representation of the State provided by Bourdieu radically differs from mainstream scientific and political representations. Contrary to certain 'democratic' interpretations, the State is not the expression of a hypothetically pre-existing civil society arising and expressing itself through the government to whom organisational power is entrusted. Bourdieu deems such a perspective and all the contractualist traditions as being completely false. As Bourdieu argues:

> It is by building this sort of unprecedented organisation, this sort of extraordinary thing which is a State, by building this set of both material and symbolic organisational resources to which we associate the notion of State, that all the social agents responsible for such constructing built the State in the sense of a unified population which speaks the same language, such phenomenon often being considered as first cause.
>
> (Bourdieu 2012: 61)

Such unsubstantiated representations have become established and propagated as to becoming at least sometime scholarly *doxa* because the State – the main producer of the instruments to construct social reality – imposes the cognitive structures by which it is thought, including the legitimate definition of any questions that concern it. Here is a common thread which spans across all of Bourdieu's work: credence as the foundation for legitimacy. If 'State actions' – i.e. 'legitimate' political acts which, ultimately, are the only tangible features when thinking about the State – are effective, it is only because we believe that there is a principle which grounds their legitimacy. The notions of official, public and universal – all attributes which the State ascribes to itself – are in fact illusions, the result of a symbolic imposition. If the State offers its citizens 'the show of the universal' and compels them to believe that the State viewpoint on the social world is a 'viewpoint with no viewpoints' – i.e. a universal and uninvolved viewpoint – it does nothing but reinforce a particular viewpoint, i.e. that of the dominant. Thus, the show of the universal derives from 'the effect of divinisation' required to provide grounds to an utterly arbitrary legitimacy. Like

Janus, the State has two faces, because 'one cannot have the universe without being a monopoliser of the universal' (ibid.: 162). Therefore, the process of concentration of the various species of capital analysed by Bourdieu is the process of dispossession (see the formation of a national language) and monopolisation: the 'monopolisation of the universal' (ibid.: 166).

The twofold social construction: State and market

In Bourdieu's view, the economy is one of the fields in which the monopolisation of the universal is mostly applied. The reason is clear enough: in order to legitimate itself and reproduce social order, the State needs to disguise its economic policies under the veil of universality and naturality. Thus, the State contributes to the existence and reproduction of both the economic field and the decisions made within it, whilst structuring the relations of force that characterise the market. This occurs chiefly through different policies which are implemented by the State

> as and when it sees fit (for example, its 'family policies' which, through inheritance laws, the tax regime, family allowances and social assistance, have their effect on consumption – particularly on the consumption of houses – and standards of living) and, at a deeper level, through the structural effects produced by budgets, expenditure on infrastructure, particularly in the fields of transport, energy, housing and telecommunications, the taxation (or exemption from tax) of investment, control of the means of payment and credit, training of labour and the regulation of immigration, and the definition and imposition of the rules of the economic game, such as, for example, the labour contract – all these being so many political interventions which make the bureaucratic field a macroeconomic stimulator, playing its part in ensuring the stability and predictability of the economic field.
>
> (Bourdieu 2000b trans. Turner 2005: 12–13)

As Bourdieu notes, it follows that economics 'is more of a State science and is, as a result, haunted by State thinking' (ibid.: 10). This issue spans across many of Bourdieu's writings, particularly in *The Social Structures of the Economy* (Bourdieu 2000b trans. Turner 2005), in which – more systematically than elsewhere – he analyses the relations between State and economics within capitalist societies. Such analysis seeks to challenge the neoliberal *vulgate*, showing that the economic rules regulating the market are by no means independent from State policies (or, in other terms, from the bureaucratic field). Just as individual dispositions, tastes and ambitions involved in economic decisions – i.e. the decision to buy a single-family house – are socially constructed, similarly the dynamics of production and distribution of goods do not comply with universal and natural laws immanent to economics but are the product of an eminently political social construction.

Bourdieu structures his analysis by considering the single-family house market, which is the main topic under investigation, and he notes that:

> the market in single-family houses is (as all markets no doubt are to varying degrees) the product of a *twofold social construction* to which the State contributes crucially: the construction of demand, through the production of individual dispositions and, more precisely, of systems of individual preferences – most importantly regarding ownership or renting – and also through the allotting of the necessary resources, that is to say, State assistance for building or for housing, as defined in laws and regulations whose genesis can also be described; the construction of supply, through State policy (or that of banks) conditions of credit to building companies, which contributes, together with the nature of the means of production used, to defining conditions of access to the market and, more precisely, a company's position within the structure of the – highly dispersed – field of house builders and, hence, the structural constraints applying to the decisions made by each of them with regard to production and advertising.
>
> (Ibid.: 16)

To argue that a given market is the product of a 'twofold social construction' – i.e. the construction of both demand and supply – is tantamount to claiming that the housing market and each of its parts are all but independent from social functioning mechanisms. In fact, as Bourdieu pointed out throughout this essay, demand and supply depend on a set of purely political and social factors:

> Economic choices in respect of housing, whether to buy or to rent, whether to buy an old house or a new one and, in the latter case, whether to buy a traditionally built house or an 'industrial' one, depend, on the one hand, on the (socially constituted) economic dispositions of the agents – particularly on their tastes – and the economic resources they can summon and, on the other, on the state of supply of dwellings. But the two terms of the canonical relationship, which neoclassical economic theory treats as unconditioned givens, depend in turn, more or less directly, on a whole set of economic and social conditions produced by housing policy.
>
> (Ibid.: 15)

According to Bourdieu, the construction of individual expectations, wishes and ambitions meets the laws and the market's interests – supported and sanctioned by the State – in the social world. Hence, contrary to what the economic discourse would like us to believe, there is nothing natural about the economic nature of such phenomena, which are the product of a purely political construction. The analysis of the housing market allows Bourdieu to broaden the scope of his research, to tackle the more general issue regarding the nature of economic dispositions and to critically discuss the assumptions maintained by neoclassical economic theories, which hold a naturalised and ahistorical perspective on market dynamics. Bourdieu aptly demonstrates, both in empirical and in theoretical terms, that economic laws are the historically determined product of the policies implemented by the State.

The effect of symbolic violence: neoliberalism as doxa

Moving from this case study, Bourdieu develops a more general analysis of the relations binding State and economy within contemporary society and harshly criticises both the neoclassical economic perspective and the sociological approaches that refer to it in different ways. The critique of the neoclassical economic paradigm echoes the criticisms which – in other writings (see e.g. Bourdieu 1997d) – Bourdieu levels against utilitarianism and the Becker-style rational action theory, because they perceive social actors as detached entities; employ the flabby notion of 'human capital'; deny the social and historical nature of economic practices; and conceive economic practices as conforming to universal and ahistorical laws – the 'universalisation effect'. Contrary to mainstream economic discourse, Bourdieu argues that the economy is all but neutral and independent from other fields. The mixture of the *effect of universalisation* and the *effect of naturalisation* disguises economic phenomena and incorporates them within a world which is legitimised by its dehistoricisation and its naturalisation. As Bourdieu argues in the 'Introduction' to *The Social Structures of the Economy*:

> [B]etween economic theory in its purest, that is to say, most formalised, form, which is never as neutral as it wishes to believe or make out, and the policies implemented in its name or legitimated through it, agents and institutions are interposed that are steeped in all the assumptions inherited from immersion in a particular economic world, which is the product of a singular social history. Neoliberal economics, the logic of which is tending today to win out throughout the world thanks to international bodies like the World Bank or the International Monetary Fund and the governments to whom they, directly or indirectly, dictate their principles of 'governance', owes a certain number of its allegedly universal characteristics to the fact that it is immersed or embedded in a particular society, that is to say, rooted in a system of beliefs and values, an ethos and a moral view of the world, in short, an *economic common sense*, linked, as such, to the social and cognitive structures of a particular social order. It is from this particular economy that neoclassical economic theory borrows its fundamental assumptions, which it formalises and rationalises, thereby establishing them as the foundations of a universal model.
>
> (Bourdieu 2000b trans. Turner 2005: 10)

Controlled, selected, distributed and legitimated by the State, a consensus about the positive effects of globalisation and liberalisation has established itself as a dominant discourse across the social space. This discourse established itself as a doxa – an unquestionable orthodoxy that operates as if it were the objective truth – colonising the discussion about economic policies. The neoliberal philosophy of development is an expression of the interests of neo-conservative restoration forces in the world, the forces of mega-capital that promote ultra-right utopia, the utopia as unrestricted exploitation (Bourdieu 1998a trans. Nice 1998: 107). Such logic leads to the extensive exploitation of labourers: job dismissal, unemployment, job insecurity, privatisation of public services, destruction of the institutions of the Welfare State and the achieved standards in the domain of labour law.

Bourdieu's theoretical critique of the neoliberal *doxa* joins the criticism of the vocabulary used in the dominant economic discourse. One of the most criticised notions is that of 'globalisation' (or '*mondialisation*'), which Bourdieu defines as 'a simultaneously descriptive and prescriptive pseudo-concept'. He stresses that 'globalisation is not homogenisation; it is, instead, continuation of the power and influence of a small number of dominant nations over the totality of the national stock exchanges' (Bourdieu 1998a trans. Nice 1998: 43).

At the same time Bourdieu claims that, whilst the nation State contributes to unify the economic space (given that the economic field constitutes itself chiefly through the creation of a national State), in the late capitalist societies a set of conjunctural factors – i.e. liberalisation, deregulation and the development of new communication technologies with the deriving mobility of capital and delocalisation of industrial enterprises – fostered the constitution of a highly *polarised global economic field.* Such process – which neoclassical *doxa* labels 'globalisation' – tends to enfeeble local and national authorities and to leave 'citizens powerless in the face of great transnational economic and financial forces' (Bourdieu 2000b trans. Turner 2005: 230).

The latter issue is chiefly addressed in Bourdieu's monumental study of those living in the French suburbs, *La Misère du monde* (Bourdieu ed. 1993 trans. Ferguson 1999). Although globalisation causes a great limitation to the economic power of any given State, the State does not cease to possess and exercise considerable power on its territory by embracing and legitimising neoliberal views and practices that lead to economic and policy measures 'which have helped create social division' (Bourdieu ed. 1993 trans. Ferguson 1999: 181). From such a viewpoint, as Bourdieu notes, the opposition between economic liberalism and statism does not hold up under close investigation.

Conclusions: a theory effect

Bourdieu calls 'theory effects' the changes of practices induced by a certain theory that corresponds to some socially legitimised representations. In other words, 'theory effect' can be understood as the effect of imposition of the principles of division which occurs whenever an attempt is made to make something explicit. Bourdieu stresses that 'theory effect' 'may be exerted by agents and organisations capable to imposing a principle of division or, if you like, of producing or reinforcing systematically the propensity to favour certain aspects of the reality and ignore others' (Bourdieu 1982a trans. Raymond and Adamson 1991: 135).

Neoliberal discourse is a paradigmatic case of this effect of theory. It is a powerful economic theory which reinforces, by the particular symbolic power bound up with its theory effect, the power of economic realities that it is deemed to express.

According to Bourdieu, neoliberal discourse is not just one discourse among the many. Rather, it is:

> a 'strong discourse' – the way psychiatric discourse is in an asylum, in Erving Goffman's analysis. It is so strong and so hard to combat only because it has on its side all the forces of a world of relations of forces, a world that it contributes to making what it is.
>
> (Bourdieu 1998e)

It does this most notably by orienting the political and economic choices of those who dominate the bureaucratic field in the nation States. It thus adds its own symbolic force to the relations of forces between economic and bureaucratic fields. 'In the name of this scientific programme, converted into a plan of political action, an immense *political project* is underway, although its status as such is denied because it appears to be purely negative' (Ibid.). This project aims to create the conditions under which the 'theory' can be realised and can function: *a programme of the methodical destruction of collectives*.

Notes

1 For an analysis of the different layers in the meaning undergone by the adjective 'symbolic' in Bourdieu's sociological thinking, see Pinto (2002). For a better understanding of the notion of 'symbolic power', see Wacquant's contribution (1993), which focuses on the relationship between Bourdieu's perspective and Marxist theory.

2 Originally published in 1977, this essay plays a crucial role in understanding both Bourdieu's theory on symbolic power and the relationships between symbolic structures and social world. Bourdieu makes reference to it in his *Masculine Domination* to explain the meaning which he attributed to the adjective 'symbolic' in the concept of 'symbolic power' (Bourdieu 1998b trans. Nice 2001: 34).

3 The way in which Bourdieu addresses the subject of domination fuels an open debate with the Marxian perspective, which always represented a constant reference point in Bourdieu's view on domination. Although Bourdieu had used the notion of 'ideology' – at least in the early stages of the development of his theory on symbolic domination – he blamed the 'Marxist perspective' for confining symbolic systems' functions exclusively to a political dimension and for attributing them to the dominant class. According to Bourdieu, Marx's theory of dominant ideology minimises the actual effectiveness of the symbolic support produced by relations of force. In other words, failing to consider the logic structure and the gnoseological function of symbolic productions prevents Marxism from thinking about the recognition of the legitimacy of domination.

4 Bourdieu explains: 'The President of the country is someone who claims to be the President but who differs from the madman who claims to be Napoleon by the fact that he is recognised as founded to do so' (1993b trans. Wacquant and Farage 1994: 12).

6 Animal spirits and habitus

Towards a convergence between Keynes and Bourdieu?

Michael Lainé[1]

Introduction

Arguably, Bourdieu's work was primarily directed against rational action theory, "paradigmatic form of the scholastic illusion" (Bourdieu 2000b trans. Turner 2005: 7), derived from mainstream economic theories, in that it created an "anthropological monster, this theoretically minded man of practice" (Ibid.: 209), the *homo economicus*. Such "scholastic illusion" consisted of putting in the decision-maker's mind the models elaborated by the scientist in order to account for her behaviour: "the scientific subject, endowed with a perfect knowledge of causes and probable outcome, is projected into the active agent" (Ibid.: 213). Bourdieu endorsed an "applied rationalism" (Bourdieu *et al.* 1968 trans. Nice 1991), which led him to make a plea for some form of realism that would not take at face value what people think of themselves. His whole theoretical enterprise revolved around avoiding those twin pitfalls, the "illusion of immediate knowledge" (Ibid.: 15) and the "scholastic illusion", a will that gave rise to the concept of habitus, i.e. the implementation of a "practical sense" by individuals in their everyday behaviour. Therefore, it should not be surprising that he kept on castigating neoliberalism and mainstream economics throughout his life, in his public statements as well as in his scientific stances.

For Keynes alike, mainstream economics' main loophole was a blatant lack of realism. In *The General Theory of Employment, Interest and Money* (hereafter, GT), he forcefully put forth that "the tacit assumptions (of the classical theory) are seldom or never satisfied, with the result that it cannot solve the economic problems of the actual world". The main contribution to what has been called the "Keynesian revolution" in economic thought was the focus on actual expectations and individual decision-making. Such focus departed from an extensive use of mathematical modelling. In fact, as early as in the book derived from his doctoral dissertation, the *Treatise on Probability* (hereafter, TP), he kept on chastising the "mathematical charlatanry" (TP: 401) of those who use probability calculus as a guide of conduct. In the GT, he added: "Too large a proportion of recent 'mathematical' economics are merely concoctions … which allow the author to lose sight of the complexities and interdependencies of the real world in a maze of pretentious and unhelpful symbols" (298). Would

Keynes still be alive today, he would heap fierce criticisms on the rational action theory and all its derivatives.

Both authors strongly reject rational action theories. Both focus on "everyday reasoning", "common sense" (Keynes) and "practical sense" (Bourdieu). Both were "political animals". Thus, this chapter aims at exploring the theoretical links between Keynes and Bourdieu on rationality, decision-making and action, with a view to laying, if possible, unified foundations for future research. In order to unite these theories, we should be certain, first, of their high compatibility, beyond the few elements contained in the introduction. Such enterprise is necessary because mainstream models have long been accused of being conspicuously flawed. The *homo economicus* desperately lacks sociological depth. On the face of it, one would be tempted to ascribe the analysis of conventions and non-rational behaviour to Bourdieu, while attributing the explanation of the specific economic rationale and the speculation motive to Keynes. But things might not be that simple. Both theories may supplement one another in a more subtle way. This chapter will hinge around four headings: 1) the little use of probability calculus; 2) the end of body/soul and rational/irrational dichotomies; 3) the sensibleness of expectations (instead of their rationality); 4) the possible deepening and underpinning of animal spirits by habitus, and vice versa.

Is mathematics the grammar of action?

Mainstream economic theories can be seen as either normative or descriptive. They always rely on an extensive use of mathematical calculations, be them conscious or unconscious. The cornerstone of such calculations is the use of probability. Basically, there are two competing views on probability (Hacking 1975, 2001; Lawson 1988). Is it *only* a form of knowledge? Then it should be called epistemic. Or is it *also* an object of knowledge? Then, it is dubbed ontological, since it exists in the world of hard facts. It should be noted that the latter view does not rule out the possibility of ignorance or imperfect knowledge; it is rather a two-stage conception of probability: there exist probable facts that can lead to probable knowledge. With regard to these points (mathematical calculations and probability reasoning), what views hold both Keynes and Bourdieu?

A guide for life? Keynes on mathematics and probability

"For Keynes, philosophy is the queen of the sciences, not mathematics" (O'Donnell 1990a). Indeed, Keynes's doctoral dissertation was philosophical. It consisted of a very dense epistemological reflection which triggered the admiration of such prominent scholars as Bertrand Russell (Dostaler 2007). In his views, logic, understood as valid thinking (i.e. philosophical rigour), was a prerequisite of any scientific reasoning. That's why he considered probability as a branch of logic, and not of mathematics. But this should not be taken to mean that his mathematical skills were below average (in fact, they were outstanding;

see Skidelsky 2004); it is a question of hierarchy: mathematics is the servant and logic (i.e. philosophy) is the master.

In the TP, Keynes endorsed a very wide view of probability. Indeed, according to him, it deals with reasoning that rests on incomplete or imperfect knowledge enabling us to entertain some degree of rational belief. Here, the term "rational" should not confuse the reader. His *Treatise* was a philosophical investigation on the stringent conditions required to make use of probability, and it was concluded that such conditions are, actually, very seldom met in real-life circumstances. Keynes's main concern was not the truth of assertions, but rather the validity of our thoughts. Therefore, a rational belief might turn out false because it was based on unreliable information. Conversely, an irrational belief might turn out true by chance. For instance, if one had concluded from the fact that the moon was full on 15 September 2008 that Lehman Brothers was about to go bankrupt, it would have been preposterous, but one would have been nonetheless right.

> The probability of the same statement varies with the evidence presented. [...] It would be as absurd to deny that an opinion *was* probable, when at a later stage certain objection have come to light, as to deny, when we have reached our destination, that it was ever three miles distant.
>
> (TP: 7–8)

To summarise, according to Keynes, probability is not concerned with degrees of truth, but rather with degrees of truth given the knowledge at hand (i.e. valid reasoning). Probability can be numerical, numerically imprecise between upper and lower bounds (e.g. $0.65 < p < 0.75$) or non-numerical (i.e. qualitative). The first two comprise the realm of mainstream economics. The third one was the most frequent case, according to Keynes. His theory was clearly epistemic: "propositions rather than events should be taken as the subject-matter of probability" (TP: 110). The conditions for a correct use of probability calculus were the following assumptions: atomism, the "limited independent variety" (namely, the hypothesis "that there were a finite number of characteristics which were relevant to the generalisation" [Bateman 1991]), the "law of uniformity of nature" (i.e. "constant causes are always at work and assert themselves in the long run" [TP: 366]), to mention but the main most unrealistic ones ... Consequently, "there is no direct relation between the truth of a proposition and its probability. Probability begins and ends with probability" (TP: 356). "At best, we are dealing with a good approximation", "subject to suitable conditions and qualifications" (TP: 419) very rarely met in actual life.

In the conclusion of the TP, Keynes equated probability with astrology. It was not precisely meant to be a compliment. Thus, it should not be very surprising that he should harshly criticise those who "measure exactly the probability of an induction" for "conceal(ing) themselves from the eyes of common sense in a maze of mathematics" (TP: 424). Indeed, "the application of the mathematical methods [...] to the general problem of statistical inference is invalid. (Such methods are) the children of loose thinking and the parents of charlatanry" (TP: 419). Descriptively speaking, rational action theories are inept.

On his way to the GT, Keynes advocated pure subjectivism, namely probability deals with *mere* rather than rational beliefs (Keynes 1978). But his conclusions continued to adhere to an existing framework (O'Donnell 2003). In a similar vein as in the TP but with greater details, he underscored in the GT the flimsiness of the great bulk of our reasoning. Radical uncertainty is the most salient feature of the world. It cannot be reduced by mathematics. That's why Keynes was opposed to the nascent econometrics discipline (i.e. the application of mathematics and statistics to economics). "What place is allowed to non-numerical factors, such as inventions, politics, labour troubles, wars, earthquakes, financial crises? One feels a suspicion that the choice of factors is influenced [...] by what statistics are available" (Keynes 1987b: 287). Moreover, economics is a "moral science" in that it deals with "introspection, values, motives, psychological uncertainties, [...] as if the fall of the apple to the ground depended on its will and on mistaken calculations as to how far it was from the centre of the earth". As a matter of fact, "[...] the only purpose of (schematic equations) is to elucidate general ideas" (Keynes 1987a: 484). Even from a normative viewpoint, rational action theories are of little use.

An ambiguous rejection? Bourdieu and probability

A philosopher turned sociologist, Bourdieu was plainly aware of what he later on labelled, following in Austin's footsteps, the "scholastic illusion" buttressing rational action theories. Indeed, they are criticised for "the use of instruments of thoughts constructed against the logic of practice, such as game theory, the theory of probability, etc." (Bourdieu 1994a trans. Johnson *et al.* 1998: 130). Game and probability theories are thus explicitly discarded. But things might not be that straightforward. Apropos his own analyses, Bourdieu writes, "the responses of the habitus are first defined, without any calculation, in relation to objective potentialities" (Bourdieu 1980g trans. Nice 1990: 53). In the same quotation, calculus is precluded but guess who is coming to dinner?: "objective potentialities". A rather odd phrase, which a sentence to be found one page later sheds some light on: "very close correlation is regularly observed between the scientifically constructed objective probabilities [...] and agents' subjective aspirations" (Ibid.: 54). Thus, it appears that probability calculus is out of the question as far as individual actions are concerned (for they have "subjective aspirations") but, at the same time, that it exists as a fact of the world ("objective probabilities"). Hence, Bourdieu endorses an ontological view on probability, unlike Keynes. Probability is an object of knowledge (there exist "objective probabilities" in the fields), but there is no using them neither *ex-ante*, since habitus is not " 'decisions' of reason understood as rational calculation" (Ibid.: 50), nor *ex-post*, after some Bayesian updating, for habitus are practical anticipations, "unlike scientific estimations, which are corrected after experiment according to rigorous rules of calculation" (Ibid.: 54).

Like Keynes, Bourdieu castigated mainstream economic theories because of their "atomism", which "reduces agents [...] to interchangeable material points, whose preferences, inscribed in an exogenous utility function [...] determine actions mechanically" (Bourdieu 2000b trans. Turner 2005: 197). But there might well be a source of misconception on Bourdieu's part. For he constantly refers to rational action theories as "the model of individual decision-making, on the basis of a conscious-calculation, consciously oriented towards profit maximisation" (Ibid.: 197), "conscious and calculated evaluation of possible outcomes" (Ibid.: 213), and other quotes of that ilk. Nevertheless, such theories do not necessarily rely on the assumption that individuals do proceed to conscious calculations, but rather that everything happens *as if* they actually did. A common analogy is the following: syntactical structures implied by the automatic use of everyday language are very intricate, and yet despite all these complexities, people are usually capable of forming correct sentences and making themselves understood, without consciously mastering such structures. So, goes the story, why will it not be the case with probability reasoning (Kahneman 2011)? Consciousness is not a pre-requisite of rational action theories. Although scholars such as Becker and Coleman regularly ran the gauntlet of criticism for their scholastic models, Bourdieu's approach is not totally at odds with them, since a "hypothesis as unrealistic [...] may seem to be validated by the facts" (Bourdieu 2000b trans. Turner 2005: 215).

Arguably, Bourdieu's analysis is not deprived of the least ambiguity. On the one hand, he emphasises that individuals cannot act on the basis of any rational action theory. On the other hand, he points out that, *statistically speaking*, they behaved almost *as if* they actually did. How could one reconcile his rejection of probability calculus as to individual reasoning and his endorsement of such calculus as to society or individuals as a whole? It is all the more troubling and perplexing as Bourdieu was not surprised by the results of Kahneman and Tversky's famous experiments showing that people are no good Bayesians. If they are very poor at probability calculus at the micro level, how could the aggregation of their behaviour be consistent with the same laws at the macro level? How could one account for such discrepancy between the macro and the micro levels? One has to convey a concept of causality at odds with the traditional one. In the wake of Heisenberg's uncertainty principle and the dramatic headways of thermodynamics, a new notion of causality surfaced (Prigogine 1997). It was to be dubbed "indeterminism" by Karl Popper. Its basic statement goes as follows: albeit at the micro level behaviour is unpredictable, it has a statistical relevance (or predictability) at the macro level. Even if one cannot ascribe a probability function at the micro level, it is possible at the macro one.

Such analysis gains considerable currency when one takes heed of the following sentence: "To speak of a tendency [...] is to say that, like Popper, one regards the values taken by probability functions as measures of the strength of the propensity of the corresponding events to produce themselves" (Bourdieu 1997a trans. Nice 2000: 215). The mention of Popper's work on probability should be abundantly clear (e.g. Popper 1989). Such work was seminal in that it proposed a new way of envisaging causality. Causality was no more seen as a succession of events, but as a success of events. "The difference the cause makes to its effect is that its occurrence increases the probability of the effect's occurrence" (Menzies and Price 1993: 190). As a result, one should bear in mind that Bourdieu's conception of causality was not deterministic in the classical sense. This is the basic meaning of his use of the word.

In a nutshell, one might argue that both were philosophers turned social scientists and that (consequently?) they cannot help but view probability calculus and mathematics with a strong suspicion. Despite the fact that Bourdieu endorsed an ontological view of probability, such a difference with Keynes is of no importance since both held that individuals do not rely on probability. Sometimes such a calculus is possible and should be implemented, for it is a good approximation of reality. But most of the time, individuals rely on other rules of conduct, which are neither rational nor irrational.

The end of dichotomies

If decision-makers seldom use probabilistic reasoning, what kinds of principles guide their action? They are not rational in the narrow, mathematical sense. Yet, they have a rationale. Even in the fields of economics, where numbers are rife, the cognitive patterns underlying decision-making are not necessarily numerical: people tend to rely on their "animal spirits" for Keynes or their "habitus" for Bourdieu. Are both concepts alike? Let's compare them.

Animal spirits in human bodies

A few prominent mainstream economists, calling themselves "neo-Keynesians", baffled by the recent crisis, tried to account for it by referring to the animal spirits, supposed to be "a restless and inconsistent element in the economy" (Akerlof and Shiller 2009: 4). In their widely acclaimed book on the topic, Akerlof and Shiller run the whole gamut of irrational decisions: animal spirits are said to give rise to confidence (and lack thereof), fairness feelings, corruption, money illusion, hyperbolic discounting and narratives (also called "empty stories"). According to their overtly subtle definition, they pertain to "noneconomic motives and irrational behaviours" (Ibid.: x) and cause "changing confidence, temptations, envy, resentment and illusions" (Ibid.: 4). Another scholar views them as the epitome of "irrational exuberance" (Farmer 2009, 2010). And when behavioural economists try to probe deeper, they still tend to see them as an "affective system" opposed to a "deliberative", rational one (Loewenstein and O'Donoghue 2004).

What should be asserted about these paltry attempts is that they are still marred by the delusive dichotomy reason/emotion or rationality/irrationality. They are at poles apart with Keynes's own views. In Latin, "animal" and "mind" both stem from the same root, "anima", which means "soul", "energy" or "breath". Albeit they are aware of the Latin roots of the concept, Akerlof and Shiller casually discard them. Thus, they might have taken it too literally, as tantamount to animal (gut feelings) as opposed to human (reason). Indeed, it was a staple theme in Renaissance philosophy, in Nicolas Malebranche or René Descartes' works, for instance. As a matter of fact, the young Keynes came to be acquainted with the notion while attending MacTaggart's lectures on Descartes. In a margin of the notes he wrote down then, he observed that "animal spirits" amount to "unconscious mental actions" (Moggridge 1992). Etymologically speaking, one can maintain that they are moving (*anima*) principles (*spiritus*). For Descartes, they were a kind of "physical force", half-wind half-fire, tantamount to "nerve impulse", responsible for *all* movements and sensations, and not only the irrational ones (Descartes 1649). There is no wondering that, according to Keynes, animal spirits are "intermediate between body and soul [...] reasonable non-deliberative actions" (Carabelli 1988: 298).

In the GT, Keynes referred to the animal spirits of the investors in a somewhat elusive manner. He used the following phrases: "spontaneous urge to action", "spontaneous optimism" (three times), "spontaneous activity", "nerves", "hysteria", "digestions", "reactions to the weather".

> Most, probably, of our decisions to do something positive, the full consequences of which will be drawn out over many days to come, can only be taken as a result of animal spirits – of a spontaneous urge to action rather than inaction.

What should be established at the very outset is that animal spirits make up their minds swiftly, for the occurrences of the word "spontaneous" are numerous. "Nerves", "digestions", "reactions to the weather"... This entire lexical field pertains to the body, as if animal spirits acted according to an embodied knowledge, susceptible of a "delicate balance". Keynes depicted them vividly, with enormous gusto:

> it is our innate urge to activity which makes the wheels go round, our rational selves choosing between the alternatives as best we are able, calculating where we can, but often falling back for our motive on whim or sentiment or chance.
>
> (GT: 163)

It should be clear that animal spirits pertain to "nonoptimising aspects of human behaviour (which can) be the subject of systematic analysis" (Gerrard 1994). Such "nonoptimising aspects" are both emotional ("whim", "sentiment") and embodied ("nerves", "hysteria", "digestions"); they act at the same time as "reasonable calculation" but more rapidly. Thus, there exist two systems of reasoning: animal spirits, on which we rely for "most of our decisions", and "mathematical expectation"; the latter needs to be "supplemented and supported" by the former, which also amounts to a sort of vital energy. Animal spirits are not merely embodied emotions, for they are triggered by our "rational selves", who choose to "fall back on" them.

Furthermore, they are not wild emotions nor random reasoning; they come in social conventions' clothing. Undoubtedly, Keynes laid considerable emphasis on conventions. It is a fact that animal spirits make the economy fluctuate. But it is also true that "economic prosperity is excessively dependent on a political and social atmosphere which is congenial to the average business man" (GT: 145). Such atmosphere, and the emotions entailed, depends on an interpretation of the situation at hand. This interpretation relies on an inductive conventional basis, developed as soon as in the TP. Indeed, "the central theme of the TP is induction. Keynes sought to formalise the inductive method and to provide a justification for its use" (Gerrard 1992: 83). There, induction was said to consist of automatic generalisations. It stems from analogical reasoning or pattern matching; it is an answer to the question "Does the current situation resemble another one which happened in the past?" Then, one combines the different resemblances so as to derive a conclusion. Basically, an individual, no matter how intelligent he may be, is said to have a tendency to deem that succession of events amounts to causation of events. Of course it can lead to erroneous thinking, but most of the time it is rather adapted, so long as most individuals reason in the same way. And, in the famous Chapter 12 of the GT, where Keynes introduced the very concept of animal spirits, he explicitly referred to his former TP. Thus, it is not foolish to contend that induction lies at the very gist of "sentiment", "nerves" and "spontaneous urge" to action. Moreover, when it comes to speculation, markets witness a "battle of wits to anticipate the basis of conventional valuation" (GT: 139). In fact, this is all what speculation is about: to outwit the crowd.

> Professional investment may be likened to those newspaper competitions in which the competitors have to pick out the six prettiest faces from a hundred photographs, the prize being awarded to the competitor whose choice most nearly corresponds to the average preferences of the competitors as a whole; so that each competitor has to pick, not those faces which he himself finds prettiest, but those which he thinks likeliest to catch the fancy of the other competitors, all of whom are looking at the problem from the same point of view.
>
> (GT: 140)

To make capital gains, one is thus compelled to take heed of the average opinion that is the conventional one. One may think that the erratic behaviour of the markets may have no anchorage in economic reality whatsoever; one cannot overlook other investors' beliefs, otherwise one would run up enormous losses. For instance, if one deeply believes the actual long-term value of a given asset to be 25 euros, it would be foolish not to buy it 35 euros today if one deems that the conventional valuation would be 40 euros tomorrow (she would then make a capital gain of 5 euros per asset sold). Consequently, "worldly wisdom teaches that it is better for reputation to fail conventionally than to succeed unconventionally" (Ibid.: 141). In any economic valuation, there is a substantial conventional component.

To summarise, Keynes held that individuals basically have two systems of reasoning. The first one manifests itself in the form of mathematical calculation. The second one, more widely used, is based on a quick embodied, emotional reason that relies heavily on social conventions. This is not tantamount to a dichotomy since the two systems can be prompted at the same time or animal spirits *can* supplement and support mathematical calculation.

Habitus or knowledge by body

Conscious calculation exists. But it is seldom used in everyday life. Instead, individuals rely on their habitus. Habitus is described as cognitive structures of preferences, perception and actions comprising what Bourdieu labelled a "practical sense", in the form of "dispositions, (derived from) a differential position in social space, that function in practice without *necessarily* acceding to explicit representations" (Bourdieu 1989b trans. Clough 1996: 2).[2] Although it can be conscious, it is not necessarily so.

> The world is comprehensible, immediately endowed with meaning, because the body, which, thanks to its senses and its brain, has the capacity to be present to what is outside itself, in the world, and to be impressed and durably modified by it, has been protractedly (from the beginning) exposed to its regularities. Having thereby acquired a system of dispositions that are coherent with these regularities, the body finds itself predisposed and ready to anticipate them practically [...]. In other words, if the agent has an immediate understanding of the familiar world, it is because the cognitive structures that he implements are the product of incorporation of the structures of the world in which he acts; the instruments of construction that he uses to know the world are constructed by the world. These practical principles [...] are constructed from the experience of frequently encountered situations and can be revised and rejected in the event of repeated failure.
>
> (Bourdieu 1997a trans. Nice 2000: 135–136)

Habitus is an inductive process ("experience of frequently encountered situations") that takes place in a social world where individuals need one another to grow and become themselves. As this process is automatic (Bourdieu likes to quote Leibniz: "we are automatons in three quarters of what we do"), it is embodied. We tend to adjust ourselves to the world as it is, in all its unwritten rules, thanks to an implicit knowledge, slowly acquired via an invisible, subtle habituation to its regularities tantamount to an inductive process. It takes the form of a quasi-reflex and functions like a potentiality. The most common phrases used to describe it are "practical sense" or "sense of the game", since it is analogous to the virtuosic "corporeal intelligence" that players usually rely on while practising sport (and the examples employed often refer to tennis, soccer or rugby). As a matter of fact, in the process of a game, players are not "consciously aware" of the very gestures they are making. Such practical sense is intermediate between body and soul, for "appropriate practice (speaking a language or riding a bicycle) is knowledge and it even contains a particular form of reflection" (Bourdieu 1997a trans. Nice 2000: 80). It is also intermediate between reason and emotion, since "there is no use of sensitivity which does not already imply the use of intellectual capacities" (Ibid.: 81).

The habitus is a matrix of classificatory schemes which generates consistent analogies (Caillé 1994) in different situations: "socialisation tends to constitute the body as an analogical operator" (Bourdieu 1979 trans. Nice 1984: 475). Put differently, through their habitus, individuals *tend* to compare present situations to past situations ("analogy") in an automatic, consistent way, and to act on the basis of a few principles susceptible to be transposed and adapted, no matter how different situations might *appear* to be (e.g. school, sport, work, family...).

> [The] *analogical practice* founded on the transfer of schemes, which takes place on the basis of acquired equivalencies facilitating the substitutability and the substitution of one behaviour for another and making it possible, through a kind of practical generalisation, to master all *problems of similar form* capable of arising in new situations.
>
> (Bourdieu 1997a trans. Nice 2000: 57, my emphasis)

As with Keynes, the emphasis is laid on induction and analogy.

Habitus is not synonymous with habit, for it is a "system of durable, transposable dispositions, [...], as principles which generate and organise practices and representations" (Bourdieu 1980g trans. Nice 1990: 53). Habitus are thus "transposable" and "generative". If it were only a posh label for "habits", it would not generate anything. It has a creative component; but creativity is not a random or chaotic process; it has principles, and such principles can be found in the habitus. Albeit first experiences are overweighed, they are a rejuvenating process, an updating power.

"The singularity of the self (is) fashioned in and by social relations" (Bourdieu 1997a trans. Nice 2000: 134). Then, since we live in a society, our experience is not only neutral or natural, but it is bound to have a social content. This truism has profound implications. Society is divided in fields, each of which has rules or rationales of its own, also called *nomos*. Each *nomos* is different, although all fields obey the same general laws, susceptible of systematic analysis. In turn, each field can be divided into many subfields. For instance, economy as a whole constitutes a field; a specific market also forms a field; a peculiar firm is a field as well. A competition takes place in each field for the highest position given by the possession of a specific "symbolic capital". Fields are not immovable; they are constantly altering, since the definition of the legitimate issues (i.e. the definition of the symbolic capital as well as that of the borders of the field) is part and parcel of the issues of the fields, "at the same time force fields and fields of struggles in order to alter this balance of power" (Bourdieu 2000c: 61).[3] Put differently, the rules of the game are not fixed once and for all; individuals constantly try to implement strategies in order to change them. What is the relation between social structures (i.e. fields) and embodied structures (i.e. habitus)? There is a dialectical movement: fields shape habitus, habitus shape fields. Habitus has a content: the accumulation of different kinds of capitals. The propensity to act depends crucially on the structure and volume of these different sorts of capitals (social, cultural, economic and symbolic) possessed, because it is such possession that makes the social position. And one cannot help but be engrossed in the *nomos*, which implies to accept as obvious the implicit rules of the field, and never to question them, a process called *illusio*. The social position entices to act in the form of a propensity; it aims at accumulating capitals. As a result, "the very structures of the world are present in the structures (or, to put it better, the cognitive schemes) that agents implement in order to understand it" (Bourdieu 1997a trans. Nice 2000: 152).

Each capital can be converted into another kind of capital. It is susceptible of two diverse uses: instrumental, as part of a strategic scheme; structural, as a fundamental driving force of the habitus. It epitomises the dualistic nature of individuals: "we are as much automatic as we are intellectual" wrote Bourdieu, quoting Pascal. "Automatic" (structural propensities), we can nonetheless implement practical strategies ("intellectual"). It should be emphasised that habitus have both dimensions: they can be described as an automatic action "programme" which generates more or less, but rather less than more, conscious strategies.

To sum up Bourdieu's views as to habitus, one might put forth the following properties: they are intermediate between body and mind, emotion and reason. They are spontaneous generative mechanisms, derived from a social position, which spur people to act in an appropriate way. Albeit they co-exist with a "rational" deliberative system, they are used for the great bulk of everyday actions.

There is no denying that habitus and animal spirits are very much in tune. Both are emotional, embodied, conventional anticipations. However, the scope of the former is wider, since it encompasses all social rules (and not only economic ones) and it has creative and symbolic, cultural components through different kinds of capital. Before going further, one should analyse how they can lead to successful actions despite the fact that they are not rational.

The realm of sensible expectations

Ironically, the similar concepts of habitus and animal spirits were the objects of severe criticisms on opposite grounds. Habitus is said to be too rational (i.e. too well adapted to the social structures). Conversely, animal spirits were said to lack rationality, a lethal blow as far as economics is concerned. To examine further the possibility of their merger, it could be interesting to qualify such contradicting views.

Radical uncertainty, time and the animal spirits

Radical uncertainty and the social conventional valuation basis of the animal spirits substantiated "Keynes's rejection of the dichotomy between rationality and irrationality" (Carabelli 1988: 219). In order to fully grasp the meaning of such an apparently fuzzy concept as radical uncertainty, one should revert to the early years of Keynes's formation. In fact, his doctoral dissertation stemmed from his will to rebut Moore's contention that one should heed long-term consequences of moral actions by means of a probability calculus and act accordingly (Rothbard 1992; Skidelsky 2004; Dostaler 2007). In the previous dissertations as well as in the TP, Keynes underscored the irreversibility of time and the intricacies of our decisions. He thought to have proved that it was "not required to have certain knowledge of the probable consequences of his actions in order to act rationally" (Skidelsky 2004: 153). Indeed, since future is not a mere repetition of the past, and since the contingencies of our actions are numerous, the possible consequences of all our behaviours were impossible to anticipate precisely, if not at all. In the TP, Keynes laid considerable emphasis on the absurd principle upon which probability calculus largely depends, that of the "uniformity of nature", "which asserts that constant causes are always at work" – i.e. the world is ergodic, which means non-unique and repetitive through time, as in natural sciences (Davidson 1991, 1996). He convincingly claimed that

> the possible contingencies are too numerous to be covered by a finite number of experiments, and exact calculation is therefore out of the question. Although nature has her habits, due to the recurrence of causes, they are general, not invariable.
>
> (TP: 402)

Undoubtedly, radical uncertainty is the most salient feature about the world. Most of the time, "we simply do not know" (Keynes 1937). In the GT, he evoked the "dark forces of time and ignorance which envelop our future", even for actions "the full consequences of which will be drawn out over many days to come" (GT: 139), rendering it necessary to rely on one's animal spirits.

Although "slumps and depressions are exaggerated in degree" owing to such actions, "we should not conclude from this that everything depends on waves of irrational psychology" (GT: 145). As a matter of fact, "certain important factors [...] somewhat mitigate in practice the effects of our ignorance of the future" (Ibid.: 146). The physical obsolescence of certain productive goods forces one to renew them. Risk can be transferred to insurance companies. And, as to public utilities, the yields are guaranteed by the monopoly authorities. Moreover, and more importantly, conventions "exert their compensating effects" (Ibid.: 145). They reduce uncertainty.

> As living human beings, we are forced to act. Peace and comfort of mind require that we should hide from ourselves how little we foresee. Yet we must be guided by some hypothesis. We tend therefore to substitute for the knowledge which is unattainable certain conventions.
>
> (Keynes 1987b: 124)

For example, the liquidity convention was said to be a proxy for knowledge (Shackle 1972). The "atmosphere congenial to the average businessman" is so vital that it led Akerlof and Shiller to conclude that there exists a "confidence multiplier": the more confident you feel ... the more confident you will feel! Hence self-fulfilling prophecies. The future may be unknown, but it is the fruit of today's decisions. The belief in the happening of a peculiar event can create the necessary conditions for that event to effectively happen! The most famous example of such a rationale is the speculative bubble: prices go up because people believe that they will go up.

Economists' lack of focus on Keynes's notion of convention stems from the fact that "Keynes's arguments are interpreted by many as being ultimately destructive of economic analysis" (Lawson 2004). Thus, it should not be startling to notice that many mainstream economists have thought animal spirits to be irrational. Conventions provide rules of predictable behaviour. For example, traffic lights are conventional, and yet most people do comply with them. Of course, many economic conventions are less compulsory and less obvious than traffic lights; yet, their role is to tame uncertainty. Expectations are reasonable instead of rational.

Are habitus and fields circular?

A widely held belief has it that habitus and fields are somewhat circular (Lahire 1998, 2001; Alexander 1995; Favereau 2001a; Caillé 1994; King 2000). As the former is the *embodied* social structures and the latter the *objective* social structures, it is tempting to conclude that. There is no denying that many statements incline us to think that this might be true: individuals

> may conduct themselves in such a way that, starting with a rational evaluation of their chances for success, it seems that they were right in doing what they did, without one being justified in saying that a rational calculation of chances was as the origin of the choices they made.
>
> (Bourdieu 1994a trans. Johnson *et al.* 1998: 76)

Besides, phrasings such as "*collectively orchestrated* without being the product of the organising action of a conductor", "the practices they generate are mutually intelligible and immediately *adjusted* to the structures", "*harmony* between practical sense and objectified meaning" abound (Bourdieu 1980g trans. Nice 1990: 53, 58, my emphasis)...

Contrary to natural science, where objects under study do not have an opinion about themselves and their surroundings, sociology (and economics) is primarily concerned with individuals who entertain a point of view, have peculiar interests and therefore can resist any attempt at unfolding the true rationale underlying their actions. That's why Bourdieu always felt compelled to exaggerate the degree to which social structures take their toll on individuals, speaking of "futile excesses", evoking "the temptation to 'twist the stick in the other direction', to overcome resistances" (Bourdieu 1992a trans. Emmanuel 1996: 185). As a result, one should not read the link between habitus and fields in too deterministic a sense. I see at least five arguments that should prevent us from doing so.

To the best of my knowledge, no critic has ever taken heed of Bourdieu's specific causality concept. It is perhaps the most fundamental argument. As we have seen earlier, causality is not a world of necessary and sufficient conditions but one of material propensities; it is not a succession of events, but a success of events. In order to fully comprehend the meaning of this point, we should take a metaphorical example. Propensity in Bourdieu's sense is equivalent to the roll of a die. If one or two obtains, then one does not act. If three, four, five or six obtains, then one acts. In either case, the result is neither rational nor irrational. It is "adapted" to the circumstances, even if it appears that, after the facts, one should have acted otherwise. Albeit the circumstances are identical (e.g. the roll of the die under the same conditions), the result might be different (each number is equally probable and unpredictable). Habitus is a tendency, not a compulsory order. It would be as ludicrous to believe that after the die is rolled it could but obtain six *because* six was obtained, as to think that habitus is very deterministic and cannot enable any margin of manoeuvre. Thus, when Bourdieu speaks of "propensities", "tendencies" or "inclinations to" (and the occurrences of such terms are numerous throughout his entire work: 39 times in *Pascalian Meditations*, 53 times in *The Rules of Art*, 62 in *The Logic of Practice*) when he refers to dispositions or habitus he is relying on such causality concept, a fact casually overlooked by all critics.

Habitus follows aggregation rules. It has statistical validity. Thus, habitus can have a standard deviation, so to speak.

> Though it is impossible for all (or even two) members of the same class to have had the same experiences, in the same order, it is certain that each member of the same class is *more likely* than any member of another class to have been confronted to the situations *most frequent* for the members of the class.
>
> (Bourdieu 1980g trans. Nice 1990: 59–60, my emphasis)

Many other quotes point in the same direction: "*in the great majority of cases*, [...] agents form reasonable expectations, that is to say, expectations matching up to the objective probabilities" (Bourdieu 2000b trans. Turner 2005: 215, my emphasis); "habitus [...] *can* be objectively adapted to their outcomes" (Bourdieu 1980g trans. Nice 1990: 53, my emphasis)... Statistically speaking, habitus from the same class resembles one another; at an individual level, there are many differences and deviations.

Furthermore, there might be hysteresis. Since the habitus overweighs our former experiences, it enhances "permanence within change". Another implication comes into play: "the screen that the habitus introduces between stimulus and reaction is a screen of time in so far as, being itself the product of history, it is relatively constant and durable, and hence *relatively* independent of history"

(Bourdieu 2000b trans. Turner 2005: 212). Consequently, there might be a discrepancy between the current state of the field and the inertia of the habitus. Hence the feeling of being displaced (Bourdieu ed. 1993 trans. Ferguson 1999). Put differently, there is a "structural lag between opportunities and the disposition to grasp them" (Bourdieu 1980g trans. Nice 1990: 59). Even though habitus tends to adapt to current situations, it adapts slowly.

Moreover, habitus can be divided or cleaved. They can be the product of contradictory social structures, as when a given society is being modernised, whereas the old structures "refuse" to die. Since the very beginning of his work, Bourdieu emphasised such cleavage in traditional Algerian communities. He reasserted such conviction in *Pascalian Meditations*.

Finally, however stringent habitus may be, there is still leeway. Bourdieu's work has elicited much confusion. One should bear in mind that it is not because his focus was not conscious deliberation that he deemed it not to truly exist. His focus was merely on habitus, or "practical sense", which accounts for the great bulk of our everyday actions. Still, Bourdieu never meant to get totally rid of conscious reflection; he rather contended that there exists two systems of reasoning. "The adjustment, in advance, of habitus, to the objective conditions is a particular case, no doubt particularly frequent (in the universes familiar to us), but it should not be treated as universal" (Bourdieu 1997a trans. Nice 2000: 159). In fact, "the homology between the space of positions and the space of dispositions is never perfect" (Ibid.: 157; also 1989b trans. Clough 1996: 183). Besides habitus, conscious strategies are possible: "the most effective strategies [...] are those which, being the product of dispositions" (Bourdieu 1997a trans. Nice 2000: 139), namely habitus... In other words, other kinds of strategies are possible, but they are, generally speaking, less effective. In fact, "it is, of course, never ruled out (the existence of) strategic calculation *tending* to perform in a conscious mode the operation that the habitus performs quite differently" (Bourdieu 1980g trans. Nice 1990: 53, my emphasis). The response of the habitus comes first, because it is embodied, spontaneous, but conscious calculation *can* go counter it, despite its *tendency* to go in the same direction as the habitus. "The principle of our actions is *more often* practical sense than rational calculation" (Bourdieu 1997a trans. Nice 2000: 64, my emphasis), but it should not be taken to mean that it "leaves no room in any circumstances to conscious intention" (Ibid.: 64). That so many scholars, even today, should continue to assert that no conscious reflection or no freedom from habitus is possible in Bourdieu's theory is somewhat puzzling... Critics turn a blind eye to the very words used: tendency, propensity, frequency, regularly, statistical analysis, and so on.

All in all, it appears that, although habitus enables reasonable expectations, it is also prone to err. Even if most of the time it tends to reproduce social structures, by means of changing the dominant social rules in a Lampedusa's way ("if we want things to stay as they are, things will have to change"), it has the ability to genuinely alter them. Once again, one should not gasp in wonder that animal spirits and habitus are very much in tune with each other. However, conventions are very briefly alluded to in Keynes's work, save for liquidity. Arguably, his views on the matter were too embryonic, even though they took centre stage in his analyses, for he was primarily an economist-philosopher. In that regard, habitus is much more developed and can provide a sociological underpinning for such a vague, catch-all notion as "conventions", as we shall see in the next section.

A fruitful dialogue: towards a unified theory?

Economics could be much enriched if it is to develop Keynesian theories in light of Bourdieu's. First of all, at a general level, there is much to be gained. Second, we could envisage the dialogue between Keynes and Bourdieu in the specific province of price formation.

Reasonable social expectations

Mainstream economics' theories have two salient characteristics. First and foremost, they purport to be based on a universal rationality, which implies that the form of the underlying equation has nothing to do with a hypothetical social position. Mainstream economics does not discard society and its rules; rather it pretends to embody them in the individuals' exogenous preferences. There are three main sets of models in mainstream economics: subjective expected utility (SEU) and all its derivatives; bounded rationality; game theory. The first one consists of maximising the multiplication of probability by utility. Since the very inception of SEU, models have evolved so that they may account for non-additive probabilities (Einhorn and Hogarth 1987; Gilboa 1987; Schmeidler 1989), non-linear (Quiggin 1982; Yaari 1987) and non-unique probabilities (Gärdenfors and Sahlin 1982; Gilboa *et al.* 2008), and even stochastic preferences (MacFadden 2000). Behavioural economics is to be attached to that set of models, since it departs only faintly from the most fundamental assumptions: indeed, no paper in that strand rules out probability calculus or preferences (Camerer and Loewenstein 2004; Thaler 2004; Harvey 1998; Rabin 1998; Kahneman 2003). They only add "distortion variables" to the basic equation of SEU, be they deformation of the probability calculus (prospect theory, support theory…) or that of "utility" (endowment effect, loss aversion…) (Kahneman and Tversky 1992; Fox and Poldrack 2009). The second set of models can also be said to resemble the first. The first alternative that crosses a certain satisfying threshold is chosen, for one cannot wait for a complete knowledge of all the relevant alternatives (Simon 1979, 1982; Gigerenzer 2001).[4] Thus, it is tantamount to the SEU in that the decision-maker still maximises under the extra constraint that he cannot know all states of nature. For sure, after the action is completed, the decision-maker can realise a better option could have been chosen. But, *at the time of the choice*, none was available. If many alternatives cross the threshold at the same time, the individual picks the best (Simon and Stedry 1969). So to speak, bounded rationality models merely have a narrower time focus. As for game theory, one has to choose the highest payoff, even if it is not the social optimum (Von Neumann and Morgenstern 1944; Binmore 1990). So, basically, all three sets of models share a similar rationale: using probability and "utility", no matter how they are defined, in order to maximise the decision-maker's satisfaction. The theoretical children of Keynes and Bourdieu would not try to use probability calculus, even in an unconscious manner, nor attempt at maximising anything when resorting to their practical sense. The principle governing their behaviour would be more qualitative. They would extensively rely on pattern matching; in this regard Keynes's very personal concept of probability (not to be confused with that of mainstream economics) points out that "we say that one argument is more probable than another (i.e. nearer to certainty) in the same kind of way as we can describe one object as more like another to a standard object of comparison" (TP: 39). An analogical and associative reasoning is more often used in everyday practice.

The second salient feature of mainstream economics' models is interaction. Others are mere parameters of a system of equations (in SEU or bounded rationality) or of an imaginative thinking experience (like the one used in game theory), if not backward induction. Only those who interact with us are being taken heed of. Bourdieu's very concept of fields helps us go beyond such narrow scope. Indeed, every decision-maker has the whole structure of the field in mind while taking action; she takes account of each and every individual in the field, whether they will be directly affected by the choice made or not. Of course, this should not imply that she ought to know each individual nor that everyone weighs equally in the decision. One should just bear in mind that other persons than those with whom we interact influence our decision. The "gravity social law": all psyches weigh upon one another constantly in unequal manners.

Overall, let's summarise the four points of departure from mainstream economics that the theoretical children of Keynes and Bourdieu (TCKB) would manifest and provide positive or constructive analyses: 1) practical sense (vs. rational calculus); 2) endogenous preferences (vs. exogenous preferences); 3) power relationships (vs. firms as homogenous entities); 4) structural effects, namely there is more to social relations and decisions than interaction (vs. interaction).

Price formation, or the mermaid's sociological song

Inasmuch as we consider companies as price makers and not price takers, status and power issues become relevant (Lavoie 1992; Eloire 2010). Thus, price can be said to be the hole through which sociology will percolate and blend with economics. TCKB will have to develop that point so as to comprise a consistent, viable, attractive, deeper alternative to mainstream. As a matter of fact, value is the greatest riddle in mainstream theories. It is a mysterious substance, said to be encapsulated in "utility". Somewhat, price can be said to convert symbolic capital into economic capital. In his case study of the restaurants' field in the vicinity of Lille, Eloire has shown how cultural capital (whose specific name is "culinary capital") converts into symbolic capital ("gastronomic capital") thanks to social capital. Hence, market positioning and profitability are accounted for (Eloire 2011).

To consider a given enterprise as a field of its own permits to explain obdurate departures from consistency and/or rationality. As a result, power relationships as to the legitimate definition of how to see the job or the mission of the firm matter. Bourdieu (2000b trans. Turner 2005) analysed the peculiar case of a construction company that had to face an uphill battle as to its *nomos*: should the trade revolve around cement, the traditional activity, concrete, which relies more heavily on chemistry, or a financial rationale? Behind the most technical choices a company has to face, there are always power relationships. Of course, this should not be taken to mean that power or accumulation of symbolic capital is the genuine underlying motivation, for it is *also* a technical matter. It is just that both aspects cannot be easily disentangled, if not at all. Thus, as for price formation, the choice of the specific techniques or models used to derive prices from costs and mark-ups involve such rationales.

Bourdieu's conceptual tools might also be useful for stock market analysis and bubble bursting. Basically, there are, according to Keynes, two kinds of investors in the stock market. The "enterprise" motive is that of the long run, people acting so as to reap dividends. The "speculation" motive is that of the short run, individuals acting in order to make capital gains. Arguably, there cannot be a pure "rationale" in the market, since everyone knows that at least some investors act according to another motive (i.e. "enterprise" if one is on the "speculation" side of the market; "speculation" if one is on the "enterprise" side). Nevertheless, the speculation motive has the upper hand over its counterpart, for "enterprise" investors would not buy an asset they believe is overvalued with regard to the "fundamentals", contrary to "speculative" investors who would continue to buy the same asset so long as they believe that the price will increase, regardless of any fundamental, long-run value. Thus, no matter how many "enterprise" investors there are (of course, the more numerous, the better), markets have an innate tendency towards speculation. Even though Bourdieu did not really talk about finance, his work could be supplemented by Keynes's analysis of stock markets, which, at the same time, could be further informed by Bourdieu's framework. It would be interesting to relate "enterprise" and "speculation" to cultural and symbolic capital. One could test, for example, the following assumptions: risk-taking is strongly correlated to symbolic capital and cultural capital. It would be fascinating, as well, to examine strategic moves in light of the field's very structure.

As a matter of fact, one would have, from now on, to take heed of the different sorts of capital, and not only of the economic one, when explaining individuals' behaviours.

There remains to be seen whether Bourdieu's analyses can supplement aptly those of Keynes upon the stock market. There, moves are erratic and swift. As embodiment of a practical sense, habitus makes up its mind quickly; it generates new behaviour. At the same time, all these new practices revolve around some kind of inertia; there remains an untouched hardcore of generating principles. Is this compatible with the actual behaviour of investors? So long as one has not completed any empirical investigation with that kind of analytical tool on the stock market, such concept remains an empty vessel and, as such, it is rather frustrating. The potency of the habitus could be to account for the feelings of "obviousness" that are rife on the markets; for example, it seems "clear" to almost all traders that an ambitious redundancy plan should be acclaimed or any announcement on the part of the central bank as to lowering base rates should give rise to an economic betterment. But there are times, as well, when the same statement or declaration prompts a different response. It does so because the field has changed; habitus ought then to explain such behaviour alteration. The chief convention on the market, liquidity, changes virtually on a daily basis. It has been forcefully pointed out that rationality there is of an auto-referential kind (Orléan 1999, 2011). Thus, mimicry and herd behaviour are widespread. How could we reconcile constant mimicry with habitus, whose basic rationale is one of distinction? First, we should bear in mind that it is disagreement that makes markets. A period of strong agreement is called "speculation": if most traders believe that assets will continue to skyrocket, then there will be more buyers than sellers and, as a result, this will elicit the rise in the values. This is called a self-fulfilling prophecy (Galbraith 1994). So, the most fundamental question becomes: what is the turning point of the upward move? Standard rationality models are totally incapable of explaining it, for markets are said to be efficient and prices embody correctly all actual information available (Mishkin 2009). Habitus should try to change the conventional valuation basis a short time ahead (as it is the case as regards fashion, beautifully described by Bourdieu in *Distinction*), so as to make huge capital gains. Besides, symbolic capitals attached to companies are more important in the interpretation of the tone of the market than economic ones. For instance, on 16 July 2010, both the Bank of America and General Electric announced profits above expectations, but the market dipped because of Citigroup, deemed to have more symbolic capital, although the first two firms are financially more powerful.

Conclusion: outlines of a general theory

Keynes and Bourdieu are fit for marriage. They may have many theoretical children. Distrust of probability calculus and mathematical expectations, reasonable expectations beyond the body/soul and reason/emotions dichotomies, the conventional basis of everyday reasoning, a certain inertia of behaviour compatible with innovation and change ... the points of agreement are numerous and fundamental. Scholars could benefit from a decompartmentalised economics. Preferences and desires could then be endogenous, instead of being left behind the smoke screen of exogeneity. Analyses could gain depth by going beyond interactions to include the whole field. Moreover, the possession of all forms of capital is pertinent to account for individuals' behaviour, even traders. Thus, one should take heed of them and cease to consider rationality as universal, independent of the social position. Besides, there are power relationships, which prevent us from considering a single firm as a homogenous entity.

This being said, much remains to be done. Especially, such unified theory is in dire need for empirical analyses so as to provide a more detailed and relevant view as to market changes. By linking Keynes and Bourdieu, we are merely pointing at a direction of future research and reminding ourselves that our understanding of economic phenomena can and should be enriched; but this is far from being over yet. We still have many children to breed.

Notes

1 Like cats, everybody has many lives. After a life of vagrancies and romantic fantasies, Michael Lainé decided to retreat into the monastic pleasures of scholarship of finishing a PhD in economics. In a previous life, he used to be a publisher. He founded his own publishing company and roamed the routes of France for knowledge and beauty's sake. In another life, he wrote books on economics (*Les 35 Mensonges du libéralisme*, 2002, *Le Marché introuvable*, 2009), politics and constitutional law (*Si Jean-Marie*…, 2006) and made anthologies on philosophy (*La Sagesse des anciens*, 2003) and literature (*Bestiaire*, 2003). He now meows and purrs at Bordeaux University, France. He has profound interests in economics, sociology, philosophy, psychology, neuroscience and literature.

2 This is my translation. Oddly enough, the word "necessarily" was totally forgotten in the original published one.

3 This is my translation, since this book has not been translated yet.

4 Even though Earl would argue that the line between mainstream and heterodoxy lies in the acceptance of bounded rationality (Earl 2001), I would rather contend that it runs inside the bounded rationality strand itself: the closer to a qualitative algorithm, the closer to heterodoxy. Hence, the theory of Reinhard Selten, for instance, has one foot inside and the other outside that border (Selten 2001).

7 Bourdieu and the Marxist economy

Bourdieu's outlook on Marx and his conception of the economic sphere

Eric Gilles[1]

Introduction

The theories of Karl Marx and Pierre Bourdieu can be reconciled. The former places in the centre of his analysis phenomena of exploitation and alienation and uses these concepts for emancipation. The latter explains the mechanisms of domination in various fields and wants to create a sociology that reveals social constructions.

According to defenders of Marx and Bourdieu, both authors belong to the same tradition and are on the same side. Thus, Corcuff, who wants to continue the Bourdieusian tradition, writes that:

> Bourdieu's sociology is one of the most important Post-Marxist critical thinking of the twentieth century … "Post-Marxist" also means that Marx and "Marxists" were major referents and interlocutors (although not exclusive and through critical screening) in the construction of this new sociology.
>
> (2003: 17, 18)

On the other hand, the newspaper of the French Communist Party pays tribute to Bourdieu, who "gives reasons and ways to influence social reality", who is "the number one enemy of all defenders of the neoliberal order" (*L'Humanité*, 22 January 2012). Similarly, some French Marxist researchers want their journal *Actuel Marx* to "confront Marx and Bourdieu in a fruitful way" (Lojkine 2003: 5).[2]

This relationship between both authors is also highlighted by Bourdieu's opponents. For example, Raynaud considers that he "tried to achieve an original synthesis of Marxist sociology, seen as a critique of domination and a theory of ideologies, and of the Bachelardian epistemology, as the 1955–65 philosophical generation understood it" (1980: 83). Ferry and Renaut see in his thinking a "distinguished variant of vulgar Marxism" (1985: 217), Alexander criticises his theory by linking it to the "Neomarxism of the Sixties" (1995 trans. Zaccaï-Reyners and Lejeune 2000: 21) and Caillé asserts that "the sociology of Bourdieu is only a development of historical materialism" (1994: 93) and that "Bourdieu's Marxism is distinguished" (Ibid.: 106).

The purpose of this chapter is to analyse and question the relationship between Bourdieu and Marx. In order to do this, we will not follow the path taken by some commentators, who have their biased vision of both authors, that is, we will not selectively compare them, and "forget" any embarrassing passage refuting our interpretation. Our point of view will be more humble and more materialistic. This will consist in identifying and analysing all statements in which Bourdieu refers to Marx in order to understand what he says explicitly in his various books and articles. We will then ask ourselves how Bourdieu uses Marx's key economic concepts, which ones he used, how he modified them, and whether his vision of the economy is close to that of the author of *Capital*.

Three tasks are necessary to report on the first dimension: first, we explain the importance of references to Marx in Bourdieu's works; then we determine whether the relevant passages are – or not – in favour of Marx; and finally we study these texts to specify their status in Bourdieu's sociological works. We will show that Marx was one of the authors most frequently and very positively cited. However, the content of these references is hardly related to Bourdieu's sociology. Hence, a paradox: despite the large number of statements in favour of Marx, they are almost independent of Bourdieu's theoretical system.

We will then look at how Bourdieu uses the key economic concepts developed by Marx and his work about the working classes. In both cases, we are brought back to the previous idea: Bourdieu's analysis of exploitation, labour value and social space are very different from that of Marx.

Analysis of the quotes in quantitative terms

In this chapter, we have virtually taken into consideration Bourdieu's whole work. It was necessary to count the number of passages that refer to Marx, whether these were in Marx's favour or not. When an author is often quoted in Bourdieu's works, then this inevitably establishes a link between the two authors in the eyes of the reader. Similarly, the fact that Marx was strongly approved of or criticised by Bourdieu created a relationship that bound them together or placed them in opposition, at least for a large portion of readers.

To estimate the number of quotations and citations, we relied on the indices of Bourdieu's various works and counted the number of references to Marx. As expected, three authors stand out: Weber being the most frequently cited, followed by Marx and Durkheim.[3] This classification cannot be considered definitive since the indices are not very well done. That said, these results clearly indicate that Marx is one of the three most highly cited authors and that the reader cannot but associate Marx to Bourdieu's sociological work.

To determine whether references to Marx are positive or negative, we classified all these statements into three categories: those where Bourdieu approves of Marx's point of view, those where he rejects it and those that are neutral. We carried out similar work for statements concerning Marxists in order to test the hypothesis that Bourdieu has a different relationship with Marx and the philosophy based on his writings.

When analysing quotations and citations to Marx and Marxist authors, Bourdieu seems to be much closer to the former, of whom he often approves, and quite distant from the latter, of whom he frequently disapproves. In other words, in quantitative terms, it is precisely as if Bourdieu wanted to be in the wake of Marx, while seeking to position himself in the theoretical field in opposition to Marxists:

- Marx is mentioned in a neutral manner on 70 occasions[4]: Bourdieu and Boltanski (1976: 15, 24, 53, 56); Bourdieu and Passeron (1964: 64); Bourdieu and Wacquant (1992: 136, 156, 219, 220); Bourdieu *et al.* (1968: 16, 30); Bourdieu (1971: 295), (1974: 4, 5), (1975a[2001b]: 379, 380, 383, 385, 390), (1980b: 40), (1980e[2002a]: 111, 112, 116), (1980g: 104, 192), (1982a: 166, 201, 202, 203), (1983[1987a]: 47, 48, 49, 50), (1984e[2002a]: 179), (1984f[2002a]: 197), (1985a[1987a]: 17, 42), (1986c[2002a]: 212), (1987a: 149), (1988: 108, 111), (1989b: 303), (1989c[2002a]: 268), (1992a: 284, 292, 310), (1992c[2002a]: 391), (1994a: 26, 28, 129), (1997a: 10, 256), (1998d[2002a]: 352), (2001b: 236), (2005b: 333), (2012: 118, 119,[5] 123, 126, 132, 134, 135, 158, 226, 234, 236, 363, 552, 560, 565, 579).
- In statements regarding Marxism[6] this kind of neutrality appears on 42 occasions: Bourdieu and Boltanski (1976: 41, 53); Bourdieu and de Saint-Martin (1987: 41); Bourdieu and Passeron (1964: 22); Bourdieu *et al.* (1964: 31, 42, 45, 70); Bourdieu (1975a[2001b]: 383, 386, 389, 390, 394), (1977b: 5), (1977c[1980b]: 90), (1977e[2001b]: 205), (1980e[2002a]: 112), (1984e[2002a]: 179), (1989b: 220, 240, 246, 247, 362), (1992b[2002a]: 240), (1994a: 32), (2012: 23, 25, 46, 123, 126, 131, 136, 140, 161, 175, 325, 334, 438, 440, 537, 563, 565).
- Marx is often praised (129 times): Boltanski and Bourdieu (1975a[2001b]: 98), (1975b[2002a]: 4, 22); Bourdieu and Chartier (2010: 61); Bourdieu and de Saint-Martin (1976: 50), (1978: 66); Bourdieu and Delsaut (1975: 7, 26); Bourdieu and Passeron (1970: 18, 19, 47); Bourdieu and Wacquant (1992: 72, 97, 98, 102, 221); Bourdieu *et al.* (1968: 14, 30, 33, 35, 43, 51, 77, 160, 193); Bourdieu (1963[2008]: 93, 95), (1971: 299, 301, 307, 334), (1972a[2002b]: 169), (1972b: 100, 166, 219, 255, 259, 356, 361), (1974: 9, 15, 23), (1975b[2002a]: 129), (1976: 127), (1977a: 29), (1977e[2001b]: 201, 202), (1977d: 55), (1979: 126, 200, 271, 280, 286, 318, 326, 437, 463, 464, 544), (1980g: 28, 52, 69, 87, 108, 192, 199, 202, 211, 215, 245, 249, 257, 280, 360), (1980d[1980b]: 23, 25), (1982a: 165), (1982b: 11), (1983[1987a]: 49), (1984b[2001b]: 261, 271), (1984c[2001b]: 295, 299, 320, 322), (1985a[1987a]: 27, 28, 46), (1985b[1987a]: 77, 85), (1987a: 148), (1988: 30), (1989b: 12, 13, 479), (1992a: 287, 295), (1994a: 27, 171, 172), (1997a: 97, 179, 198, 291, 362, 370), (1997b[2002a]: 322), (1998b: 98), (2000b: 273), (2001b: 71), (2012: 17, 28, 83, 126, 128, 144, 161, 232, 237, 318, 326, 542, 554, 559, 560, 564, 587, 589).
- Marxism is approved of only six times: Bourdieu (1990[2002a]: 75), (1994a: 165), (2012: 71, 133, 268, 559).

- Marx is criticised on 26 occasions: Bourdieu and Passeron (1970: 19); Bourdieu (1972b: 230), (1974: 25), (1979: 390), (1980d[1980b]: 25), (1983[1987a]: 49, 64), (1984a: 47), (1984d[1987a]: 127), (1987a: 148, 153), (1989a[2002b]: 222), (1992a: 508), (1994a: 27, 53, 131), (1997a: 179), (1998b: 62, 63), (2001b: 329), (2012: 17, 231, 275, 542, 545, 559).
- Marxism is criticised on 63 occasions: Bourdieu and Chartier (2010: 36, 81); Bourdieu and Wacquant (1992: 102, 220); Bourdieu (1971: 299), (1972b: 279, 361), (1975a[2001b]: 385), (1977e[2001b]: 208), (1980g: 28, 70), (1980c[2001b]: 194, 195), (1980d[1980b]: 24, 25, 26), (1980e[2002a]: 109), (1980f[2001b]: 292), (1982a: 201, 202), (1982b: 11), (1982c[2002a]: 175), (1983[1987a]: 64), (1984c[2001b]: 293, 299, 314, 322, 323), (1984f[2002a]: 191), (1985a[1987a]: 13, 27, 28), (1989b: 373), (1990[2002a]: 75), (1992b[2002a]: 242), (1993a[2002a]: 271), (1994a: 27, 129), (1997a: 255, 256), (1997c[2002a]: 338), (1998d[2002a]: 350), (2012: 17, 18, 19, 110, 117, 134, 158, 221, 224, 234, 235, 236, 255, 265, 268, 269, 277, 425, 441, 545, 559).

Judging from the number of citations, Marx is five times more praised than criticised, while Marxists are ten times more contradicted than valued. This relationship with Marx and Marxists is present throughout Bourdieu's sociological work. Thus, statements that favour Marx are 14 times greater in number than those opposing him in the periods 1963–1970 and 1971–1980. The proportion of favourable statements to opposing ones dwindles to 2.7 and 2.8 for the periods 1981–1990 and 1991 onwards, respectively. Similarly, the Marxist school of thought is not valued before 1981 and is 16 times less approved than it is disapproved between 1981 and 1990, the proportion increasing to 6.6 from 1991.

This laudatory assessment of Marx and devaluation of Marxism is deeply consistent: very favourable quotations for Marx enable Bourdieu to be in line with him; he criticises Marxists, who are competitors in the sociological field. Doing science and valuing Marx is an efficient way to justify the criticisms he addresses to Marxists.[7]

Furthermore, the evolution of the relationship between statements that favour Marx and those that are against him is not surprising. The fact that the proportion of the former to the latter is equal to 14 until 1980 and around 2.8 thereafter is quite logical: Bourdieu no longer needs to enhance Marx to criticise his competitors, because his sociological works are sufficient to call into question the Marxist school of thought. The statistics, which clearly show that Bourdieu is less favourable to Marx from 1980, challenge the accuracy of Bourdieu's statement in his interview with Wacquant:

> I notice that I have never cited Marx as often as I do nowadays, that is, at a time when he has been made a scapegoat of all the ills of the social world – no doubt an expression of the same rebellious dispositions that inclined me to cite Weber at the time when the Marxist orthodoxy was trying to ostracise his work.
>
> (Bourdieu and Wacquant 1992: 102)

Analysis of the content of quotations and citations

The previous findings are based on quantitative methods of frequency and rank. We will now analyse the diversity of the passages' contents in which Bourdieu refers to Marx, distinguishing those in which he approves of Marx and those in which he is critical of him.

Our thesis is that the statements that are favourable to Marx do not express a strong link between the two authors; that the major part of them is not related to Bourdieu's theoretical system and is acceptable by non-Bourdieusian contemporary sociologists.

This thesis is paradoxical, since it apparently contradicts the previous quantitative analyses. So far, we have demonstrated that Bourdieu has increased his citations of Marx. What we are asserting is that these references are independent of Bourdieu's theoretical system because they do not contribute to the specificity of his sociological work.

Bourdieu refers positively to Marx on 129 occasions. As he sometimes cites the same quotes in several texts, we can consider that there are 64 different statements favourable to Marx in our corpus of Bourdieu's works. We decided to classify them into nine relatively homogeneous categories[8]: characteristics of particular individuals; methodology and epistemology; history; property and economic capital; other economic phenomena; state and politics; knowledge and consciousness; specific social groups; and other social phenomena.

We chose to repeat those 64 items to allow readers to test our thesis. References to pages from Bourdieu's texts will enable them to check whether the passage is favourable to Marx and whether each item corresponds to comments made by Bourdieu. Similarly, they can confirm (or not) that all these items can be defended by non-Bourdieusian sociologists and the validity of some of these items is independent of Bourdieu's theoretical system.

Overall, statements that are favourable to Marx or his comments include:

Characteristics of particular individuals

1. Type of Proudhon's anger (Bourdieu 1979: 280)
2. Link between Seneca and the asceticism of the wealthy (Bourdieu 1979: 286)
3. Marx who is a theoretical and practical inventor (Bourdieu 1980d[1980b]: 23; 1984c[2001b]: 322)
4. Criticism of Andrew Ure and his laudation of managers (Bourdieu 1989b: 479)

Methodology and epistemology

5. Distinction between the things of logic and the logic of things (Bourdieu and Wacquant 1992: 98; Bourdieu *et al.* 1968: 193; Bourdieu 1972b: 255; 1984c[2001b]: 299; 1985b[1987a]: 77; 1994a: 27)
6. Marx who has a consequent objectivist point of view (Bourdieu and Passeron 1970: 19; Bourdieu and Wacquant 1992: 72; Bourdieu *et al.* 1968: 30, 33; Bourdieu 1987a: 148)

7. Concepts that must break with realism (Bourdieu *et al.* 1968: 51, 77, 193)
8. Criticism of the spontaneous analogy (Bourdieu *et al.* 1968: 43)
9. Persons who personify positions or general provisions (Bourdieu *et al.* 1968: 14; Bourdieu 1975b[2002a]: 129)
10. Complex forms enabling us to understand simple forms (Bourdieu 1971: 307)
11. Understanding the world entails an active analysis of practices, knowing the real activity (Bourdieu 1972b: 100, 219; 1977e[2001b]: 202; 1980g: 87, 245, 280; 1997a: 198)
12. Possibility of thinking the logic of naked interest, of the egoistical calculation (Bourdieu 1972b: 363)
13. Analyses of typical, pure phenomena (Bourdieu 2012: 144)
14. Critique of idealism (Bourdieu 2012: 83)

History

15. Idolisation of nature which fails to grasp what history produces (Bourdieu *et al.* 1968: 35, 160; Bourdieu 1971: 301)
16. Oversight of history, as classical economists do, is in the interest of the ruling class (Bourdieu *et al.* 1968: 160)
17. Inability to explain Greek mythology and art by technical phenomena (Bourdieu 1976: 127; 1980g: 215)
18. Greek art as eternal charm (Bourdieu 1980g: 28)
19. Interest to analyse a social phenomenon from the movement that gave birth to it (Bourdieu 1980g: 52)
20. Historisation of concepts (Bourdieu 1985a[1987a]: 27)
21. Criticism of the retrospective worship of past revolutions (Bourdieu 1997b[2002a]: 322)
22. Analysis of the end of feudalism (Bourdieu 2012: 126)

Property and economic capital

23. Link between heritage and land in traditional societies (Bourdieu 1972a[2002b]: 169; 1980g: 249, 257; 1985b[1987a]: 85)
24. Presentation of private property as a means of personal existence, distinctive, as essential life (Bourdieu 1979: 318)
25. Existence of a concentration and monopolisation process in the economy (Bourdieu 2000b: 273)
26. Subjective evaluation of needs, based on owned economic capital (Bourdieu 1972b: 259)

Other economic phenomena

27. Concept of simple reproduction (Bourdieu 1963[2008]: 93; 1977a: 29)
28. Link between the intellectual work and material work division and the distinction city/countryside (Bourdieu 1971: 301)
29. Distinction between work time and production time among the peasantry (the time between sowing and harvesting) (Bourdieu 1971: 301; 1972b: 356; 1980g: 199, 360)

30. The many contingencies that maintain or question working conditions (Bourdieu 1972b: 166; 1980g: 202)
31. Credit that is the economic assessment of the morality of a man (Bourdieu 1974: 23)
32. Indirect and impersonal domination in capitalism, and not in the pre-capitalist economy (Boltanski and Bourdieu 1975a: 98; Bourdieu 1980g: 211; 2012: 128, 237)
33. Strong separation of the different craft branches before the emergence of large-scale industry (Boltanski and Bourdieu 1975b[2002a]: 4; Bourdieu 2001b: 71)
34. Reduction of the work done by workers to simple work (Bourdieu 1977a: 291, 370)
35. Purchases depending on income and social positions, some having nothing (Bourdieu 1979: 437, note 4; 1984c[2001b]: 295, note 3)
36. Definition of effective demand as a realistic relationship to possibilities (Bourdieu 1974: 5; 1980g: 108)

State and politics

37. State as an instrument of domination and a concentrated, organised social force (Bourdieu 1983[1987a]: 49; 1997a: 179; 2012: 17, 232, 326, 589)
38. State regarded as an illusory community (Bourdieu 2012: 28, 587)
39. Political ideas reflecting interests (Bourdieu 2012: 161, 559)
40. Distinction between human rights and citizens' rights (Bourdieu 2012: 564)
41. Philosophy of assimilation, which characterises French citizenship (Bourdieu 2012: 554)

Knowledge and consciousness

42. Ethnocentrism of the Church Fathers (Bourdieu and Wacquant 1992: 102, 221; Bourdieu 1963[2008]: 95; 1972b: 361; 1980g: 192)
43. Naive, ideological, socially limited consciousness, imbued with the old world (Bourdieu and Chartier 2010: 61; Bourdieu and Passeron 1970: 19; Bourdieu 1971: 334)
44. German socialism that is characterised by a work of philosophical universalisation (Boltanski and Bourdieu 1975b[2002a]: 22)
45. Ideas crossing borders (Bourdieu 1977e[2001b]: 201)
46. Marx, founder of the sociology of knowledge, the latter not being a simple reflection of underlying economic mechanisms (Bourdieu 1979: 544; 1982b: 11; 1992a: 295)
47. Opposition between French thinkers who are political theorists and German thinkers who ask universal and abstract questions (Bourdieu 1985a[1987a]: 46; 1997a: 97, 362)

Specific social groups

48. Educators who need to be educated (Bourdieu and Passeron 1970: 47)
49. Luxury that is a business requirement and must be displayed by certain

social groups (Bourdieu and Delsaut 1975: 7; Bourdieu and de Saint-Martin 1976: 50; Bourdieu 1979: 326)

50. French aristocrats who become the dancing masters of Europe (Bourdieu and Delsaut 1975: 26; Bourdieu 1979: 126; 1992a: 287)
51. Workers whose appearance consecrates them as a capital property (Bourdieu 1979: 200)
52. "Petit-bourgeois" trapped within the limits of his brain (Bourdieu 1979: 271)
53. Agents who must universalise their personal interest (Bourdieu 1984b[2001b]: 271)
54. The dominant who are themselves dominated (Bourdieu 1989b: 12; 1998b: 98)
55. The poorest who, as a first approximation, have an interest in the universal (Bourdieu 2012: 542)

Other social phenomena

56. Social constructions that appear independent and masked, the utopia allowing to question them (Bourdieu 1977d: 55; 1979: 463; 1980d[1980b]: 25; 1984b[2001b]: 261; 1984c[2001b]: 320)
57. Domination as a class phenomenon (Bourdieu and Passeron 1970: 18)
58. Religion fostering social order (Bourdieu 1971: 299)
59. Dull pressure of economic relations (Bourdieu 1974: 15; 1980g: 69)
60. Language as the real, practical consciousness (Bourdieu 1979: 464)
61. Marx who gave the elements of a socio-linguistic pragmatics (Bourdieu 1982a: 165; 1985a[1987a]: 28; 1988: 30)
62. Mediation of certain social relations by things (Bourdieu 1989b: 13)
63. Marx's analysis and its compatibility with the habitus concept (Bourdieu and Wacquant 1992: 97; Bourdieu 1994a: 171, 172)
64. Differentiation process of social worlds (Bourdieu 2012: 318).

We argue that the aforementioned statements, which are favourable to Marx, express only a tenuous link between the two authors. Some of these items are contradicted by Bourdieu's statements in other parts of his work. Therefore, they cannot characterise Bourdieu's thinking and his relationship to Marx. In particular, let us analyse successively items 6, 52, 18 and 1:

- On the one hand, Bourdieu writes that Marx has a substantial objectivist point of view:

  > We know that Durkheim is no doubt, together with Marx, the one who expressed the objectivist position in the most consistent manner: "We believe this idea to be fruitful, he wrote (Durkheim 1970: 250), that social life must be explained, not by the conception of those who participate in it, but by deep causes which lie outside of consciousness".
  >
  > (Bourdieu 1987a: 148–149; 1987b trans. Wacquant 1989: 15)

On the other hand, he is opposed to Marx as an activist, who promotes the consciousness of individuals: "one can equally apprehend this mechanical sequence of gestures and words 'from a subjective point of view', as the Marx of the *Theses on Feuerbach* somewhat rashly puts it" (Bourdieu 1972b: 230; 1972b trans. Nice 1977).

- In *Distinction*, he approves of Marx's point of view on "petit bourgeois": "To say with Marx that 'the petit bourgeois cannot transcend the limits of his mind' (others would have said the limits of his understanding), is to say that his thought has the same limits as his condition" (Bourdieu 1979: 271; 1979 trans. Nice 1984: 244). A few pages later, Bourdieu criticises this point of view when he claims that an objectifying reduction

  has nothing in common with class contempt – which is flagrant in so much writing on the petite bourgeoisie, the traditional whipping boys of aestheticising prophecy and the favourite target for political anathemas (one only has to think of Marx's attacks on Proudhon…).

  (Bourdieu 1979: 390; 1979 trans. Nice 1984: 338)

- These contradictory statements of Bourdieu can also be seen when he describes the relationship between Marx and Proudhon, since in the same book (*Distinction*), he approves of it (Bourdieu 1979: 280; 1984: 244) and then criticises it (1979: 390).
- In *Le Sens pratique*, Bourdieu agrees with Marx in saying that Greek art has an eternal charm (Bourdieu 1980g: 28), while adopting the opposite position in *The Rules of Art*: "'eternal charm' of Greek art that Marx described (rather casually…)" (Bourdieu 1992a: 508; 1992a trans. Emmanuel 1996: 311).

On several occasions, Bourdieu suggests that Marx is a pioneer, because he is the initiator of the sociology of knowledge, he gave the elements of a sociolinguistic pragmatics and he carried out analyses close to the concept of habitus (items 46, 61 and 63). These three statements can be easily accepted, given the vagueness of the terms used, the uncertainty associated with the use of the words "initiator", "elements" and "close". That said, they do not relate to the central concepts of Marx's works (surplus-value, links between production relations and productive forces, communism…) and thus cannot establish a strong link between the two authors.

The analysis of item 11 confirms the significant difference between Bourdieu and Marx. Here Bourdieu explicitly cites passages from the *Theses on Feuerbach*. However, there is a significant discrepancy between Bourdieu's theoretical system and this 1845 text, in which Marx affirms that knowledge cannot be objective and can only originate from revolutionary practice. In his sociological work, Bourdieu does not attempt to transform the social world, but to analyse it, objectify it, understand it scientifically – even if his works have political and social effects and help fight against domination. Quite the opposite, in the *Theses on Feuerbach*, Marx says that knowledge of social reality has to be partially subjective[9] and comes from revolutionary transformation: "The chief defect of all hitherto existing materialism – that of Feuerbach included – is that the thing, reality, sensuousness, is conceived only in the form of the object or of contemplation, but not as sensuous human activity, practice, not subjectively" (thesis n°1); "Man must prove the truth – i.e. the reality and power, the this-sidedness of his thinking in practice" (thesis n°2); "The coincidence of the changing of circumstances and of human activity or self-changing can be conceived and rationally understood only as revolutionary practice" (thesis n°3); "The philosophers have only interpreted the world, in various ways; the point is to change it" (thesis n° 11). There is a series of items in which Bourdieu appears to approve some of Marx's factual analyses: the end of feudalism (item 22), opposition between French and German thinkers (48), French aristocrats as the dancing masters of Europe (51), to mention a few. But these statements do not create strong links between Bourdieu and Marx, since Bourdieu's theoretical system is completely independent of the analysis of these phenomena.

Lastly, some items enjoy acceptance by a large number of non-Bourdieusian contemporary sociologists. Therefore, they are not related to the specificities of Bourdieu's way of thinking. These items indicatively include: the critique of spontaneous ideology (item 8), the historisation of concepts (20), the process of concentration and monopolisation of the economy (25), credit as the economic judgment on the morality of men (31), political ideas reflecting underlying interests (39). As such, these items do not allow us to associate the particularity of Bourdieu's sociological work with statements made by Marx.

Content of the statements against Marx

We have established that the numerous statements expressed in favour of Marx do not show a significant link between the two authors. In this section, we come to highlight the few passages in which Bourdieu criticises Marx in order to demonstrate that there is a significant discrepancy between the two theoretical systems. Criticism of Marx is located in the following:

- a In Marx's work, there is no analysis of the recognition of legitimacy (Bourdieu and Passeron 1970: 19; Bourdieu 2012: 161, 275, 559)
- b He displays imprudence when, in the *Theses on Feuerbach*, he wishes to adopt a subjective point of view (Bourdieu 1972b: 230)
- c Contempt for class, political anathema towards Proudhon (Bourdieu 1974: 25; 1979: 390)
- d Adoption of a specific point of view, the objectivist position (Bourdieu 1980d[1980b]: 25; 1987a: 148)
- e Weakness of Marx's religious sociology (Bourdieu 1983[1987a]: 49)
- f Marx's unsatisfactory theory of social classes (Bourdieu 1983[1987a]: 64; 1987a: 153; 1994a: 53)

- g Erroneous pretension of being able to seize the totality of historical data (Bourdieu 1984a: 47)
- h Criticism of the labour theory of value (Bourdieu 1984d[1987a]: 127)
- i Constant singularity of the political standpoints of farmers, which is not due to spatial dispersion (Bourdieu 1989a[2002b]: 222)
- j Marx's thoughtlessness when he evokes the eternal charm of Greek art (Bourdieu 1992a: 508)
- k False alternative between utopianism and sociologism (Bourdieu and Wacquant 1992: 169)
- l Marx has no analysis of the "theory effect" (Bourdieu 1994a: 27)
- m He is oblivious of the effects of a state that appears as the site of universality and general interest (Bourdieu 1994a: 131; 1997a: 179; 2012: 231)
- n Marx's statements expressing his social properties and slightly criticising Marxism (Bourdieu 1994a: 28; 2001b: 329)
- o Emancipation, which is not necessarily the result of class consciousness (Bourdieu 1998b: 62, 63)
- p No explanation of the existence of the state (Bourdieu 2012: 17)
- q No mechanical link between public interest and the proletariat (Bourdieu 2012: 542)
- r The French revolution thought as the real bourgeois revolution (Bourdieu 2012: 545).

Some statements go beyond Bourdieu's theoretical system and do not give further information on a link between Marx and Bourdieu: the relation between farmers' political position and spatial dispersion (i); Marx's standpoint linked to his social position (n); Marx's pretension to be able to seize the totality of data (g); and emancipation which he analyses as the mechanical consequence of consciousness (o).

Most of the remaining items contain criticisms relating to key points of Marx's work and thus show strong opposition between the two theories. According to Bourdieu, the analysis of social classes is not satisfactory (f) and leads Marx to make mistakes regarding public interest (q). Similarly, he rejects Marx's vision of the economy since he opposes his labour theory of value and his conception of exploitation (h). Furthermore, Bourdieu criticises his analysis of the state, which fails to explain its existence (p), or its effects as a site of general interest (m). Lastly, Marx does not consider the recognition of legitimacy (a), the theory effects (l) and analyses religion in an unsatisfactory way (e).

Overall, we observe that in quantitative terms, Bourdieu was particularly in favour of Marx. Nonetheless, by analysing the content of these statements, we arrive at a radically different conclusion: the passages in favour of Marx do not offer support to a meaningful connection with Bourdieu. Moreover, our analysis of the relatively fewer critical remarks inclines us to think that there is a quite strong opposition between the two theoretical systems.

The economic concepts of Bourdieu and Marx

We now wish to clarify the way in which Bourdieu uses Marx's main economic concepts. He uses them in diverse ways. Sometimes Bourdieu appears to be in line with Marx, or to slightly modify his concepts. In other cases, he significantly transforms these concepts or does not use them at all. The way these concepts are used could offer an indication of the closeness between these two theories: as long as Bourdieu does not share Marx's theoretical views, he has no reason to adopt them; the more distance he takes from Marx, the more he tends to transform these concepts, even to the point of forgetting them.

We focus on four key economic concepts developed by Marx: commodity, exploitation, the pair labour/labour-power, and alienation. We chose them for two reasons. First, these particular concepts characterise Marx and distinguish him from other socialist approaches and from economists. Second, they are central to the economic theory he develops in his maturity,[10] so that other economic notions he discusses (e.g. currency, reproductive patterns, falling rate of profit, crisis of overproduction, production price) partially result from these four basic concepts.[11] Let us briefly recall the characteristics of these four concepts.

The concept of commodity – that is, the conjunction of exchange-value and use-value – is a concept found in classical political economy. Marx adds an element allowing him to criticise the market. Value is a substance, a quantity of abstract labour, which imposes its logic to men: they obey the market, even though they have created it (see Marx 1867a, b; ch. 1).

Exploitation is based on the labour theory of value. Only work creates value: all income comes from work, be it wages, profit, rent and interest (in the capitalist economy), or drudgery and tithe (in feudal economy). The concept of exploitation is closely linked to the relationship between two social groups: some obtain a surplus (capitalists, lords) because others have worked for free or for less than the exchange-value of the commodity they contribute to (proletarians, peasants).

The pair labour/labour-power is related to the two previous concepts. Labour-power is a commodity that is similar to other commodities: it has value, which is determined by the labour-time socially necessary to produce the means of subsistence; it has use-value, a social use-value (labour); and it is bought at its value and is used according to its use value. As a result, the capitalist does not buy labour but labour-power; he is not a thief as he pays for labour-power at its value. Hence, surplus-value, which is equal to the difference of the value of labour provided and the value of labour-power, is a necessity in capitalism (Marx 1867a: 1031–1036; 1867b: 677–681).

The concept of alienation is present throughout Marx's work, even if it appears more frequently in his earlier texts. By analysing the different dimensions of the capitalist economy, Marx argues that man is alienated, which means that he is deprived of his humanness. This alienation, this inauthenticity, will disappear with the advent of communism, which will include "free men, working with the means of production held in common, and expending their many different forms of labour-power in full self-awareness as one single social labour force" (Marx 1867a: 613; 1867b: 171).

Now let us examine how Bourdieu treats such notions in his work. We begin with the concept of exploitation. Although Bourdieu uses this word, he never uses it as Marx intends it – that is, in the sense of added value and free labour. He uses the term in its usual meaning: there is exploitation when workers have particularly hard working conditions and very low wages, whereas for Marx, there is exploitation when there are profits, even if wages are high. Throughout our collection of works, Bourdieu consistently refuses to use the concept of exploitation *à la* Marx. Here are some examples:

- "Manoeuvres left to exploitation due to their lack of qualifications and the constant threat of unemployment" (Bourdieu 1958: 124); "Exploitation of job-candidates takes various forms: we may 'require the payment of a sum of money' (5,000 francs according to various testimonies) or in-kind gifts" (Bourdieu *et al.* 1963: 273);
- "In the absence of a rational organisation of the placement and lack of control of recruitment processes, some employers may exploit (or let exploit) with manoeuvres 'deprived of specialty' " (Bourdieu 1977a: 50).

Since Bourdieu does not share Marx's notion of exploitation, it logically follows that Bourdieu does not adhere to Marx's distinction between labour and labour-power and to his conception of surplus-value. Indeed, Bourdieu never wrote, explicitly or implicitly, that the worker sells his labour-power at its value and that the entrepreneur utilises the use-value of this commodity, that is, labour.

By refusing to adopt the aforementioned concepts, Bourdieu questions the labour theory of value. Marx's perception of the value and exploitation of labour are linked: since labour is the only source of value, income earned outside of work necessarily comes from others' "free" labour. Hence, the notion of exploitation in slavery, the feudal or capitalist economy, is based on labour as the sole source of wealth. Conversely, Bourdieu, who does not share Marx's notion of exploitation, does not need to defend the labour theory of value.

Bourdieu takes the argument further and criticises this theory:

> the structure of the economic field determines everything that occurs in the field, and in particular the formation of prices or wages. The effect of this is that the so-called political struggle to modify the structure of the economic field is at the heart of the object of economic science. Not even the criterion of value, the central bone of contention between economists, can escape being an object of conflict in the very reality of the economic world. So that, in all rigour, economic science should include in its very definition of value the fact that the criterion of value is an object of conflict, rather than claiming that this struggle can be decided by an allegedly objective verdict and trying to find the truth of exchange in some substantial propriety of the

goods exchanged. It is no small paradox, indeed, to come across the substantialist mode of thought with the notion, of labour-value, in Marx himself, who denounced, in fetishism, the product par excellence of the inclination to impute the property of being a commodity to the physical thing and to relations it entertains with the producer and the potential buyers.

(Bourdieu 1984d[1987a]: 127; 1987a trans. Wacquant and Lawson 1990: 89–90)

This critique of the labour theory of value[12] confirms that Bourdieu's theoretical system differs from the one developed by Marx. According to Bourdieu, wages and prices are not determined by the logic of the value of labour, or by the quantity of labour, but by the structure of the economic field. In other words, the value of commodities is not mechanically fixed, but is the object of major struggles. That said, it seems difficult to follow Bourdieu in his criticism of the text of Marx on commodity fetishism. He writes that Marx's view is paradoxical because he accepts pricing according to the labour theory of value, which makes it a property of things, a substance, and at the same time he denounces the belief of a naturalised value held by the advocates of the markets. However, we believe that there is no paradox in Marx's analysis: the notion of value as substance is merely a social feature, a property of the commodity, based on market participants' belief. Market actors will question the logic of the market and the logic of value when they become aware of their alienation.

Marx's theory of alienation has two features: on the one hand, man is alienated when he is deprived of his humanity, when he is a stranger to himself; on the other hand, it is consciousness leading to the establishment of communism that will question and then suppress alienation. Bourdieu resumes Marx's first idea, but will never associate communism with the authenticity of individuals.

He uses the term "alienation" in Marx's sense and applies it to many aspects of social life:

- Alienation is a matter of granting to individual agents the share that effectively falls to them in the preservation or transformation of structures, and

  returning to them the responsibility they unknowingly assume when, in letting themselves be guided by unconsciouses we may justifiably call *alienated*, since they are but internalised externality, they agree to make themselves the apparent subject of actions that have the structure as their subject.

  (Bourdieu 1989b: 47)

- It is at the centre of political struggles: individuals can only come into being as a political group capable of representing its interests once that group selects a spokesperson, so "they must always risk political alienation in order to escape from political alienation" (Bourdieu 1984b[2001b]: 186, my translation, since the actual translation, to be found in *Language and Symbolic Power*, 1991: 249, preferred "dispossession" instead).

- It is associated with social differences: the experience of "'the alienated body', embarrassment, and the opposite experience, ease, are clearly unequally probable for members of the petite bourgeoisie and the bourgeoisie" (Bourdieu 1979: 228); "Awareness of alienation is a privilege for those who are not so completely insane they can free themselves" (Bourdieu *et al.* 1963: 310).
- It allows us to analyse specific cases, like Flaubert, who

> was unable to be a sociologist while he tried to be one (it is something we forget: he wanted to be both master of the language and of the form and also – you've only got to look at his documentation work – he wanted to tell the truth about the social world), knowing prevents from dreaming about a speech which is actually an alienated speech. I think that, to some extent, the novelist Flaubert was not able to do completely what he wanted to.
>
> (Bourdieu and Chartier 2010: 101, 102)[13]

Moreover, Bourdieu never says that communism will abolish alienation and restore authenticity, since for him it constitutes a utopian project. When he defends the concept of a communist society, he does this to explicate the arbitrariness of social constructions and motivate people to think about new political and social alternatives by examining the facts.

According to Bourdieu:

> Perhaps the most radical approach to the problem of politics is to ask of it the question that Marx and Engels raised in relation to art. Having analysed the concentration of the capacity for artistic production in the hands of a few individuals and the correlative (or even consequent) dispossession of the masses, they imagine a (communist) society in which "there are no painters but at most people who engage in painting among other things",[14] and in which, thanks to the development of the productive forces, the general reduction of working time (through an overall decrease and an equal distribution) allows "everyone sufficient free time to take part in the general affairs of society – *theoretical as well as practical*".[15] There are no politicians but at most people who engage in politics among other activities: here, as elsewhere, a utopia is scientifically (and, no doubt, politically) justified by the way it demolishes self-evident appearances and forces one to bring to light the presuppositions of the usual order.
>
> (Bourdieu 1979: 463; 1979 trans. Nice 1984: 397; see also Bourdieu 1977d: 55)

Therefore, apart from the concept of alienation, Bourdieu tends to reject Marx's main economic concepts. This opposition between the two authors is consistent with our previous analysis. Since we have little space to explain all theoretical divergences, we focus on a fundamental issue, that of social class.

Class struggles and social space

To compare both authors' views on social classes, we analyse Marx's theory, and then ask whether Bourdieu agrees with him. Marx's theory on social classes is based on five statements, which are found in several of his texts and have occasionally been subject to change throughout his work. We juxtapose Bourdieu's point of view against these statements, in order to identify similarities and differences with Marx.

First, let us briefly describe Marx's social class theory by delineating these five statements:

a *Classes are defined in the production process, the so-called infrastructure, tantamount to the underlying economic processes, and they exist in themselves, apart from the consciousness of individuals.*

This idea will be repeated many times in Marx's texts. In *The Poverty of Philosophy*, he writes that the mass of workers is "already a class as against capital, but not yet for itself" (Marx 1847: 177). Referring to the defeat of the Parisian insurrection of 1848, he says that "the time had come to deal more closely with the relations themselves on which the existence of the bourgeoisie and its class rule, as well as the slavery of the workers, are founded" (Marx 1849: 202). Similarly, in *The Eighteenth Brumaire*, he analyses the peasants as a class that has neither a common representation nor a kind of organisation:

> a whole superstructure of different and specifically formed feelings, illusions, mode of thought and views of life arises on the basis of the different forms of property, of the social conditions of existence. The whole class creates and forms these out of its material foundations and the corresponding social relations.
>
> (Marx 1852: 40)

b *Agents are increasingly aware that they belong to a class, which causes them to engage in struggle on the political level.*

This statement is linked to the first one. Individuals, who belong to a class defined in the economic instance, become aware of their class through struggle only gradually.[16] For example, workers first and foremost want their wages to be increased, which leads them to create a workers' association, which in turn shows its inadequacy; in the face of employer repression, this association takes on a political nature (Marx 1847: 177; see also Marx and Engels 1848a: 170). For example, as discussed in *The Eighteenth Brumaire*, if material conditions define the landlords and the bourgeoisie, their opposition will lead to a political struggle between the legitimate monarchy and the July Monarchy, which are the political expression of these two classes, respectively (Marx 1852: 40).

c *The main social conflict opposes two antagonistic classes, the proletariat and the bourgeoisie, which are defined in their relation to the surplus-value.*

This idea is clearly expressed in *Capital*. Marx discusses some other classes, he characterises the proletariat as the class that produces the surplus-value, he shows that the bourgeoisie obtains its income through free labour and he frequently emphasises the antagonism between these two social groups. He adopts a slightly different position in previous works: although Marx defends the idea that the class struggle is structured by the opposition between workers and the bourgeoisie, the concept of added value is not yet permanently stabilised.

In the *Communist Manifesto*, he says:

> Our epoch, the epoch of the bourgeoisie, possesses this distinctive feature: it has simplified the class antagonisms. Society as a whole is more and more splitting up into two great hostile camps, into two great classes directly facing each other: Bourgeoisie and Proletariat.
>
> (Marx and Engels 1848a: 162; Marx and Engels 1848b: 220)

For example, he writes: "Labour, being itself a commodity, is measured as such by the labour time needed to produce the labour-commodity" (Marx 1847: 45); "Labour was NOT always a commodity. Labour was not always paid work" (Marx 1849: 205); "On the basis of the present system labour is only a commodity like others. It must, therefore, pass through the same fluctuations to fetch an average price corresponding to its value" (Marx 1865: 526); "There are some peculiar features which distinguish the value of labour-power from the values of all other commodities" (ibid.: 562).

d *Other social classes that participate in the class struggle and come together take sides more or less strongly with the bourgeoisie or with the proletariat.*

In *Capital*, Marx only drafted his chapter on social classes without further explaining their different characteristics or their links. In empirical texts, different classes and fractions of classes depend on specific historical configurations and take part in the struggle between the bourgeoisie and the proletariat. Thus, Marx distinguishes five classes and fractions of classes in the *Communist Manifesto*, seven in *Struggle of Classes in France* and eight in the *Eighteenth Brumaire.*

e *The class struggle is increasingly favourable to the proletariat, it transforms social conditions and leads to communism.*

For Marx, the proletariat will become conscious of the hardness of their exploitation, create unions, become more numerous (with each economic crisis), understand the insufficiency of material struggle, choose the political struggle for communism and build this new society: "the class struggle necessarily leads to the dictatorship of the proletariat"; "that this dictatorship itself constitutes no more than a transition to the abolition of all classes and to a classless society" (letter of March 5, 1852 written by Marx to Weydemeyer) (Engels and Marx 1864: 59).

Bourdieu rejects four of the five previous aforementioned statements: social classes are not defined in the economic instance; there is no passage from the class-in-itself to the class-for-itself because the first does not exist; classes are not structured based on the surplus-value; the class struggle does not lead to communism. The opposition between the two authors is more nuanced when one considers that Bourdieu gives a key role to the economic sphere, as will be shown later on, and links real social relations to the theoretical social space.

Bourdieu's opposition to Marx is explicit in the beginning of the reference article dedicated to social classes: "Constructing a theory of the social space presupposes a series of breaks with Marxist theory" (Bourdieu 1984c[2001b]: 293; see also Bourdieu 1984c trans. Nice 1985). We must therefore reject the definition of theoretical classes. The first break is that one should not characterise social classes on the economic plan, but from the various dimensions of society. It is thus necessary to reject the Marxist definition of theoretical classes "whose number, limits, members, etc., one claims to define", and which leads one to reduce the social field "solely to the economic field, to the relations of economic production" (ibid.: 293). On this point, one of Bourdieu's contributions, compared with the other sociologists, is that he introduces the symbolic capital concept: the actors perceive themselves mutually through words, symbols; they are so classified in the social space and are more or less valued; the symbolic capital is imperative upon the agents while being produced by them; and this symbolic logic leads actors to accept, to legitimise their social positions, their social groups.[17]

Opposed to the concept of "class-in-itself", Bourdieu can only refuse the passage from this class to the "class-for-itself", particularly because "there is no mention of the mysterious alchemy whereby a 'group in struggle', a personalised collective, a historical agent assigning itself its own ends, arises from the objective economic conditions" (Ibid.: 299). However, Bourdieu adopts a similar rationale to that of Marx when he gives the economic dimension a key role and links the social space and the theoretical space, based on the social positions of different agents:

- "the hierarchy that prevails among the different kinds of capital and the statistical link between different types of assets are responsible for the fact that the economic field tends to impose its own logic on the other fields" (ibid.: 295, my translation); "the social space is a multi-dimensional space, an open set of fields that are relatively autonomous, i.e., that are more or less strongly and directly subordinated, in their functioning and their transformations, to the field of economic production" (ibid.: 314, 316).
- "one can separate out *classes*, in the logical sense of the word, i.e. sets of agents who occupy similar positions and who, being placed in similar conditions and subjected to similar conditionings, have every likelihood of

having similar dispositions (habitus) and interests and therefore of producing similar practices and adopting similar stances and a shared world view" (ibid.: 296–297); "probability of assembling a set of agents, really or nominally – through the power of the delegate – rises when they are closer in social space and belong to a more restricted and therefore more homogeneous constructed class" (ibid.: 297–298); "groupings grounded in the structure of the space constructed in terms of capital distribution are more likely to be stable and durable, while other forms of grouping are always threatened by the splits and oppositions linked to distances in social space" (ibid.: 298).

Bourdieu's point of view regarding Marx's statements c, d and e are less difficult to understand:

- As he refuses the Marxist conception of surplus-value, it is logical that social space should be based on "different species of power or capital that are current in the different fields" (ibid.: 294), and not on labour. Concretely, the social space and the social classes are constituted by three dimensions: the volume of the capital possessed by the various agents, the structure of capital, and the social trajectory of the agents (cf. Lenoir 2004). It is enough to know the social trajectories and the different types of capital possessed by various actors to statistically represent social differences between individual and groups (by using factor analysis in particular), to detect the various social classes, their fragilities and their heterogeneity, and to clarify the kind of oppositions that develop between social groups.
- Bourdieu agrees with the idea that different classes are positioned between the dominant group and the subordinate group,[18] although these groups vary according to the different fields and cannot be identified systematically to the members of the proletariat and the owners of the means of production.
- He never asserted that class struggle would lead to communism.

On the question of Bourdieu's alleged "Marxism", this depends above all on how we define this school of thought. Bourdieu cannot be considered as a Marxist if this school of thought is seen as the theory that serves the communist party or analyses capitalism and the advent of communism. The conclusion is radically different if Marxism is defined as the theory which favours the economic dimension or emphatically criticises domination and social inequalities.

Alexander views Marxism as a kind of historical and critical materialism (1995 trans. Zaccaï-Reyners and Lejeune 2000: 20, 21, 25, 36, 54), which incorporates the positive sciences (ibid.: 23) and underlines the structuring of society by the dominant social class (ibid.: 94, 95, 105). At the same time, he does not consider characteristics inherent in this school of thought that Bourdieu opposed: the idea of the communism; the notion of exploitation based on the labour theory of value; the opposition to the other socialist trends. Since he could not label Bourdieu as a Marxist, Alexander qualifies him as neo-Marxist (ibid.:

21), which is less than satisfactory. On the one hand, his definition does not represent Marxism: an anti-Marxist can be a materialist (it suffices to think of the construction of the European Union, a project which aims at creating a common economy to move closer to the superstructures of the various European states), can incorporate the positive sciences (like Durkheim and Caillé) and think that social classes structure the society. On the other hand, considering the neo-Marxism of the authors who wish to update Marxism, we could say that Bourdieu does not belong to their sphere of influence because they defend communism, the labour theory of value and exploitation, and oppose the other socialist trends (at least in the French intellectual field).

Close criticisms can be directed to other commentators who qualify Bourdieu as a Marxist. For example, Ferry and Renaut are completely wrong to write that the sociology of Bourdieu is "a distinguished variant of vulgar Marxism" (1985: 217). Bourdieu criticises constituent elements of Marxism (communism, labour theory, etc.), so his sociology cannot be a variant of this school of thought. Similarly, when Caillé qualifies Bourdieu as a Marxist (1994: 66, 93, 106, 112), he sets him up against a number of fundamental aspects of this school of thought: Marx's communist ideal that runs against Bourdieu's eternal submission to the law of capital (ibid.: 71); the issue of economic exploitation which is analysed by Marx and not at all by Bourdieu (ibid.: 127); the scholastic demarcation of the classes in Marx's work and the adoption of a hierarchical continuum in Bourdieu (ibid.: 127); the metaphoric use of political economy concepts by Bourdieu, contrary to Marx (ibid.: 118).[19]

Conclusion

In the present chapter, we focused on three points: Bourdieu's citations of Marx, his use of Marx's key economic concepts and their theories of social class. We observed that, when we counted the number of citations, Bourdieu appears particularly favourable to Marx and opposed to Marxism. The result was very different when we examined the content of citations: on the one hand, the many statements in which Bourdieu approves of Marx do not show any strong link between the two theoretical systems; on the other hand, the few critical statements are about major issues in sociology, namely the effects of theory, the recognition of legitimacy, religion, and the State as the site of general interest. The difference between the two authors is exacerbated when we compare their positions on the theory of value, exploitation, the distinction between labour and labour-power, the abolition of alienation and their analysis of social classes.

We also noted that Bourdieu had a strategy in the field of social science theory: he multiplied citations that were favourable to Marx to better oppose Marxism. This interpretation deserves further merit.

We should explain the different strategies related to our subject and used by Bourdieu in the field of social science knowledge. Let us mention three. First, Bourdieu uses citations in a way to reference certain authors who are independent of the argumentation and to overlook the essential ones.[20] Meanwhile, he refuses to specify his relation to Marxism in the name of science. For him, sociologists should use the work of their predecessors objectively, so they would not need to choose (beyond what is required by scientific rigour). In the same way, they should combine the various concepts developed by prior sociologists for a given topic.[21] Lastly, by giving his point of view on Marx, his different concepts and his evolution, he would be taking sides with his opponents, specialists of Marx, and thus risking some delegitimisation.[22] He therefore abstains from creating such upheaval: "saying, for some, that Marx and Parsons are not very different, I understand that it may upset, but I have neither the time nor the desire to do it" (Bourdieu 2012: 123).

It would be necessary to analyse further the relation between Bourdieu and Marxism: Bourdieu founded the Committee for the Defense of Freedom at the École Normale Supérieure, which was denounced by the communist group of the ENS; he was close to Louis Althusser (invitation to his seminar in 63–64, Althusser's text in the first edition of *The Craft of Sociology*) before criticising him radically in the 1970s (see, for example, Pestaña 2012); he had major conflicts with the French Communist Party while working with members of the party; he worked with Marxist activists even though he criticised neoliberalism; etc.

The relation between Bourdieu and Marx is necessarily one of affiliation and rupture.[23] Our analysis showed that the opposition between the two authors is clear: explicit criticism from Bourdieu on key issues, disagreements with Marx on economic concepts and social classes. These disagreements should also enable us to confront and investigate further the concepts of both authors. Let us consider the notions of exploitation and domination. Sharing Marx's point of view and his vision of exploitation inevitably leads to many difficulties, since it is based on the labour theory of value, which is incompatible with the logic of price and income.[24] On the other hand, it is difficult to adopt Bourdieu's point of view and consider that prices can be explained by the structure of the economic field, at a time when current globalisation seems to defend Marx and his commodity fetishism, as men and governments obey the market, even though they are the ones to have created it. Similarly, if it is legitimate to criticise Marx and his idea of man's authenticity in communism, can we be content with simply describing domination and denouncing it, or must we consider transforming it?[25]

Notes

1 Eric Gilles teaches sociology and economy at the University of Poitiers. He is responsible for the professional curriculum/course of the Master's degree "Methods of analysis of the social" at the University of Poitiers, and he is a member of the laboratory GRESCO (Sociological Group of Research and Studies of the Centre-West). He is author, with C. Tourelle-Randon, of the book *TEJS: Exposé sur un thème économique juridique et social* (ed. Corroy, 2001). He has also written several regional sociological inquiries on topics such as associative commitment of young people, articulation of personal life and professional life, and access to housing for vulnerable populations. He currently works on the relationship between sociology and economic theories.

2 Bourdieu's early work had been radically criticised by some Marxist researchers:

> *La Nouvelle Critique* [the French Communist Party review] wrote – we are not making this up: "Like the Synod of Bishops (...), those ideologues [the authors of *La Reproduction*] with their analyses push teachers, parents, students towards apocalyptic mirages, behaviours of withdrawing and fleeing, despair that demobilises"
>
> (Bourdieu 1980e[2002a]: 109)

3 Results are similar when we derive information from the site "Pierre Bourdieu a tribute" (see http://pierrebourdieuunhommage.blogspot.fr/2011/12/en-ligne-pierre-bourdieu-propos-de-marx.html, retrieved on August 21, 2012).

4 When Marx or Marxism is mentioned in a neutral way on several occasions on the same page, we have selected only one reference. In other cases, when two significantly different ideas appear on the same page, they are recorded as separate references.

5 Bourdieu refers to section 8 of *Capital*, Vol. I, on primitive accumulation (see Marx 1867a, b).

6 We recorded only the statements where the Marxist current is mentioned in its entirety and explicitly. We therefore did not include passages where Bourdieu refers to the different trends of Marxism (Gramsci, Althusser's disciples, etc.). Taking into account all the citations concerning Marxists would not have modified our conclusion, but would have, on the contrary, reinforced it since Bourdieu generally criticises those authors.

7 On several occasions, Bourdieu will value Marx and attack Marxists in the same reasoning:

> Marxist theory makes a mistake quite similar to the one Kant denounced in the ontological argument or the one for which Marx criticised Hegel: it makes a "death-defying leap" from existence in theory to existence in practice, or, as Marx puts it, "things of logic to the logic of things".
>
> (Bourdieu 1994a: 27; 1994a trans. Johnson *et al.* 1998: 11)

In another passage referring to transhistorical concepts, Bourdieu writes:

> For instance, in France, they have just published a *Dictionnaire critique du marxisme* in which three-quarters (at least) of the entries are of this type (the few words which do not belong to this category were made by Marx himself).... Many "Marxist" philosophers perpetuate them, wrest them out of their historical context and discuss them independently of their original use.
>
> (Bourdieu 1985a[1987a]: 27, 28; 1987a trans. Wacquant and Lawson 1990: 17)

He adds that "Marxism, in the reality of its social use, ends up by being a mode of thought completely immune to historical criticism, which is a paradox, given the potentialities and indeed the demands inherent in Marx's thought" (1985a[1987a]: 28; 1987a trans. Wacquant and Lawson 1990: 17).

8 Each statement is classified in a certain category. However, in order to avoid overestimating some categories, we set to ten the maximum number of items for each.

9 Here Marx talks about the theorist's subjectivity. Bourdieu does not say that the scientist must be subjective, but that he must take into account the subjectivity of agents:

> Marx evacuated from his model the subjective truth of the social world, against which he posits the objective truth of that world as a system of power relations. Now, if the social world were reduced to its objective truth as a power structure, if it were not, to some extent, recognised as legitimate, it wouldn't work. The subjective representation of the social world as legitimate is part of the complete truth of that world.
>
> (Bourdieu 1980d[1980b]: 25; 1980b trans. Nice 1993: 12)

10 We focused on the writings of his maturity because they are the most interesting and most relevant (see, for example, the three volumes of *Capital*).
11 There is no unanimity on this issue among commentators of Marx. For example, Althusser has for a long time asserted that Marx did not use the theme of alienation in his maturity, until he retracted towards the end of his life (Althusser 1976: 171).
12 In another passage, he criticises some of the opponents of the labour theory of value: "works of art provide a golden example for those who seek to refute Marx's labour theory of value (which anyway gives a special status to artistic production)" (Bourdieu 1977b: 5; Bourdieu and Nice 1980: 263).
13 All other passages develop along similar lines.
14 Engels and Marx (1845/1846: 433–434) as cited by Bourdieu.
15 Engels (1878: 214) as cited by Bourdieu.
16 "Singular individuals do not form a class so far as they lead a common struggle against another class" (Engels and Marx 1845/1846: 93).
17 We join the analysis of Wacquant (1993: 37).
18 For example, in *Photography: A Middle-Brow Art* (Bourdieu *et al.* 1965 trans. Whiteside 1990), he connects the properties of the middle class and examines their social position between the ruling classes and the dominated classes.
19 These comments follow a certain pattern. Bourdieusians, as Mauger (2012) and Wacquant (1996) are particularly and strongly critical of Alexander. On the other hand, Alexander (1995 trans. Zaccaï-Reyners and Lejeune 2000: 21) partially approves of Ferry and Renaut. Caillé (1994: 9) considers that his theses converge with those of Alexander (1995 trans. Zaccaï-Reyners and Lejeune 2000: 74) and endorses criticisms of Bourdieu by Ferry and Renaut. There are nevertheless differences in every camp. Alexander writes that Ferry and Renaut do not do justice to Bourdieu and "his authentically reconstructive impulse" (ibid.: 21). Caillé explains that Ferry and Renaut do not sufficiently cover "the question of the condition of possibility of a sociological speech" (Caillé 1994: 74).
20 For instance, let us take Veblen, and his *Theory of the Leisure Class*, which is not quoted in the 19 pages of the index of *Distinction.*
21

> Whether or not to be a Marxist or a Weberian is a religious alternative, not a scientific one … Marx claimed enough his title of scientist to honour him in using what he did and what others have done with what he did in order to go beyond what he thought to do.
>
> (Bourdieu 1983[1987a]: 64)

Gérard Mauger places this argument at the centre of his article regarding the relation between Bourdieu and Marx: "Bourdieu is no more 'Marxist' than 'Weberian' or 'Durkheimian': he is nothing of that or he is everything at the same time. He inherits from Marx, Weber and Durkheim, he adopts them" (Mauger 2012: 39).

In another text, Bourdieu gives a more satisfactory version, since it assumes that different sociologists are adopting different points of view regarding Marx, in the context of scientific work: "*the question of affiliation* of a sociological research to a specific theory of the social field, that of Marx, Weber and Durkheim, for example, *is always second compared to* the question whether this research belongs to sociological science" (Bourdieu *et al.* 1968: 16).

22 Criticising Marx's theory of exploitation would probably have weakened the position of Bourdieu and his collaborators.
23 Cf. Wacquant (1993: 36, 37).
24 Marx did not resolve the problem of the passage from values to production prices (that is, from the concepts in Vol. I of *Capital* to those of Vol. III). Suggestions initiated by his successors have not been convincing, which induces heterodox economists to rely less and less on Marxist concepts in their work (see Pouch 2001).
25 Wacquant (1993: 38) poses a similar question at the end of his article.

8 Change and not only reproduction

Pierre Bourdieu's economic anthropology and *régulation* theory[1]

Robert Boyer[2], translated by Michael Lainé

Introduction

Bourdieu's language seems to borrow from economics many of its basic notions; furthermore, he broached this disciplinary field in one of his books dedicated to the analysis of the social structures of the economy. The aim of this chapter is, precisely, to scrutinise Bourdieu's economic anthropology, to try to dispel misunderstandings and also to put forth a range of arguments in favour of a thesis which some critics would find paradoxical: far from straining himself to the analysis of reproduction, he provides a series of factors of change, particularly institutional ones. Incidentally, one may establish certain parallels with the objectives, if not the concepts and methods, of the economic research programme on the modes of *régulation*.

Bourdieu's work and its evolution have elicited many comments. Almost ritualistically, they bring into conflict the fervent admirers and heirs, who view him as the founder of a reflexive sociology with a strong scientific commitment, and on the other, the detractors, who play down – if not deny – the sociologist's insights in the comprehension of contemporary societies. In this debate, two recurring themes run through the controversy. On the one hand, Bourdieu is said to have sunk into an economism which would barely distinguish him from neoclassical theory to the point of being presented as one of Gary Becker's disciples. On the other hand, the emphasis laid on the concepts of habitus and field would only enable the analysis of social reproduction and not that of social transformation.

This chapter aims at answering these two symmetrical criticisms. First of all, it is shown that Bourdieu's detractors have too often taken at face value the titles of his books, which as a matter of fact underscore the permanence of the reproduction of social roles, even though, beyond the definitions of basic notions, the purpose is by no means to be reduced to a purely economic rationale. Moreover, it is important to stress that Bourdieu's proponents have insufficiently shed light on the deeply dynamic nature of virtually all his works, from his earlier research in Béarn and Kabylia, to his more recent analysis of the individual housing market, the university, literature, art, not to mention state nobility.

The same criticisms have been addressed against many contemporary institutional theorising. On one side the emphasis upon rules, norms, institutions and organisations would finally deny any choice to actors, simple agents constrained by an overwhelming society-wide structure. On the other side, this strict determinism, in turn, would imply the domination of pure reproduction over changes and transformations, features that are typical of market economies and individualist societies. This is especially so concerning *régulation* theory, an approach in political economy which emerged in France in the 1970s[3] out of the failure of ongoing theories to explain the end of post-World War II fast and stable growth in industrialised countries: the concept of Fordism was far too functionalist and it was thus impossible to capture the consequences of liberalisation and laissez-faire ideologies. Only methodological and ontological individualism was able to overcome this intrinsic limit of institutional and *régulationist* approaches.

This chapter proposes an unconventional but rigorous reading of Bourdieu's work and defends a core proposition: the concepts of field and habitus are able to explain not only reproduction but also changes and even innovation and this was his major concern, the study of reproduction being only the first and necessary step towards the analysis of the transformations of the various fields he investigated. In addition, the founding works in *régulation* theory had mobilised the concept of habitus as a better alternative than substantive economic rationality, while subsequent investigations focused upon the process of emergence of new institutional configurations. Therefore, a second part suggests the existence of a homology between the two paradigms, operating at different levels, either meso or macro, and gives an example of symbiosis between them.

A misuse of canonical economic notions?

It has been conventional wisdom to criticise Bourdieu for importing, consciously or not, categories of economic analysis into social sciences in general and sociology in particular. After all, his work would merely outline another variant of standard neoclassical economics. A more careful, literally and figuratively loyal, analysis unfolds quite different perspectives. Indeed, the economic field is nothing but one of the domains in relation to which action and conflicts are structured, while economic institutions fall under a construction much in the tradition of Norbert Elias.

The origins of a misunderstanding

In most of Bourdieu's books and articles, terms referring to economics abound: *interest*, *profit*, *capital* and even *market* are frequently summoned in fields alien to the economy. It is the recurring use of such terms that have elicited the criticism often levelled against Bourdieu: finally, beyond his explicit blueprint, he is said to have expanded economic reasoning to a set of other domains (artistic milieu, academia, linguistic practices, gender relations, and so on), leading astray the very rationales of these disciplines. Such interpretation displays a misunderstanding, both literal and figurative. These terms borrowed from economics have a different meaning in each of the specific fields; they are merely the starting point of analyses introducing factors that are much different from those posited by standard neoclassical theory or its extension to an analysis of social facts *à la* Gary Becker and those whom he inspired. In fact, Bourdieu works on a sociology of interest, as opposed to a purportedly general sociology.

> What may mislead people is that, like the neo-marginalist economists, I refer all social behaviours to a specific form of interest, of investment. But we are only using the same *words*. The interest I am talking about has nothing to do with Adam Smith's notion of self-interest, an a-historical, natural, universal interest, which is in fact simply the unconscious universalisation of the interest engendered and presupposed by the capitalist economy.
>
> (Bourdieu 1980b: 33; trans. Nice 1993: 18)

Indeed, there are as many ranges of such key-notions, borrowed from economics, as there are fields. By 'field', one must conceive of a delimitation of the social world, governed by specific laws and codes, be it university, journalism, literary, artistic or political milieus, which constitute just as many worlds of connivance and role-playing.

According to Bourdieu, each *field* is characterised by a specific, differential form of *interest*. It is true that interest, as defined by economists, is present in the economic field, but one does not find it playing a key role in most of the other fields. In some cases, the action that seems to be the most disinterested abides nonetheless by the logic of the field (e.g. be it academic or artistic). As a matter of fact, economic interest is not the general equivalent of the various interests that fan out in all the diverse fields, and this is a fundamental difference with works in sociology that are inspired by the rational choice paradigm. Wouldn't the application of the *homo oeconomicus* rationale spawn multiple misinterpretations in most fields? Suffice it to take but two examples. What could be the scope and accuracy of the assumption that a noble attached to the court of Louis XIV is viewed as a contemporary capitalist entrepreneur maximising his intertemporal profit? Or could we describe a scientist as a typical entrepreneur whose activity aims at profit maximisation?

As far as *profit* is concerned, its use is more metaphorical than typically economic. In fact, the term pertains to the outcome of the specific action that takes place in each field. Consequently, 'profit' may be as or even more symbolic than economic. Everything depends on the nature and organisation of the field in which individuals act. A more precise term would undoubtedly be 'unequal distribution of attributes', or even 'benefits' (within a given field). For instance, in the academic field, profits are highly symbolic: peer recognition through the number of citations, responsibilities borne in learned societies, and so on. In the academic market, such recognition tends to be converted in divergent incomes, monetary and fringe benefits only in societies and epochs where the economic rationale prevails.

The same applies to the very notion of *capital*, which cannot be reduced solely to economic capital. Indeed, there are other forms of capital a priori endowed with a rather radical autonomy, be it encapsulated in the features of cultural capital (e.g. grades, knowledge, good manners) or in the social capital linked to agents' network relations. The operating logic is even more different for symbolic capital: in fact, it enables agents to gain the equivalent of what other forms of capital, such as economic capital, provide. Admittedly, these diverse forms of capital could potentially be converted into one another, but the process has by no means the automaticity posited by the theory of human capital in its Beckerian variant. It is therefore unwise to refer to such a problematic neoclassical category, all the more so because the 'Cambridge capital controversy' demonstrated that there is no theoretically grounded measure of economic capital. The relevance of such a notion in the Bourdieusian construct is to account for a differentiated accumulation in relation to the positions occupied in a given field. Thus, it pertains to a relation of domination, as economic capital expresses the domination of capital over labour. In this regard, Bourdieu breaks with rational choice sociology, according to which only equals are interacting, at least by law, if not de facto.

The limits of the transposition are even more obvious as regards the use of the notion of *market*, whose meaning is clear for the economic field. Nonetheless, while research in economic sociology stresses that this mode of coordination stems from a construct involving certain key actors, the notion is used in a more metaphorical manner in most other fields. Can we really talk about a matrimonial market, unless we posit that the power of the economic rationale will prevail in all fields to the point of turning them into markets strictly speaking? Presumably, such risk of confusion is borne by Bourdieu, who thus practices an art similar to that of the judoka: importing a key notion in the analysis of contemporary societies in order to better bring out the logic of interactions within a field. In academia, even if the logic of interest specific to the economic sphere is replaced by a logic of disinterestedness, these are opposing logics which nevertheless abide by an a priori invariant model across fields. However, by so doing, Bourdieu exposes his theory to a possible misconception: that a sketchy reading might give the impression that he endorses a standard neoclassical theory variant.

A remedy to an extensive use of the notion of rationality

In their everyday decisions, do economic agents implement the same cognitive maps as the professional economists? Can we really summarise economic relationships solely as trading relations between individuals endowed with the same powers, capabilities and information? Doesn't the *homo oeconomicus*, considered as a representative agent, conceal the absence of a solution to the micro–macro bridge? Why consider that, everywhere and virtually always, the State destabilises the course of economic activity? Moreover, do equilibrium theories enable us to think about historical time and the transformations it implies?

Finally, is it reasonable to posit economic laws that are invariant in space and time?

To all these questions, Bourdieu gives bouts of answers, not only through an epistemological and methodological criticism of the anthropological prejudices of rational choice theory, but, even more so, through an original conceptualisation of the diverse fields and their interplay. Such a construct can be applied to the analysis of economic activity. In a very generous fashion, the *neoclassical theoretician* actually ascribes to concrete economic agents the *same rationality* as she herself assumes to account for a pure economy. Beneath an analysis which pretends to be positive, one perceives that a normative scheme is bursting: if observation data does not fit with the presumptions of the theoretical framework, then this is due to some degree of irrationality in agents' choices or to the incompleteness of markets. One will recognise here the project of neoclassical fundamentalism, which itself opposes a methodological use of rationality and equilibrium assumptions, leaving open the question of the existence of a Pareto-optimum market equilibrium.

Furthermore, time sets a formidable challenge to virtually all economic theories. Indeed, the *time* taken heed of by the economist is one of calculus, expectation and convergence toward equilibrium: it is a *cinematic time*, by and large virtual since it offers mere support to a thought experiment of the neoclassical theoretician. And yet, the question of historical time lies at the heart of the economic agent construct, as emphasised by Bourdieu in the very definition of habitus. A second factor of change comes into play through the evolution of the rules of the game that govern the functioning of a field, and more generally the historical transformation of economic institutions. Thus, the economic sociology that is concerned with genesis of categories, institutions and markets provides a starting point for the historicisation of economic analysis. This constitutes an alternative to neoclassical theory, whose predictions are permanently thwarted by the recurrence of innovations sometimes seen as radical, but in fact minor, or the other way round, of marginal initial changes that give rise to a metamorphosis of the entire mode of régulation outlined by the Régulation School.

Most economic theories have problems accounting for the role of politics and the State. Indeed, in its very essence, an analysis that formalises interactions between rational agents solely through markets is bound to view state intervention as harmful. If one takes at face value the teachings of standard neoclassical theory, the economist has no alternative but to be the defender and advocate of markets. Conversely, if one takes a look at economic history, there appears a remarkable symbiosis between the State and the market. In numerous cases, and not only those which, like France, are characterised by some kind of state capitalism, it is government policy that makes the institution of markets possible. A purely economic theory of markets appears to be a contradiction in terms – even the monetary institution at the basis of a market economy is inseparable from state sovereignty and legitimacy. Thus, the assumption of a pure theory regarding the possibility of closure of the economic field on itself – namely, the explanation of the economy by economic factors alone – is extremely untenable, because it assumes a separability that vast empirical evidence tends to invalidate. Be it only because the emergence of markets amounts to a process that mobilises the strategy of diverse social agents and very often the State power of legitimation.

Economics and the economy as constructs

With a few exceptions, like industrial economics, most economic research posits the existence of a market and then studies its features without ever proposing a general theory. Too often, we assume that agents' common interest will make the market institution emerge once they realise its superiority over an economy where transactions would be ruled by barter. It amounts to overlooking, as Alfred Marshall already showed, that a market takes its shape only insofar as intermediaries are able to convert news about suppliers and demanders into a profit source, precisely because of market structures for which they are responsible. During the last two decades, economists themselves have pointed out the limits of coordination by markets owing to the imperfection and asymmetry of information, the impact of representations upon the very functioning of markets or even the constitutive character of certain social norms. Still, once markets are established, there is no guarantee that they will achieve equilibrium on their own, since in certain configurations characterised by returns to scale, differentiated quality and the coordination of numerous agents, they cannot provide solutions to the coordination of a series of decentralised actions.

To illustrate, most economists consider that the market is the *solution* to coordination problems between interdependent agents, while, for social sciences as a whole, the shaping of the market is the *problem* which should be analysed. Function and functioning on the one hand, emergence and structuring on the other: economic research actually posits a central mechanism for which no theory is provided, let alone for its genesis, whereas papers of economic sociology account for the emergence of markets. In the electronic bid market for agricultural products ('marché au cadran' in French)[4] studied by Marie-France Garcia, it is the alliance between an official of the Chamber of Agriculture trained in neoclassical theory and local producers, who are in conflict with wholesale retailers, which made a market form more akin to perfect competition. A much subtler mechanism is at work in shaping the image and markets for Burgundy wine, according to a study by Gilles Laferté. While in the beginning of the 1920s traders organised the market to their advantage by wiping away their registered designation of origin and creating new brands, the irruption of a few new actors, like Jules Lafon, enabled the (re)invention of a tradition and the dramatic reshaping of the market in favour of landowners and those with a registered designation of origin, thus building a new image for Burgundy wines. This example of a market, analysed as a social construct, denies the conception of a field as a mere space for reproduction. A third example is to be found of course in Bourdieu's analysis of the individual housing market: it is the outcome of a double social construction of both the demand, through the formation of individual preferences and aid in terms of access to credit and public benefits, and supply, through a policy aimed at the constructors themselves. In both cases, the State contributes to the re-shaping of these two components into what would *ex post* appear to be a market.

The dominant/dominated relationship is structuring the diverse fields

In most economic theories, the market is presented as the cardinal, if not exclusive, entity of the behavioural coordination of an entire set of decentralised agents. This mechanism is perceived as a horizontal relationship between agents endowed with the same power on markets, power that is nullified since competition is assumed perfect. Moreover, not only is the market often presented as efficient, but also as fair, to the extent that each agent contributes to the formation of prices proportionately to her income/wealth. Once again, on this point, Bourdieu's economic sociology insists on a fundamental property: whatever the field, some have more power than others, so that competition does not serve the equalisation of opportunities but the reproduction of an unequal distribution of capital. In this regard, all fields are undermined by the opposition between the dominant and dominated, which defines as much their structure as their momentum and transformation. In principle, such opposition is rather reminiscent of Marx's distinction between commercial relations and production relations, but it cannot be reduced to that. As a matter of fact, between fields, there prevails a division in the working of domination: each field is characterised by specific power relations, based on the possession of one form of capital or another. Thus, capital differentiation is a guarantee against the imposition of a unique hierarchy that would be based on the concentration of all powers. On this point, Bourdieusian theory is in contrast with those Marxist conceptions that would, for instance, view political power as the mere embodiment of economic capital domination. For Bourdieu, if all the different fields are united by a certain solidarity based on homological positions, they also stand in opposition owing to the relations of competition and the conflicts concerning, for example, the formation of the conversion rate between the different sorts of capital that are constitutive of the diverse fields. That is why one cannot build a global capital index independently of the field within which the agent acts.

So, the heterogeneity of social positions largely shapes habitus and life styles. Whereas the economist tends to consider the heterogeneity of individual preferences and skills as exogenous, the approach undertaken by Bourdieu is concerned with the factors that determine the very distribution of the diverse forms of capital as well as their evolution through time. It sheds some precious light on the famous, unresolved dilemma of relations between microanalysis and the unveiling of macroscopic regularities. In fact, Bourdieu helps the economist to better comprehend the reasons for failing to produce an approximate aggregation, if not a perfect one, on the basis of serialised individuals that would distinguish themselves from one another only in terms of incomes. It is the dynamic relations between unequal agents that define the features of a field, a characteristic that applies also to the diverse markets.

Another benefit of the divide between the dominant and dominated is to introduce from the outset a dynamic aspect in the analysis. Each field is the site of struggles in order to conserve or transform the distribution of capitals, a feature that prevails even in the scientific fields. The dominant are in a good position to implement strategies enabling them to preserve their position and expand their capital. On the contrary, the dominated, as well as newcomers, are better off destabilising acquired positions and consequently developing innovations devaluing the capital possessed by those who hold power. It is clear that the destabilisation of a given field is not a frequent phenomenon, but it would be erroneous to conclude that each is the site of an *ad infinitum* reproduction of the same structure. It is worth asking why so many critics of Bourdieu have viewed him as a theoretician of reproduction. In virtually all his books, doesn't he repeatedly claim that 'analysis of structure, the statics, and the analysis of change, the dynamics, are indissociable' (Bourdieu 2001c: 121; trans. Nice 2004: 61)? Many readers thus seem to confuse the contention that invariable laws rule the functioning of all fields with the impossibility of an analysis of the historical momentum that is under play within each field.

Under the veil of reproduction, a theory of change

It would be tempting to defend a paradoxical interpretation of Bourdieu's work: while a sketchy analysis suggests the inevitability of social reproduction, in fact his entire analytical endeavour is devoted to the unveiling of change and transformation factors. As is the case in his earlier works on Algeria that essentially dealt with the analysis of economic and social transformations, the crisis theme does not cease to be carried over to other terrains. Besides, the concepts of habitus and field invite a historical approach aimed at grasping the *genesis*, the process of institutionalisation, the factors of transformation and finally the crisis of a field.

When it comes to the concept of habitus, critics' misconception is at its utmost: habitus is said to be nothing other than habits, thus the mechanical reproduction of invariants leading to the disappearance of individuals' autonomy, thus to a motionless history marked by the permanent domination of the same capital holders over dominated agents, without paying attention to the letter of Bourdieu's texts, according to which the habitus is 'that which has been acquired, but which has become durably incorporated in the body in the form of permanent dispositions' (Bourdieu 1980b: 134–135; trans. Nice 1993: 86). It constitutes an '*invention* principle that, produced by history, is relatively detached from history: dispositions are *lasting*, something that leads to all sorts of effects of hysteresis (delay, discrepancy)' (ibid.: 134–135, 87).

History is also percolating by the fact that investment in a given field stems from the interplay between a game space that defines the issues at stake and a disposition system adjusted to this game. 'In other words, investment is the historical effect of the harmony between two realisations of the social: in things, through institution, and in bodies, through incorporation' (Bourdieu 1980b: 35; trans. Nice 1993: 19). Hence, the adjustment of one to the other is but one special case when institutions and habitus have been engendered by the same historical process. And yet in his early work Bourdieu dealt precisely with the mismatches and failures in the functioning of a field whose logic went then unnoticed.

> What appears to have happened is that the special case of habitus and structure has often been taken as a principle of repetition and conservation. In fact, the concept of conservation, like that of habitus itself, was the only way in which I could describe the sort of discrepancies to be found in an economy such as that of Algeria in the sixties [...] between objective structures and incorporated structures, between economic institutions imported and imposed by colonisation (which today would take the form of market constraints) and the economic dispositions held by agents whose origin was in the pre-capitalist world.
>
> (Bourdieu 1987a: 189)

Furthermore, against the identification of habitus as a monolithic and immutable principle, stands the example of the Algerian underclass, which shows 'the existence of cleft, tormented habitus, bearing in the form of tensions and contradictions the mark of contradictory conditions of formation of which they are the product' (Bourdieu 1997a: 79; trans. Nice: 2000: 64).

> Habitus is not necessarily adapted to its situation nor necessarily coherent. [...] It can happen that, in what might be called the Don Quixote effect, dispositions are out of line with the field and with the 'collective expectations' which are constitutive of its normality. This is the case, in particular, when a field undergoes a major crisis and its regularities (even its rules) are profoundly changed.
>
> (Ibid.: 190; 160)

Such theoretical insight could be found throughout Bourdieu's work, be it employment in Algeria, the evolution of the peasantry in Béarn, university crisis, the conversion strategies of the French elite, not to mention gender issues. One should not overlook the symmetrical problem, namely that of the emergence of a new field, as in the case of the individual housing market, for example.

One cannot help being struck by a certain analogy between biased interpretations of Bourdieusian theories and the reception of régulation theory. The level of analysis is of course different: more microeconomic as far as habitus and field are concerned; macroeconomic as regards the régulation approach. Although the latter has its origin in the realisation of the – then rampant, now ostensible – crisis of the growth regime in the aftermath of World War II, critics have never ceased to blame it for its alleged steadfastness and for the identical reproduction of capitalism's institutions. By and large, such an assessment stems from the connotations associated with the term 'régulation' (homeostatic reproduction of a system), which tends to overcome the precise definition of what a mode of régulation is, since it is conceived as a transient equilibrium between forces leading to the endogenous destabilisation of an accumulation regime. In both cases, the notions developed to account for the social construction of individuals and institutions by history are interpreted as a defence and an illustration of identical reproduction, with no possibility for incremental or substantial change. Such rebuke has continuously been levelled against Bourdieu even though his purpose was, through a reflexive analysis, to provide the tools that would enable one to have a chance to overcome the apparent fatality of domination relationships that manifest themselves in each field.

The genesis of fields and markets

Thus, one essential tool is none other than the use of history to characterise contemporary patterns and guard against any attempt at naturalisation. For instance, Bourdieu's analysis of Gustave Flaubert's work shows the *autonomisation* process of the literary field in the nineteenth century. Likewise, one of his contributions to economics consists of underscoring the social conditions of the emergence of markets from the specific, albeit illuminating, example of the individual housing market. The outcomes accumulated by these diverse studies (see Table 8.1) trace a research path that is explored by economic sociology and paradoxically is conducted in a more systematic manner in the United States than in France.

The multiple factors of change: a taxonomy

Once a field is constituted, its functioning sets in motion a series of forces of change which trigger historical movement. In this regard, one cannot help but regret that few economists read the section entitled 'Principles of an economic anthropology', which closes the book on the *Social Structures of the Economy*. At least five factors contribute to change and such typology goes beyond the scope of the specific market studied (Figure 8.1).

The first factor stems from the fact that dominant actors in a field have a certain capacity to set 'the tempo of transformation [...] and the differential use of time is one of the main levers of their power' (Bourdieu 2000b: 248; trans. Turner 2005: 202). Indeed, one must recall that the reproduction of positions in the field supposes the permanent recreation of the unequal distribution of *the* discriminating form of capital. Thus, the perpetuation of domination cannot be based on the identical reproduction of strategies, since it also implies innovation. In this regard, one might think that the artistic or literary fields are cases in point of such pressure towards novelty, which becomes their major feature.

Besides, the entry of new agents is susceptible to modify a field's structure. Such a factor is of course crucial in the economy, since the pressure to innovate so as to give rise to new sources of profits leads to an upheaval of productive

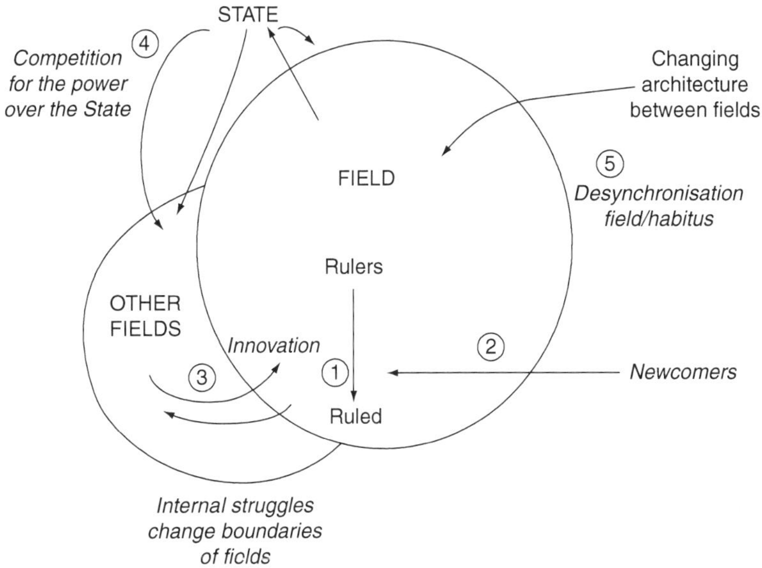

Figure 8.1 The factors of change for Pierre Bourdieu.

structures in certain historical periods. This momentum is further reinforced by economic competition from other nations or sectors. This factor of change is found in most fields: generalised access to education for new social classes changes the functioning of the system; similarly, the renewal of university faculties does not fail to affect these dynamics.

In turn, 'the changes within a field are often linked to changes in the relations to the exterior of the field. To these boundary crossings must be added also *redefinitions of boundaries* between fields' (Bourdieu 2000b: 249; trans. Turner 2005: 203). In the economy, the constitution of new sectors by way of specialisation is observed: in the information technology industry, for instance, the production of software is being autonomised with regard to the production of hardware to the point of inverting the hierarchy within the sector, as demonstrated by the evolution of profit distribution. Conversely, certain radical innovations can lead to the creation of a new sector by the fusion of old ones: for example, the coalescence of information technology and telecommunications has turned upside down the most established monopolies of the 1960s. This movement or redefinition of boundaries is especially prominent in the economy, but it also characterises most other fields. Thus, the field of the media increasingly alters the academic field, and trade relationships are penetrating the artistic field, and so on.

Among the exchanges of a field with the other fields, Bourdieu highlights the importance of interactions with the State. Indeed, the *competition for power over state power* introduces a potent factor of change. Once again, this factor is crucial for the economic field, if only because the same market-oriented strategies are in fact based on state power. Likewise, the contemporary evolution of diverse fields is marked by struggles over state interventions. No doubt, Bourdieu's awareness of these factors explains the increase in his public interventions, which were particularly frequent after 1995. They fall within continuous reflections over the meaning and features of state nobility and over the opposition between the administration and the private sector.

Finally, the de-synchronisation between habitus and field, owing to changes in the structure of the distribution of capitals across fields, constitutes a frequent source of change, if not crisis. Such is, for instance, the case with general transformations regarding demography, life style or gender relations, which are diffracted throughout the social world. Or even, quite simply, a change in the conversion rates between the diverse forms of capital can reverberate in a set of fields, which destabilises the responsiveness of a habitus formed in an entirely different context. In some cases, the complexity of the interdependencies between fields can give rise to crises altering more or less directly the conditions and factors of domination within them.

Thus, the conceptual framework, which seems to favour the notion of reproduction, always raises the question of the transformation of the field. According to Bourdieu's terminology, the field is endowed with a certain plasticity and in this way it distinguishes itself from the concept of apparatus, for '[a] field becomes an apparatus when the dominant agents have the means to nullify the resistance and the reactions of the dominated' (Bourdieu 1980b: 136; trans. Nice 1993: 88). Or:

> the permanent struggle within the field is the motor of the field. It can be seen, incidentally, that there is no contradiction between structure and history [...] the structure of the field [...] is also the principle of its dynamics.
>
> (Ibid.: 200; 135)

Actually, revisiting Pierre Bourdieu's work should convince the reader that this vision is present in quite any empirical research (Table 8.1).

The analysis of change and crises

If one holds the view that has just been expounded, Bourdieu's work contains a paradox. On the one hand, he did not have the time to achieve the general theory of fields that he constantly announced, worked upon and reframed over the years but never fully formalised. On the other hand, his theoretical construct favoured a sketchy interpretation which tends to underestimate his contribution to the understanding of change and crises, the characteristic of which is to shed light on the hidden laws of reproduction.

The de-synchronisation between a field and a habitus is analysed in many field studies: the incapacity of eldest bachelors to adapt to a matrimonial market

Table 8.1 Markets and fields genesis – a few examples

Fields/Markets	*References*	*Factors of emergence*		
		Specialisation/ autonomisation	*Dominant actors*	*State power*
Artistic	*The Love of Art* (Bourdieu *et al.* 1966 trans. Beattie and Merriman 1990)	•		
Agricultural bid market	*La Construction sociale d'un marché parfait* (Garcia 1986)		•	•
Literary	*The Rules of Art* (Bourdieu 1992a trans. Emanuel 1996)	•	•	
Media	*On Television* (Bourdieu 1996a trans. Ferguson 1998)	•	•	
Individual housing market	*The Social Structures of the Economy* (Bourdieu 2000b trans. Turner 2005)	•		•
Burgundy wine	*Folklore savant et folklore commercial* (Laferté 2002)		•	•

which is no longer local in the Béarn society of the 1960s; the rending of the Kabyles in the face of colonial domination over the economy and the heteronomy of the notion of work; the crisis of the university, as a result of the change in the student population and the growing heterogeneity of newly hired teachers; the malaise and disillusionment of the various categories of wage-earners because of the changes in the nature of work during economic crises; the troubles of feminism in view of the permanence of the invisible structures that rule gender relationships. These examples call for a reassessment of his contribution to the comprehension of contemporary societies and show that his theoretical construct has not lost its capacity to give rise to an original research programme (see Table 8.2). Likewise, Bourdieu's increasing public interventions could be interpreted as additional evidence of the importance attached to change, so that disclosing the general laws of reproduction is but one of the conditions for a genuinely transformative collective action.

Régulation theory: filiation and homology with Bourdieu's project

By criticising mainstream theory's assumptions regarding rationality, time and equilibrium, the Régulation School has not failed to meet with Bourdieu's sociology in its quest for a logic of action which would be compatible with a historical, institutional approach. In particular, the concept of habitus appeared as a reference consistent with the emphasis laid on the determination of agents' logic by the institutional context or, to put it more precisely, by institutionalised

Table 8.2 Change in the core of field theory

Fields/markets	*References*	*Factors of emergence*				
		Desynchronisation between habitus and field	*Dominant actors' strategy*	*Newcomers*	*Endogenous shift of boundaries between fields*	*Competition over power over state power*
Béarn peasantry	'Célibat et condition paysanne' (Bourdieu 1962), *Bachelors' Ball* (Bourdieu 2002b trans. Nice 2008)	Incapacity of the elderly to adapt to a matrimonial market that is no longer local		Competition of non-peasants	Consequence of the advancement of the market economy over the access to marriage	
Kabyle society	*Outline of a Theory of Practice* (Bourdieu 1972b trans. Nice 1977)	The Kabyle socialisation process renders the notion of work alien to agents	Imposition of colonial norms			Consequence of the colonial domination over the organisation of social relations
Academia	*Homo Academicus* (Bourdieu 1984a trans. Collier 1988)	The opening of the access to college studies destabilises the field		Growing heterogeneity of teachers due to the expansion of recruitment	The change in the social composition of the student population affects relations between the university and the economy	
Economic elites	*State Nobility* (Bourdieu 1989b trans. Clough 1996)	Transformation of the economic regime and its impact on the elite education system	Reconversion strategies of children from bourgeois families	Creation of new courses and business schools	The internationalisation displaces public boundaries	
Workers	*The Weight of the World* (Bourdieu ed. 1993 trans. Ferguson 1999)	Divorce between the expectations engendered by a prior pattern of a field and the constraints associated with the new economic regime	Technological, social innovations of companies and managements			Change in the economic policies towards neoliberalism

compromises. The development of a research programme led to an encounter with Bourdieu's other contributions that address factors of change, especially under the influence of the opposition between the dominant and dominated, politics and the symbolic, not to mention the role of the school in the reproduction of inequalities.

From the habitus to an institutionally situated rationality

From the outset, works mainly dedicated to macroeconomics – the nature and evolution of the accumulation regimes and the modes of régulation – have felt the necessity to specify which theory of action should be adopted. The rejection of the *homo oeconomicus*, which is endowed with a wide, substantive rationality, an exceptional ability to calculate and a virtually perfect anticipatory capability, entailed the endorsement of the concept of habitus, which is understood as a matrix of behaviour formation, strongly marked by history. In a more implicit than explicit way, the implementation of the Régulation School's research programme induced its proponents to detail and redefine this concept.

First of all, the notion of habitus presupposes *a restriction of the scope* of action. Whereas the substantive rationality hypothesis contends that each agent knows the whole set of prices, in fact, since gathering the relevant information is costly, agents form routines enabling them to find their way in the economic sphere in which they usually operate. Thus, workers and, even more so, collective organisations such as labour unions, take heed only of a limited set of variables – consumption prices, unemployment, productivity – without generally being capable of internalising the indirect consequences that are transmitted through the macroeconomic impact of a combined series of decentralised negotiations. So to speak, behaviours are specified with regard to five institutionalised forms: the monetary regime, the wage system, the forms of competition, the relations between the administration and the economy, and the form of international integration.

Second, prices are not the only indicators taken heed of, since the internalisation of the rules of the game and the induced effects on other actors are essential. Once again, the example of wage negotiations sheds some light in this regard. One can show that, for the same preferences and objectives of employees on one side and employers on the other, the wage level and, by extension, the level of employment, depends on the modalities of interaction between the actors. Depending on which side is organised – employers or employees – or on the fact that a professional organisation negotiates with a unique labour union, macroeconomic results will be totally different. Economists from the Régulation School are therefore tempted to ascribe certain precedence to the rules of the game over the habitus, without by the same token denying the importance of the latter in the explanation of social differentiation and heterogeneity. Indeed, if, on account of political upheavals, the institutional context changes significantly, it is possible to account for the alteration of macroeconomic regularities without positing an equivalent change in the objectives pursued by the actors. One example among others: French peasants, who were supposed to be Malthusians in the interwar years, became productivists in the 1960s, and they gave rise to over-production and, in the end, to criticism from environmentalists. Régulation School theory tends to focus on institutional change with regard to individual incorporation of learning, so far as the transformation of macroeconomic regularities is concerned.

Such a conception does not bar us from recognising that agents' objectives and preferences are shaped in and by history, as a strong variant of institutionalism maintains. This flexibility of habitus adds a factor of evolution to supplement the institutional one spurred by politics. Once again, an example illustrates such duality. To account for the transformation of French capitalism in the 1990s, not only should we analyse the impact of financial deregulation and the opening towards new standards of good governance, but one can also invoke a change in the visions of the largest French companies and their leaders and stress the omnipotence of the *conatus* of capital, which might be due to a generational renewal of high-level civil servants and entrepreneurs. In any event, the huge takeover bids could not have taken place with such a high frequency were it not for the change in the institutional context. Thus, institutional forms appear to prevail in the genesis of macroeconomic regularities.

Beneath an apparent invariance, two analyses of historical change

Bourdieu and régulationists alike have been criticised for analysing the reproduction of a field or an economic system, in which actors would be subject to a relentless determinism that would leave no room for any change. In both cases, critics take at face value the very wording of habitus on the one hand, and that of régulation on the other. But this amounts to forgetting that, in both cases, the project aims at examining the conditions that make change possible. One sees it when Bourdieu writes that his refusal to talk about 'subjects', as in the traditional philosophies of consciousness, does not amount to

> annihilating agents to the benefit of a hypostasised structure, like certain structuralist Marxists do, even though these agents are the product of this structure and continually make and remake this structure, which they may even radically transform under definite structural conditions.
>
> (Bourdieu and Wacquant 1992: 114–115, my translation)

Such intent is also apparent in the founding work of régulation theory:

> To speak of the régulation of a mode of production is to try to formulate in general laws the way in which the determinant structure of a society is reproduced. [...] A theory of social regulation is a complete alternative to the theory of general equilibrium. [...] The study of capitalist regulation, therefore, cannot be the investigation of abstract economic laws. It is the

> study of the transformation of social relations as it creates new forms that are both economic and non-economic that are organised in structures and themselves reproduce a determinant structure, the mode of production.
>
> (Aglietta 1976 trans. Fernbach 2000: 13–16)

In some way, from the beginning, the régulation research programme has never ceased to identify changes of institutional forms and to try to diagnose the accumulation regimes as well as the modes of régulation in gestation.

These similarities can be found on a more analytical level. It has already been pointed out, as far as Bourdieu is concerned: 'In a field, there are struggles, thus history' (Bourdieu and Wacquant 1992: 78, my translation), whereas for Régulationists, it is the architecture of institutional forms that orients and polarises conflicts. Most of the time, these conflicts are the very expression of the functioning of régulation but may, during certain crucial historical periods, become determinative of the constitution of institutional forms. While Bourdieu is concerned with the shifting of borders and relations between fields under the effect of internal strife, régulation theory instead insists on the alteration, through time, of the mode of régulation, under the effect of its very rationale and the success of its economic reproduction. This stems from a difference in scale between the two research programmes: largely meso/micro for the former; essentially meso/macro for the latter.

A final area of convergence between the two approaches concerns the role ascribed to the State. In both cases, administrative power lies at the heart of change in most fields and institutional forms, such as the economic field studied by Bourdieu, or the transformation of the wage system, forms of competition and international integration studied by the Régulation School. This role is even more obvious when it comes to institutionalised compromises that shape social security, the fiscal system and the nature of public spending. While for numerous economic theories, government intervention generally plays a disturbing role, they have here a constitutive, establishing role.

Social stratification and emergent growth regimes

Bourdieu's analyses of the role of the education system in social reproduction would not cease to be reworked over time. From these works, a key idea stands out: the school and, more generally, the education system are the matrix of the reproduction of dispositions and, consequently, of the positions occupied in the diverse fields. But such an invariant is compatible with notable variations in the organisation of the school, the university or the *Grandes Écoles*. Nevertheless, the pivotal hypothesis is that the social heterogeneity that results from the conjunction of belonging to a family and school curriculum – these two factors being linked – manifests itself in the dominant/dominated relationship across fields.

The contrast with the founding works of régulation theory is striking. Here it is the company that lies at the heart of the wage system reproduction and differentiation, during the so-called 'fordist' growth regime as well as in the previous historical ones. That's why most research by the Régulation School still focuses on the wage system. But the demise of the 'fordist' wage system from the late 1970s is heading towards greater differentiation in the wage relationship, that is, variation in the wage system according to sectors, individuals or companies. Hence, what is the factor that accounts for the differentiation of the trajectories of workers over the 1980s and 1990s? So far as France is concerned, there is little doubt that school and college history plays a decisive role. This has led to a generalisation of the notion of the wage system in favour of the *employment and training relation*. As a matter of fact, one can analyse the long-run history of the wage system as the result of the interaction between the dynamics of the education system and the evolution of the division of labour.

When an economist from the Régulation School reads Bourdieu's work published up to the 1990s, a remarkable absence strikes him: the wage relationship does not seem to structure the diverse fields, even the economic one, which is quite surprising when one bears in mind that Bourdieu was a careful though critical reader of Marx. And yet, in his book on employees' sufferings from, and their political commitment against, the social and human harms of conservative, market-oriented policies, contemporary domination appears to lean extensively on the wage system in practice, if not in theory. One notices the trail of transformations in French society under the effect of Fordism's crisis, which is not surprising if one notes that Bourdieu always insisted on the historical character of the social sciences.

Hence, we can speak of a mutual exchange between the two research programmes. The former takes heed of the action exerted in all fields by the economic crisis and is compelled to integrate the fact that the wage system is the essential determinant of employees' individual situation. The latter, as we have shown, is prompted to take heed of the consequences of skills differentiation and the movement of specialisation on the trajectories that would lead out of the crisis. Thus, the reference to a canonical wage system, defined by the typical workers' contract in the fordist industries, is fading away, which calls for a re-examination of the diversity in wage relationships and its role in maintaining the consistency and responsiveness of the mode of régulation. As a result, the bargaining power of wage earners is weakened; the more so, the more intense the opening to world competition. Firms can thus argue that they need more 'labour flexibility', i.e. wage concessions, more hours worked and a reduction in welfare coverage, and that the State generally fulfils their demands: the search for a competition-led growth has replaced the fordist regime via a shift in the hierarchy of institutional forms.

Another contemporary example: the conversion of the economic power of Wall Street into a control of state intervention

Let us apply the framework depicted by Figure 8.1 to a core issue investigated by régulation research: how and why has competition-led growth been replaced by a finance led one during the 1990s (Boyer 2000)? The first step takes place within academia, when mathematicians and statisticians invent a model in order to set a price for sophisticated financial products such as options. It was adopted by some investment banks since it allowed the creation of new markets and easy profit (MacKenzie and Millo 2003), given the huge informational asymmetry between the quants that design these instruments and the buyers that discover them at their risk and peril. Thus newcomers bring a major innovation that alters the previous equilibrium between commercial banks, which live out of deposits and credits, and investment banks, which manage portfolios. The second can capture a growing market share at the detriment of the first one. Wall Street becomes the leading actor since it sells its new products to Mean Street banks and it becomes the rule-setter since no public authority masters the intricacies of these complex financial instruments. The lobbies of finance thus convince public authorities that a full deregulation is necessary to reap the benefits of these innovations (Boyer 2011).

Simultaneously, non-financial firms have adopted a type of governance that favours shareholder value, the stock market valuation being the only relevant criteria of performance (Boyer 2007). This way, accounting principles are updated from historical cost to fair value and mark to market valuation and this allows a greater appropriation of markets and profit by Wall Street (Boyer 2007).

The industrial relations are directly affected since the stabilisation of the capital rate of return implies more flexibility for employment and remuneration (Amable 2003). In the context of recurring booms of the stock market, pension funds progressively replace pay-as-you-go systems. This was permitted by an early reform of legislation that meant the submission of welfare and by extension of labour to finance (Montagne 2006). The domination of finance is then quasi complete in other spheres of economy, society and polity (Figure 8.2). Four of the five mechanisms proposed by Bourdieu have been operating: entry of newcomers (quants), innovations that change the relations between the dominant and the dominated, shift in the hierarchy of fields and, last but not least, power to control the State so as not to be controlled by any external authority. The message of Bourdieu, extended at the macro level by régulationist research, can still provide a way to comprehend the transformations of our social world.

A place for the symbolic in régulationist

In earlier works on régulationist that fall within a critical reassessment of the Marxist legacy, actors' ideologies and representations are admittedly present in the daily functioning of institutional forms, but they are not subject to explicit analyses. By contrast, in Bourdieu's work, symbolic capital is an essential category that was introduced as soon as his first publications and is a landmark in the social sciences. Régulationists have focused on the treatment of economic capital, all the more so as they have wanted, in the beginning at least, to explain essentially economic phenomena such as inflation, growth, productivity or even the evolution of the profit rate in the long run.

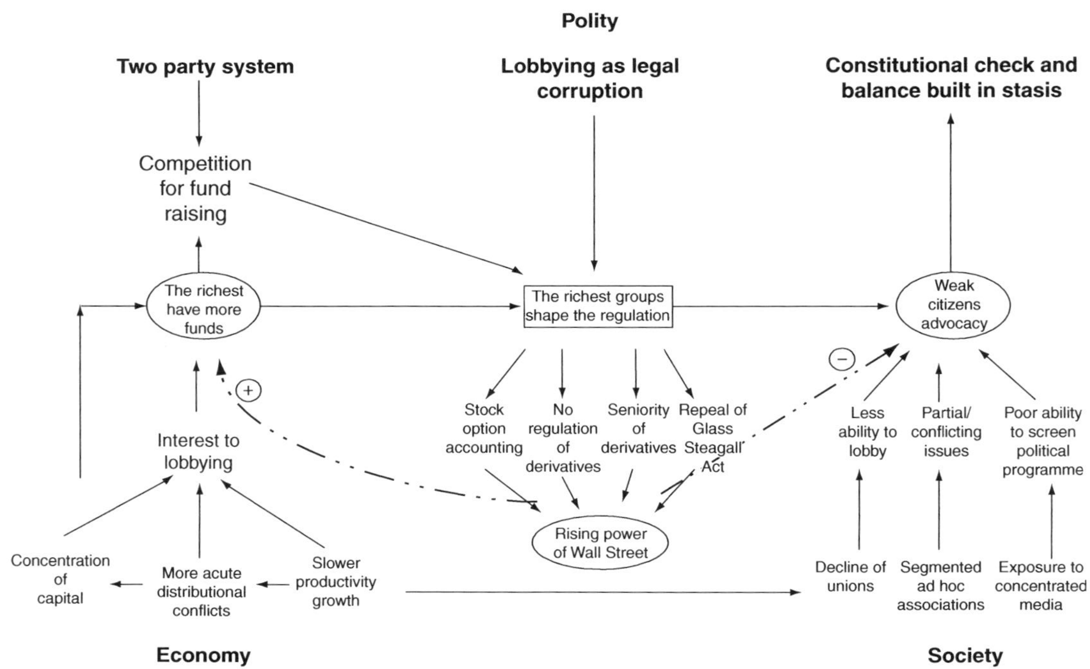

Figure 8.2 How the US financiers have captured State power and promoted a new growth regime and its crisis.

Nonetheless, the development of both research programmes points to a certain convergence of concerns. On the one hand, over time, Bourdieu takes more and more heed of the impact of the proper economic form of capital which percolates and expresses itself in each field. As we have already underscored, his references to economics and the economy with regard to the functioning of all other fields have multiplied since the mid-1990s. On the other hand, research on the theoretical foundations of the five institutional forms outlined by régulation theory, along with observations made in the 1990s, led to explore notions that, directly or indirectly, relate to the symbolic. Such is the case when one is looking for the representations that legitimise the forceful resurgence of neoliberal ideas. One broaches directly the question of symbolic power when one tends to account for the inflection, and then the total reversal, of economic policies that characterised the post-war boom. The very development of research that shows the impossibility of an individualistic foundation of money resulted at first in the question of violence, and then in an even more general interrogation on legitimacy and sovereignty. Analyses of innovations in technology (the information and communication technologies) and/or in organisation (the start-ups), or even more analyses of the evaluation process of financial assets in the new sectors, outline the decisive role of beliefs.

Thus, at the very core of the supposedly emblematic field of sheer economic rationality – the financial markets – we find beliefs, the symbolic, in short representations that are largely extra-economic and yet have an impact on the evolution of stock markets, exchange rates, and consequently on macroeconomic evolution. Willingly or unwillingly, régulation theory is committing itself to one of the most difficult research programmes in contemporary social sciences. The crucial importance of the symbolic emerges in light of the transformations being observed during the last two decades, particularly in the domain of the legitimisation of economic policies. So to speak, it legitimises social mediations and crowns the macroeconomic regime. Conversely, it appears that the most severe crises certainly are those which affect the very symbolic order.

Conclusion

Putting into perspective Bourdieu's work authorises us to reassess and highlight its convergence with certain institutionalist approaches in economics. More precisely, the arguments expounded so far point at four major propositions.

1 Recourse to an *economic vocabulary*, with the use of notions like interest, profit, capital and market, elicited a reductionist interpretation of Bourdieu's theory. *Interest* comes in a variety of forms according to modalities that are in no way the projection of the utilitarian, economistic conception. *Profit* simply designates the rewards that are specific to each field and not their monetary conversion. *Capital* designates the accumulation of useful skills in a field and not the accumulation of a fundamentally economic capital. Finally, the preponderance of relationships between the dominant and

dominated is far from buttressing the irenic vision of markets developed by theories positing an equality, *de jure* thus de facto, between agents in these markets. Field theory, progressively devised, constitutes an original construct, and it can inspire *alternative economic research.*

2. It would be misleading to consider that Bourdieu cannot think of anything else than the reproduction of invariant positions in a field. Indeed, the working of the fundamental concepts through historical analysis and field study shows on the contrary a multiplicity of factors of evolution, change, or even open crisis. Most books and papers actually converge towards the analysis of a crisis deriving from the innovative strategies of the dominant in a field, or from the entry of new actors endowed with a habitus that was formed in other fields and contexts, or from the endogenous redefinition of boundaries between fields as a result of struggles that take place within them. Also, one should not overlook the essential role played by competition for power over state power, that is, the action of the latter on the constitution and evolution of a field. Finally, alterations of the general context can elicit a de-synchronisation between habitus and field, a pattern frequently observed in contemporary societies.
3. In so doing, Bourdieu's theory reflects in certain *economic research programmes*, like régulation theory. Indeed, in the beginning, the concept of habitus appeared to be relevant to account for the historicity of what economic theories dub 'preferences', on the one hand, and their evolution as soon as the institutional context changes, on the other. The deepening of this issue has since then led to the development of an approach according to which any kind of *rationality is situated* with regard to the context, particularly the institutional context. In the long run, the structuring of institutional forms happens to have a determining impact on the dynamics of habitus. But such harmony is always approximate and limited in time.
4. It is clear that Bourdieu's sociology and régulation theory do not share the same objectives and do not develop identical notions and concepts. It is all the more remarkable to note a convergence as to the hypothesis of the *central role played by politics*, be it constitutive of a group's social identity or the guarantor of institutional compromises that lie at the heart of modes of régulation and growth regimes. So, it is impossible to fence either sociology – which would aim at explaining the social by social – or economics – which insists on a discipline founded strictly on the basis of economic rationality. The link to politics is essential in order to comprehend the functioning of a field or the features of a mode of régulation as well as to analyse crises.

Mainstream economics is in disarray in analysing the origin of, and unfolding ways out of, the systemic crisis revealed by Lehman Brothers' collapse. This originates in its inability to deal with structural change and the interactions between economy, society and polity. In this context, Bourdieu's work is still a source of inspiration and a possible starting point for a socio-economics of the contemporary world.

Notes

1 This chapter is the translation and the updated version of the French article 'L'anthropologie économique de Pierre Bourdieu', *Actes de la Recherche en Sciences Sociales*, 2003, 150: 65–78. The editors would like to thank the publishers and the author, who have kindly given permission for the use of this article.

2 Robert Boyer is Economist at the Institute of the Americas (Paris) after a career at CNRS (*Centre National de la Recherche Scientifique*) and EHESS (*École des Hautes Études en Sciences Sociales*). He is a contributor to *régulation* theory, which investigates the factors that shape institutional and technological long-term evolutions. Among various publications: 'The present crisis. A trump for a renewed political economy', *Review of Political Economy*, 2013, 25(1): 1–38; 'The quest for theoretical foundations of socio-economics: epistemology, methodology or ontology?', *Socio-Economic Review*, 2008, 6(4): 733–758; *Régulation Theory: The State of the Art* (with Y. Saillard, eds, Routledge, 2001).

3 In this chapter 'régulation' means the dynamic adjustment of accumulation and economic activity. It is not to be confused with the English term 'regulation' that relates to the methods for state monitoring of some key markets.

4 At the local level and for each batch of product, farmers and buyers exchange their bid via an anonymous electronic system in order to prevent any collusion and favour transparency and speed in transactions. The bids appear on a wide screen, 'un cadran' in French, and they can be compared with the prices set in other localities.

Part IV

Capitals and institutions

9 Capital conversion in post-modern economies

Michael Grenfell[1]

Introduction

This chapter discusses *capital* and the role it plays in financial markets at a stage of late capitalism – termed 'post-modern economies'. It contrasts Bourdieu's understanding and use of the term *capital* with the conventional Marxist one.

It refers to the underlying philosophy and epistemology of *capital* in terms of class reproduction and the role of economic processes in such social evolution. What constitutes the 'economic' is considered with respect to underlying issues of the *symbolic*, *moral* and *social* aspects of capital in a situation of rapid economic transformation. The economic as symbolic and the symbolic as economic is highlighted by drawing an analogy between modern economics and financial markets and the field of contemporary art; this is to show how they both operate according to distinct but similar logics of practice, which share 'post-modern' characteristics. Preliminary notes towards a 'field analysis' of financial practice is offered by way of an examination of *economic hysteresis* in the light of the financial crisis that hit the world in 2007/2008. A key observation is that traditional structural relations with respect to *time*, *honour* and *exchange values* have been reconfigured in late-capitalist economies. This discussion is exemplified with reference to those involved in the *economic field* and contemporary economic processes. Reference is made to the *forms of rationality* prevalent in such fields; again, with Bourdieu's own reflexive account being contrasted with those inherent in rational action theory and classical economic theory. The discussion will then lead to further examination of other forms of 'capital' – *informational*, *juridical* and *political* – to show the *ways* in which capital is now converted in 'post-modern economic systems'. The chapter closes with a discussion of the inherent inner tensions and contradictions of such conversion rates.

Working capital

For the Love of God is a sculpture by Damien Hirst, the leader of the Young British Art (yBa) movement, which so dominated the international art world for a time from the 1990s (see Adams *et al.* 1997 and Muir 2010). It is a platinum cast of a real human skull encrusted with 8,601 flawless diamonds (see http://en.

wikipedia.org/wiki/For_the_Love_of_God). Reputedly, it cost £14 million to produce and went on display at the White Cube Gallery in London in 2007 in an exhibition entitled *Beyond Belief*. On sale at an asking price of £50 million, the highest price ever paid for a living artist, rumour had it that a purchaser willing to pay $100 million for it had already been found. Beyond belief, indeed … perhaps.… A work of art?… Perhaps. In fact, the deathly theme was nothing new to Hirst's oeuvre as he had made his name in works which exhibited dead sharks, cows and sheep in formaldehyde, a cow's head being consumed by flies, pharmaceuticals, and piles of smoked cigarettes (see Gallagher 2012). The art historian Rudi Fuchs wrote this about it: 'The skull is out of this world, celestial almost. It proclaims victory over decay. At the same time, death is relentless. Compared with the tearful sadness of a vanitas scene, the diamond skull is glory itself' (www.wired.com/beyond_the_beyond/2011/01/for-the-love-of-god-its-damien-hirst/).

For some maybe and such a *momento mori* certainly has its aesthetic appeal, but I want to consider it as a piece of artistic *capital*. Of course, the diamonds and platinum have capital value in themselves, based on scarcity, approximately £14 million worth, but what of the rest, the £36 million that made up its asking price? This value was really the price of Hirst himself, the added value, of the *symbolic* value he held in the art field as its leading artist. Was Hirst simply trying it on? Well, maybe. As a 'post-modern' conceptual artist, painterly work in the traditional media would be far from his worldview. Rather, he, as all the yBas, would 'play' with their audience, go against rules and expectations, posture, shock and provoke. Indeed, one might say that Hirst's engagement with the art world *is* his art. Accordingly, it is perhaps of little surprise that when the skull was eventually sold it was to a consortium of which Hirst was a member. Thus, he was able to claim that it was sold while retaining ownership itself. As David Lee, editor of *The Jackdaw* noted: 'Everyone in the art world knows Hirst hasn't sold the skull. It's clearly just an elaborate *ruse* to drum up publicity and rewrite the book value of all his other work' (Owen and Dunbar 2007, emphasis added). These were prophetic words since, in September 2008, Hirst took an unprecedented move for a living artist by selling a complete show, *Beautiful Inside My Head Forever*, at Sotheby's by auction and thus by-passing his long-standing galleries. The auction exceeded all predictions, raising £111 million ($198 million), breaking the record for a one-artist auction as well as Hirst's own record with £10.3 million for *The Golden Calf*, an animal with 18-carat gold horns and hooves, preserved in formaldehyde. The exhibition took place on 15–16 September – 15 September also saw the collapse of Lehman Brothers in the US, thus sparking the financial crisis which subsequently threw Western economies into disarray. Some said that buyers of Hirst's work were spending like there was 'no tomorrow' – literally 'out of time'. Was Hirst simply 'having a laugh' – a ruse? If he was, it was certainly a profitable one. But what has all this to do with capital conversions and post-modern economies? I want next to consider 'capital' in more detail.

Capital

In traditional economics, capital, capital goods or real capital are those already-produced durable goods that are used in the production of goods or services. The capital goods are not significantly consumed; and they may depreciate in the production process. Capital is distinct from land in that capital must itself be produced by human labour before it can be a factor of production. In a fundamental sense, capital consists of any produced thing that can enhance a person's power to perform economically useful work – a stone or an arrow is capital for a caveman who can use it as a hunting instrument, and roads are capital for inhabitants of a city. Capital is an input in the production function. Homes and personal autos are not capital but are instead durable goods because they are not used in the production effort. Capital therefore is both the product and process of work. Accumulated wealth, in the traditional sense, simply went to those who worked harder, thus accruing more capital. This may seem quite a benign, just, process but such is not the case from a Marxist perspective; there are three key aspects to consider. First, that capital is used to buy in order to sell to realise a financial profit. So, labour itself is bought at a cheaper rate than the actual value of work it provides – since surplus value is an essential part of capitalism. Capital therefore only exists as part of a financial exchange process. Wealth is created not simply by working harder but by generating greater surplus value; for example, by selling at a higher value than cost, either by reducing capital/wage costs or by convincing buyers that goods are worth a greater value than they actually are. Second, issues of time and place are critical to the generation of capital. Third, all capital needs to be considered as 'economic' since it all begins and ends in economic (ultimately financial) power. Of course, in classic Marxist texts, crisis in capitalism is inevitable because it is not possible ultimately to create something from nothing; so, the logic of surplus value through cutting costs and raising profits cannot be sustained.

Bourdieu and capital

Bourdieu both accepted this basic analysis whilst insisting that the economic logic extended beyond the purely economic:

> orthodox economics overlook the fact that mechanical practices have principles other than mechanical causes or the conscious intention to maximise one's utility and yet obey an immanent economic logic. Practices form an economy, that is, follow an immanent reason that cannot be restricted to economic reason, for the economy of practices may be defined by a wide range of functions and ends.
>
> (Bourdieu and Wacquant 1992 trans. Wacquant 1992: 119)

In other words, the economic logic of practice described above equally applied to the social world as a whole since the same was differentially valued according to its own symbolic systems. Time and space would be included in this world-view; indeed, they would form an integral part of economics since such took place precisely in time and place. Bourdieu found this situation applied time and time again in his analyses of traditional societies in the Béarn, a rather rural area in south-western France, and Algeria. For example, marriage between couples itself operated according to precise matrimonial strategies which disclosed specific interests in the outcome over and above emotional and domestic compatibility (see Bourdieu 2000a, 2002b; Bourdieu and Darbel 1966). Marriage was not governed by individual free choice or strict rules, but strategies with mostly unconscious calculations of profit; so, there was a personal *interest* (see Grenfell 2012: chapter 9) in the outcome. That interest needs to be understood as *habitus incarnate* – those subjective, structuring structures which shape behaviour in a dynamic with objective (structured structures) environmental conditions (ibid.: Part II). That such structures are socially differential means that reproduction of social classes, fractions, groups and categories is always operating according to its own 'economic' logic. Time and space simply offer the conditions for such reproduction.

Time for Bourdieu is always *made:* human time is not the same as biological or astronomical time. He uses Husserl's distinction between *project* and *protension*: 'project' is a conscious aiming at the future; 'protension' is a 'pre-reflexive aiming at a forth-coming which offers itself as a quasi-present in the visible … as what is directly perceived' (Bourdieu 1997a trans. Nice 2000: 207). So, the past is projected into the future and is present in the present. It follows visible trends, and exists not simply for individuals but for whole classes.

In Algeria, he saw how time featured in carrying interests as expressions of kinship. This is why marriage patterns could not simply follow rules and customs. It was not enough to unite individuals, especially in a socially turbulent world. Rather, individuals also needed 'shared interests', which themselves could be expressions of the social collectivity, its property and strength, or vulnerability, with respect to the future. Conflicts of interest reflected conflicts of groups or individuals and their respective positions in the field, as well as their view of the future. Strategies are then developed to regularise these interests, so that the individual is adjusted to the collective interest – this occurs or the individual appears unreasonable. There were indeed significant differences in economic exchanges between pre-capitalist and capitalist societies.

> [P]ractice never ceases to conform to economic calculation even when it gives every appearance of disinterestedness by departing from the logic of interested calculation (in the narrow sense) and for playing for stakes that are non-material and not easily quantified.
>
> (Bourdieu 1972b trans. Nice 1977: 177)

In pre-capitalist societies – Bourdieu uses Algeria and his home territory of rural Béarn as examples – the *good-faith economy* operates to conceal the economic logic of social exchange. Gift, honour and virtue are placed above profit.

The man of good faith takes pains to distribute the best fresh food to friends and neighbours rather than selling them to other peasants. In this way, social networking is built up – *social capital* – with the explicit expectation of reciprocality – and a symbolic currency established: 'Thus the interest at stake in the *conduct of honour* is one for which economism has no name, and which has to be called symbolic, although it is such as to inspire actions which are very directly material' (ibid.: 181). Such honour, in a similar fashion to 'the gift' (see Mauss 1990), sets a premium on the future, rather more a 'you-owe-me' than 'I-owe-you', that establishes a certain social relation with a future pay-off that has to be respected. Time-honoured relations, therefore, have economic consequences.

In modern economies, such traditions are superseded by capitalist exchanges. The more money is likely to be the currency of exchange, the more impersonal the exchange becomes; this trend can be seen across Europe during the process of industrialisation in the eighteenth and nineteenth centuries. Where this occurred, money – *economic capital* – replaced the exchange value of local networks and their systems of honour and virtue – *symbolic capital*. The irony for Bourdieu is, of course, that economic capital has itself now been displaced in the contemporary world where *cultural capital* (and increasingly *social capital*) takes precedence as the medium for the expression of field interests. Whilst the medium is symbolic, the substantive rationality is economic. As Bourdieu states, 'most actions are objectively economic without being subjectively economic' (Bourdieu 1987a trans. Wacquant and Lawson 1990: 90–91), and:

> the concept of *cultural capital* which, being elaborated and deployed at more or less the same time as Gary Becker was putting into circulation the vague and flabby notion of 'human capital' (a notion heavily laden with sociologically unacceptable assumptions), was intended to account for otherwise inexplicable differences in academic performance with children of unequal cultural patrimonies and, more generally, in all kinds of cultural or economic practices; the concept of *social capital* which I had developed, from my earliest ethnographical work in Kabylia or Béarn, to account for residual differences, linked, broadly speaking, to the resources which can be brought together *per procurationem* through the networks of 'relations' of various sizes and differing density...; the concept of *symbolic capital*, which I had to construct to explain the logic of the economy of honour and 'good faith' and which I have been able to clarify and refine in, by and for the analysis of the economy of symbolic goods, particularly of works of art; and lastly, and most importantly, the concept of *field*, which has met with some success....
>
> (Bourdieu 2000b trans. Turner 2005: 2)

Bourdieu therefore notes the association he shares with the 'new Economic Sociology'. However, Bourdieu and Becker's views of capital differ considerably. Both draw on economic metaphors in their theoretical constructions of social practice. As noted above, however, the nub of the argument for Bourdieu is an opposition to what he considers to be crude 'economism'. The argument goes as follows. Since Adam Smith, men have been seen to be motivated by *self-interest* and to be acting accordingly for financial gain. Becker extended this economic approach, which defined action in terms of 'rational choices' towards the maximisation of financial profit, to all areas of life. However, for Bourdieu, Becker did so literally, whilst his use of the economic analogy was quite different. For example, both write about the 'cost' of having children. Whilst Becker sees individuals acting according to 'norms' of calculated costs and profit, Bourdieu understands actions in terms of *interests* (cultural and social benefits and loss, as well as economic) – the *illusio* – and *strategies*. For Bourdieu, '…economists deserve credit for explicitly raising the question of the relationship between the profits ensured by educational investment and those ensured by economic investment' (Bourdieu 1989b trans. Clough 1996: 275). However, such a relationship is not simply expressed in terms of explicit rational choices over the economic but involves moves with respect to mobilising the entire holdings (present and anticipated) and configuration of *social*, *cultural* and *economic capital*, as well as whole-scale orientation to the past, present and future. So, to take the example of having children and their education, Becker is criticised for not recognising that social reproduction is involved – as well as individual monetary outlay and yield – in such investment. 'Ability' and 'academic aptitude' depend on the home culture and the extent to which it matches that of schools such that the interests of schools and pupils are drawn together by a process of *elective affinities*. It is not, as Becker argues, simply a calculation of the material cost of schooling options.

Bourdieu is therefore against any view of economic behaviour which restricts itself to a rational, conscious choice of costs and profits in purely financial terms. He extends his critique to rational action theory (RAT) or rational choice theory (RCT), which seems to do just that. Advocates of this approach take individuals to act according to clear alternatives with visible, calculated outcomes. For Bourdieu, RAT and RCT are at best idealistic. They both overlook the fact that any individual habitus acts 'rationally', or at least reasonably, because this is a precondition of possessing economic and cultural capital appropriate for a particular social time and place. Calculations of chance – what is probable, possible and potential – are all made with respect to specific social and economic conditions and the consequential perceived opportunities: 'because it must postulate ex *nihilo* the existence of a universal, preconstituted interest, RAT is thoroughly oblivious to the social genesis of historically varying forms of interest' (Bourdieu and Wacquant 1992 trans. Wacquant 1992: 125). Bourdieu goes on to argue that, nevertheless, because it is an approach which 'conceives of action as determined by conscious aiming at explicitly posed goals', it is a 'well-founded illusion' (a phrase coined from Durkheim and used elsewhere by Bourdieu [see Bourdieu 1989b trans. Clough 1996: 335] to describe the granting of reality to fiction, and perceiving the *illusio* in its truthfulness). The sense of the game implied in an anticipated adjustment to the future through habitus when faced with the necessities and probabilities of the field can be construed to be 'aiming at the future'. Moreover, collective action can appear to represent a convergence attributable to common interest rather than a conscious group intention or plan. In this way, Bourdieu argues that teleological phenomena pose major problems for RAT, set as it is in explaining action in terms of direct efficacy of cause or the 'choices of a pure mind commanding a perfect will' (Ibid.).

For Bourdieu, the essential problem is that RAT can be 'empirically sound' whilst being 'anthropologically false'. In other words, those working with RAT are noting something that is true but are giving a wrong interpretation of it. He concludes:

> There is an economy of practices, a reason immanent in practices, whose 'origin' lies neither in 'decisions' of reason understood as rational calculation nor in the determinations of mechanisms external to and superior to the agents ... this economy can be defined in relation to all kinds of functions ... only one of which is monetary.... In other words, if one fails to recognise any form of action other than rational action or mechanical reaction, it is impossible to understand the logic of all the actions that are reasonable without being the product of reasoned design ... adjusted to the future without being the product of a project or a plan.... And, if one fails to see that the economy described by economic theory is a particular case of a whole universe of economies, that is, fields of struggle differing both in the stakes and the scarcities that are generated within them and in the forms of capital deployed in them, it is impossible to account for the specific forms, contents and leverage points thus imposed on the pursuit of maximum specific profits and on the very general optimising strategies (of which economic strategies in the narrow sense are one form among others).
>
> (Ibid.: 51)

To re-emphasise in summing up: 'economic' practice for Bourdieu needs to be understood in terms of the symbolic and strategic as well as the monetary and the conscious calculation of profit. In considering capital, we must be aware of other forms – social and cultural – which act with and against the economic in mediating social space. I now want to take this position to the financial field itself. There are key issues to note by way of introduction. First, that the operations of financial – economic – capital need to be set beside cultural and social capital in the first instance. Second, that the function and form of each of these must necessarily have changed in contemporary financial systems, and both in themselves and with respect to each other. Third, that other forms of capital need to be considered as the changing taxonomy of capital has evolved in post-modern economies. Fourth, that the very term 'post-modern economy' implies structural change away from traditional operations to ways which can now be termed 'post-modern', and thus sharing characteristics with other manifestations of the same – for example, the art field. Fifth, we need to focus on capital morphology, and also issues of time and space in the financial field in order to understand how it is valued, and how this valuing mediates the field.

The modern field of capital

At one point, Bourdieu argues that in order to construct a field, one has to undertake a 'sort of hermeneutic circle' (Bourdieu and Wacquant 1992 trans. Wacquant 1992: 108) in order to identify the specific forms of capital that operate it, and in order to do this, one needs to understand the specific logic of the field. In one sense, this question is quite easy in terms of the financial field since its specific capital is economic/financial and its specific logic is financial profit. My analysis represents examples so as to understand this and how it is brought about in 'post-modern economies'. Elsewhere, I have argued that in order to conduct a Bourdieusian study, one needs to follow a three-stage methodology: Construction of the Research Object; Field Analysis; Participant Objectivation (see Grenfell 2012: chapter 13); and that Field Analysis itself involves three levels. The latter are summed up by Bourdieu as follows: level 1, 'to analyse the position of the field vis-à-vis the field of power'; level 2, 'to map the objective structure of the relations between the positions occupied by agents or institutions who compete for the legitimate form of specific authority of which this field is the site'; level 3, 'the habitus of agents, the different systems of dispositions they have acquired by internalising a determinant type of social and economic conditions, and which find in a definite trajectory within the field under consideration a more or less favourable opportunity to become actualised' (Bourdieu and Wacquant 1992 trans. Wacquant 1992: 104). These might be abbreviated to as studying: the field within the field of power; the field itself; and the habitus of those occupying the field. Clearly, it is not possible to elucidate all three stages in the present context of a single short chapter; although they have been undertaken. Moreover, even to include all three levels of a field analysis would involve analyses outside of the scope of this chapter. I shall add comments with respect to levels 1 and 3 in what follows. However, the main focus is on level 2 – the field itself. Furthermore, for the purposes of the chapter, I propose to concentrate not so much on the structural morphology of the field (for which see Lebaron 2008) but the capital conversions, both economic and otherwise, within it; this is in order to show up principal practices of the field and how its specific logic is played out.

Capital conversions in post-modern economies

This term itself needs unpacking by way of introduction to the analysis. Above, we have seen how, for Bourdieu, one form of capital invariably led to other forms of capital. In this respect, they were/are inter-convertible. So, social capital, for example, allows entrée to elite fractions of society, which may be important in accruing economic capital through business, jobs, etc. Furthermore, it is possible to see weight and configurations of capital from a historical perspective. So, economic capital predominated in terms of the holders of wealth in France in the nineteenth century, which needs to be understood as position, and thus influence, in the field of power itself. A key notion for Bourdieu was that this money wealth – economic capital – had been eclipsed in the second half of the twentieth century in France by cultural capital: individuals holding academic (itself producing cultural) capital, which was needed to fuel the new technological, commercial world. Such capital has value in the field of power in the new technological society, and does manage and attract economic capital, whilst not directly aiming at financial acquisition. As societies develop, capital configurations will be in constant flux, so that patterns of capital holding are always shifting according to current social and economic needs: the dynamic of capitalism. Both capital holdings – their weight – and their relationship to each other are thus changing in response to the economic logic of practice of the fields in which such are being played out. As noted above, first all capitals, as symbolic, have economic consequences in terms of actual money wealth – for example, the art market (see Grenfell and Hardy 2003). Second, one capital rarely works on its own but is combined with other forms of capitals to maximise profit: the art market is again a good example of this as, although it functions primarily through cultural and social capital, ultimately its *raison d'être* is economic as works of art are sold at high prices, as the case of Damien Hirst demonstrates. Here, I focus on economic capital per se and the financial field in which it operates in late capitalism. This approach does not mean that social and cultural capital do not feature in the analysis; quite the contrary as will be shown. Rather, it is concerned with the forms of economic capital, how its very nature has changed in contemporary systems, the reasons and consequences for these changes, and how that change was brought about.

In a traditional, *modernist*, world, the financial sector of a country centres on the stock market where stocks and shares are sold. In its simplest form, the price of these stocks and shares is set simply by the profitability of a company. A company with large profits will have more expensive shares since they offer a higher return to investors. In selling new shares, companies raise finance to develop and expand; individuals and groups get returns from yearly dividends from companies as a result of profits gained and also by selling stocks and shares which, if they have gone up in value, offer profits to holders of portfolios. Money is merely the lubrication of the system as, ultimately, there is actual production; this, as noted above, is a pre-requisite for capital and capitalism. In traditional worlds, early industrialisation, for example, more objects were produced – textiles, machines, etc. Clearly, in modern settings, we observe an expansion in the production of immaterial goods. What about retail outlets, for example? Or, services – like banks, computing, insurance? In these cases, there might not be direct material production as such, but they deal with systems that do have the same at some point further along the food chain. Without over-simplifying the stock market, it would also be true to say, at least in its conventional form, that principles of time and honour operated in a way not dissimilar to traditional economies described above. Investment in purchasing stocks and shares carried with it an aspect of honour, in terms of both the buyer and the seller, against future action – time was also implicated in the transaction. Clearly, what began as local, national industrialisation grew to become much more internal in outlook during the nineteenth century and the first half of the twentieth century whilst maintaining its local priorities. All this changed in the latter decades of the twentieth century.

For Bourdieu, a sure-fire precursor to fundamental changes in field structure is growth in its size. Such was the case of painters in the art field of nineteenth-century France, or student numbers in education in the 1960. It is, therefore, perhaps unsurprising to note that an important characteristic of financial markets during the last decade of the twentieth century was growth in size. Of course, other markets – in New York and Tokyo – had already grown to challenge the dominance of the City of London as the most important financial sector in the world. However, other markets had also established themselves to complement and compete with these, and the amount of business they all carried increased substantially. Capitalism was booming – so larger markets – but a different form of capitalism, one based much more on finance and services as opposed to actual material production. Neoliberal economics had also freed markets from traditional constraints that aimed to link finance and production, so that one closely reflected the other in the way described above. Free markets became the by-word in financial dynamism, which quickly took on global proportions. More money was needed to fuel this growth and vitality, so the growth of financial services also exploded. To make it clear, it is not so much that the logic of practice changed: the logic of practice – to make a profit – stayed the same; it is the ways and the means of making that profit which altered so radically. But, why should we label this change as 'post-modern'?

The term 'post-modern' can be traced as far back as the 1870s when it was used by John Watkins Chapman to describe a particular style of painting. From that time, the term was often used in connection with architecture, urban planning and culture in general. But it was not until the 1970s, and with the publication of *La Condition post-moderne* by Jean-François Lyotard, that both the term and the 'attitude' it implied became such a dominant way of thinking in a whole range of social and cultural activities.[2] It also became increasingly associated with the new generation of French philosophers, which included Derrida, Foucault, Deleuze, Baudrillard, along with Lyotard himself. Of course, their individual philosophies probably had more that separated them than brought them together. However, they each grounded themselves in the space that had been opened up by Saussure earlier in the century when he posited the separation of linguistic sign from what was signified, thus announcing the arbitrariness of meaning. The way content now became dependent on context necessitated a move from *modernism*, where such were stable and static, to *post-modernism*, implying the relativisation of ... well ... everything! Ruled essentially by a philosophy of and to language, other characteristics included Appropriation, Hybridisation, Euphemism, Temporality, Intensification, Ruse, Decentring, Posture and the Arbitrary. Now, it would be wrong to suggest that everything post-modern must include all of these – one does not necessary involve another – but one does at least implicate the other. Much that goes in the name of post-modernism can be understood in terms of this set of principles; not least the work of the yBas and Damien Hirst. So, let us explore the financial field and examples of economic capital behaviour keeping these principled terms in mind.

1 Decentring
2 Intensification
3 Language
4 Ruse/Posture
5 Hybridisation
6 Temporality

As noted above, language, the way it operates, and indeed its function and form, is a ruling feature in post-modernism; it is necessary always to see the analogy between social systems – economic, artistic, etc. – and linguistic systems. In a sense, in the twentieth century, the philosophy of man became the philosophy of language. Language in the economic field is significant; first, because of the way one can see an operational analogy between the two and, second, in the very way it is used to represent both the logic of practice in the field and its operational manifestations. Further, as noted, the growth in the size of a field will inevitably lead to a radical restructuring of its morphology. This is exactly what happened from the late 1990s and in the 2000s when there was a huge expansion in money wealth available. The fall of the Berlin wall and Soviet Communism irrevocably altered the world order. China too positioned itself as a full, international capitalist economy. Large amounts of finance entered the markets; mostly coming from Asia/China and the oil nations of the Middle East. Between 2002 and 2008, 70 per cent of finance coming into British markets came from abroad. Moreover, it entered on different terms; of free money market economies with the removal of regulations and the central control. The result was a reshaping of the social space of finance itself because there was a lot more capital, its nature had changed, and many more participants were active within the field. Free trade barriers, a crucial principle of neoliberal economics, also increasingly began to have an impact. Commercial and industrial companies ceased to think of their operations in national terms but instead structured their activities at a global level. For example, the way BT (British Telecom) in the UK moved its back-up services to India, or the way a traditional British car company – Rover – was purchased and managed by the German company Volkswagen. In fact, more and more British firms had foreign owners. These transformations meant that the field of economic control shifted from being national to being international in nature.[3] In other words, neither financial nor economic field participants saw their field of operations or support as existing within a national field context. To this extent, their allegiance was first to international companies rather than the state field of power (government, local economics, etc.). Indeed, some companies became more powerful than national governments in shaping economic activity; for example, an Asian car manufacturer may or may not locate its building plants in one country – and region – or another. The fact that this occurred with the tacit and explicit support of national governments attests to the way that neoliberal economics ruled at a global level.

To an extent this is understandable, since such world-level changes were unstoppable from a national perspective. However, it also had the advantage of relieving government of prime economic management, which it had increasingly shown itself unable to effectively undertake anyway. In terms of control, there was a curious paradox. In one sense, no-one was in control; everything had been *decentred* away from government, individual companies and banks. Everything was in a post-modern realm of 'free-play'. Yet, such centrifugal forces were reined in the opposite centripetal forces of concentrating ultimate power in fewer and fewer operators: banks took over other banks to form super banks; industrial and commercial companies merged to form multinationals – *intensification* – this in order to 'buy' extra power in the economic field.

Clearly, such mergers offered opportunities for rationalisation, a term (*language*) itself used to mean redundancies and restructuring made possible in a deregulated labour market. This process was not only the means to the end of greater economic profitability but in some cases became the end of profit making itself. So, such private equity firms (PEFS) as Kohlberg Kravis and Roberts (KKR) operated by borrowing money to purchase companies in order to sell them on after necessary restructuring had taken place. Governments – in a government-light neoliberal world – were happy for this to happen as it removed the responsibility, and thus social and political consequences, of making difficult decisions which would affect employees. PEFS were happy since they made money – almost out of nothing. So, for example, when KKR bought Alliances Boots (a popular British pharmaceutical company) in 2007, of the £11 billion paid for it, £9 billion of it was borrowed. The idea is then for the PEF to keep the company for 2–5 years before selling it on, at a profit enhanced by low capital gains tax, which government granted to them to support the process. Moreover, interest on the debt from original borrowing itself is then offset against future profits. For example, in 2003 the retail company Debenhams paid £40 million in tax. In 2005, under a PEF, they were allowed a tax credit of £13 million.

This strategy to buy underperforming companies in order to strip assets and sell at a profit within a short period of time (*intensification*, *temporality*) was not restricted to private companies. Indeed, it became a means to move companies from the public to the private sector (*hybridisation*, *blurring of boundaries*); again, something that governments supported as it removed costly, often underperforming activities from the expenses of the exchequer, thus allowing greater freedom in reducing taxes – always a popular move in national politics and in a world that becomes atomistic. ('Society', Margaret Thatcher famously claimed, 'does not exist' – thus, by implication, only individuals competing in social space – a very Bourdieusian image. Incidentally, the philosopher of the 'the open society', Karl Popper, claimed that Thatcher was the first post-modern politician, and indeed, her eschewing of modernist notions of state and societal support in favour of individual 'freedom' would support such a view.) This public to private blurring is identifiable in the purchase of Qineteq (who managed the research arm of the Ministry of Defence) by the PEF Carlye for £42 million in 2003, only to be sold on for £400 million on the Stock Market in 2006.

In one sense, there might seem to be no problem with such procedures. PEFS, after all, are taking risks in buying these companies and are able to raise the finance. Anyone who buys a house – by taking on debt – and does so with a view to selling it on at a profit is acting in a similar way. However, with a house there is a material object at source. In financial matters, even companies disappeared in the quest to make money. How so?

Clearly, in order to finance PEFS, a lot of money is required. However, even with the influx of Asian and Middle Eastern money, this was not enough to finance the level of activity. Governments had been dedicated to restricting the money supply under monetarism in order to avoid high inflation. Their main means of doing this was the ability to raise and lower interest rates through control of the central bank. But, they increasingly ceded control over the banks, giving the latter greater independence; for example, in Britain under the New Labour Chancellor Gordon Brown, who allowed the then Governor of the Bank of England, Mervyn King, to set interest rates as he saw fit to control inflation. Paradoxically, and somewhat contrary to monetarist principles, at a time when there was a huge increase of money finance in markets, both rates of inflation and interest were relatively low. But, interest rates, in the market, are largely irrelevant when the speed of financial transactions intensifies. Inflation also implies lack of supply, which was not the case when what was being sought was money itself. In other words, money increasingly became the product, both the means and the ends of economic activity. In this way, there was a kind of post-modern stripping of economic capital to financial capital in its purest form, which was managed as such in order to supply the money for … more financial transactions. Money ultimately is lent to people to buy other financial products; for example, mortgages on houses which, in such cases as Ireland, were themselves being constructed by firms on whose board of directors sat the same individuals who were also bank directors and prominent politicians. Inflation, a rise in house prices, was then used to justify the purchase of further financial products to buy additional houses and the like. Remortgaging became the norm. But what to do with all that debt? Why not sell it on – as a product – to generate more money?

Under the system of sub-prime loans (*language*!), money is lent to individuals with poor credit record; they therefore pay a higher rate of interest. Indeed, in this case, individuals do not even have to prove their credit status. In popular vernacular, such 'Liar Loans' were, in the language of the bankers, euphemised to 'Pay as You Earn' or 'Stated Asset Loans'. Such loans are sold to individuals by brokers with little or no permanent link with the bank provider in return for a commission. If loans could not be paid back, another loan could be taken out to pay for it. Thus, debt repayment is continually deferred (*time*). The equivalent of £600 billion of such loans was lent to American households in 2006 by major investment banks – Morgan Stanley, Merrill Lynch, Goldman Sachs, UBS and Barclays. A further advantage of such loans is that they could be bundled into Bonds (*language/obfuscation/euphemisation*) and sold on. This allowed for the full vent of centripetal forces as debt was 'homogenised', often at high speed, and 'disposed of'. In other words, loans are sold at a premium against the potential of future payment. Bonds can also be bundled into bonds, which in turn can be bundled into bonds. As such, there is a disconnection between the financial product itself and the economic activity to which it is linked. Bonds become an end in themselves. Of course, individuals could default on loans. However, historically, data suggested that the percentage of 'toxic waste' (*language/euphemism*) was manageable within normal margins and, anyway, could be insured against – a further source of capital generation. If bonds are bought and sold at a high speed – *intensification/temporality* – the future need never happen. In fact, the future is collapsed with today as long as buying and selling continues. European banks further avoided control of lending by buying bonds linked to sub-prime loans and putting them into enormous funding vehicles – *euphemised* as Conduits. This was also another way to borrow short-term funds from the money markets backed up by various forms of securities – Asset Backed Commercial Paper. As the economist Maynard Keynes stated when questioned about the ultimate outcome of macro-economic stimulation to cure unemployment, 'In the long term we are all dead' – a principle taken to heart by bond dealers, PEF financiers and loan brokers. In the immediate term, salaries rise and bonuses are gained. The system intensifies and becomes hyperventilated: sub-prime loans went up by 18 per cent in 1995 and were $1.3 trillion in 2007. It is not so much that debt replaces profit but becomes it in its own right.[4] It is a form of simulacrum, as the post-modernist philosopher Baudrillard argued, 'the hyperreal' detached from reality, which in this case would be the traditional economic activity of production, profit and loss – a hyperreality which is also unreal as there is a separation between content and context, function and form (as is always the feature of post-modernism). Such is the need for profit that debt gets literally 're-presented' as profit, and so it is, to generate profit from debt.

Everything works as long as everything is working. Like some sort of wild financial game of 'pass the parcel', all is fine as long as any one individual is not left with the debt. The parcel stopped in August 2007, when the French BNP bank declared that it could no longer value with confidence the US asset-backed bonds in three of its funds. In other words, there was just not enough overall money to cover the value of the debt implied by such. In the intense world of post-modern economics, confidence is all. If there is no confidence, there is still a need to feign – to *posture* – confidence. Moreover, such confidence can be communal; while the whole is working, why listen to any one individual? No one thanks anyone for pointing out misrecognitions. In August 2007, that is exactly what BNP did. The rest is history: Lehmann brothers collapsed in 2008, the world banking crisis followed.

Working the field/work in the field

We know from the methodological discussion above that it is necessary to approach a field analysis through three levels: the field and the field of power, the field itself, and those working within the field. The topic of this chapter is more the capital configurations within the field – the medium of financial dynamic. However, I want to add some complementary comments in order to raise issues about the structure of the field itself and the individuals who operate within it.

We know, for example, that field theory predicts that fields strive to attain autonomy, since this is the way to exert power both within its own constituency and between fields. This is exactly what has occurred in recent decades, with banking institutions gaining greater and greater independence. The logic of practice of neoliberal economics insists on deregulation and financial freedom. As noted above, such can be remarked in the British case where New Labour Chancellor Brown was happy to cede monetary policy to the Governor of the Bank of England and openly welcomed deregulated financial activities. PEFS were explicitly supported by Brown and Prime Minster Blair; they had the advantage of progressing the sell-off of public assets by stealth and the implementation of profit seeking asset stripping away from public scrutiny and accountability. Financial control was certainly *decentred*, *euphemised* and *hybridised*. Moreover, and as a result of such changes, banks moved to become the main generator of economic activity by being the source of finance and, as shown above, raised large amounts of money from the 1990s to pay for expansion in a number of fields across society: industrial, commercial, art and media, and political. In a way, the financial field rose to challenge the field of power in terms of socio-political control; this phenomenon is noticeable in the way banks, post collapse, had to be bailed out by government – to put it briefly, whatever their mistakes, states cannot exist without their banks; they must be protected and allowed to operate. This economic 'trump card' – a kind of implicit *posture* – was clearly understood by bankers, but perhaps less so by governments keen, as they were, not to question too deeply where the money is coming from while it continues to pour into the pockets of their voters. Also, as noted, the countervailing forces – both centripetal and centrifugal – formed concentrations of banking institutions: for example, the Royal Bank of Scotland consolidated its assets by taking over NatWest (2000) and Ulster Bank (2000), and also became a major shareholder in the Citizen Financial Group (1998 – the eighth largest bank in the US) and the Bank of China (2004–2009); and the Spanish financial group Santander, which took over a range of British building societies (Abbey National 2010; Bradford and Bingley 2010; Alliance and Leicester 2010).

It is important to keep in mind that all such changes do not just originate from multinational corporations but ride on the back of individuals. Just as sub-prime loans are sold by brokers who set the size of their salary through dividends accruing from the number of mortgages sold, so central banking movements are determined by individuals – chairmen, directors, etc. – who gain large six-figure bonuses as a result of growth in business, no matter that a large proportion of it is virtual. As Lebaron (2008) has shown, such bankers are far from being a homogeneous group. If we consider the educational, academic and professional backgrounds of central bankers, governors and monetary board members, we see different types of capital competing for 'symbolic power'. 'Insiders', who come from central banking institutions, compete with 'outsiders' from the economic, political and academic fields for dominance. Legitimacy is therefore contested between the financial/private sector and the political/academic. Consequent capital configurations – expressed in and through habitus – compete with each other, confront and combine, and result in the individuals involved assuming specific positions in the economic field. Just as Damien Hirst's capital holding offered him a 'royal flush' in terms of British Art, thus allowing him to take on pole position in the yBas (Grenfell and Hardy 2003), so key individuals in the financial world hold pivotal points of control by virtue of their habitus-based capital holdings. One example will suffice: Lord Dennis Stevenson (http://en.wikipedia.org/wiki/Dennis_Stevenson,_Baron_Stevenson_of_Coddenham).

Lord Stevenson went to two independent Scottish schools (Edinburgh Academy and Trinity College – *cultural capital*) before going to Kings College Cambridge as an undergraduate (*cultural* and *social capital*). Eventually, he was himself to become Governor of Imperial College, London, a highly prestigious science and technology university (*economic capital*). He was given a CBE in 1981, a knighthood in 1997 and a life peerage in 1999 (*symbolic* and *social capital*). He has been Chair of the House of Lords Appointment Commission and is a friend with the New Labour 'fixer' Peter Mandelson (*social/political capital*). The fact that he sits as a 'cross-bench' peer, thus *blurring the boundaries* between conventional political allegiances, shows the way he has entry to a wide spectrum of political and social power positions. He has been active as Director in media and communications: British Technology Group (1979–1989), Tyne Tees Television (1982–1987), Thames Television (1991–1993) and BSkyB (1994–2001) (*informational/social capital*). He is also a trustee of the Tate Gallery in London and a Director for Pearson Publishers (*cultural capital)*; thus, underlining his inroads into the art field as well. He has 'played' this *educational*, *political*, *social*, *cultural* and *informational capital* together with the symbolic power gained from being active in a range of economic/business consultancy situations: Manpower Plc (1988–2006), Rothchild Assurance Plc (1991–1997), English Partnerships (1993–2004), and Lazard Bros (1997–2002). Little surprise, therefore, to learn that Lord Stevenson was also Director of former building society Halifax Plc (from 1999), which then merged with the Bank of Scotland in 2001 to become HBOS, which he also chaired until it collapsed in 2008. It might be felt that it is indeed a *ruse* to suppose that one individual could do so many jobs, could be competent in such a wide range of activities. The subsequent Parliamentary Banking Standards Commission Report (2013) referred to his chairmanship of HBOS as a 'model in self-delusion'. But, that is not the point. In the long term, that is what may well be concluded. In the short term, what Lord Stevenson sells is significant *social*, *political* and *cultural capital* to facilitate business and economic activity (*economic capital)*. For example, when Philip Green wanted to buy the retail company Marks and Spencer in 2004, he formed a company specifically to do this – Revival Acquisitions – and appointed Lord Stevenson as a Director. What he bought was the legitimacy, consecration and ultimate field power that Lord Stevenson's capital holding represented symbolically with the field, which itself was evidence by his field position. As Bourdieu writes: 'There are positions in the field that admit only one occupant but command the whole structure' (Bourdieu and Wacquant 1992 trans. Wacquant 1992: 243).

Conclusion

What this chapter has sought to show is the way that capital has operated in the contemporary financial field. Much of Bourdieu's work on education is underpinned by the notion that *cultural capital* had eclipsed *economic capital* as the main purveyor of social position. However, he also makes it clear that economic is both the final determiner of power, and all forms of capital are ultimately reducible to it. In global capitalism, *economic capital* is the multinational *passe-partout*. But the nature of that *economic capital* has itself changed, both in form and function, from traditional practices. The logic of practice of financial markets has remained the same – to make profit – but the form this *economic capital* takes has radically altered. More virtual than real, it is based on a temporary belief in the reality underpinning financial operations. In a world where *hysteresis* is endemic – everyone is by definition 'behind the time' as everything speeds up – the only way to deal is to 'make believe' as if it is real. Debt can become profit in this world. And, of course, whilst everyone is believing it so and the money is pouring in, this *posture* is reinforced in the hearts and minds – and pockets! – of those involved. The future is now and now is the future. Indeed, normal oppositions – profit/loss, asset/debt, future/now, centripetal/centrifugal, speed/stasis, homogeneity/heterogeneity – are collapsed.

I began this chapter by referring to Damien Hirst and the art world by way of drawing attention to the 'post-modern' conditions that dominate in many fields in the contemporary world, underlying its defining generating principles of language, appropriation, hybridisation, euphemism, temporality, intensification, ruse/posture and the arbitrary. The rest of the chapter has gone some way to demonstrate how these play out in the economic field that is the modern financial sector. As Hirst claimed: 'The value of something is simply what someone is prepared to give you for it ... creativity is the point of conception.' *For the love of god*, he has perfectly demonstrated the truth of this statement in his own 'field manoeuvres'. As the ace poker player he is, he 'saw out' the art world in 2008 when he sold his catalogue for £111 million. This was tacit recognition that the 'game was over' and it was time to leave the field. Sadly, in the economic field, when faced with the financial crisis of the same year (and subsequent years), those affected by its consequences do not have a comparable field position to make the same choice.

Notes

1 Michael Grenfell is Professor of Education at Trinity College, University of Dublin, Ireland. His background is in French Studies and he has a long research association in areas including education, language teaching and sociology, especially with respect to the application of the approach of the French social philosopher Pierre Bourdieu to a range of research topics. He knew and collaborated with Bourdieu for over 20 years and was three times 'visiting scholar' at the *École des Haute Études* in Paris. Besides a number of articles on Bourdieu, he is author of: *Bourdieu and Education: Acts of Practical Theory* (Falmer, 1998, with D. James); *Bourdieu: Agent Provocateur* (Continuum, 2004); *Bourdieu, Education and Training* (Continuum, 2007); *Arts Rules: Bourdieu and the Visual Arts* (Berg, 2007, with C. Hardy); *Bourdieu, Language and Linguistics* (Continuum, 2007); *Bourdieu: Key Concepts* (Acumen, 2008).

2 Of course, Bourdieu was against post-modernism as a philosophical stance and argued that it was dangerous in that it undermined many 'humanistic' principles and institutions. I am using its characteristics here to enhance Bourdieu's account of capital since I believe that this highlights the way that capital now operates compared with the past.

3 This is, of course, not to say that the whole trend of modern capitalism was not toward internationalisation. But, during the period under consideration, this trend intensified and important structural shifts moved the balance from national to international control.

4 Of course, debt has always been an important part of capitalism. What was new here was its forms, and the underlying level of economic activity it represented, or at least purported to.

10 Revisiting field theory

On taking Bourdieu to envisioned futures

Doris Hanappi[1]

Introduction

The question of how social forces intersect with human conduct has puzzled social scientists for centuries. The founders of American and European sociology welcomed the emphasis on the impact of social forces as *the* research programme for sociology. In the early twentieth century, such emphasis matched well the efforts to 'institutionalise' sociology as an academic discipline and in parallel distinguish it from behavioural psychology. Behaviourists consider human conduct as resulting from precisely controllable stimulus–response events. Similar to behaviourism in this respect, neoclassical theories have not sufficiently accounted for social forces in human conduct. Rather, they stayed locked into a mechanistic conception of economic and social processes (Mirowski 1991). This mechanistic view is embedded in an institutional structure in which empirical evidence provides the make-up for a Kabuki dance, i.e. an event that is designed to create the appearance of conflict or uncertainty where outcomes are decided upon beforehand. As a critique to such mechanistic view, the work of Pierre Bourdieu has stimulated new interest in the intersection between social forces and human behaviour. His concept of field has become a leading reference in the growing literature on theories of human action and social context.

This chapter is dedicated to revisiting Bourdieu's concept of field as a framework to link the wider social context, social relations, and cognitions without analytically merging them. Its aim is to show the position of the concept of field with respect to major schools of sociological thought, and in particular to the embeddedness tradition which also addresses similar questions on the social structuring of human conduct. This debate goes counter to the way that methodological individualism is used in economics. In what follows, the discussion will focus on key authors of an embeddedness approach, such as Marc Granovetter (1985) and Karl Polanyi (1944[2001]), whose arguments on social relations and structural regulation of action seem most valuable to show in what way economists and social scientists may have full gain if adopting a Bourdieusian field perspective for their analysis of human behaviour.

By 'embedding action' in social structures and processes, economic sociologists and also some heterodox economists have repeatedly elaborated in their works on what one can label the structural, relational, and cognitive dimensions of human action (Fligstein and Dauter 2007; Dobbin 2004; Beckert 2009). Whereas structural and relational forces reflect the idea that social action is embedded in pre-given social structures and networks, the argument of existing cognitive forces is that only the individual can interpret what goes on in the social world (Granovetter and Swedberg 2011). Empirical applications in network analysis do show either how the structure of action is conceived or how external factors influence the action processes ongoing within networks and finally do relate these to certain outcomes (e.g. flow of information, distribution of power in networks). The subsequent section addresses continuity and change of fields. It builds on previous arguments that the field notion provides a framework that accounts for mediating field effects on behavioural outcomes, and at the same time enables scholars to address field opportunities and constraints which are mediated by human conduct (Swartz and Zolberg 2005). The notion of habitus is revisited by focusing on the role of imagination as a key to better understand the intersection between field and human behaviour. John Dewey's study of moral imagination is central in this respect – in particular as concerns the sociology of habit and its malleability. Even if Bourdieu was sceptical towards moral or normative explanations as found, among others, in Dewey's works, his explanations of the malleability of the habitus deserve some reflection about possible parallels and to question how agents seize upon possible new relations for thought and action from social, unconscious experience (that shapes their 'practical sense' embodied in the habitus) on the one hand, and from their conscious physical experience on the other hand.

Bourdieu's field notion as critical response to the embeddedness tradition

The notion of field grows out of Bourdieu's attempt to address the following question: How do social forces influence human action? More precisely, how do social forces mould human conduct even to the point of reproducing regular patterns by generating new ones? With the concept of field, Bourdieu developed an important theoretical framework. Its origins are directly linked to Bourdieu's later strategy of situating himself in the French intellectual world in the 1950s and early 1960s, and of developing a critical distance vis-à-vis purveyors of other traditions, such as behaviourism (Skinner 1953; Watson 1924), structuralism (Lévi-Strauss 1947, 1958), and existentialism (e.g. Sartre 1943) or, more generally speaking, narrow forms of materialism and idealism (see also Pinto 2002). A main argument in Bourdieu's field theory is that individual action is for the most part not conditioned by some stimulus–response sequence.[2] Rather, human behaviour is fundamentally motivated by a continuous (re-)enactment of past learning that is adaptive to external structures as well as constitutive of the field itself. As such he also distinguishes himself from the *structuralism* of Lévi-Strauss that lacks agency, and in particular the generative power of human conduct. For Bourdieu, fields do not only structure human conduct but are constituted by the fundamental human capacity of its agents to see and generate new opportunities and ideas through their past experiences to present and future situations. At the same time, Bourdieu takes distance vis-à-vis Sartre's *existentialism*, because he rejects analyses accounting for behaviours only in terms of reasons and wills (Bourdieu 1987a trans. Wacquant 1990).

On these grounds, one may expect similarities between Bourdieu's field theory and *embeddedness approaches*, which are familiar to most economists. Because Bourdieu's theory of fields suggests a way to link social structures and relations to human agency, *Polanyi's structural approach* and *Granovetter's relational approach* to embeddedness are of particular interest to show why economists and social scientists will all gain if adopting a field perspective. I will develop this argument by looking first at the two conceptions of embeddedness and show how Bourdieu's field notion differs from and eventually goes beyond these conceptions, especially when cognitions and its link to the wider macro-structures are considered. The concept of embeddedness was first invoked by Karl Polanyi (1944[2001]), and received wider attention in the early 1980s with the publication of a theoretical essay by Marc Granovetter (1985). In the sociological discourse, purveyors of the Polanyian understanding of embeddedness are concerned with integrating the economy into broader social systems and share a focus on the mutual constitution of state and market (Polanyi 1944[2001]; Polanyi *et al.* 1957). Polanyian scholars reject the idea that markets can exist outside of state action, and adhere to the argument that economic actions become destructive when they are 'disembedded', or not governed by social or non-economic authorities. What partly exempts Polanyi's concept from a strict sociological critique of the neoclassical model of economic action is his acceptance of the generic notion of *homo economicus* as (historically specific) institutionally based.

Instead, the Granovetterian understanding of embeddedness involves identifying the relational basis of social action in economic contexts. In his view, transactions are entangled in a net of personal relationships that explain economic action (Granovetter and Swedberg 2011). A Granovetterian embeddedness approach rejects the *homo economicus* in its purely determinist version that disallows any influence of social structure and social relations. Granovetter went even so far as to say that 'behaviour and social institutions are so constrained by ongoing social relations that to construe them as independent is a grievous misunderstanding' (Granovetter 1985: 482). The Granovetterian conception of embeddedness was empirically tested by using network analysis, which examines the structure of relationships between social entities. Nevertheless, network analysis focused on 'objective structures' rather than on social content and subjective expectations. One prominent exception is Brian Uzzi (1997, 1996), for instance, who stressed the quality of network connections by differentiating between 'arm's length ties', i.e. corresponding to anonymous market exchange, and 'embedded ties' based on enduring exchange relationships shaped around non-market ties. In this regard, Uzzi discussed trust between parties, in-depth information transfer, and joint problem-solving. We should not omit works dealing with the polyvalent nature of networks, which draw attention to potential limits of beneficial effects – for instance, when connections turn into a liability; or the work of Portes and Sensenbrenner (1993), who studied network complementarity in immigrant economies, in particular the impact of network closure on credit circulation and on individual mobility. Moreover, Fuhse and Mützel (2010) introduced the idea of *cognitive structures*, i.e. agents' interpretative frames by which they assign meaning to their connections depending on the wider structural and cultural context of their networks.

For Bourdieu, networks represent the analytical aspect of fields which are made of temporary or durable relations, formal and also informal relations. In his field concept, he ascribes power and meaning to the 'objective structures' of fields so that he calls networks parts of a field. According to his perspective, fields are not only comprised of relations within them, but also of relations between and across fields. In modern societies, the social space is made up of a number of relatively autonomous but often hierarchically ordered social microcosms, or spaces of objective relations in which specific logics prevail that are a necessity and irreducible to those that regulate other fields e.g. the economic field, or the artistic field. While fields are also governed by the general laws (e.g. reproduction, hierarchisation), which are stable laws of functioning, each field defines itself partly by specific interests which do not necessarily correspond to the interests of other fields (Bourdieu 1993b trans. Wacquant and Farage 1994). We find in *An Invitation to Reflexive Sociology* (1992) a definition of fields as networks in which Bourdieu points on the one hand to the objective relations of positions constitutive of fields, and on the other hand, introduces the dimension of power, or the regulative role of power derived from the distribution of capitals.

> In analytic terms, a field may be defined as a network, or a configuration, of objective relations between positions. These positions are objectively defined, in their existence and in the determinations they impose upon their occupants, agents, or institutions, by the present and potential situation (situs) in the structure of the distribution of species of power (or capital) whose possession commands access to the specific profits that are at stake in the field, as well as by their objective relation to other positions (domination, subordination, homology, etc.).
>
> (Bourdieu and Wacquant 1992 trans. Wacquant 1992: 97)

Implicit to this definition is the assumption of an underlying symbolic process as part of the conversion of capital to power. For Bourdieu and Wacquant fields are spaces of objective relations between 'positions defined by their rank in the distribution of competing powers or species of capital' (Bourdieu and Wacquant 1992 trans. Wacquant 1992: 114). Therefore, fields are different from networks since the latter are understood as the mere manifestation of these objective relations. Similarly, Martin (2003) describes fields as a topological *space of positions*, a field of *relational* forces, and a *battlefield of contestation*. With the latter,

Martin refers to the political dimension of battlefields, which is manifested by a struggle for power to improve one's position. Bourdieu defends the idea that human action is adaptive to and embedded in fields, but to be sure, it is not entirely determined by it. While network approaches, and particularly comparative and historical approaches in economic sociology, argue that institutions generate meaning for people and to this extent determine action, Bourdieu sets against such explanation a notion of field that opens possibilities to action. More precisely, economics and social science scholars adopting a Bourdieusian field perspective would need to consider actors neither as being forced by their social surrounding into their choices nor as conforming to rules externally imposed on them. Rather, these actors engage in a 'game' whose rules orient action. Implicit in this 'game' metaphor Bourdieu often used is the political dimension of fields in which *agency* is assumed to be subject to a struggle for power.

The Bourdieusian agents enter a field of relational forces well aware that they will have to struggle, negotiate, bargain to advance their positions within the existing field-specific power structures (Swartz and Zolberg 2005). As they struggle for power, their behaviour gets structured by the field but at the same time their conduct becomes constitutive of the future field structure. In order to describe this process, Bourdieu used the language 'structured structures' and 'structuring structures' representing his view of the relationship between the individual and society. While society shapes the individual habitus through socialisation, the very continuity and evolution of society depends on the permanent actions of individuals. Bourdieu describes this in *Outline of a Theory of Practice* as follows:

> The structures constitutive of a particular type of environment (e.g. the material conditions of existence characteristic of a class condition) produce *habitus*, systems of durable, transposable *dispositions*, structured structures predisposed to function as structuring structures, that is, as principles of the generation and structuring of practices and representations which can be objectively 'regulated' and 'regular' without any way being the product of obedience to rules, objectively adapted to their goals without presupposing a conscious aiming at ends [...].
>
> (Bourdieu 1972b trans. Nice 1977: 72)

Games, likewise, order play through rules and players invest in the game and agree by their belief that the game is worth playing. These analogies serve to explain two behavioural mechanisms: on the one hand, the resorting to common practices which have their grounding in the past following the behavioural principles individuals derive from incorporated knowledge and beliefs; and on the other hand, strategic improvisation (Powell and DiMaggio 1991; Meyer and Rowan 1977). The strengths each individual can put into the game depend on the value and meaning of the types of capital.[3]

Structural, relational, and cognitive explanations of action in field theory

There is more to social contexts than their converging effects with past field structures. Economists and social scientists adopting a Bourdieusian perspective have to employ two main concepts to understand action and how it is moulded by field structures: capital and habitus (the element of agency). Bourdieu identifies what Widick calls two moments: first, there is an *objective moment* referring to the power-laden structure and patterned systems of objective forms, objects (*capitals*), positions, and action that constitute groups and institutions; second, there is a *subjective moment* (which is organised under the term *habitus*) used by Bourdieu to locate individuals into the social context by interlinking them in a kind of dialectic of cognitive and social structures. This dialectic consists in the encounter of individuals and their opportunities as the objective conditions of possibility of action. Widick (2005) argues in psychological terms, that the 'self is mediated by the social that shapes expressions of the subjective commitment to the external dimension of lived institutions that order, structure, and constitute the world of collective necessity' (Widick 2005: 199). Whereas the view that action takes place within social order is also shared by most embeddedness scholars, their conceptions on the underlying forces are different (Granovetter 1985). We may say that Bourdieu sees 'social power' as the main element of the structure and logic of any given field and thus attributes high importance to the role of conflicts over resources that shape the functioning of the field, and in the end decide upon who gets what.

Capital and power in field theory

The dimension of power is central to Bourdieu's relational analysis of behavioural outcomes and transformation processes of fields. People's power depends on the amount and configuration of resources and the extent to which these resources are valued in a field. Ultimately these resources affect their dispositions to act, their strategies, and the way they impact on common practices. Bourdieu has identified different kinds of capital – educational capital, social capital (such as useful contacts and networks), technological capital (such as innovative technical equipment), commercial capital (such as brands), and organisational capital (such as a firm's reputation) (Bourdieu 1979 trans. Nice 1986). He distinguished cultural, technical, and commercial capital as the objectivised capital (equipment, instruments), from those embodied kinds, such as personal competencies and skills.

Since people do not act in a social vacuum, fields are competitive arenas. The idea of competition is much less prominent in network approaches, where network connectors in similar positions would rather be considered redundant. The strength an individual can compete with, or more generally the possibilities of action an individual has, depend to some part on the stock of capital. Fields are characterised by heterogeneity of their agents differently equipped with capital (Bourdieu 2005a). Not only is the stock of total capital important (i.e. its volume, or total amount), but also its structure (i.e. the relative proportions of the different types of capital). For instance, firms with similar total stocks of capital can occupy dissimilar positions if the share of the diverse forms of capital (e.g. economic, cultural capitals) is different between firms – see, for instance, in this volume, Chapter 11, written by Fabien Eloire. The basic idea of how fields are structured can well be illustrated by one quote from a book chapter entitled 'Principles of an economic anthropology', where Bourdieu describes the structure and capital distribution of the specific field of the market as follows:

> The structure of the distribution of capital and the structure of the distribution of costs, itself linked mainly to the scale and degree of vertical integration, determine the structure of the field, that is to say, the relations of force among firms: the mastery of a very large proportion of capital (of the overall energy) in effect confers a power over the field, and hence over the firms less well endowed (relatively) in terms of capital; it also governs the price of entry into the field and the distribution of opportunities for profit.
>
> (Bourdieu 2005a: 76)

The concept of field posits that the distinctive value attributed to capitals remains marked by its earliest conditions of acquisition. Capitals whose transmission is 'best hidden', receive higher weight in the reproduction of the field than direct, tangible forms that are more strongly controlled.[4]

One type of capital that is also prominent in network approaches, and that has been mentioned earlier in this volume, is social capital, which comprises the totality of resources, including financial capital and information, that may be activated through a 'more or less mobilisable network of relations that procures advantage by providing higher returns on investment' (Bourdieu 2005a: 76). In other words, we may consider the volume of an agent's social capital as dependent on the size of the network of connections that the individual can mobilise, and on the volume of capital possessed by the other members to whom the agent is connected.

In a field theoretic view, struggle is symbolic because agents attribute certain value to capital. The definition of social capital makes this abundantly clear. Social capital involves relationships of mutual recognition and knowledge. As a power in terms of brand loyalty, or commitment to a firm in the case of employees, symbolic capital functions as a form of credit that presupposes trust and belief of those upon which it bears because they are supposed to grant it credence. The extent to which capital can be converted in a field adheres to common laws of conversion and of securing field functioning (reproduction). For instance, in markets which are sub-fields of the economic field, manpower can be converted into financial capital, and its rate of conversion highly depends on whether it serves to secure the firm's and the overall market functioning.

Opportunities, interpretation, and imagination

The basic idea of field struggle is that individuals try to stabilise or improve their positions in the field by using their capital (Boyer 2008). They may influence the functioning of the field – holding back, maintaining expectation, or hustling and surprising – to exert power (Bourdieu 1981). For instance, if a group could use its social capital to exploit some of its properties that could serve as (symbolic) capital in the new state of the field, then they would be able to modify the rules of the game to their advantage. This vision is well expressed in 'Principles of an economic anthropology', in which Bourdieu argues that interactions depend on indirect conflict, on the socially constructed structure of the relationships of force that agents modify through those resources they control (Bourdieu 2005a).

Bourdieu holds the view that the conflict over structure by virtue of the volume and structure of the capitals at hand shapes the space of opportunities of action. However, the idea that this space constrains the choices of strategies (Fligstein 2001a; Bourdieu 1972b trans. Nice 1977) would not separate the agent from the field, rather it is said to inscribe the actor into the field logic who follows written scripts he can do little about. This would emphasise a 'taken for granted' reality, a routine social order and reproduction in which all actors share the same perceptions of their opportunities and constraints. Therefore, Bourdieu and even more so Fligstein and McAdam (2011) avoid this pitfall to reduce the field actor to a 'socialised cipher' (Widick 2005). In contrast, for them, field actors constantly adjust to the conditions in the field given their position and the action of others. Fligstein and McAdam (2011: 7) define 'strategic action as the attempt by social actors to create and maintain stable social worlds by securing cooperation of others'. They emphasise that strategic action is about control, which is achieved by the creation of identities, political coalitions, and interests. But the ability to reach such agreements requires that actors are capable of role-taking.

This idea is consistent with Bourdieu's *habitus* that links any given field to the *cognitive capacities* of the agents operating within it, without confusing them analytically. The conception of the habitus is that of a repository of classifications, schemata of perception, dispositions, and scripts (Bourdieu and Wacquant 1992 trans. Wacquant 1992). It serves as a repertoire of meanings and orients action structured by and synchronised with the fields. An essential point of his view is that individuals as social agents operate in the fields and make them operate insofar as 'a field can function only if it finds individuals socially predisposed to behave as responsible agents, to risk their money, their time, sometimes their honor or their life, to pursue the games and to obtain the profits it proposes' (Bourdieu 1982b: 46; trans. Adamson 1990: 194). Individuals choose strategies on the basis of these repertoires, which operate out of the intersection of perceptions, appreciation, and action inclination moulded by their past experience (Crossley 2001). Figure 10.1 provides a simplified illustration of the relationship between Bourdieu's basic concepts of habitus, capital, field, and behavioural outcome. While the force of habitus is mediated by fields, the constraints and

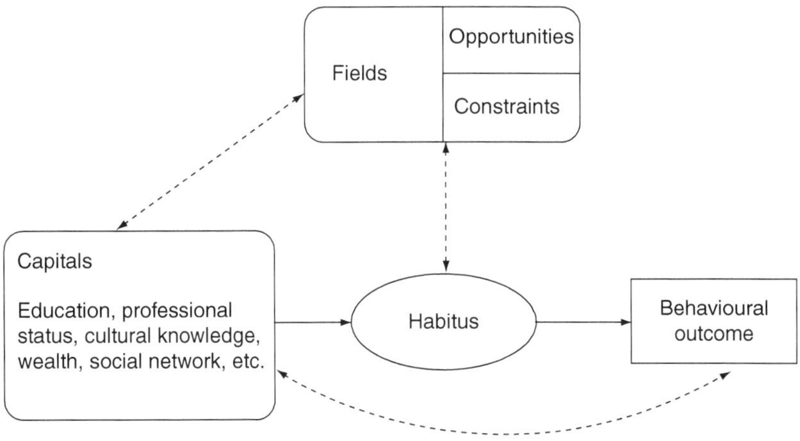

Figure 10.1 Simplified overview of the relationship between capitals, fields, habitus, and behavioural outcomes.

opportunities imposed by fields, such as their power structure and the possibilities they open to agents, are mediated by the dispositions of the habitus. Accounting for an interplay between field and habitus allows purveyors of this perspective to better understand how existing social structures came about, and thus go beyond situating or embedding action within a pre-given social context as proclaimed in the embeddedness tradition.

In Bourdieu and Wacquant (1992), the internalisation of external structures, or the somatisation of social relations, helps agents to identify and interpret their social environment. Field actors regress to 'virtually prevalent situations' within the body (habitus) that can be reactivated and serve as an *interpretative device* as part of the pre-logical, spontaneous logic of practical action (Widick 2005). In other words, individuals chose strategies out of their pool of options and on the basis of prior experience, both of which are shaped by their social environment and incorporate shared understandings.

Emphasising the *interpretative capacity* is to suggest that people are always acting informed by the sense of the game, mostly in an unconscious way and with an inborn *interest* to practically master their lives. They construct their own relation to the field[5] – their own personality and identity. Out of prior experience, based on values and knowledge of game rules, they derive their strategies. However, the habitus is subject to permanent stimulation and conditioning by the social process, so that it is the product of history, 'an open system of dispositions' that is durable but not eternal; not a reflex but conditioned limited spontaneity (Bourdieu 2000b trans. Turner 2005). It is also consistent with this logic that actors with presumably an identical habitus will generate different outcomes because their biographical trajectory and attachment to other actors affects their cognitive capacity to make sense of people's actions and environments.

Key to the idea of interpretative capacity is that individuals must be able to use their interpretative repertoires at any given moment. This kind of competence however requires a second capacity, which links the subject to the network of social relations, and is the capacity of imagination and identification (Widick 2005), or as Fligstein puts it, the social skill of reading people and environments (Fligstein and McAdam 2011). This *imaginative capacity* is consistent with Bourdieu's notion of the generative nature of the habitus because it bears the idea that strategies are oriented by the constraints and possibilities built into their position (Bourdieu 2000b trans. Turner 2005: 78) and by the representation the individual is able to form of that position and the position of competitors. These strategies result from the information at their disposal and their cognitive structures (Bourdieu 2005a).

The imaginative capacity that Bourdieu did not explicitly mention, rather his works refer to improvisation (Bourdieu 2000b trans. Turner 2005), bears the core motivation of field actors to identify themselves with others. This desire, or investment, and the instantaneous influence it has on the mental structure inculcate social typifications, categorisations, and schemata. Here, one can observe similarities to John Dewey (1910), one of Bourdieu's major sources of inspiration, who thought of imagination as an activity to test alternatives to resolve conflicting situations in thought by envisioning them to be carried out. The imaginative process continues until a suggested solution meets all the conditions of the case and does not run counter to any feature of it. Dewey calls this imaginative process 'dramatic rehearsal', which is a taking-in of the full scope of the situation, including its socio-cultural meaning (Dewey 1930). It differs from imaginary flights of mind-wandering, which are totally separated from the concern of the current situation. Through imaginative activity, individuals' perception is amplified because people are able to form anticipations of the future in the present. This has repercussions on how a field evolves because individuals deliberately rehearse ways to settle difficulties or ambiguities and by doing so open up a situation so it is perceived in a new way. The attention Bourdieu drew to the individual field agent, including his capacities and potentialities in taking action and by doing so contributing to the structuring of the field, goes far beyond socially embedded agents who build on trust and reciprocity as one of their core motivations of action (Granovetter and Swedberg 2011).

Two sites of transformations are possible, the *intra-subjective* and *inter-subjective sites*, both of which shape the structure and logic of the field. In the *intra-subjective site*, individuals are able to imagine being the other, which transforms their mental structures by the image of the other. Consequently, it creates an image through which later the social environment will be imagined. An example would be observing the successful manager in a company; the observer lives through this other – being part of his or her career in an instance of identification that transforms the observer's mental structures, e.g. qualifying the perception of one's position and worldview relative to others. In the *inter-subjective site*, imaginative capacity aids individuals not only to transpose themselves into others, but to mobilise people by identifying their 'frames' and those of the environment, and to make them act on behalf of these frames (Fligstein 2001b). By doing so, they need to take distance from their own and the group's interest, and consider multiple interests which are socially constructed to converge strategies for shared views with wider ranging structural effects (e.g. social movements).

Permissiveness of fields

Coming back to Bourdieu, he suggests that individuals who imagine futures form implicit understandings about how competition is dealt with, what roles and internal hierarchy and interests a field has. If these understandings are undermined, fields become permissive to change. Indeed, in turbulent times, strategically acting individuals, which in Bourdieu's conception can be powerfully generative and innovative, challenge and question the rules and positions governing the field (Bourdieu 1980g trans. Nice 1990). A major signal of this turbulent time is a high level of uncertainty. This uncertainty influences what someone deliberates as rational to do. It may cause non-foreseeable behaviour, which is not necessarily irrational. In other words, someone may show behaviour which is not pre-given in its direction in the stimulus and that is not deducible from knowledge of the appropriate rules, even if individuals knew most of them; such behaviour is presumably shaped by the trace of one's past trajectory that does not necessarily match the existing field structure and the collective conceptions that control its working (Bourdieu 1997e). A mismatch between habitus and field often leads a field into crisis and disrupts regularities, which increases the field's permissiveness to transformation, changes to the configuration of laws of functioning, and tempo of transformation. Additionally, it increases changes in the relation between fields, which in turn may affect the overall configuration of the vertically and horizontally organised field structure.

The disruption of regularities can be a *consequence* of a de-synchronisation between field and habitus, i.e. the lack of correspondence between the two (Florian and Hillebrandt 2006); or it can be considered as a *cause* for further field–habitus transformations (Hanappi 2011). In this sense, we recall, field structure inculcates the habitus, and these mental structures in turn reproduce or change social structures. This view is consistent with Crossley (2001), who explains that patterns and underlying principles of social contexts are incorporated in the habitus as both an inclination and a *modus operandi*. Disruption can often feed on itself. Individuals incorporate a generalised feeling of uncertainty (about threats, opportunities, and benefits of action), which leads them to question existing laws of functioning of the field and which hinders anticipations of field relations (McAdam and Scott 2005). This weakens the integrative power of the existing laws which hold together the field, and which define its boundaries towards the outside world. As a consequence, the field becomes permissive as a response to such disruptions, and new people (with their habits) can intrude to change the existing logic.

At the same time, dominant individuals attempt to safeguard or regain the former position and re-stabilise the former system by taking (innovative) action.

This brings in an almost perpetual spiral of adjustments in the objective (field) and mental (habitus) structures by virtue of cognitive acts. These acts include the recognition as reasonable of the agent's practices and rules of thumb, and a pre-reflexive, unconscious style on the one hand, and the practical acts of mastering a situation, on the other hand. In a field perspective, continuity and change are thus not the mere result of an innovative activity. Rather, as a result of an adjustment to novel situations and the enactment of past experience, it is a highly interwoven dynamic between field and habitus which by nature has stabilising and destabilising social forces. Part of this dynamic is that individual mental adjustments do not just occur *to* the environment but *of* the environment and generate relatively independent field forces. This makes fields non-ergodic (North 1999) – the present means (averages) are no good proxy for future means – which continue to change in novel ways. Therefore, it does not put an end to the attempt to anticipate future possible outcomes among even the most sophisticated and experienced individuals.

Final remarks

The chapter has presented approaches which embed action to help better explain the relationship between human conduct and the structured social context by referring to relational, institutional, or cognitive forces. Applications to embed action in networks often consider the role of institutions and cognitions as secondary, or inscribe action into institutional settings and take social networks and cognitions for granted.

The field theory of Bourdieu has been offered as an alternative way to link human conduct and social structure, providing a framework to consider structural, relational, and cognitive elements together without analytically merging them. Bourdieu departs from the game metaphor that sees individuals in permanent competition over positions and power. Their goal is to safeguard or improve their position in the field, by either stabilising or de-stabilising the current state and resorting to more or less innovative strategies. Individuals may influence the very rules of the field – holding back, maintaining expectation, or hustling and surprising – to exert power. By considering the objective moment adherent to all fields as the power-laden structure and patterned systems of objective forms, objects, positions, and action that constitute groups and institutions, the subjective moment which refers to habitus in Bourdieu's work locates competent agents into their objective social structure. This interrelationship between field and habitus is fundamental, and embodiment is an irreversible process, i.e. all external stimuli and conditioning experience are perceived through already constructed past experience.

The idea that conflict over structure and past trajectories shapes the space of opportunities is however too narrow since strategic action is achieved by the creation of identities, political coalitions, and interests. In other words, cognitive forces are fundamental. To identify and interpret their social environment, individuals refer to internalised knowledge (not necessarily thought) that can be reactivated and serve as an interpretative device. Individuals build images as kind of representations of the other, which allows them to locate themselves in the social structure (out of the position they currently inhabit), and to take sufficient distance to identify others' interests. These images have been argued to be central to link individual cognitions to social and institutional structures. They either confirm the general field functioning or in times of social change they disrupt the existing field laws, which lowers compliance with existing rules and renders the field permissive to change.

Notes

1 Doris Hanappi is a social scientist, specialising in work and family sociology, social theory, and fertility, as well as management sciences, work and family studies, comparative longitudinal research, and field analysis. She is currently a Visiting Scholar at the Demography Department, University of California Berkeley, and she is also affiliated with the Swiss National Centre of Competence in Research LIVES at the University of Lausanne. She is a member of FamiliesAndSocieties ('Changing families and sustainable societies: policy contexts and diversity over the life course and across generations'), a project financed by the EU (February 2013–January 2017). Relevant works on the book's topic include: 'Economic action, fields, and uncertainty', *Journal of Economic Issues*, 2011, 25(4): 785–803; 'Field, habitus, and economic reason: prospects for conceptualising economic action', *LIVES Working Papers*, 2011/6. The author acknowledges financial support from the Swiss National Centre of Competence in Research LIVES.

2 In some of his works, he contends at the metaphorical level that the screen the habitus introduces between stimulus and response is a screen of 'time' and that this is most effective in as much as no conscious reflection is involved (Bourdieu 2005a). In *An Invitation to Reflexive Sociology*, he described his understanding of this stimulus–response relationship as follows: 'We must think of it [the habitus] as a sort of spring that needs a trigger and, depending upon the stimuli and structure of the field, the very same habitus will generate different, even opposite, outcomes' (Bourdieu and Wacquant 1992 trans. Wacquant 1992: 135).

3 A prominent scholar in American sociology who took up this field concept was Neil Fligstein, who used it to analyse several empirical topics, e.g. differences between national employment systems, or governance in the field of international relations (see Fligstein 2005: 183–204). In his view, field actors are confronted with different rights, laws, and conceptions of control, which result in strategic practices, similar to those strategies resulting out of a 'feel for the game' as suggested by Bourdieu (see Bourdieu and Wacquant 1992 trans. Wacquant 1992).

4 Bourdieu's view may be conceived as being rooted in an anticipation of the distinction between the two states of capital, the objectivised and the embodied, as spelled out in Thorstein Veblen's work on the instinct of workmanship (1898).

5 At least complementary to the principle of rationality are the principles of *adaptation* and *practical* mastery that guide the reasonable agent in any of his or her actions. Bourdieu argued that an economic habitus generates behaviours that are particularly well-suited to those conditions from which they arise and that they tend to reproduce (Bourdieu 2000b trans. Turner 2005).

11 The effects of social capital on economic and symbolic profits

An analysis of the field and networks of restaurant owners

Fabien Eloire[1]

Introduction

In his work, Bourdieu appears to have dedicated less space to the concept of social capital, even though he considers it as one of the principal forms of capital in social life, alongside cultural and economic forms of capital (Bourdieu 1986a). A thorough investigation reveals that in 1980 he wrote and published a text entitled "Notes Provisoires", which contains an innovative theoretical and empirical research programme that provides an accurate definition of social capital and several hypotheses for empirical analysis. More importantly, if we want to take serious account of Bourdieu's statements in this short two-page text, we have to break with some of the recent works on social capital (Ponthieux 2006).

Indeed, from Coleman (1988) to Burt (1995) to Putnam (1993a), who popularise the notion before its appropriation by the World Bank and the OECD, we observe various conceptions of social capital: for Coleman, social capital is conceived as an attribute of the social structure which cannot be appropriated by any individual; for Burt, social capital relates to the way an individual's personal network is structured to achieve efficiency; for Putnam, social capital is a norm of generalised reciprocity which promotes the institutional performance of a society. A common thread that runs across these definitions is that, at the level of interpersonal interactions, there is some kind of personal network configuration that makes social capital efficient. However, there is disagreement on what forms of configuration are most efficient: while Coleman considers that efficiency comes from network *closure*, Burt strives to demonstrate that the *brokerage* position is the most profitable.

There are two reasons why Bourdieu does not address this debate in his "Notes Provisoires": first, this debate emerged after the article was published; second, it relates to the *interactionist* paradigm, of which Bourdieu was critical. Indeed, his reservations towards the interactionist dimension focuses on the tenets of both *network analysis* and the *American new economic sociology*. For Bourdieu, agents have limited leeway to create more or less durable interactions between them in order to establish some exchanges which express and maintain the existence of networks, because such leeway is determined by the structure of the field which is ubiquitous and operates in a permanent and invisible manner

(Bourdieu and Wacquant 1992). He further argues that one of the disadvantages of network analysis is that it centres on interactions, which removes the effects of structure and objective power relations. In other words, this type of analysis ignores the structural constraints exerted by the field, and tends to see only "influence effects" where in fact power relations, struggles, and domination are at play (Bourdieu 2007).

This is the reason why the question posed by the "Notes Provisoires" is that of integrating the two paradigms, *relational* and *interactionist*, that is, of compounding the *objective relations* which structure a field, on the one hand, and the *inter-subjective relations* which compose a social network, on the other. This integration of these two paradigms has yet to be explored. We attempt to tackle this issue in the present chapter, by conducting a case study of a sample of restaurant owners which reconstitute a complete network (Eloire *et al.* 2011). In the first part of the paper, we present our idea of Bourdieu's research programme as it was developed in the "Notes Provisoires". In the second part, we apply this research programme empirically by proposing an accurate measure of social capital, and by showing the effects of this measure on the accumulation of symbolic capital.

An alternative research programme for social capital

Our first objective is to show that Bourdieu's article contains a detailed research programme on social capital, one that has never been applied before. To this end, we begin by returning to the definition of social capital that this article develops. Then we describe the analysis model, and finally we present the hypotheses that emerge from this model.

The Bourdieusian definition of social capital

Within the field–habitus–capital theoretical architecture, the notion of social capital was employed to describe all the situations in which cultural capital and economic capital are not sufficient to explain what agents or groups are doing when they "work" to establish and maintain connections which are durable, permanent, and useful. Social capital constitutes a theorisation of what common sense means by "having relationships". The idea is that connections allow agents and groups to accumulate a form of capital, which are not their own, but accessed indirectly through interpersonal ties, and which can be mobilised when necessary (Bourdieu 2007). Thinking in terms of social capital refers to the *interactionist* paradigm, which focuses on visible, palpable *interactions*, and manifests in meetings or concrete exchanges within the physical space. Hence, this conception invites us to consider as "work" a whole set of practices generally equivalent to idleness, leisure, sociability: exchanges of visits, letters, presents, marriages, etc.

Social capital therefore constitutes the way by which the notion of exchange, as the basis of a "network" of *connections* or *alliances*, finds its place in Bourdieu's sociology. This does not happen automatically. In fact, the concepts of cultural and economic capital are specifically fitted to the application of the *relational* paradigm (Bourdieu 1980g), in which the objective properties of agents directly contribute to the structuring of the social space (Bourdieu 1979) and to the objectification of social relations. What is different about the notion of social capital is that it is situated at the intersection of the two paradigms, *relational* and *interactionist*, which tends to promote a dual reading and assessment: it could either be considered as a "meta-capital" without a specific content (Godechot and Mariot 2004), acting in a rather indirect way, by multiplying the effects of other forms of capital and improving their profitability; or it could be seen in terms of what it produces in the social world, that is, in terms of all the practices that induce agents in each field to accumulate social resources, transmit them, and reproduce them.

These two dimensions are inseparable. Indeed, for Bourdieu, while social capital is never "completely independent" of the economic and cultural forms of capital, there also exists an "irreducibility" of *inter-subjective interactions* compared to objective relations of proximity within the social space. This is what constitutes the specificity of social capital. Thus, to construct an empirical measure of the latter, it does not suffice to study the objective structure of a field (in terms of economic and cultural capital); attention should also be given to network relationships, that is, to the whole set of durable and useful connections that each particular agent or group establishes and sustains with other social agents or groups. Here we are confronted with a methodological issue which remains largely unexplored and relies on the task of determining the relationship between empirical data on agents' objective properties and their inter-subjective interactions. We address this issue in more detail in the following sections, where we describe the analysis model and conduct our case study.

The analysis model in "Notes Provisoires"

As mentioned above, social capital holds a dual meaning, so its empirical reconstruction necessarily requires different indicators that will allow us to reconstitute both objective relations and inter-subjective interactions that are inherent in social capital. Godechot and Mariot purport that, even though researchers roughly agree on the "volume dimension" of social capital, which renders it an "increasing function of the number of relations" possessed by an agent, they seem to disagree on which of the two ideal-typical configurations of a network, namely brokerage and closure, would potentially be the most profitable. This controversy (which, in fact, might only be resolved if we consider that the effectiveness of one or the other configuration depends on the context, as stressed by Burt 2005) ultimately overlooks the fact that, in addition to its volume and interactionist dimensions, social capital also possesses a structural dimension, linked to the distribution and weight of the other forms of capital (economic and cultural) in the composition of social capital.

Network analysis has widely contributed to the development of some tools and empirical measures that take into account the volume dimension of social capital (Lazega 1998). To incorporate the structural dimension in measures of social capital, we must first construct the structure of the field to determine the objective position of agents and the composition of their capital in terms of volume and structure; then we must construct the network of connections of agents within their field. As an indirect form of capital, which is mobilised when necessary, social capital could be measured, according to Bourdieu's definition, as the sum of the volumes of the other forms of capital (economic and cultural) possessed by each agent to whom a given agent is linked. To this measure of social capital that reflects its volume dimension, we must add another structural measure (expressed in percentage terms) that reveals the orientation of the network either towards agents who possess more cultural capital, or agents who possess more economic capital.

Hence, the analysis model applied here requires: first, the construction of a field as a contextual social space; second, adequate measures of the social capital of each agent, which appear in the model as independent variables; and third, some measures of efficiency, performance (economic and symbolic), and differential profitability of agents that appear in the model as dependent variables.

Hypotheses on the effects of social capital

For Bourdieu, the concept of social capital is used to describe a mechanism, which is not only economic, but also applicable to several other dimensions (cultural, symbolic, or social), and which is based on two ideas, the idea of accumulation, and the idea of time, because time is necessary to accumulate capital. Thereby, each accumulated capital is the product of the history of its accumulation (Bourdieu 1986a). In the case of economic and cultural capital, it is the relationship between habitus and field that determines how the accumulation process occurs and why it generally takes the shape of a reproduction process. In this process, according to Bourdieu, interactions tend to play a secondary role, because "networks" primarily emanate from the objective structure, and depend on power relations and struggles within the field. However, as Bourdieu suggests, in some cases we need to introduce the concept of social capital in our analysis. In his "Notes Provisoires", not only does he propose a definition of social capital, but he also suggests two generic hypotheses: the first one relates to the *interdependence* of social capital with other forms of capital, and the second one relates to the *multiplier effect* of social capital.

As regards the first hypothesis on interdependence, we recall the idea that social capital is "never completely independent" of the other forms of capital. According to Bourdieu, interactions actually emanate from objective structures, because the "choices" which guide the forms of inter-recognitions between agents presuppose a minimum of "objective" heterogeneity: this is related to the classical hypothesis of "social and cultural homogamy" (Girard 1964). Girard claims that, statistically, people marry from their own socio-economic group; likewise, in our study, we expect that people are friends with those who are similar to them by the *homophily* principle, which means that "birds of a feather flock together". Thus, on the one hand, we expect a significant and positive correlation between the volume of social capital and the volume of the other forms of capital (economic and cultural); on the other hand, we expect a significant and positive correlation between the volume of cultural (or economic) capital of an agent and the share of cultural (or economic) capital possessed by the agents of his/her network.

As regards the second hypothesis on the multiplier effect of social capital, the idea is to consider social capital as a "meta-capital", acting indirectly and multiplying the profitability of other forms of capital. This idea is clearly developed in the "Notes Provisoires", where Bourdieu stressed that: at a nearly equivalent level of (cultural or economic) capital, a higher level of social capital explains a higher profitability of (cultural or economic) capital. The underlying rationale is that differences in profitability could be explained by the capacity of some individuals to indirectly mobilise the capital of a group. Thereby, we expect a significant and positive correlation between the volume of social capital and the indicators of differential profitability studied, a phenomenon to be observed at both the macro and the meso level, that is, at each level of (cultural or economic) capital.

However stimulating, this hypothesis complicates the description of the accumulation process of capital. Indeed, the aim is to show that "relationships" can effectively exert a "multiplier effect" on agents' own capital (Bourdieu 1980a). Methodologically, testing this hypothesis requires that we design a specific survey, which will allow us to conjoin correspondence analysis (statistical tool used to describe a field, e.g. Leroux and Rouanet 2010) and network analysis (tool used to report regularities in interactions, e.g. Wasserman and Faust 1994; Freeman 2004; Lazega 1998).

The effect of social capital: a case study in the gastronomic field

Bourdieu's research often predisposes us to think about social capital in relation to the "dominant classes" (elites, upper-class bourgeois, heirs, nobility). But it should not be forgotten that the effects of social capital can be understood at all levels of the social space and within each field. A *generic* analysis model of the functioning of social capital becomes possible when we apply the principle of the structural homology of fields, which postulates that each field reproduces, at its own level, the structure and the mechanisms of the social space (Bourdieu 1979). An example is the sub-field of commercial gastronomy in Lille (Northern France), which we consider here as an empirical case study.

Positions and stances in the gastronomic sub-field of Lille

In Figure 11.1 (see Annex), we observe that restaurant owners are distributed along two axes, reminiscent of those that shape the social space. In particular, the vertical axis represents the overall volume of capital, that is, "the set of actually usable resources and powers – economic, cultural, social capital" (Bourdieu 1979 trans. Nice 1984: 114), while the horizontal axis represents a "chiasm structure", so that "the structure of the distribution of economic capital is symmetrical and opposite to that of cultural capital" (Bourdieu 1979 trans. Nice 1984: 120). The general trends that we discover in the structure of the gastronomic sub-field, suggest that, on the one hand, there is an opposition between the dominant and dominated, and, on the other hand, among the dominant, there is an opposition between two poles: the first one is controlled by the material interests of monetary profitability that restaurants pursue as firms; and the second one is controlled by the symbolic interests of gastronomic recognition that skilled professionals pursue as "chef". To better explain our method of multiple correspondence analysis (MCA), we conduct two separate analyses for cultural capital and economic capital.

With regard to cultural capital (Figure 11.2 in the Annex), the horizontal axis contains a summary of the cultural capital hierarchy between restaurant owners. As we move towards the left of the axis, we encounter those who have no diploma in catering and no experience as an employee in this business before being themselves owners of a restaurant. As we move toward the right of the axis, we come across those who, before opening their own restaurant, had a diploma in catering, had gained multiple skills (in cooking, serving tables), and had extensive experience in a number of successive jobs (up to four) at different gastronomic restaurants nationwide (including highly rated, *Michelin-starred* establishments). Towards the centre of this axis, we find those who have some, but less prestigious, experience as an employee, serving tables in places like *brasseries* or traditional, regional restaurants. This MCA underlines the weight that a certain state of cultural capital has within this professional *milieu*, one that Bourdieu refers to as the *institutionalised state* of cultural capital, or cultural capital in its objectified form as a title, such as an education degree, which is conceived as a certificate of cultural competency that "confers on its holder a conventional value" (Bourdieu 1986a: 248). Indeed, in Figure 11.2 we observe that the modalities that derive from one's diploma, know-how, and work experience (diamond-shaped points in the figure) contribute more to the configuration of this axis than those that are concentrated in the dotted circle (triangular points in the figure) and are related to an *embodied state* of cultural capital, which is inculcated and assimilated through time and by heredity. Finally, family background, region of origin, having created or reclaimed the business, and the number of years in this line of work appear weakly discriminating variables in the formation of cultural capital.

With regard to economic capital (Figure 11.3 in the Annex), the horizontal axis highlights the organisational and legal principles that shape firms. As we move towards the left of the axis, we encounter small restaurants that: have a capacity to host less than 40 guests and to employ one or two workers; have a single proprietor; are open less than seven times a week; and have a maximum turnover of €250,000 per year. As we move towards the right of the axis, we come across larger establishments that: can host over 90 guests and employ more than ten workers; are open more than ten times per week (up to seven days a week, lunch and dinner); have a turnover above €800,000 per year; and are registered as partnerships or simplified joint stock companies (but not private limited companies, aka SARL), where investors extend beyond the family circle and owners are likely to have other restaurants.

As we show in our analysis of the field, *stances* are never independent of the *positions* which restaurant owners have at the moment they start up their business, and which are determined by the volume of the cultural capital owners possess and its relative weight to their economic capital. In the MCA of the gastronomic sub-field, we add some supplementary variables to these active variables, in order to capture the effect of the two forms of cultural and economic capital on restaurant owners' *stances* toward their culinary style and their access to symbolic capital (Figure 11.4 in the Annex). The analysis demonstrates that the reconciliation of material and symbolic interests, money and food, is much more difficult to achieve as one rises in the hierarchy of capital and gains market power. The nature of this power differs depending on where a restaurant is placed along one or the other pole of the field.

As far as restaurants' stances towards culinary style are concerned, we note that the volume of cultural capital possessed by restaurant owners determines their choice of culinary style. In the "gastronomic pole" of the sub-field, an informal hierarchy between culinary styles appears: from the "traditional" style adopted by restaurants that are relatively less endowed with cultural capital (e.g. diplomas, experience), to the "gastronomic" style adopted by restaurants that are well endowed with cultural capital. Conversely, in the "economic pole", we note that restaurant owners that are better endowed with economic capital tend to choose a "brasserie" style, or specialise in certain foods (potatoes, fish, crepes, etc.), so they cover the bottom range of low-priced dishes. By standardising the production of meals and controlling costs, these establishments are relatively larger in size and exploit economies of scale. In this way, they have more leverage in negotiations with their suppliers and their employees (Gadrey *et al.* 2002).

Similarly, with regard to the accumulation of *symbolic capital*, we observe that the higher the rank of a restaurant owner in the cultural capital hierarchy, the higher is his/her rank in the symbolic capital hierarchy (which is objectified through professional rewards, including references in and awards from gastronomic "guides", as well as peer co-optations for entry in "honorary associations" of chefs). Thus, in the gastronomic pole, we discover restaurants that cover the top-range, high-priced dishes and get their reputation from the signature name of the chef. The size of these restaurants is smaller than those located in the opposite, economic pole, and their owners are committed to stringent quality requirements, which favour neither higher economic returns, nor greater leverage in their transactions with suppliers and employees ("we can't compromise on quality", "the quality comes at a price"; Dallery *et al.* 2009).

To construct our indicator of symbolic capital, we used a series of gastronomic guides, each of which offers its own annual awards: stars for the *Michelin* or the *Bottin Gourmand*; notes for the *Gault & Millau*; points for the *Champerard*; and plates for the *Pudlo*. Our MCA shows that, while gastronomic restaurants obtain awards, some restaurants situated in the economic pole are also likely to possess symbolic capital, but they are not distinguished by awards, only by references in one of the specialised guides. For our indicator, we also consider honorary associations, particularly those that have some members in the metropolis of Lille, but exert national influence. These associations are run by co-optation and sponsorship. They all work to defend gastronomy, but each has its own conception of what it is: for instance, the so-called *Générations. C, Cuisine & Cultures* adopts a very modern and "nouvelle cuisine" outlook; the *Ordre International des Disciples d'Auguste Escoffier* or the *Club Gastronomique Prosper Montagné* promote a more traditional cuisine; and the *Jeunes Restaurateurs d'Europe* and *Maîtres Cuisiniers de France* have an interest in traditional cuisine as well, but enjoy a more prestigious position.

Professional friendships as a matrix of social capital

Findings from our social network analysis demonstrate that restaurant owners are more isolated from each other in the economic pole of the gastronomic subfield. To the contrary, in the gastronomic pole, informal contacts between restaurant owners are numerous and frequent. It is these contacts that in 1999 led to the establishment of a formal association, the *Club des Tables Gourmandes*, which is considered as the most emblematic association in our study. The club brings together about 40 chefs, who are exclusively from the Lille metropolitan area, and have been co-opted among the most prominent and most recognised for their expertise. The existence of such an association is in a way the outcome of all these informal activities of *relational investment* that we have been investigating. The underlying network of professional friendships between restaurant owners constitutes the basis for the construction of our social capital indicator.

The contradictory expression of "professional friendship" aptly captures relational activities between restaurant owners. These relations indicate the establishment of durable relationships of trust between agents in a professional, yet objectively competitive, market framework. These professional friendship ties function as the reciprocity cycles that Bourdieu describes in his generator model (Bourdieu 1980g: 171). They facilitate exchanges of various useful resources (material or symbolic), without reducing these exchanges to their pure utilitarian or commercial expression:

> Professional friends are people I have known since my studies and maintained contact with, irrespective of whether I had the chance to work with them or not. In addition to our friendship, we are in the same line of work, so we continue to phone each other to say, hey, I need some advice, some help, and some exchanges. In this way, we created a professional side to supplement the friendship we already had.
>
> (Restaurant owner, traditional cuisine)

This exploratory interview extract is consistent with our individual survey results. Indeed, we find evidence that social resources circulate through friendship ties: there is a strong statistical correlation between considering someone as a friend and exchanging with that person different social resources (e.g. information, help, customers) (Eloire 2010). This reveals the importance of friendship and network relations in our analysis of social capital. These durable, permanent, and useful connections structure exchanges between agents, because they induce regularities in the circulation of social resources and they constitute the visible expression of this form of capital, which is obtained by proxy, and mobilised when necessary. The usefulness of an empirical knowledge of these networks is reinforced when the survey protocol allows us to capture the reciprocity that lies in these connections, as is the case in our survey. The reader can consult the methodological annex for a more detailed description of our fieldwork research (survey questionnaire, choice of sample and variables, construction of the field and networks, and calculation of indicators).

To construct our indicators of social capital, in terms of both *volume* and *structure*, we chose the network that consists of links of mutual friendship between restaurant owners: this network (Figure 11.5 in the Annex) consists of 566 links between 164 restaurant owners from the 283 owners that are included in our sample. In other words, 58 per cent of our sample of restaurant owners claims to have relationships of mutual friendship, while 42 per cent claim they do not. Of the 58 per cent, 22 per cent have only a single friend with whom they have mutual relations, 17 per cent have two or three friends, and 20 per cent have four or more. The maximum number of mutual friends identified in our study is 13. We now have all the information we need to test the hypotheses derived from the analytical model of the "Notes Provisoires".

Testing the hypotheses of interdependence and multiplier effects

We first test the hypothesis concerning the *interdependence* of social capital with the other forms of capital. In Table 11.1 (see Annex), we provide evidence of a strong and positive correlation between cultural capital and social capital, as well as between economic capital and social capital. This result indicates that social capital is never completely independent of the other forms of capital.

However, to have a more precise idea of the link between the objective structures of the field and the interactionist process of the social construction of gastronomy, we can examine the link between the structure of the individual capital of an agent and the structure of his/her social capital. This relates to the social *homophily* hypothesis. Indeed, our results in Table 11.2 (see Annex) reveal a positive correlation between the volume of cultural (or economic) capital that is individually owned by an agent and the volume of cultural (or economic) capital that can be accessed through his/her personal friendship network. In other words: the higher the volume of cultural (or economic) capital that belongs to the agent him/herself (to the *ego*), the higher the share of cultural (or economic) capital in his/her social capital (his/her *alters*). This implies that connections are not randomly established, but follow a specific social logic: agents that belong to a certain pole in the sub-field are more likely to choose their friends from the same pole. But if these interactions reinforce the structural effects of the field, then the specificity of social capital is to be sought elsewhere, particularly in its multiplier effect, which we now turn to.

Social capital does not rely on a purely utilitarian conception of agents' interactions. It perceives social relations as an act of investment, the efficiency of which is precisely based on the essential principle that such investment goes unseen as an activity and unrecognised as a source for useful and efficient capital. But the efficiency in question here is not the one economists talk about. The social resources exchanged daily between restaurant owners (e.g. information, help, customers) are not only material but also symbolic, and they facilitate access to monetary profit as well as access to symbolic profit. Thus, the efficiency of social capital must first be considered in its dimension of symbolic capital accumulation, as indicated by the first axis of Figure 11.6 in the Annex (principal components analysis, PCA). Indeed, the figure brings to the fore an opposition between two groups of correlated variables: one group includes three variables, namely the volume of an agent's economic capital, the share of economic capital in his/her structure of social capital, and monetary profit; the other group also consists of three variables, namely the volume of cultural, social, and symbolic capital of restaurant owners.

These findings reveal that social capital exerts two opposite effects: the higher the volume of social capital, the higher the volume of symbolic capital, while the monetary gain achieved is lower. Apparently, restaurant owners must choose between these two conflicting goals. However, social capital has the capacity to impact monetary profits, as long as one takes into account its volume, as well as its structure. Indeed, an important element of social capital is the share of economic capital in the structure of social capital: the more significant this share is, the higher the monetary profit. In other words, our results demonstrate that having some friends (even a few) who are situated in the economic pole is positively correlated with economic success. But, in the final analysis, the correlations produced from our PCA with concern to social capital appear as secondary, since there are deeper trends which link symbolic profit and the volume of cultural capital, on the one hand, and monetary profit and the volume of economic capital, on the other. So, our analysis tends to confirm that social capital acts, in an indirect way, as a sort of "meta-capital".

To complete our analysis, we must still show that social capital is likely to have a *multiplier effect* on cultural capital and economic capital: if two agents have almost the same amount of cultural (or economic) capital, then the one that has more social capital will be able to accumulate more symbolic (or economic) capital. To conduct this test we must create groups with equivalent amounts of cultural capital and economic capital, and then examine within each group whether a higher volume of social capital is effectively associated with a higher level of symbolic or economic profit. First of all, with regard to economic profits, results are depicted in Table 11.4 (see Annex). They reveal no multiplier effect on the part of social capital. This can be explained by the idea that the accumulation of economic profit in the market seems to obey other logics beyond that of the instrumental use of friendship relations (Dallery *et al.* 2009).

To the contrary, with regard to symbolic profit, our results are depicted in Table 11.3 (see Annex). They offer evidence that social capital produces a rather strong multiplier effect. In the case of economic capital, we observe that, in each group (except one), the more social capital one has, the more symbolic profits one gains. Results are similar for cultural capital (though there is an insignificant effect in the two first groups, which can be explained on the basis that symbolic capital is nearly missing at these levels of cultural capital). Overall, these results offer evidence of the specificity of social capital relative to other forms of capital, as well as the specific modalities of its functioning.

Conclusion

In this article, we tried to reconsider Bourdieu's propositions on social capital. From our attentive review of his "Notes Provisoires", published in 1980, we discover not only a definition of social capital, but also an innovative research programme, in that it combines two definitions of "social relations" and two paradigms: *relational* and *interactionist*. Methodologically, the operationalisation of the Bourdieusian definition of social capital establishes a specific device of scientific inquiry which allows us to conjoin correspondence analysis and network analysis.

There are certain steps we need to follow to apply the alternative model developed here: first, we construct the field as a social and structured contextual space; second, we accurately measure each agent's social capital, which functions as the explanatory variable in the model; third, we adopt measures of economic profit and symbolic efficiency that are used as dependent variables. To complete these steps and offer an empirical foundation to our model, we test two hypotheses derived from the "Notes Provisoires": the *interdependence* and the *multiplier effect* hypothesise. Our case study provides strong evidence that social capital is interdependent with other forms of capital, and also possesses a kind of specificity. As a "meta-capital", it exerts indirect effects, which makes it all the more effective because they are largely denied on the basis of friendship, social exchange resources, and reciprocity cycles.

Methodological annex

Fieldwork research and survey

Our empirical data on the gastronomic sub-field of the metropolis of Lille was derived from fieldwork research that was conducted from February to October 2006 and was based on a face-to-face survey questionnaire. We interviewed about 300 restaurant owners. To construct the questionnaire, we conducted a pilot-survey, which took place from April to October 2005 and consisted of ten semi-structured interviews with a fairly open framework of qualitative questions. The questionnaire was separated into three parts, each of which corresponded to a specific set of variables: (1) the social attributes of restaurant owners; (2) the economic characteristics of their establishments; and (3) several network variables, including: transfers or exchanges between restaurant owners; social resources identified during the pilot-survey; informal discussions about economic conditions; transmission of interesting information; sending over customers; mutual support.

Choice of sample

To define our sample of restaurant owners, we used different criteria: to be located in the metropolis of Lille; to be owner of a traditional-type restaurant as opposed to a "fast-food restaurant" (according to the French Trade Sector Code NAF); to be legally independent (we excluded restaurants that belonged to a chain or franchise). Some of them would also need: to participate in a network where social resources are transferred and exchanged between restaurant owners; to take part in certain institutional relationships in the business, such as being a member of an honorary or commercial association, or a member of a trade union, or being referenced in a gastronomic guide (Eloire *et al.* 2011). We must note that restaurant owners did not need to fulfil all these criteria to be included in the sample. Satisfying several of the aforementioned criteria sufficed for the purposes of our analysis.

Construction of the field

We construct the field by using the two parts of our questionnaire dedicated to "the social attributes of the restaurant owners" and "the economic characteristics of their establishments". By means of a multiple components analysis (MCA), we describe the social space of the restaurant owners in its various aspects (economic, cultural, symbolic) and develop its objective structures. The MCA is composed of 18 active variables (61 items) and five supplementary variables (20 items). The active variables are used to measure cultural capital (nine variables, 30 items) and economic capital (nine variables, 31 items). The supplementary variables are related to culinary style (one variable, seven items) and symbolic capital (four variables, 13 items). Two additional MCAs were conducted: one only with cultural capital variables, and the other only with economic capital variables. A principal components analysis (PCA) was also conducted with the variables of symbolic capital. These complemental analyses allow us not only to offer a better interpretation of MCA results for the entire gastronomic field; they also provide for a quantitative measure of the three forms of capital (economic, cultural, symbolic) by using axis 1 of each of the MCA and PCA. These measures can then be used to test for correlations with quantitative measures of social capital.

Social network analysis

The sociometric part of our inquiry centres on the reconstitution of interactions between restaurant owners and forms the basis for the construction of our social capital indicator. While social attributes allow us to retrace the field of objective relations, the study of interpersonal contacts and social resource circulation enables us to reconstitute networks.

The name generator used in the questionnaire was: "who are the restaurant owners you personally know, and who know you personally too?" Thus, respondents are asked to list the restaurant owners with whom they are linked. This is an open-ended question that is only intended to provide a list of contacts and stress aspects of reciprocity: respondents are not called upon to cite people who are considered "popular" (as in the media, for example), but people with whom they are likely to interact. Once the list has been established, specific questions are asked about the type of link maintained with each person cited: length of the relationship; the nature of the relationship – familial or friendship; and the potential exchange of social resources.

Another point worth mentioning is that our sociometric survey uses respondents' memory and subjectivity, and so the questionnaire records agents' perceptions of each other. But our survey follows an iterative process: when one individual is cited, then this person is also interviewed, so that for each interaction we possess information about both sides of the relationship. Thus, while the point of view of *ego* is *subjective*, by having the point of view of *alter*, we give the *inter-subjective* relation an *objective* character. It is when the relationship is reciprocal that the two subjectivities meet and a reciprocity cycle is at work.

Calculating social capital

Our goal is to measure social capital of Rest40, who has cited as friends Rest26, Rest36, Rest32, Rest53, and Rest27, each of which has also cited Rest40 as a friend. In Table 11.5 below, columns *Capitcult* and *Capiteco* depict scores of cultural capital and economic capital, respectively, of Rest26, Rest36, Rest32, Rest53 and Rest27. These scores are equivalent to the value that the two forms of cultural and economic capital obtain on axis 1 of the corresponding MCAs. The volume of Rest40's social capital is the sum of these ten scores and is equal to 11.44276. The structure of social capital is the share of cultural capital (64 per cent) compared to the share of economic capital (36 per cent) in the volume of Rest40's social capital.

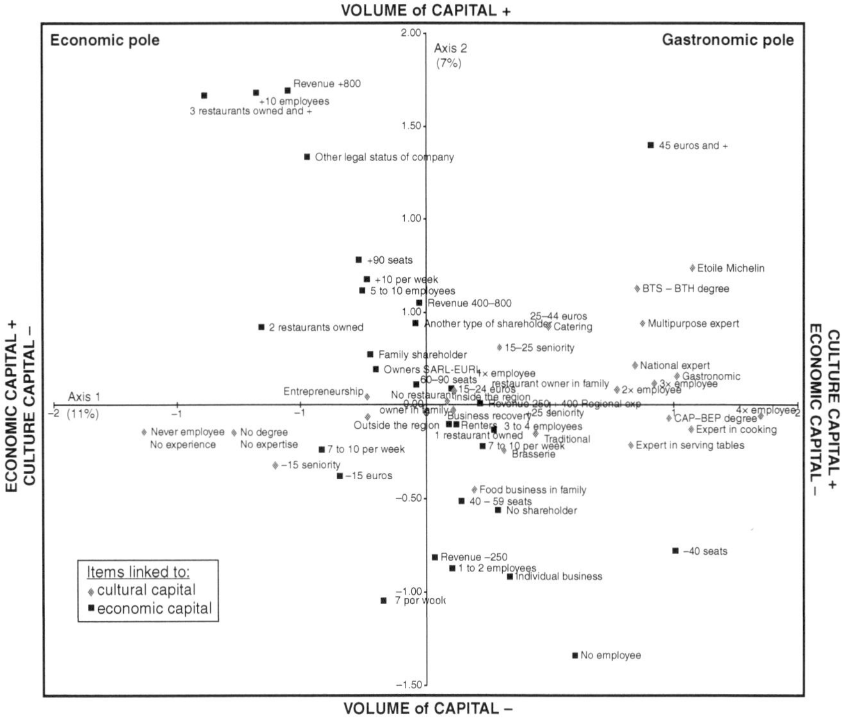

Figure 11.1 The structure of the gastronomic sub-field in the Lille metropolis.

Notes
The abbreviations in the figures stand for:
SARL: limited liability company.
EURL: sole proprietorship limited liability.
CAP: certificate of professional skills.
BEP: vocational studies certificate.
BTS: higher technician certificate.
BTH: bachelor of technology hotellerie.

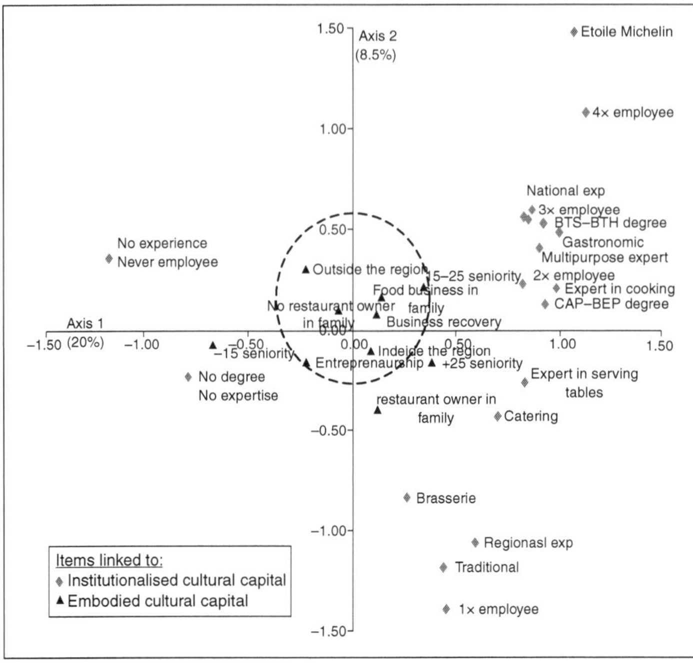

Figure 11.2 Cultural capital.

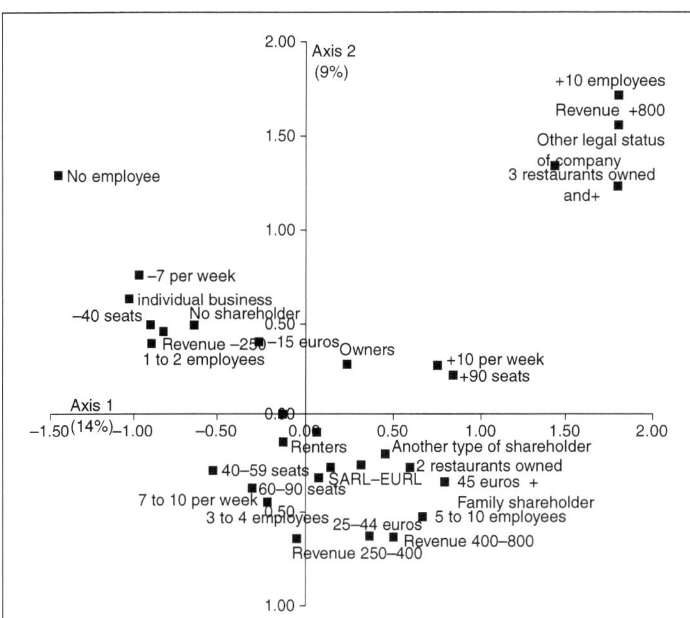

Figure 11.3 Economic capital.

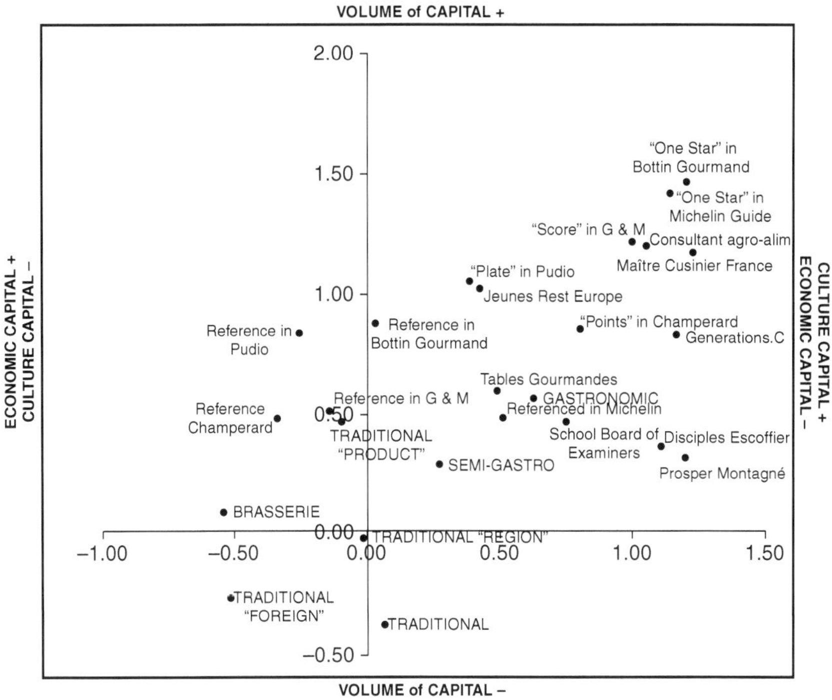

Figure 11.4 Symbolic capital.

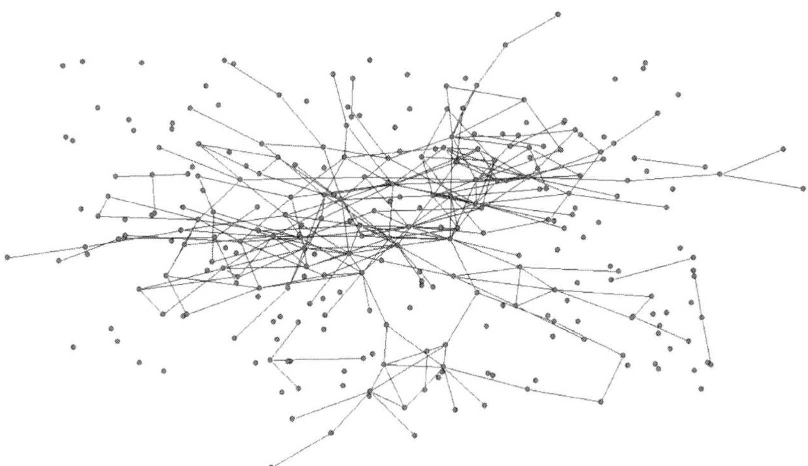

Figure 11.5 Network of links of mutual friendship.

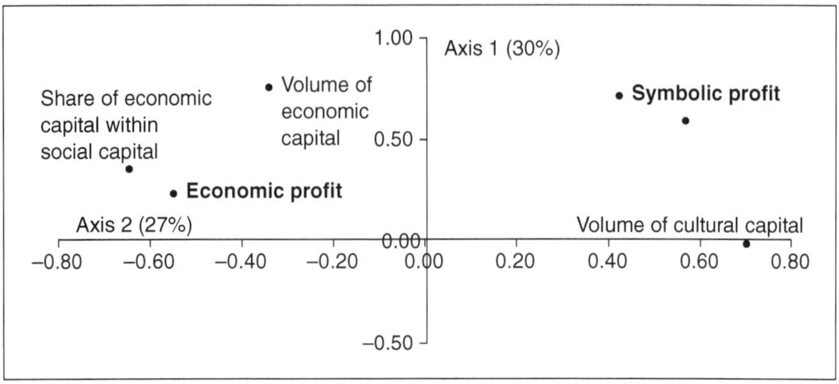

Figure 11.6 The effect of social capital (PCA).

Table 11.1 The volume of social capital is interdependent with the other forms of capital

	Volume of social capital
Economic capital	**0.16 (<0.01)**
Cultural capital	**0.23 (<0.01)**

Table 11.2 The interdependence of social capital with economic and cultural capital

	% of economic capital between social capital	*% of cultural capital between social capital*
Economic capital	**0.36 (<0.01)**	**−0.36 (<0.01)**
Cultural capital	**−0.31 (<0.01)**	**0.31 (<0.01)**

Table 11.3 Multiplier effect – correlations between social capital and symbolic profit

Classes of…	*…cultural capital*	*…economic capital*
1	0.06 (0.66)	**0.50 (>0.01)**
2	0.06 (0.70)	**0.28 (0.05)**
3	**0.26 (0.05)**	0.06 (0.65)
4	**0.40 (>0.01)**	**0.77 (>0.01)**
5	**0.35 (>0.01)**	**0.45 (>0.01)**
6	**0.77 (>0.01)**	**0.51 (>0.01)**

Table 11.4 Multiplier effect – correlations between social capital and economic profit

Classes of…	*…cultural capital*	*…economic capital*
1	0.05 (0.75)	−0.02 (0.93)
2	−0.23 (0.28)	−0.28 (0.16)
3	−0.30 (0.06)	−0.08 (0.71)
4	0.27 (0.25)	−0.10 (0.57)
5	−0.07 (0.68)	−0.19 (0.22)
6	−0.31 (0.09)	0.23 (0.14)

Note

Tables 11.1, 11.2, 11.3 and 11.4 present statistical correlation analyses. The first number is the correlation coefficient (i.e. the intensity of the link between two variables). The second number in parentheses is the *p*-value (i.e. the significance level of the link between two variables). The correlation coefficient has a statistically significant effect when the *p*-value is less than 0.05 or 0.01 (whenever this is the case, we put the numbers in bold type).

Table 11.5 The volume and structure of social capital

Ego	*Alters*	*Capitcult*	*Capiteco*
Rest40	Rest26	1.63524	1.36955
Rest40	Rest36	1.75473	0.82746
Rest40	Rest32	0.60013	1.01786
Rest40	Rest53	1.75084	0.00163
Rest40	Rest27	1.57352	0.91180
Total		7.31446	4.1283
Structure of capital =		64%	36%
Volume of capital =		11.44276	

Note

1 Fabien Eloire teaches sociology and does research at the University of Lille 1 and at the Clersé-CNRS laboratory. He has done research on the restaurant industry in an economic sociology perspective, and has used social network analysis. He has written about cooperation between competitors ("Une approche sociologique de la concurrence sur un marché. Le cas des restaurateurs lillois", *Revue française de sociologie*), and about price mechanisms in collaboration with post-Keynesian economists ("La fixation des prix en situation d'incertitude et de concurrence: Keynes et White à la même table" *Revue française de socio-economie*).

12 Toward an alternative framework for social capital as social change

Reflections on Bourdieu's approach

Asimina Christoforou[1]

Introduction

Over the past three decades, the literature on social capital has associated norms and networks of trust, reciprocity and cooperation with improvements in economic development, social cohesion and democratic governance. Critical views of social capital claim that the literature overlooks the role of power relations, hierarchical structures and social inequalities, which are reflected in and sustained through social norms and networks that are established and imposed by the dominant classes (for an overview, see Christoforou 2014). Some of these authors point to the much neglected work of Pierre Bourdieu.

According to Bourdieu, social networks are a resource individuals have access to and exploit to their interest by transmitting various forms of capital and credit (social obligations) among members. In this way, the holders of capital possess the strategies and powers to reproduce the hierarchies and inequalities of the capitalist system, which, contrary to contemporary views on social capital, fail to enhance individual and community welfare. In this chapter, we argue that limited attention has been given to the fact that Bourdieu's notion of capital – including cultural, social and symbolic – has an active part in processes of social transformation, that is, in changes of social structures, as much as in the reproduction of these structures. Even though social capital appears to be the type of capital that Bourdieu focuses relatively less on, it always operates in relation to the other types of capital he introduces in his analysis. In fact, social capital could only be fully appreciated and studied as part of the mechanisms of the transmission of material and immaterial resources, the reformulation of groups and the restructuring of society.

In the next section of this chapter, we briefly discuss how recent studies on the relationship between development and social capital have overlooked or distorted Bourdieu's radical conception of capital. Due to the influence of mainstream economics, the literature adopts a reductionist view of social capital and thus fails to explain social transformation. In the third section, we try to restore this loophole in the literature by reflecting on Bourdieu's approach that could be summarised in his notions of field and habitus. Our objective is to reconstruct from a Bourdieusian perspective the basis for an alternative theoretical framework that would promote the study of social capital by incorporating the role of contextual factors. We will see how these factors are determined by the structure of the diverse forms of capital (first subsection), and the influence they exert on group formation, social struggles and change (second and third subsections). By focusing on some of Bourdieu's representative works in this area of research, we wish to provide a more careful reading of his ideas and re-educate ourselves in his alternative way of thinking. We close with some concluding remarks.

Bourdieu, social capital and development research

During the heyday of social capital research at the World Bank in the late twentieth century, social capital was identified as the 'missing link' in development. Researchers at the Bank argued that the economic backwardness observed in less developed regions compared to the industrial world is attributed to factors beyond those predicted by traditional capital accumulation theories, which centred on the relative stock of physical and human capital resources. They turned to less economically oriented resources in the form of norms and networks of cooperation and trust that individuals have access to and use to overcome the conditions of market inefficiency and government ineffectiveness that condemn regions to their backwardness. Focus shifted to how collective action is organised: what formal and informal rule systems individuals apply to control for fierce atomism and achieve social order; whether they actively and voluntarily participate in social and political groups and organisations; whether they vote or pay their taxes or respect common pool resources; whether they trust market and state institutions; and how effectively they work with government officials. In the 1990s, World Bank development programmes recommended and funded structural change that was conditional on the availability of a 'stock' of social capital in less developed regions. Communities, grassroots associations, self-governed networks and NGOs were encouraged to take active part in the planning and implementation procedures.

The rationale behind this was that norms and networks of association and trust would be used to exploit the benefits of social resources, namely, to combat the asymmetric information and transaction costs involved in exchanges among economic agents, government officials and representatives of international organisations in development programmes, and thus provide for a more efficient and welfare-enhancing allocation of funds. Social capital was treated as another productive resource alongside standard types of physical, human and financial capital that feature in economics. But it was mainly considered as a resource that made up for the absence of other types of capital in less developed regions, by inducing individuals to draw from shared interests, pool the meagre resources each had at hand, and rely on each other to improve their living standards. In fact, social capital emerged as a means to universalise a vision of the empowerment of the poor. Moreover, researchers at the World Bank, including Anthony Bebbington and Michael Woolcock, claimed to employ the 'capital' metaphor in order to speak in the language of the economists at the Bank and convince them to take account of the social dimensions of the development process (Bebbington *et al.* 2006). As a powerful organisation, the World Bank influenced development practitioners across the globe and set the standards on how development and social capital were to be perceived and assessed.

However, many authors have questioned the success of this approach. Indeed, in their evaluation of World Bank community-based and -driven projects, which relied heavily on social capital, Bebbington and his team discover that very few projects managed to achieve the aspired objectives of building networks and promoting local development (Bebbington *et al.* 2006). They attributed these failures to problems in the incentives of local private and public agents, project directors and Bank employees. However, in their critical overview, Mansuri and Rao, also World Bank researchers, offer an alternative explanation: they point to setbacks imposed by elite groups, which dominated these projects and thus compromised public welfare objectives, particularly within communities that were more unequal (2003: 10–25, 30–31). The authors argue that this is due to a naïve application of terms such as participation, social capital and community without considering the effect of contextual factors driven by: local structures of power; social divides based on gender, caste, race or ethnic identities; and uneven interests in a specific public good or the uneven distribution of resources (19). Moreover, they observe that sustainability of community-driven initiatives could only be achieved within an enabling institutional environment that was characterised by the transparency, accountability, commitment, knowledge and skill of national governments, community leaders, international organisations and project managers. Thus, community-based development is conditioned by local cultural and social systems (24–26, 31).

In this regard, Mansuri and Rao suggest a more nuanced understanding of social capital, based on Bourdieu's perception of capital as power and of networks as transmitters of power (13–14). Here social capital is linked to the possession of a durable network, which provides each of its members with the backing of collectively owned capital, a 'credential' which entitles them to a kind of credit, be it economic, social or cultural (Bourdieu 1986a: 249–250). Contrary to mainstream approaches, conceptions and measures of social capital derived from Bourdieu's analysis are not restricted to the interactionist aspects of networks – how many individuals belong to a group or an organisation or how frequently they meet, or even how many groups and organisations function in a certain community or society. Bourdieu extends his analysis to the kind of exchanges that take place within the group and particularly the structure and volume of capital resources that members share (see also Eloire's chapter in the present volume). More importantly, he looks into the role of contextual factors, determined by the transmission and distribution of various types of material and non-material resources, and into the differential effect they exert on agents' power to build networks, form groups and promote social change. We return to these issues in the next section where we discuss in more detail the ways in which these 'connections' can reproduce the differential distribution of material and non-material resources across social groups, and at the same time influence the struggles among groups for the re-distribution of resources and the transformation of society.

So, even though Bourdieu is often acknowledged to be an early purveyor of social capital, his radical approach was subsequently lost. With the increasing influence of both neoliberalism and rational choice methodology, especially in US sociology and political theory, Bourdieu's notion of social capital was discarded from the contemporary social capital literature and replaced by the rational choice perspectives adopted by the sociologist James Coleman (1988), the political scientist Robert Putnam (1993b) and the economist Gary Becker (1996). As a result, recent literature tends to round up the symbolic and the cultural into the social, and equally drop the class and contextual content for universal notions of any collectivity across time and place (Fine 2010: 4). Eventually, it is Bourdieu and his radical conception of social capital that constitute the 'missing link' in the theory and practice of development research.

Some attempts to bring Bourdieu back in appear in the works of Svendsen and Svendsen (2003, 2009) and Lin (1999, 2001). However, their 'neo-capital theories' fail to take distance from mainstream implications and applications of transaction costs, economic growth and social networks. In these theories, any kind of 'change' in society appears to take place at the individual level, given the social structures within which individuals interact. At best, as Lin predicts, labourers will become capitalists by investing in the human and cultural capital that the market offers returns to. Such conclusions are unable to grasp Bourdieu's perception of social transformation, as we shall see in the next section. For even when he spoke of economic calculations and strategic choices hidden behind cultural and social activities, Bourdieu did not rule out the presence of alternative contexts and interests, beyond those implied by rational choice, that participate in social struggles and change. Ultimately, these 'neo-theories' miss the complexities of the relation between habitus and field in the Bourdieusian context (for a detailed analysis, see Christoforou 2014).

As a final note, Bebbington (2007) wonders whether Bourdieu's notion of social capital, understood as product and producer of cultural and political economy, has any chance of travelling into development policy. He agrees that Bourdieu's analysis provides distinct ways of reconceptualising social capital to incorporate considerations of network resources. A deeper understanding of network relations would shed light on contextual factors, which highlight the historically, geographically and ideologically situated aspects of social capital. More importantly, it would draw attention to the 'downside' of social capital, as social groups function to produce prejudice and social exclusion, sustain dominant worldviews, and reinforce existing hierarchical and unequal social structures (156–157). However, Bebbington purports that, even if Bourdieu's conflict-based reading of social capital is useful in critiquing and re-assessing contemporary perceptions of social capital and development policy, his failure to analyse the emergence of 'disinterested, cooperative or solidaristic action' is an issue that needs to be investigated further (160). Apparently, it is Bebbington that fails to foresee the transformative capacity of Bourdieu's notion of capital.

In fact, one of the functions of Bourdieu's field theory is to eliminate the opposition between reproduction and transformation, statics and dynamics (Wacquant 1989: 36–37; Lebaron 2003: 561). We discuss this in more detail in the sections that follow.

Reflections on Bourdieu's approach to capital and transformation

The forms of capital

As mentioned previously, most authors in the literature adopt a rational choice approach. This offers a narrow interpretation of the profits that adhere to the individual by virtue of his/her membership in certain groups. Norms and networks are reduced to outcomes of economic calculation, so the transformation of social groups and structures can only partly be explained. In the present section, we engage in an in-depth reading of some of Bourdieu's articles to discuss the aspects of social capital that have been overlooked. We shall see how social capital influences the structuring of society not independently, but in conjunction with the other forms of capital, namely economic, cultural and symbolic capital. Furthermore, we explore from a Bourdieusian perspective the contextual factors that are at play. These factors are determined by the transmission and distribution of the various forms of capital and contribute to the formation of groups as the driving force of social struggle and change.

We begin with 'The Forms of Capital' (Bourdieu 1986a).[2] In this article, Bourdieu describes the forms of capital he usually refers to across his works, namely economic, cultural, social and symbolic capital. Generally, for Bourdieu, capital is accumulated labour – in its materialised, objectified form or its incorporated, embodied form – which, when appropriated on a private basis by agents or groups, enables them to appropriate social energy in the form of reified or living labour (1986a: 242). Also, capital contains a tendency to persist in its being, as a force inscribed in the objectivity of things, by a specifically political action of concerted conservation, namely demobilisation and depoliticisation, which keeps the dominated 'united' by 'orchestrating' their dispositions and individual acts (242; 255, fn. 1). As such, capital and power amount to the same thing (243). In this regard, Bourdieu does not depart from Marxist conceptions of capital. He takes the argument further by asserting that economic production and exchange should not be conceived as a unique source of capital and power: for instance, social networks constitute forms of social capital, whereas educational qualifications represent instituted forms of cultural capital, which endow agents and groups with various powers, interests and strategies that are not reducible to those derived from economic capital (241–242, 252–253).

Furthermore, the real efficacy of capital depends on the unequal distribution of the means of appropriation and of the power to impose the laws of the functioning of the field that are most favourable to the reproduction of capital. The symbolic efficacy of capital lies in the logic of its transmission, especially across generations. The transmission of social and cultural capital receives a proportionately greater weight in the reproduction strategies of agents and groups (see Bourdieu's article in this book for a detailed coverage of reproduction strategies). This is because the transmission of these forms of capital is heavily disguised, or even invisible, compared to the transmission of economic capital that tends to be more direct and visible and thus more strongly censored and controlled. Indeed, these mechanisms exemplify the role played by the family and the educational system in the socialisation of individuals and the 'unconscious' acquisition of these forms of capital. Also they allow those who possess such forms of capital to conceal their underlying interest through a symbolism that makes them look disinterested. This is particularly the case for the field of cultural production, such as art or science, which is presented in opposition to the field of economic production, such as business or finance, where economic interest appears in its restricted sense as the self-interested pursuit of monetary profit (242, 244–246).

Thus, forms of social and cultural capital are predisposed to function as symbolic capital. This means that they are to be unrecognised as capital and misrecognised as legitimate competence and authority, when they are actually employed by agents and groups endowed with these forms of capital to serve their interests, produce profits and sustain power. Of course, this is also true for economic capital, which, despite its material state, contains aspects of symbolic capital, because it is subject to processes of misrecognition that legitimise structures of ownership and distribution (245; 255, fn. 3, 17). Often authors have taken such mechanisms of social transmission and symbolic processes of misrecognition to provide support to a 'reproductionist theory'. However, it is precisely these mechanisms and processes that bear the dynamics for contradiction with and transformation of dominant values and institutions.

Indeed, capital exists as symbolically and materially active, effective capital insofar as it is appropriated by agents and implemented as a stake in the struggles that take place not only in specific fields (e.g. field of cultural production, such as art and science), but also in the field of the social classes in the global social space. That is, similar to Marxist notions, capital is only as such if it is used as a stake in the struggles between the dominant and the dominated, between conservation and transformation. For Bourdieu, however, there is no one-for-one correspondence between immaterial forms of capital and economic capital: even though social and cultural capital are to a certain extent determined by economic capital, they are not reducible to it, especially when agents can obtain them by relying on various resources beyond economic capital, or even more so when they can convert them into economic capital (247, 252–253). Moreover, agents and classes struggle to maximise their material as much as their symbolic profit, which 'consists in the fact of feeling justified in being (what one is) and being what it is right to be' (Bourdieu 1979 trans. Nice 1984: 228).

In particular, social capital is portrayed not as a natural or even social given, but as a product of an unceasing effort of sociability, a continuous series of material and symbolic exchanges, like bequests and gifts, between the members of a network that can secure material profits – such as all types of services accruing from useful relationships – and symbolic profits – such as those derived from association with a prestigious group. Even though these exchanges reproduce the group by recognising and reaffirming the group's membership and limits, new entries that seek to benefit through some form of misalliance (e.g. matrimony 'outside' of one's class or league) can modify the group by modifying the limits of legitimate exchange (1986a: 250–251).

Likewise, cultural capital, either in its embodied form (as cultivation and manners), in its objectified form (as books, paintings, photos, instruments and machines) or in its instituted form (as educational qualifications), can be appropriated materially and symbolically. For example, the acquisition of educational qualifications depends on the social capital developed through familial and community ties, which offer access to an inherited stock of both cultural and economic capital. Since all agents do not have the resources for prolonging their children's education, social divisions can be reproduced by the scarcity value that cultural capital derives and the material and symbolic profits of distinction that it yields for its owner. In fact, agents who derive profit from their own cultural capital, but do not possess the means of production in the strict economic sense, are classified among the dominated groups; they are opposed to those who draw their profit from economic capital and are classified among the dominant groups. Nonetheless, holders of cultural capital can increase their collective strength as the cultural capital incorporated in the means of production increases (247).

Given that economic capital remains a dominant type of capital and one of the principal means of reproduction (247, 252), similar to Marxist notions of capital, Bourdieu expresses his concerns with regard to the potential of cultural capital to actually challenge the power and privilege of economic capital and provoke a change in social structures. The holders of economic capital might set the holders of cultural capital in competition with one another by attaching a monetary value to different levels of qualification and legitimising a pecuniary reward for cultural production (that is, by converting cultural capital into economic capital) (247, 248). Furthermore, they could use social capital in the form of string-pulling or old boys' networks to correct for the effect of academic sanctions that would arise from questioning social realities, revealing underlying truths, and thus threatening the legitimacy of resources and their transmission (258, fn. 21). Overall, as Bourdieu argues, when the subversive critique, which questions dominance by bringing to light its arbitrariness, is incorporated in institutionalised mechanisms that control the official, direct transmission of power and privilege, the holders of economic capital have a greater interest to resort to better-disguised reproduction strategies that ensure the appropriation of and convertibility with forms of social and cultural capital (254).

Bourdieu adds to this statement that resorting to reproduction strategies that provide better-disguised transmission comes at a cost. Everything that helps to disguise the economic aspect also tends to increase the rate of loss, particularly during intergenerational transfers. On the one hand, forms of cultural capital such as educational qualifications become the condition for the legitimate access to dominant positions, and in this way the educational system tends to increasingly dispossess the group that monopolises the transmission of power and privilege. On the other hand, the declared refusal of calculation and of guarantees in the production of social capital, that is, in social obligations or network relations, necessarily entails the risk of ingratitude or embezzlement (253–254).[3] Thus, non-material forms of social and cultural capital that are meant to conceal the underlying material interest and profit and thus sustain the dominance of economic capital can, at the same time, create an opening to contest and refute its power and privilege. For example, the controversial concept of corporate social responsibility might be used by firms to disguise 'business as usual', guided by conventional practices of maximising monetary profit, especially in a market where consumers have developed 'finer' tastes for ecological considerations and environment-friendly products. Nonetheless, this might also create an opening for more socially oriented production and consumption practices, as agents' continuous efforts in the social and ecological movement would compel firms to take further measure for the satisfaction of community needs and the preservation of the environment.

One might argue that even the social and ecological organisations will be comprised of agents who participate in networks to serve their own hidden agenda and influence the effectiveness of the social movement, because the pursuit of a self-oriented interest, based on economic calculation and strategic choice, remains paramount. Throughout his work, Bourdieu points to the existence of interests beyond those dictated by a restricted sense of economic capital. Specifically in 'The Forms of Capital', he argues that the profits which accrue to membership in a social group or network are the basis of the solidarity which makes these profits possible (249). Yet he emphasises that investment in social capital is not necessarily conceived as a calculated pursuit of gain, but is experienced in terms of an involvement, which is necessary, emotional and disinterested. Even if the most 'sincerely disinterested acts' may be those best corresponding to objective interest and the essential principles of the field, especially in the field of cultural production (255, fn. 18), this does not rule out the existence of differentiated interests that could challenge the values and institutions that sustain the power and privilege of capital.

Generally, symbolic practices should not be conceived of as explicit strategies of domination or 'calculated acts of class appeasement' (249, 255, fn. 18). Bourdieu offers the example of national liberation movements and ideologies, which cannot be accounted for solely by reference to economic profits derived from wealth redistribution and highly paid jobs. These profits would only explain the nationalism of the privileged classes. For those who are lower down the social hierarchy and thus more threatened by the economic and social decline, Bourdieu suggests that we add the very real and very immediate profits derived from membership and solidarity (255, fn. 14).

In this article, there are questions that remain unanswered: What are these real and immediate profits that are derived from membership and accrue to those who are lower down the social hierarchy? Are these profits the kind of benefits that provide those threatened most by economic and social decline with some of the resources they need to 'get by' or with the power they need to 'get on'? Can social groups account for alternative interpretations of the social world, which would help agents to promote the redistribution of resources and the restructuring of the social space?

Symbolic power and the genesis of groups

We derive a more elaborate presentation of the conditions for social transformation and the role of social groups mainly from three articles: 'The Social Space and the Genesis of Groups' (Bourdieu 1984c trans. Nice 1985), 'Social Space and Symbolic Power' (Bourdieu 1987b trans. Wacquant 1989) and 'What Makes a Social Class? On the Theoretical and Practical Existence of Groups' (Bourdieu 1987c). Here social change is determined by struggles for symbolic power, that is, the power to produce and impose a vision and division of the social world, and thus to preserve or transform objective principles of classification, association and dissociation, in matters such as gender, nation, region, age, and social status or class, through the language used to designate or to describe individuals, groups or institutions. Put differently, symbolic power, perceived in its multiple forms as both common-sense knowledge (e.g. 'folk theories') and scientific social theories,[4] is the power to change the ways of world-making, to make groups and manipulate the objective structure of society. Hence, symbolic struggles are political struggles *par excellence*, since they involve the theoretical and practical struggle for the power to conserve or transform the social world by conserving or transforming the categories through which it is perceived. In this sense, according to Bourdieu, symbolic power becomes a power of constitution or construction of society, and the diverse forms of capital play a crucial role in this process.

To begin with, Bourdieu argues that social reality identifies not with substances, but with relations (Bourdieu 1984c trans. Nice 1985: 723; Bourdieu 1987b trans. Wacquant 1989: 15–16). The social world can be represented objectively as a symbolic space which is organised according to the logic of differentiation and distinction, by what one owns in terms of material assets, but also by what one drinks, how one speaks or whom one associates with.[5] The active properties selected as principles of construction of the social space are the different kinds of capital that are active in the different social fields. The distribution of different forms of capital defines the state of power relations in the global social space, as well as within the different social fields. The global social space is described as a field of power. It is characterised by the power relations between different kinds of capital, or between the agents who possess a sufficient amount of one kind of capital (especially cultural capital and economic capital) and are in a position not only to dominate the corresponding field, but also to question the relative value or exchange rate between the different forms of capital and impose the principle of social differentiation in the global social space (Bourdieu 1994a trans. Johnson *et al.* 1998: 32–34). In these struggles, agents rely on their symbolic power, which is the specific form of symbolic capital in the field of power (Bourdieu 1984c trans. Nice 1985: 724–725, 729; Bourdieu 1987b trans. Wacquant 1989: 19–20).

The social world is not only comprised of relations between groups based on certain material and non-material principles of differentiation and distinction that determine one's position in the social space. Social reality is also determined by the relation between habitus and field, a relation which operates in two ways: it is a relation of 'conditioning' as the field structures the habitus; and it is a relation of knowledge or cognitive construction as the habitus contributes to constituting the field as a world of meaning, endowed with sense and value (Wacquant 1989: 43–44). Therefore, the perception of the social world is the product of a double structuring: on the objective side, it is structured by the unequal distribution of properties attributed to individuals, which pertain to the field; on the subjective side, it is structured by the schemes of perception and appreciation, especially those deposited in language, which relate to the habitus (Bourdieu 1984c trans. Nice 1985: 727–728; Bourdieu 1987b trans. Wacquant 1989: 20).

However, Bourdieu stresses that the objects of the social world can be perceived and uttered in different ways, because they always entail a degree of indeterminacy, uncertainty and plurality. On the objective side, the plurality of visions and divisions is due to the relative indeterminacy of the reality which offers itself to perception; on the subjective side, it is due to the plurality of the principles of visions and divisions that are available at a certain moment and are based on different criteria beyond the economic (Bourdieu 1987c: 11). For instance, even though social groupings, which are grounded in the structure of the space and constructed in terms of capital distribution, are more likely to be stable and durable, this does not exclude the possibility of organising agents in accordance with other principles of division – ethnic, religious, national, etc. Moreover, as historical objects, they may be subject to variations in time, so that their meaning, insofar as it depends on the future, is open to alternative perceptions of the social world. Therefore, even though social position, adequately defined, gives the best prediction of practices and representations, status and habitus, these are social objects that can be changed with more or less difficulty by history (Bourdieu 1984c trans. Nice 1985: 726, 728, 739; Bourdieu 1987b trans. Wacquant 1989: 20). This provides a basis for symbolic struggles over the production of the common-sense or over the power to impose the legitimate vision of the social world.

Still, according to Bourdieu, symbolic struggles have a specific logic which endows them with a real autonomy from the structures in which they are rooted, and determines their effectiveness in the transformation of these structures.

First, all the symbolic strategies through which agents seek to impose their perception of the social world and their position within it, can be located between two extremes:

1 In one extreme, we observe the insult, or 'idios logos', with which an individual tries to impose his own point of view at the risk of reciprocity and retaliation.

2 In the other extreme, we have the power of legitimate or official nomination, which identifies with an act of symbolic imposition – or symbolic violence. It is ultimately performed by a delegated agent of the State and incorporated in the official principle of vision and division, the word of law, or 'nomos' (1984c trans. 1985: 731–732; 1987b trans. 1989: 21; 1987c: 13).

Second, symbolic struggles over the perception of the social world may take two distinct forms (1984c trans. 1985: 726, 729, 732; 1987b trans. 1989: 20–21):

1 On the objective side, one may act by ways of representation, collective or individual, to display alternative realities. At the collective level, agents may participate in demonstrations to make a group exist visibly, while at the individual level they may apply strategies of presentation that manipulate one's self-image and position in the social space. For instance, though there is more chance of mobilising the set of workers than the set composed of workers and employers, it is possible, in an international crisis, to provoke a grouping on the basis of links of national identity, which redefines the national social space and the hierarchical distances within the economic field.
2 On the subjective side, one may act by trying to transform categories of perception and appreciation of the social world, and change the cognitive and evaluative structures through which it is constrained. At the individual level, agents are endlessly occupied in the negotiation of their own identity by means of accusation against the state or other groups and institutions (*kathegorein* – or accuse – via 'categorisation'). At the collective level, they can use strategies of political struggle that aim at imposing a new construction of social reality by jettisoning the old political vocabulary designed to describe the social world. The capacity to make entities exist in the explicit state, to publish and make public what had not previously attained objective and collective existence, represents a formidable social power.

Third, the way in which symbolic power obtains the capacity to impose alternative visions and provoke social change rests on two conditions (1984c trans. 1985: 741; 1987b trans. 1989: 22–23):

1 Symbolic power has to be based on the possession of symbolic capital, that is, it depends on the social authority agents have acquired in previous struggles. Symbolic capital is a power granted to those who have obtained sufficient recognition to be in a position to impose recognition. In this way, the power of constitution, a power to make a group by speaking on behalf of the group as an authorised spokesperson, is the outcome of a long process of institutionalisation.
2 Symbolic efficacy depends on the degree to which the vision proposed is founded in the objective relations that bring agents together and are determined by the distribution of the various forms of capital (field) and by the

> internalisation of these structures (habitus). In this sense, symbolic power becomes the power to consecrate or reveal, to know and recognise what is already *there*, not something that is outside of these realities. Politics is the site *par excellence* of symbolic efficacy, the action that can promote alternative meanings of the social world and produce social objects and groups.

As Bourdieu puts it, the problem of social change, whereby dominated visions can be constituted and come to prevail in social struggles, is one of knowing how to obtain the power for *legitimate naming* or the power *over words* used to describe groups or the institutions that represent them. He argues that: 'words can make things and, by joining in the objectivised symbolisation of the group they designate, they can, if only for a time, make exist *as groups*, collectives which already existed, but only in a potential state' (1987c: 16). The dominated have a practical mastery, a practical knowledge of the social world, which can exert an effect of revelation and constitute a creative power, because it represents a vision of the social world that is grounded in reality. But the task lies in the hands of the 'ministerium', the spokesperson or representative of the group, who carries the 'mysterium', that is, the means to contribute to the making of the group and the social world: the slogan, the watchword, the command, or even his/her mere existence. In this way, people recognise and identify themselves as members of a class, a trade union or a nation, and mobilise to pursue the interests of the group. The work of symbolic production and the function of making-explicit, particularly in times of crisis, confer on collective representatives major political functions.

By means of what Bourdieu terms homology, those who occupy the dominated positions within the social space are also located in the dominated positions in the field of symbolic production,[6] which imposes further constraints on their potential to promote the (re)construction of the social world. Yet it is the specific logic of cultural production that can provide the means for challenging the representations that reproduce social structures. Professionals in the field of cultural production, such as academics and particularly sociologists and social theorists, provide a theoretical mastery or objectified representations of the social world (or, more precisely, of methods of objectification) and, therefore, give power to the truth that has been concealed by the dominant (1984c trans. 1985: 729, 735–736; 1987b trans. 1989: 23–24; 1987c: 15–16). The crucial role Bourdieu reserves for producers or creators of 'cultural capital' lies in the constitution of the 'collective' intellectual, whereby writers, artists, philosophers and scientists make their voice heard directly in all areas of public life. Professionals would fulfil their function of public service by means of argumentation and refutation, which characterise the logic of intellectual life. In this way, they contest the logic of political life, which is determined by denunciation and slander, 'sloganisation' and falsification of the adversary's thought (Bourdieu 1998a trans. Nice 1998: 9).

Hence, knowledge not only buttresses the hierarchies of the social world; it can also be an effective part of the struggle to change that world, even if it is never produced from a standpoint outside it (Calhoun 2013). At the same time, Bourdieu points out that professionals must take caution and avoid the 'illusion of the lector'. In other words, one must not show excessive confidence in the power of language, and thus 'regard an academic commentary as a political act or the critique of texts as a feat of resistance, and experience revolutions in the order of words as radical revolutions in the order of things' (Bourdieu 1997a trans. Nice 2000: 2). Indeed, for Bourdieu (1987c: 7–8) the movement from probability to reality, from theoretical class to practical class, that is, the politics and political work of imposing a principle of vision and division of the social world, is never given, even if it is well-founded in reality. This is because the principles of vision and division of the social world, which are employed for the construction of theoretical classes and are supported by the affinity of the habitus, will have to compete with other principles – ethnic, racial, national, communal and occupational. Moreover, the political work aimed at producing classes in the form of objective institutions has its own specific logic, that of symbolic production, which supplies these institutions with recognition and legitimacy through representation, symbols, acronyms and constituents. In this way, classes and social groups in general are a genuine product of history, borne out of the action of interest groups and sanctioned by legal consecration.

For instance, as Bourdieu argues, 'the working class' has come into existence only inasmuch as agents, including trade unions, social movements and social theorists such as Marx, have historically transformed what could have remained an 'analytical construct' into a folk category. Yet Marxist theory does not describe the process whereby a 'group in struggle', a personalised collective and a historical agent assigning itself its own ends, arises from the objective economic conditions. On the basis of the knowledge of the social space, one can separate out classes, that is, sets of agents who occupy similar positions, and therefore are more likely to have similar dispositions and interests, practices and stances. However, this does not suffice to shed light on the processes of transition from a constructed to an actual class. In Marxist theory, these processes are assumed to arise inevitably and naturally from an 'awakening of consciousness' determined solely by the similarity in economic conditions and the enlightened guidance of the Party (Bourdieu 1984c trans. Nice 1985: 725; 1987b trans. Wacquant 1989: 17–18; 1987c: 7).

Therefore, representatives of groups, social scientists included, are those who take lead in the political action for the creation or the 'construction' of groups, and coordinate the process by which classes on paper become real classes, or by which objective constructs finally become a subjective perception, individually and collectively. If, as mentioned previously, social capital, as resources based on connections and group membership, is very strongly correlated with symbolic capital, then there is a role for social capital in the process of social transformation. This lies in communicating 'the word' through network relations not only to reveal the vices of established social structures that sustain relations of discrimination and subordination; but also to make groups, to invite members to recognise the virtues of cooperation and solidarity and to persuade them, through the 'mastery' of collective representatives and social scientists, to seize their powers and pursue social change.

Groups and desynchronisation: some thoughts

Beyond the struggles for symbolic power, there are certain conditions in the social space that enable agents and groups to exploit opportunities for social change. One of the major sources of change discussed by Bourdieu lies in the desynchronisation of habitus and field.

The field represents the objective social structures that depend on the distribution of capital and determine agents' economic and social conditions and positions, whereas agents' habitus identifies with the internalised, embodied social structures that are converted into a disposition, which generates meaningful practices and meaning-giving perceptions, subjectively experienced and objectively attuned to the differences between conditions and positions. Thus, the dialectic between field and habitus forms the basis which transforms the distribution of capital and the structure of power relations into a system of perceived differences, a distribution of symbolic capital, or legitimate capital, which makes social differences appear natural, but whose objective truth remains misrecognised (Bourdieu 1979 trans. Nice 1984: 170–172).[7]

A desynchronised habitus and field creates a crisis whereby the habitus fails to generate those practices and perceptions of practices that accord to the objective structures of the field. This could be a result of: innovative strategies adopted by the dominant and the dominated of the field; new entrants whose habitus has been formed in other fields or contexts; struggles within the field that lead to a redefinition of the boundaries between fields; demographic, cultural and economic shocks, that is, social changes that appeared far more rapidly than the habitus can adapt to, hence phenomena of hysteresis. Such events can change or even radically transform what had previously been determined and can open up struggles for the reconstruction of agents and groups and the redefinition of the principles that structure the field or its institutional architecture. It is clear that the destabilisation of a field is not a very frequent phenomenon, but it would be an error to conclude that every single field is the scene of a reproduction *ad infinitum* of the same structure (Adkins 2003; Wacquant 2004; Boyer 2008).[8]

To show the dynamics of desynchronisation between habitus and field and the struggles of agents and groups to reconstruct the social world, Bourdieu studies four major social transformations that took place in the course of history (Calhoun 2013): (1) The way state power and market expansion and intensification produced a deracination of traditional ways of life – specifically peasant life – in the Kabylia tribe of Algeria and in his own native region of Béarn in the Pyrénées Mountains of Southwest France. (2) The creation of modern society by the differentiation of state and market power and more generally by the making of the fields as a domain of relative autonomy marked off from others by distinctive hierarchy, values, struggles, life-styles and forms of capital. (3) The great economic expansion and welfare state project of the post-World War II era, called in France *Les Trente Glorieuses*, a period that promised greater equality, opportunity and participation, but also reproduced old inequalities in new contexts and structures and often legitimated them by apparent meritocracy and the logic of individual responsibility. (4) Neoliberalism portended a destruction of social fields, especially those dependent on public support, and a violent reduction of the pursuit of different values to the market logic. This turned Bourdieu's attention more directly to what the different fields and the State itself had achieved, and what hopes they still offered, despite the limits imposed by their frequent conservatism.

What is important to note in these transformations is that they do not follow from the mere reformulation of habitus to accommodate an ever-changing field. According to Bourdieu, the habitus is not only a structured structure, as the product of the internalisation of objective social structures and divisions, but also a structuring structure, as a generative principle of practices and perceptions of practices (Bourdieu 1979 trans. Nice 1984: 170). He argues that to understand the habitus and its capacity to generate products – thoughts, perceptions, expressions and actions – one must transcend the usual antinomies of determinism and freedom, conditioning and creativity, consciousness and the unconscious, or the individual and society (Bourdieu 1980g trans. Nice 1992: 54–55). The habitus implies practices and perceptions of practices that can be objectively regulated without being the product of obedience to rules; that objectively adapt to their goals without a conscious aiming at ends; and that are collectively orchestrated without being the product of an orchestrating act of a conductor.[9] Thus, practices cannot be directly deduced either from the objective conditions or from the principle that produced them; they can be accounted for only by relating the objective structure defining the social conditions that produced the habitus, to the contextually defined conditions in which this habitus is operating and which represent a particular state of the structure, objectively adjusted to alternative practices and their principles. Language is one such example of the relation between official, grammatical rule and implicit, practical necessity (Bourdieu 1972b trans. Nice 1977, 27th edn 2012: 28, 78–79).

Returning to our discussion on development programmes, we argue that these projects can better serve their objectives for empowerment of disadvantaged groups if researchers, practitioners and policy-makers recognise and uncover the influence of persisting hierarchical structures and power relations. Their efforts must be accompanied by change in people's perceptions of what constitutes 'collective' interests, and how the 'collective' power of dominated groups can be resumed and reclaimed for their own benefit, rather than be further manipulated by dominant groups to perpetuate conditions of hierarchy and inequality. Therefore, researchers, practitioners and representatives of social movements that act at a local and global scale[10] must create networks and invest in forms of political struggle to raise social awareness and promote a new 'vision' of the social world. This is consistent with key elements of Bourdieu's approach to social transformation, which relies on processes of symbolic re-orientation, political competition and network relations, led by dominated groups and supported by scholars and activists, to reveal the truth of inequality and subordination, which is concealed by dominant forces in order to sustain existing social structures.

Some concluding remarks

In this chapter, our main task was to provide the basis for an alternative theoretical framework in the study of social capital as a source for social transformation. To this end, we reflected on Bourdieu's approach to shed light on the contextual factors that are at play and determined by the transmission and distribution of other forms of capital. We argue that in the contemporary social capital literature and in the social sciences in general limited attention has been given to Bourdieu's notion of capital, especially forms of social, cultural and symbolic capital, as an active part in processes of social transformation. Instead, rational choice explanations of network-building, social participation and collective action prevailed and reduced these processes to a product of economic calculation. This resulted in naïve applications of social capital in community-based and -driven development programmes, led mainly by the World Bank, which overlooked the impact of hierarchical social structures on the unequal distribution of capital and power, and ultimately failed to achieve its main objectives for the empowerment of the poor. Our aim is to go beyond these explanations by adopting a Bourdieusian perspective.

Indeed, the social space is characterised by forces of preservation and conservation exerted by the structure of the field (i.e. by the possession and distribution of the different forms of capital), and by the transmission mechanisms of misrecognition and symbolic violence (i.e. by processes of internalisation and legitimation). Yet these very social conditions are those that create opportunities for social transformation, as symbolic dimensions of capital, located particularly in immaterial forms of social and cultural capital, carry forces of contestation and resistance, through the re-evaluation and re-making of groups that serve multiple and diverse interests and express alternative principles of perception and practice of public welfare. Bourdieu's framework of social transformation can explain the failures of prior development projects and guide our efforts to enhance the role of dominated groups by building networks of local groups and professionals with an obligation to voice local needs and reconstitute social structures to preserve social welfare.

Surely we do not claim to have covered the richness or uncovered the complexity of Bourdieu's analysis on social change and the role played by the diverse forms of capital. There are two crucial aspects of this analysis that require further research: one is Bourdieu's conception of reflexivity, whereby agents develop the capacity to shape the habitus of the field and thus the field itself, particularly at times of crisis; another is the specific mechanisms that relate the 'makings' and 'workings' of groups to the social resources they have access to, such as networks and their underlying norms and connections.

Moreover, if we are to re-introduce Bourdieu's approach in social capital research, we must engage with the essentially transformative dimensions of his notion of capital. Here we focused on sketching the theoretical foundations of Bourdieu's analysis to gain a better understanding of these dimensions. However, a great deal more research needs to be done by consulting his empirical works from his early 'Algerian' studies to his later activist writings against neoliberalism. There one can see the transformative nature of his own way of thinking, and thus unravel the Ariadne's clue for developing a fuller account of his much neglected and misunderstood approach.

Notes

1 Asimina Christoforou has a PhD in economics and does research on topics such as social capital, economic and regional development, European integration, ethics in economics, voluntary associations and social institutions. She has taught at the Athens University of Economics and Business (Greece), the University of Crete (Greece) and Boğaziçi University (Turkey). Some of her publications include: 'On the identity of social capital and the social capital of identity', *Cambridge Journal of Economics*, 2013, 37(4): 719–736; 'Social capital, inequality and power from a Bourdieusian perspective', in A. Christoforou and J. B. Davis (eds), *Social Capital and Economics: Social Values, Power and Social Identity* (Routledge, forthcoming). The author would like to thank Wolfram Elsner and Peter Kriesler, editors of the Routledge book series, and participants of the AHE/FAPE/IIPPE Conference (Paris, July 5-8, 2012, panel on 'Pierre Bourdieu and his contribution to economics') for their wholehearted support and constructive comments. The editors would like to thank Vassilis Balkizas for his invaluable assistance in preparing the index.

2 This is one of Bourdieu's most cited works in the literature for his nuanced definition of social capital, but rarely for anything beyond that.

3 What is referred to as 'ingratitude' and 'embezzlement' within the context of established social structures and obligations might actually concur to a break with these structures. For example, within a partitocratic system, especially in the ranks of the public sector, a breach of loyalty to the political party might be considered by members as an act of 'ingratitude' and 'embezzlement' from the part of the instigator, who ceases to receive further support from party cadres and is banned from the echelons of the public sector. However, the 'instigator' might have simply showed resistance to submit to party cadres' means and objectives, because he/she may believe their influence overrides considerations of fairness and favours special interests. It may even be to his/her knowledge that the party cadres can legitimately justify their reaction by appealing to 'the word of law', which has been constructed in accordance to their requirements.

4 Bourdieu (1987c: 10–11) stresses that ideologies, preconceptions and folk theories that the objectivist, theoreticist rupture set aside to construct the objectivist space of social positions must be brought back into the model of social reality, because they participate in the struggle for imposing alternative visions and divisions of the social world and thus contribute to the construction of that very world.

5 The social space thus tends to function as a space of life-styles and status groups characterised by different life-styles.

6 Bourdieu (1977e trans. Nice 1979: 80, 81) defines the field of symbolic production as 'a microcosm of the symbolic struggles between the classes'. The different classes pursue these struggles either directly in the symbolic struggles of daily life or through the struggles between the specialists of symbolic production, like academics and artists.

7 For example, as mentioned previously, the field of cultural production requires a habitus oriented to a kind of disinterestedness.

8 For a superb account of such changes in the context of the current financial crisis, we refer the reader to chapters by Boyer, Grenfell and Lebaron in the present volume.

9 Bourdieu illustrates this by bringing forth the polysemous nature of the word 'rule', as expressed in Wittgenstein's question: What do I call 'the rule by which one proceeds'? He clearly argues of the naïveties of legalism, which sees practices as the product of obedience to rules, and of intellectualism, which transfers the scientific objective truth into a practice which, by its essence, rules out the stance of an imposed theoretical model (Bourdieu 1972b trans. Nice 1977, 27th edn 2012: 27, 29).

10 One might wonder what role is left for the various forms of capital in light of mass movements. These movements historically rely on the dynamics of associational interaction and reaction at a lower level in order to organise collective action and political struggle at a larger scale. On the other hand, movements that have a history and wider representation have the capacity and power to collaborate with local associations and give them the leverage they need to promote their own means and objectives to confront their contextual constraints.

Part V

Politics and policies

How to transform the world

13 The sociology of domination

Critical perspectives

Franck Poupeau[1]

Introduction

Would Marx have written *Das Kapital* had it not been for the insurrectional and organisational context of the times in which he lived? The simplicity of such a question suggests that the project to 'rebuild the left' will not emerge from the brilliant reflections of enlightened intellectuals working calmly in their offices, but will, instead, be fuelled by the sound and fury of social struggles that find an echo in certain intellectual spheres that support them. In fact, today, left criticism is not lacking in contact with the militant world, a nebulous configuration that encompasses not only committed researchers (who often have no partisan filiations but are nevertheless often in touch with anti-capitalist organisations), but also militant publishers and professional militants (attached to associations or unions) involved in intellectual struggles against neoliberalism.

And yet, over the last twenty years, left criticism in France has found it difficult to mobilise support in areas other than identity politics and the defence of public services. With the possible exception of protests against the CPE (First Job Contract) in 2006, the social movements that emerged after the strikes that swept France in 1995 constitute a sad litany of political defeats, not only because of the intransigence of the government but also because of a lack of popular support. The eventual failure of the various strikes against the supposed pension and social security reforms throughout the first decade of the century in France, and the difficulties encountered by the Indignados and Occupy movements at the beginning of the decade in arousing – in spite of the importance of the debates about inequality that they promoted – anything other than a well-circumscribed media interest, express the impotence of these social movements and their analysts in the face of the current economic system and the 'inevitable' austerity programmes by which it is accompanied.

Beyond the failures of recent protest movements, one has to ask why there is no *mobilising* alternative to capitalism and, more precisely, why protest movements and the social criticism that they express have so far failed to provide a counterweight capable of modifying the institutional and intellectual orientations of governments and leaders – particularly those of the social-liberal left – in a political field overdetermined by electoral issues. The tendency to believe that merely condemning the misdeeds of capitalism is enough to persuade the rest of the population to share in its 'refusal' of that system and make 'a different world' possible prevents left criticism from taking into account the biases that affect its perspective on social reality, a field that it now explores with the aid of the social sciences, which tend to exclude all analysis of domination from their intellectual and political horizons.

Such an analysis is one of the main contributions of Pierre Bourdieu's sociology, which makes it possible to examine the reasons for which a certain type of left criticism which contents itself with ritually denouncing the ravages of capitalism has managed to paint itself into a corner. However correct its tenets may be, the approach applied by this current of thought is unable to generate automatically actions subverting the established order, since consent to that order is not merely an affair of reason or self-interest. According to Bourdieu, consent is inscribed in the heart of bodily dispositions, a notion described by the concept of the *habitus* (Bourdieu 1980g, 1997a). It was with a view to explaining the mystery of the dominated classes, who should not exist, that Bourdieu forged the notion of symbolic violence, an invisible violence contained in the self-evident nature of the existing order conveyed by schemas of thought supported by language and institutions. Every time a judgment seems 'natural' or 'obvious', there is a high probability that it masks an implicit vision of the social order and, consequently, contributes to perpetuating it. Symbolic violence goes beyond physical constraint: it encompasses the contribution that the dominated classes make to their own domination by accepting the categories of perception and analysis that occlude the arbitrary nature of the established order, categories by which the principles of vision and division of the social world are imposed. Bourdieu's sociology thus represents a break with theories according to which revolt is based on a spontaneous flowering of awareness, and which consequently ignore the effects of symbolic violence. But the domination effects outlined in Bourdieu's theory are not ineluctable and the objective of this chapter is to study the conditions of access to politicisation, arguing against essentialist interpretative approaches that share with mainstream economics the vision of the individual as an informed, lucid and calculating 'actor'.

It is in this perspective that an entire current of thought developed, the advocates of which assimilate the sociology of domination to the domination that, they claim, sociologists exert over the 'ignorant', a category supposedly coterminous with the 'People'. The social sciences, a field previously decried for its emancipatory pretentions, is now accused by various currents of left criticism of appropriating a monopoly of knowledge with a view to legitimising its own existence and its position in the social space. However simplistic it may be, such an accusation is, perhaps, symptomatic of the fact that, leaving to one side the disputes that have always characterised the radical factions of the intellectual world – struggles the main motive of which, need we recall, is to define what a 'left intellectual' is today – sociology is confronted with a genuine problem, a problem that cannot be reduced to a mere breakdown in communication.

Of course, left criticism likes to use the intellectual tools of the social sciences in order to gain an understanding of what it terms 'contemporary social problems'. Alas, it often selects a kind of sociology whose orientations remain unquestioned, whether in terms of its political presuppositions or the methods associated with them. This is 'state sociology', characterised by a mainstream approach emphasising the importance of 'actors' and their 'capacities for action'.[2] This defence of the independence of individuals in regard to contextual determinisms leads, in the end, to an overemphasis on their personal responsibility for their social destiny, while at the same time ignoring – conveniently enough – the mechanisms of social reproduction perpetuated by the state.

In this sense, state sociology is remarkably well suited to contemporary evolutions in the regulatory systems by which the social world is governed. Although the academics involved in this kind of sociology often think of themselves, in terms of European – and, particularly, French – political classification systems, as being of the 'Left', the kind of approach they take is, according to the same principles, fundamentally of the 'right': if you are poor, scruffy and lacking in qualifications, it is not the state's fault, but, rather, yours – you get what you deserve. But the main particularity of state sociology is that it highlights and promotes the power of negotiation and compromise: in the magic and fluid world of 'actors', conflict does not exist. Everything happens at the local level in spheres of communication in which social conflicts are diluted by dialogue and negotiation, as if sociology were adjusting itself to the needs of 'social rebuilding'. Everything in this world is agreement, contract, governance.

In regard to the education system, for the proponents of state sociology, the fight against inequality takes place exclusively in schools, and the academic failure of students is the sole responsibility of teachers, who should thus be managed in terms of projects and results (Poupeau 2003). In the management of the common goods that are natural resources, the capacity of 'actors' to find local compromises occludes, on the one hand, the problems inherent in articulating national and international administrations with markets – markets for urban water distribution services or any other form of natural resource, such as timber transformed into an economic good[3] – and, on the other, the relationship between economic and political forces governing the implementation of regulations.

State sociology finds its most complete expression in the theories of methodological individualism and the rational actor. An expression of an anthropology of economic liberalism which, as we are now aware, is less concerned with destroying the state than with transforming its modes of action (Dardot and Laval 2010), these theories are born of the programmes of surveillance and social control developed by government administrations following the Second World War (Guilhot 2001; Mirowski 2001). They have since been reprised in the contemporary form of an economic sociology, the self-imposed objective of which is to diagnose social 'malaises' (social divisions, taxation, etc.) and to develop a 'new social criticism'. It is surprising to see those left critics who are apparently the most vehemently opposed to state sociology share its most fundamental presuppositions. While it could be argued, with Luc Boltanski and Ève Chiapello, that criticism always contains something of what it rejects,[4] that is not enough to explain why state sociology has achieved the status of 'common sense' in the French intellectual arena.

The convergence between left criticism and state sociology is based on two presuppositions that function in a complementary fashion. The first implies the rejection of any idea of constructing a scientific object, a notion reduced to the vision of an 'epistemological break' that has very little to do with the way research is really carried out or with its social dimension. This rejection leads to a tacit acceptance of a social philosophy of 'actors' envisaged as subjects free of all determining factors. The second presupposition, which concerns the autonomy of the various 'classes' of the dominated (from the working classes to the masses to the 'indigenous', either of the French Republic or of the 'South') gives rise to a form of 'populist knowledge' (Jeanpierre 2012) that effectively denies the very possibility of any knowledge of the social world emanating from points of view other than those of the 'actors' who compose it. This explains why critics can objectively support a system they believe they are fighting by providing it not only with the 'justifications' it requires to develop a 'new spirit of capitalism', but also by helping it to postpone the idea of emancipation to a future the objective conditions of which it claims, against all evidence to the contrary (crises, debt, bankruptcies, etc.), gradually to be implementing. A future, characterised by superficial 'negotiations', that belongs to 'actors' who attempt, with a heroic perseverance that recalls the travails of Sisyphus, to keep a lid on the tumults provoked by ongoing socio-economic transformations, of which Greece, in the wake of the devastation wrought on Africa, represents Europe's catastrophic avant-garde.

The implications of a sociology of domination

It should be observed that when sociologists attempt to explain 'current problems' by means of an authoritative discourse that recycles rudimentary explanatory schemas – for example, the supposed link between the riots in France in 2005 and urban poverty – they do little to promote a trust-based political relationship between intellectuals and the working classes. First, because the only thing that can be achieved by reducing the social movements in the *banlieues* (lower-classes suburbs) to forms of economic privation – the analytical framework most frequently employed – is to produce somewhat less simplistic 'cultural' interpretations and an 'ethnic' reading of social problems. An example of this is provided by Robert Castel's comment that 'youths from the *banlieues*' are no more 'excluded' from society than they are 'included' in it, in the sense that the economic precariousness with which they are confronted does not cut them off from 'dominant French culture' and the concomitant attractions of consumer society (Castel 2007: 42). Left criticism runs the risk of returning to forms of social philosophy that extol, in the face of contingency, the autonomy of groups such as the 'youths of the *banlieues*', which is one of the root causes of their 'unsatisfactory relationship with citizenship'. From this viewpoint, 'ethno-racial discrimination' in regard to 'visible minorities' leads automatically to a revolt against the government's need to constitute, as in the past, 'dangerous classes' on which all fears can be focused.

In this interpretation, which leans towards culturalism, 'state racism' becomes the indispensable explanatory key to preserving the dignity of struggles reduced to the dimension of ethnic identity: the dominated classes are, in the end, assimilated to 'visible minorities', while the 'silent majority' supposedly votes for the right or is, at least, fundamentally conservative. Here, we can clearly see the degree to which, beyond their apparent differences, the sociologism applied to urban poverty and the culturalism applied to ethnic discrimination contribute to reducing the properly political struggle to an autonomous subject incarnated, in the first case, by the politicised working class, to which the 'youth of the *banlieues*' are said not to belong, and, in the second, by visible minorities, largely constituted by those youths. It is the delimitation of the social frontiers of the working class world that defines which side left critics lean towards.

If the issue at hand is, therefore, to take into account various ways of accepting or rejecting domination, the question to be asked is *why the dominated classes accept, and even contribute to elaborating, in a more or less active way, the modes of domination to which they are subject*. This thesis is not only morally insupportable for critics on the left but also unthinkable for them due to their idealisation of working class milieus and their (pre)supposed autonomy. In presenting the work carried out by sociologists as a monopolisation of power/knowledge and a stigmatisation of the supposed ignorance of the dominated classes, left criticism in effect forbids itself the right to consider the degree to which a knowledge of the mechanisms of domination can constitute a condition of social emancipation.

Paradoxically, the idea that the dominated classes are autonomous leads to a form of populism[5] that, due to its emphasis on the quasi-ontological centrality of the working classes to relationships of exploitation, is not only hostile to identity struggles but also rejects any possibility of a rigorous knowledge of the social world. The emphasis on the autonomy of working class milieus makes it quite simply impossible to understand the difficulties involved in mobilising against the capitalist system in the sense that any appraisal of the contribution of the dominated classes to the relationships of domination in which they are inscribed is strictly off limits. In particular, the inability to take into account the effects of 'symbolic domination' in the sense of a combination of processes of miscognition and recognition of domination, an approach replaced by a vision of the omnipresence of the power and spontaneity of the resistance that supposedly results from them,[6] leads to a neglect of what, in the revolutionary movements of the past, was due to the mobilisation of the most dominated fractions of the population. It is, of course, possible for this kind of spontaneity to emerge in exceptional moments of protest, those during which analysts believe that they are able to grasp the autonomous dynamic of the revolt (Gobille 2008), but an attempt must also be made to inscribe those moments within a wider temporal framework ranging from the construction of an organised popular movement to the exercise of government. On the subject of the role of collective solidarities in the democratisation of modern societies, Catherine Colliot-Thélène speaks of 'the repeated failure of attempts made to install on a long-term basis egalitarian, or, in other words, domination-free communities' (Colliot-Thélène 2011). This brings us back, in Weberian terms, to the impossibility of rendering charisma 'quotidian' and the exceptional nature of revolution.

The question is, therefore, whether or not the social sciences are forever doomed to oscillate between a type of sociological miserablism that is always suspect in terms of its inability to recognise the autonomy of the working classes defined negatively with regard to dominant forms, and a kind of populism that, on the contrary, presupposes such an autonomy in order to confer on the dominated the subversive potential that subaltern, postcolonial and post-modern theories have often sought to highlight, without, however, being able to produce anything other than pure statements of principle spiced up with radical political rhetoric (Grignon and Passeron 1989). These 'populisms of knowledge', as Laurent Jeanpierre (2012: 150–164) calls them in his study of the relationship between political and epistemological forms, have undeniably contributed to anthropology and the social sciences by helping to reveal the ethnocentrism underpinning their approaches and by calling their sometimes complacent positions into question; but they have often done so at the price of a simple inversion of dominant values and styles of thought.

The question of the political effects of the kind of knowledge made accessible by the sociology of domination concerns the 'unveiling' of issues such as symbolic violence, class, labour and gender relations. But what kind of unveiling are we dealing with here? Isn't the deconstruction of modes of domination itself an effect of domination? The most immediate response to this question is to reaffirm that sociological knowledge has an intrinsic emancipatory potential, similar to Spinoza's second kind of knowledge. 'Men believe that they are free in their actions, but ignore the causes that determine those actions', wrote the Dutch philosopher, employing a rhetorical device characteristic of materialist philosophies. But it is by no means certain that the problem of the domination effects of knowledge can be solved merely by inscribing ourselves in this tradition. And, in fact, sociology provides elements of discussion that can never be genuinely discussed as long as we remain trapped within a framework in which separate fields of knowledge are insufficiently distinguished.

An initial point of displacement is the idea suggested and proven by Pierre Bourdieu, notably in his article 'L'opinion publique n'existe pas' (Bourdieu 1980b: 222–235; see also 1979: 463–542), that the link between access to politicisation and cultural/educational capital is not a universal one but, rather, an observed relationship, or, in other words, a relationship constructed statistically and characterised by historical and social conditions of possibility. In contemporary, so-called differentiated societies, where education and the state serve a legitimising role in terms of social inequalities and forms of domination, individuals with a substantial educational and cultural capital feel more confident in becoming involved in politics than those who do not. The question therefore arises as to how to account for political commitment or forms of politicisation that are not dependent on that statistical relationship. Such phenomena are often treated as 'exceptions', but it would be well for sociologists to think of them in terms of more general social mechanisms. It is easy to understand the importance, in this context, of the structures framing the workers movement, namely local unions and party sections, organisations serving as a substitute for traditional educational establishments in terms of developing a militant capital and making it possible to acquire, by alternative means, in microcosms not governed by the ordinary laws of the social world, the skills, techniques and 'authority' needed to be effective in the field of politics and to express social malcontent or revolt in a political manner. It is also in this sense that we can interpret the role of popular collectives in Bolivia, for example, the local committees in El Alto – the *juntas vecinales* who waged the 'Gas War' in 2003, and the farmers' committees of Cochabamba, the *regantes*, who unleashed the 'Water War' in 2000. The protests organised by the 'Bolivian people' against the neoliberal regime have nothing to do with the spontaneously anti-capitalist nature of the 'good Indian' living in harmony with the Pachamama, a vision that militant researchers, either *in situ* or abroad, promote without always realising the degree to which it is influenced by a profound colonial heritage (Poupeau 2008).

A second point of displacement is the transition from critical thought to the analysis of forms of mobilisation. The impossibility of transforming the left into a popular emancipatory movement, as demanded by critics, derives from the lack of social conditions of access to politics, particularly in popular milieus in which protest votes are too often seen as examples of 'populism', be it of the right or the left. This is a fairly strong thesis – or hypothesis – which, however, does no more than acknowledge the consequences of the first point of displacement. It is not enough to rehash the critique of the separation between the professionals and the profane in the field of politics (Bourdieu 2002a). The problem should be presented in somewhat different terms. Is knowledge, or revelation through knowledge, the exclusive precondition of politicisation or of the political strength of a social organisation or collective? The problem does not consist solely in determining whether access to knowledge has 'hidden meaning' effects which encourage the political field to focus exclusively on its own issues, but in also asking oneself, in the wake of Bourdieu's claim that there is no 'intrinsic force in a true idea', if the awareness permitted by knowledge is effective in and of itself.

At this point, the arrogance of academic sociology and the kinds of inhibitions that can be engendered by symbolic violence should be acknowledged, and other forms, not only of the diffusion but also of the production of scientific knowledge and of the construction and appropriation of intellectual tools useful for social struggles, could be possible and should be explored.[7] While the limits of knowledge and the importance of a sociology aware of its limits in terms of the elaboration of social movements must be recognised, so too must the ways in which knowledge can exercise such effects on 'the people' and, more generally, determine the conditions of politicisation of the popular classes. But, indeed, the two displacements produced by sociology make it possible to understand the effects of the symbolic violence of knowledge and the efficiency of policies of depoliticisation, the mechanisms of which Bourdieu analysed in his work on the evolutions of the state (Bourdieu 2001a).[8] Since politics is an activity one of the main issues of which is to impose legitimate principles defining the vision and division of the social world (principles used to implement public policy in the spheres of health, welfare, etc.), it is clear that promoting a fragmented vision of that world in which 'actors' are equipped with autonomous capacities for action unaffected by contingent determinants (they are, therefore, 'responsible') contributes to the efficiency of policies of depoliticisation. Left criticism fails to understand that, in rejecting the sociology of domination, it favours, in spite of itself, the economic forces against which it believes it is struggling.

Critiques of criticism

Sociologists' pretentions to monopolising the truth are rejected in the name of the dominated classes' capacity for self-organisation, previously referred to as the autonomy of the popular classes. The fact that this is a speculative argument with no empirical foundations provides the conditions of possibility for an implicit transition from the cultural to the political: if the dominated classes are able to exist culturally, it is because they are politically autonomous. This presupposition is never questioned. But it is a postulate that runs counter to the idea according to which access to public discourse and politicisation is – as pointed out by Bourdieu in his critique of the presupposition that everyone has not only the right to have but also an actual political opinion (Bourdieu 1980b: 222–235) – subject to social conditions. In this perspective, the idea of equality at the heart of Jacques Rancière's political analysis (Rancière 1998) echoes, paradoxically, the anthropological foundations of a liberal philosophy that, since the first studies on social collectives carried out by Durkheim (social labour, collective representations, suicide rates, etc.), have refused to countenance the holistic aspect of society other than in terms of aggregates.[9] We can see here the degree to which the anti-totalitarianism which has had such a deep impact on the French left since the 1970s has influenced Marxist thinkers (Christofferson 2009). Research focused on providing explanations for social determinants is assimilated, without reservation, to a desire to reduce the individual to those determinants in a 'totalitarian' approach that denies both freedom and subjectivation.

A critique of criticism must also take into account the arguments – and not just the presuppositions – of the theses it examines. The decisive argument of the advocates of the autonomy of the dominated classes is, in reality, 'factual'. According to this argument, since forms of popular politicisation do in fact exist, so too do possibilities of emancipation that cannot be reduced to an awareness of domination. Unlike the kind of vision to be found in, for example, the work of Rancière, who deals only with the most cultivated and militant members of the working class, it is a question here of explaining how individuals or groups who are not equipped with educational or cultural capital can still become politicised in apparent contradiction to the law correlating cultural capital and politicisation.

Numerous studies shed light on the way in which some social microcosms, particularly partisan or organisational configurations, make it possible, at the local level, for people who would at first sight seem to be the most unlikely candidates, to acquire political skills (see, amongst others, Rimbert and Crespo 2004; Pudal 2009; Renahy 2010; Mischi 2010). The idea of elaborating a 'militant capital' (Matonti and Poupeau 2004) capable of replacing educational capital explains the differentiated political commitment of those most dominated by social frameworks and forms of popular education, which also function as social conditions of access to political autonomy. Above all, by studying the social and institutional microcosms that suspend the ordinary laws of the social world – for example, the law linking cultural capital to politicisation – sociology makes it possible to highlight the fact that domination has nothing ineluctable about it and that the social conditions of emancipation, both as an idea and as a political practice, really exist.

The critique of the division between the knowledgeable and the ignorant casts common sense as the exclusive preserve of the dominated classes. However, it neglects the fact that the sociology of relationships of domination can also be applied to those who produce the dominant ideology (Bourdieu and Boltanski 1976; Bourdieu 1989b; Boltanski 2008: 85, 113–114) and to the field of power organised by dominant mental structures. More tellingly perhaps, it also makes the implicit claim that the desire for sociological objectivation is accompanied by a value judgment about popular milieus according to which, in the eyes of sociologists, the dominated classes are either too 'lacking in qualifications', 'uncultured' or 'stupid' to notice the domination to which they are subject. Social scientists can thus be disqualified as haughty and arrogant, even though they are merely attempting to explain an important aspect of relationships of domination, namely that, as Alexis Spire has shown in his work on tax avoidance amongst the rich (Spire 2011), the dominant can more easily act on mechanisms of domination because they have more resources (financial, institutional, etc.). On the other hand, the dominated classes may, due to what Richard Hoggart would term their 'nonchalant' relationship with political and cultural affairs, contribute, without being aware of it, to maintaining a social order that militates against their interests. They are also obliged to engage in much more costly forms of resistance, at both the collective and the individual levels, which sometimes condemns them to a form of 'heroism' (I am thinking here of Didier Eribon's description, in Eribon 2010: 84–85, of 'the naked violence of exploitation' perpetrated on the body of his working class mother, of the overtime he had to work to make ends meet and his failure in the entrance exams for the ENS – the most famous French elite school).

In this context, it is highly revealing that the theory of symbolic violence is never discussed as such by the critics of sociology. Numerous empirical studies suggest that the dominated aid and abet the dominant by contributing to their own domination (Bourdieu 1989b). But instead of examining the validity of this idea, opponents of the sociology of domination merely repeat the unexplained mantra that the dominated are autonomous. This presupposition generates a highly reductive vision of domination that, in left criticism, is conceptualised exclusively in terms of oppression, be it in the form of physical coercion or ideological propaganda (we will not linger on the misinterpretation of the Gramscian notion of hegemony).[10] But what symbolic violence describes above all is the incorporation of cognitive structures and categories of thought that produce an adjustment or, more precisely, a form of consent to the social order which is all the more powerful because it is presented as self-evident. It is characteristic of crisis situations that they call into question this ordinary acceptance by generating 'gaps' between the real and the schemas of perception and appreciation with which it is viewed. Another effect of sociological research, through the implementation of techniques as varied as statistics, questionnaires, social history and thoroughgoing interviews, is to create a reflexive distance in regard to ordinary approaches to understanding the real.

The advantage of the sociology of symbolic violence elaborated by Bourdieu is that it demonstrates that mechanisms of domination are perhaps more insidious than might be imagined, since they operate at the heart of language and of categories of thought to produce forms of consent to the principles of vision and division on which the existing social order is based. To elaborate a scientific problem against the background of the social problems in which it is initially located is to unveil the mechanisms of symbolic violence inherent in social relations by deconstructing the categories spontaneously used to imagine them. It is not a question of grabbing a 'monopoly of power' but, on the contrary, of diffusing knowledge without which men and women are doomed to live in servitude, to use a word much employed in Spinoza's time. And in this materialist vein, there is reason to believe that a knowledge of the determinants of actions and thought contribute to whatever degree to liberating those who are exposed to it. By rejecting the idea according to which 'men believe that they are free in their actions, but ignore the causes that determine those actions' (Spinoza 1994, Appendix to Book II), theories postulating the autonomy of the dominated or popular classes are, without wanting to be, much more than just a form of political spontaneity; in fact, they partake in an idealist philosophy which is rarely accompanied by emancipatory policies and which, indeed, has always tended to support the existing order.

Lastly, critiques of the pretention of sociology to impose a monopoly of knowledge focus on an 'epistemological break' as the condition of any social science. To counter the impossibility of applying the kind of demands characteristic of the so-called 'hard sciences' to the study of the social world, a postmodern vision is invoked of the 'great sharing' of men and things that will take place in the modern era of triumphant rationalism. Indeed, Bruno Latour provides a description of this phenomenon, the exaggerated simplicity of which doubtless contributed to its success, that, with no empirical scruples whatsoever, ignores decades of meticulous work on the history of science (Latour 1991).[11]

It would seem that this situation is characterised by a serious misunderstanding. The reference to the Bachelardian theme of the 'construction of the object' developed by the French school of historical epistemology and represented, in particular, by Georges Canguilhem, can in no manner be assimilated to the invocation of the 'uncertainty principle' applied to politics that Jacques Bouveresse had already criticised in *Prodiges et vertiges de l'analogie* (Bouveresse 1999). It is not an unfounded comparison, but, instead, a research practice. In fact, this misunderstanding is linked to the very idea of what it is to analyse the social world: the sociologist, like the journalist and the politician, uses linguistic and conceptual categories to decipher meaning.

To maintain that sociology should elaborate concepts with a view to explaining certain phenomena has, therefore, nothing to do with a desire to plagiarise the natural sciences. It is an act of classifying and ordering the real similar to the analyses described by Marx as the elaboration of a model capable of encompassing the real which, at first, appears in the falsely concrete form of an indistinct population, and which is then categorised according to the division of social labour of the social classes of which that population is composed, before the structuring force of capital is finally revealed and the real attained as 'concrete thought' (Marx 1857; new edn 1965: 254–256). This meticulous process of 'modelisation' has nothing to do with a radical doubt introduced by an omniscient *scientist* or with an inaugural *epoche* that puts the world on hold. On the contrary, it is a long and patient process of inquiry, involving a comparison between intellectual categories and the social world that they order by observing it, a process corresponding to the initial stage of the 'construction of the object'.

The epistemological break with common sense as a vector of the structures of thought in which domination resides is linked to a specific conception of the construction of the object in the initial stage of inquiry (Pestaña 2011). The sociological survey is a *social relation*, something that the presupposition of the autonomy of the dominated obscures: merely because someone occupies a particular position in the social space does not mean that he can express its truth. What is expressed is a point of view, probably *a* truth, but at best a partial truth, which needs to be positioned in 'the space of points of view' (Bourdieu ed. 1993: 9–11) and in its social conditions of enunciation, conditions that are not always spontaneously accessible. What, for example, a farmer expresses about his living conditions does not necessarily reflect the truth of the agricultural world; to restore meaning to his observations, we have to place them in the context of the crisis of family reproduction that affects his sector of activity, and the universe of meaning associated with it (Champagne 1993: 533–549; 2002). Neither are the members of the working classes omniscient or immediately capable of expressing anything other than the experiential truth of the person expressing him- or herself.

According to Didier Eribon, who it is difficult to suspect of scientism or hostility to ethnocentric struggles:

> any kind of sociology or philosophy that places the 'point of view of the actors' and the 'meaning that they give to their actions' at the heart of its approach runs the risk of offering nothing more than a stenographic record of the mystified relationships that social agents have with their own practices and desires and, consequently, of doing nothing more than contributing

> to the perpetuation of the world as it is: an ideology of justification (of the established order). Only an epistemological break with the way individuals spontaneously imagine themselves makes it possible to describe, by reconstructing the system as a whole, the mechanisms by which the social order is reproduced and, notably, the way the dominated ratify that domination by accepting the educational exclusion to which they are doomed. The strength and interest of a theory are to be found precisely in the fact that the theory in question is never content with merely recording the comments of the 'actors' on their own 'actions,' but, on the contrary, aims at enabling individuals and groups to take a different approach to seeing and thinking what they do and who they are.
>
> (Eribon 2010: 51–52)

If one takes into account the social aspect of the relationship between the researcher and his work, it is possible to appreciate that the likely distorting effect of the interaction between the two on the production and reception of discourses can only be corrected by an analysis and self-analysis of the position of the researcher and the subject of her research. This constitutes another component of the construction of the object. In eschewing this rudimentary form of epistemological prudence and in emphasising the immediacy of the 'voice of the voiceless', populo-workerist, postcolonial and post-modern currents, as well as the highly academic – and academically dominant – pragmatic sociology, obscure social relations under the portmanteau concept of the 'indigenous' knowledge that actors have of the social world in which they live. According to these approaches, 'indigenous' knowledge encompasses the totality of knowledge about the social world. In this sense, they share one of the main postulates of state sociology: individuals are, as matter of principle, free to choose their lifestyles, their social compromises and their forms of self-justification since they have knowledge of them.[12] Such approaches presuppose that the dominated classes are autonomous and that the most dominated amongst them have a natural tendency towards political emancipation. However, if we are to accept this postulate, it becomes impossible to understand why they continue to live in social worlds that, logically, they should reject out of hand. In the end, taking into account the social conditions of politicisation as revealed in sociological surveys makes it possible to take a position that is not only much more modest, but also more amenable to imagining practical forms of emancipation.

In the end, the issue of the political functions of sociological analysis should be addressed from a different perspective. Sociology, a necessarily incomplete form of knowledge, the gaps of which Jean-Claude Passeron's 'theoretical plurality' does not succeed in filling, nevertheless contains corpuses of methods and techniques, imperatives of empirical validation and obligations of collective evaluation. All of these serve as criteria that, even if they are often challenged or shoddily applied by many people in the 'profession', nevertheless express the existence of an agreement about potential disagreements, a precondition of the constitution of a 'community of peers' and, in the long-term, of a discipline equipped with its own rules and principles of operation.[13] Such a situation – which corresponds to the definition of a scientific field – remains far beyond the reach of sociology in its current form.

The fact that sociology does not yet function in entirely the same way as a science does not mean that its pretentions to attaining full scientific status are unfounded; what it does mean, however, is that, as things stand, it is not rigorous enough in terms either of its practices of inquiry or of its collective operational rules. Indeed – alas – it is unlikely that the new evaluation criteria introduced in recent years will do much to alleviate this state of affairs (Collectif P.E.C.R.E.S. 2011; Laval *et al.* 2011). Ensuring that sociology attains scientific status thus depends on constituting an autonomous scientific field, a task that is not without its ambivalent aspects.

The act of defending the scientific validity of sociological analysis can be interpreted, in a somewhat simplified manner, as a monopolisation of knowledge on the part of a group of specialist academics, to monopolise knowledge, a process supposedly incompatible with the production of popular knowledge. But beyond the often neglected fact that the project to rehabilitate this form of popular knowledge is rooted in the sociological project and would in all probability not exist without it (Muchielli 1998; Heilbron 2006), it can be argued that the elaboration of a body of collective techniques, methods and norms should remain separate from their appropriation and diffusion by non-specialists. Indeed, the appropriation of the knowledge produced in the field of sociology is the main precondition of any future production by non-specialists of knowledge that could serve as an integral part of the redefinition of a popular political project.

The issue at hand thus concerns the ways in which sociologists intervene politically, how the results of their work are diffused and how knowledge produced by the social sciences beyond the immediate circle of 'professionals' and 'initiates' are currently being reappropriated. Left criticism's presupposition that the dominated classes are autonomous obscures the fact that political autonomy is the product of a process of elaboration or, expressed in a more combative vocabulary, of a process of social conquest, and that knowledge of the social world is one of its preconditions. In the meantime, it has to be admitted that we are still at the laborious stage of the conquest of scientific autonomy, which, needless to say, is just as far from our grasp as is an emancipatory politics. It could be objected that we are dealing with an impossible ideal and that there is no time to waste in terms of breaking down the barriers between specialists and non-specialists. In fact, the issue at hand is to discern, in a potentially shared process of knowledge production, what is linked to a field of knowledge and what isn't: truth criteria should then be defined applying the standards of scientific legitimacy in order to avoid ideological relativism and undifferentiated knowledge.

However, it should perhaps be admitted that sociology finds itself caught between a rock and a hard place. On the one hand, it is confronted with a demand for it to be constituted as a science (and therefore as a scientific field regulated by 'peers' from the academic world who do not always act out of the purest of interests), and, on the other, by a demand for the knowledge it produces to be diffused in the social world. It is not beyond the bounds of possibility – and it is a possibility that is well worth exploring – that, thanks to a potential break with common sense and the forms of domination by which it is characterised, the more scientific sociology is, the more potentially political it is. In that case, according to Bourdieu, sociology, as a critical activity, could serve as a motor for the construction of a social science shared beyond a circle of professionals:

> The sociologically armed epistemological vigilance that individual researchers are able to apply themselves can only be reinforced by the generalisation of the imperative of reflexivity and the divulgation of the kind of tools needed to impose it; only this kind of vigilance can establish reflexivity as a common law in the field, which would thus be devoted to a sociological critique of everyone by everyone else capable of intensifying and redoubling the effects of the epistemological critique of everyone by everyone else.
>
> (Bourdieu 2001c: 178–179)

Beyond miserabilism and populism

After this critique of criticism, we can return to the problem of dominated cultures, the study of which, according to Claude Grignon and Jean-Claude Passeron, oscillates ineluctably between a miserabilist approach that reductively characterises popular culture in a negative manner and a form of populism that, on the contrary, highlights its active and autonomous aspects. It is worthwhile taking a closer look at this dichotomy. Because the concepts developed in *Distinction* are said to insufficiently address the practical aspects of relations of domination, the miserabilism characteristic of the theory of cultural legitimacy outlined in the book would fail to properly take into account popular culture. Meanwhile, in the populist approach, the desire to do justice to dominated cultures can be said to be based on the

> anti-intellectualism of intellectuals in difficulty who, by accepting the existing hierarchy of objects of study in order to carve out a small degree of glory for themselves, help to ensure that their own object of study is regarded as belonging to the Second Division in terms of research.

It is understandable that, by presenting an unbridgeable gap between intellectuals and the working classes, Grignon and Passeron experience genuine 'embarrassment' when confronted with sociological or romanticised evocations of 'the people'. In seeing no more than, on the one hand, an expression of passivity in the face of domination and, on the other, the capacities for creation or revolt on the part of the dominated, they are quite simply unable to entertain the idea that the dominated might contribute to their own domination, a phenomenon that defines the problem of *consent*.

Nevertheless, Jean-Claude Passeron also observes that 'the problem of the consent of the dominated classes to domination and to the legitimacy of dominant values is, in all social orders, the political enigma to which sociology most directly leads' (Passeron 2003: 59, quoted by Gobille 2008). And if he does not arrive at the same conclusions as Pierre Bourdieu concerning the link between the sociology of domination and the necessary engagement of the academic, he nevertheless notes that the analysis of common sense and, more exactly, of 'naïve opinions' borrowed from the anthropology of Pascal, makes it possible to explain the contribution of the people to the maintenance of the social order without recourse to the philosophies of alienation that have, since Hegel and Marx, defined the horizon of left criticism. But without taking symbolic power into account, Passeron is unable to perceive the degree to which consent is linked to an anthropology of practices that goes far beyond debates about interest and disinterest, the exchange economy and the theory of the gift, of which disinterest and the gift define, at present, one of the only social alternatives to left criticism.[14]

To escape the grasp of the capitalist system and the violence inherent in economic relations, there may be no alternative to developing a society founded on the gift and on disinterest, symptoms of a revived sense of community.[15] That is precisely Bourdieu's analysis of the gift, an analysis that doubtless provides an interpretative key to the problem of consent: in the interval between giving and receiving a gift, the truth of exchange is denied. The objectivist description of the exchange of gifts, which reduces the transaction to a give-and-take scenario, is therefore unable to provide a foundation for the difference between an exchange of gifts and a credit transaction. This process of dissimulation of the objective truth of the practice can be revealed by sociology, but if sociologists fail to take on board the existence of social agents, they run the risk of reducing a disinterested act to the status of a cynical, calculated manoeuvre. As Bourdieu writes:

> The unfortunate thing is that sociologists tend to favour the first, purely objectivist approach, which demystifies or disenchants; people often become sociologists because they want to be clever and distinguish themselves from those naive individuals who believe that a gift is just a gift.
>
> (Bourdieu 1994b: 11)[16]

Practices are thus a vector for double 'truths' that have to be considered in tandem if their social significance is to be properly understood. This ambiguity stems from agents' denial, which itself derives from a process of mis-knowledge, of what could – if the concept did not connote an implicit finality – be termed individual and collective self-deception. The denial of the economic truth of exchange is, in fact, linked to a process of presentation and euphemisation: individuals must provide signs that they are observing the rules, a respect accorded to the social order itself that Spinoza refers to as *obsequium*. This logic of denial of the economic:

> is accomplished by means of a process that focuses objectively on transfiguring economic relations and, in particular, exploitative relations (men/women, elder/younger, master/servant, etc.), in both word (by means of euphemism) and deed [...]. The most interesting example of this kind of symbolic alchemy may well be the transfiguration of relationships of domination and exploitation. Gifts can be exchanged between two equals, a transaction that strengthens communion and solidarity by means of a process of communication that creates social bonds. But they can also be exchanged between parties who are not equal, as in potlatch, which, if those who describe it are to be believed, institutes long-term relationships characterised by symbolic domination, relationships of domination based on communication, knowledge and recognition.
>
> (Bourdieu 1994a: 186)

The problem of consent can thus be defined, in a different way, as the possession of identical categories of perception and appreciation that make possible cognitive acts of knowledge and recognition that transfigure acts of domination (that can include the exploitation of women by men, of younger people by older people, of domestics by masters) in affective relationships, or, more exactly, in 'domestic relationships of familiarity' that mask the truth of domination. In differentiated societies, paternalism provides an example in that economic transactions do not entirely eliminate the economy of symbolic exchange. The adjustment of categories of perception and appreciation to their conditions of production makes it possible to create a capital of recognition, a symbolic capital that can then function in a quasi-magical manner by extorting 'types of submission that are not even perceived as such' because they correspond to collective expectations and socially inculcated beliefs. These beliefs are based on a process of socialisation in which agents equip themselves with schemas of perception and appreciation that enable them to 'perceive the injunctions inscribed in a situation or discourse and to obey it', and that provoke an immediate acceptance of what is said and done. Consent is a form of submission to the injunctions of the world, a product of the adjustment to mental structures involved in the relationship of domination.

The strength of a theory is measured in terms not only of its explicit content, but also of the degree to which it allows us to think beyond the parameters of the initial issue. Because, like ethnic identities in differentiated societies, symbolic capital is shared by all the members of a group, the sociology of symbolic domination does not imply that consent is irredeemable or irreversible. Individual and collective strategies to conserve, overthrow or appropriate symbolic capital can lead to the emergence of strategies of, on the one hand, reproduction or, on the other, subversion that call the established order into question. The latter are capable of undermining consent:

> Due to the fact that structures of perception and appreciation are essentially dependent on the incorporation of objective structures, the structure of the

> distribution of symbolic capital tends to be extremely stable. And symbolic revolutions presuppose a more or less radical revolution in terms of instruments of knowledge and categories of perception.
>
> (Bourdieu 1994a: 191)

In this context, the kind of *collective intellectual* in which academics and leaders of social movements could work jointly to 'produce and diffuse instruments of defence against symbolic domination, which more often than not today arms itself with the authority of science' (Bourdieu 2002a; Champagne and Christin 2004) that Bourdieu called for in *Raisons pratiques* would be unlikely to fit into the analytical framework of left criticism since its aim would be to construct a sphere of political and scientific autonomy without presuming that it already exists. In the end, such a perspective is, as has already been underlined, far more modest than the incantatory reference to 'the coming insurrection'. On the one hand, *it lays no claims to establishing a political line*: its ambition is to unveil mechanisms of domination that ensure that alternative propositions remain mired in forms of thought imposed by existing social relations; on the other, it creates the *possibility of a convergence* between organisations and collectives that already reject forms of expert knowledge that serve the interests of capital and its state apparatuses of transmission, and attempts instead to develop more realistic forms of mobilisation more relevant to social struggles.

At a time when, with the Indignados and Occupy movements having been left high and dry by the media, it seems that the existing capitalist order no longer needs to resort to propaganda in order to justify itself, an intellectual collective, working within the framework of the *European* social movement, of the kind Pierre Bourdieu called for at the turn of the millennium, would make it possible to unite movements and develop solidarities at the supra-national level, where they are now needed to strengthen local resistance struggles.

Notes

1 Franck Poupeau is CNRS Senior Researcher and Director of the International Joint Unit iGLOBES, CNRS/University of Arizona. His research developed at the intersection of the sociology of urban segregation and the political analysis of social movements. His work on inequality of access to water in urban peripheries in Andea cities constituted the first step of a larger multidisciplinary project focusing on the conditions of political mobilisation in urban areas, which articulated variables usually considered separately by the social science disciplines (anthropology, urban geography, political science, management of urban services). He is the coordinator of several programmes on water management and conflicts for natural resources in the Andes. Since 2003, he has been the editor of the journal *Actes de la recherche en sciences sociales*. He has authored more than 40 peer-reviewed articles.

2 In an example of breathtaking epistemological innocence, 'pragmatic sociology' claims to be able to do without 'theoretical frameworks' and focus on 'letting the facts speak for themselves'. For a charitable reading, see Bénatouïl (1999).

3 It is not by chance that the Nobel Prize for Economics was given to the woman who defended such ideas in the field of environmental conflicts. See Ostrom (1990) and Burger *et al.* (2001).

4 According to Boltanski and Chiapello (1999: 87), the impossibility of developing a critique completely articulating the four sources of indignation that are inauthenticity, oppression, poverty and egotism explains 'the intrinsic ambiguity of criticism, which always shares – even insofar as the most radical movements are concerned – "something" with what it seeks to criticise'.

5 If, for Ernesto Laclau, populism is a political logic in which the people constitutes itself as a historical agent based on antagonistic situations, the concept is often used reductively to refer to a movement representing a specific social category, such as workers, farm workers or smallholders.

6 Inspired, notably, by a singular interpretation of Michel Foucault's biopolitics. On this point, see Revel (2010).

7 This type of question was at the heart of the project to construct a European social movement initiated by Pierre Bourdieu in the 1990s and to which only a few unionists, including Annick Coupé, thought it worthwhile to contribute: in my opinion, this project went well beyond the formation of an 'collective intellectual' comprising committed researchers. All that now remains of the project are two separate publishing houses.

8 These politically committed texts are largely based on articles published in *La Misère du Monde* (Bourdieu ed. 1993) and *Les Structures sociales de l'économie* (Bourdieu 2000b).

9 See, in particular, Durkheim (1990: 138) for a distinction between collective opinion, as produced by a shared project of elaboration, and the vote as a statistical aggregation of individual opinions.

10 On this point, see Ramzig Keucheyan's (2012) introduction to Antonio Gramsci; also see Amselle (2011: Chapter 8).

11 For a more closely argued view, see Latour (2006).

12 In this perspective, Boltanski's pragmatic sociology can serve, in the same manner as Rosanvallon's analyses, as a theoretical framework for advocates of postcolonialism and populo-workerism.

13 Following Fabiani (2010), it should be recalled that a recourse to specific methods and forms of rationality has always been rejected by spiritualism. For example, conservative spiritualism, which got a second wind after the Paris Commune, managed to undermine the efforts of those attempting to build the organisational and theoretical foundations of social emancipation. See also, Léonard (2011).

14 For an analysis of the gift that eschews this political mythology, see Alain Testart and, above all, Athané (2011).

15 See, amongst other examples, the analysis of the 'gift cycle' carried out by Michéa (2007: 138). According to the author, Orwellian 'common decency' finds, in this anthropological perspective that escapes the self-interested logic of giving in order to receive, its true philosophical and moral coherence. But it is precisely the 'moral claim' of the working classes not to 'idealise delinquency and transgressive behaviours' that 'the French extreme left' is, Michéa claims, incapable of understanding (ibid.: 157).

16 See also Bourdieu (1994a: 175–213) and Bourdieu (1980g).

Part VI

In the words of *Pierre Bourdieu . . .*

14 The future of class and the causality of the probable[1]

Pierre Bourdieu, translated by Michael Grenfell

The theory of practice that human sciences operate, most often in an implicit way, when they have to account for the economy of practices, that is, the immanent logic of actions and the objective meaning of works and institutions, oscillates, beyond divergences between theoretical traditions, between mechanism and a generally intellectualist version of finalism. In the absence of recognising something other than different variations of *rational action* or *mechanical reaction* to a determination such as the constraint of prices mechanically set by the market, one bars oneself from understanding the specific logic of all actions which are reasonable without being the product of reasoned design or, all the more so, of rational calculation; inhabited by a sort of objective finality without being consciously organised according to an explicitly constituted end; intelligible and coherent without stemming from an intelligent intention and a deliberate decision; adjusted to the future without being the product of a project or plan.[2] The power of the alternative is such that those who expect to react against the mechanism of a certain economic tradition, without falling into the intellectualism of 'economic calculation' (or the 'psychology' a priori inherited from utilitarianism and pragmatism) with which it commonly alternates, rarely escape the naïveties of subjectivism with its personalist kits of 'aspirations' and 'projects'; and that, conversely, those who expect to break with the naïveties of subjectivist theories of action fall again rather inevitably into a mechanism hardly any less naïve than that of the theory which, transposing to economics the axiomatic of classical mechanism, treats economic agents as indiscernible particles submitted to the laws of a quasi-mechanical equilibrium. Indeed, it is not enough to do away with the old alternative, to come back to a better concealed form of mechanism, similar to those of the structuralists who treat agents, amusedly reduced, through an over translation of Marx, to the role of 'structural support' (Träger), as redundant reflections of structure or to locate the principle of practice in an unconsciousness defined as a *mechanical operator of finality*.[3]

In fact, for most of their actions, economic agents do not constitute a rational calculator, obeying the only rational evaluation of chances, any more than an automat, mechanically determined by the laws of the market. As a generating principle of *objective strategies*, as sequences of structured practices which are orientated with reference to objective functions, habitus embodies the solution of the paradoxes of objective logic without subjective intention, because amongst other reasons – the words say it – it poses explicitly the question of its own individual and collective genesis. If each of the moments of a series of ordered and orientated actions which make up objective strategies can appear to be determined by an anticipation of the future and in particular of *its own consequences* (which justifies the use of the concept strategy), it is because practices which are engendered by the habitus and which are controlled by the past conditions of production of their generating principle are already adapted to the objective conditions each time that the conditions in which the habitus functions remain identical (or similar) to the conditions in which it constituted itself. Adjustment to objective conditions is indeed immediately and perfectly successful and the illusion of finality, or, more or less the same thing, of a self-regulated mechanism, is complete *in the case and only in the case* where conditions of production and effectuation perfectly coincide.[4]

The endurance, in the form of habitus, of the effect of primary conditions, implies that the immediate correspondence between structures and habitus (with representations – the doxic experience of the social world – and the expectations – the amor fati, i.e. the love of fate – that they engender) is only one particular ***case*** *of the system of possible relational cases between objective structures and dispositions. Also, it explains equally well the cases where dispositions function as a setback (according to the paradigm of Don Quixote, so dear to Marx) and where practices are objectively inadapted to present conditions because they are objectively adjusted to bygone or abolished conditions: it is enough to quote the particularly paradoxical case of social background where a permanent change is seen in objective* conditions *– therefore, a permanent time-lag between conditions to which habitus is adjusted and the conditions to which it has to adjust – at the same time, as a simple translation of the structure of class relations, the hysteresis of habitus being able to lead in this particular case to a time lag between expectations and the objective conditions which induce impatience with these objective conditions (this is the case, for example, when those who hold academic titles which have become devalued, because of their commonality, even though they remain identical, hope for real advantages which, in a previous time, were attached to these titles). But there is more: among everything that marks the primary conditions that habitus 'expects' and 'calls', even if as a setback, because it assumes them to be a condition of its function, nothing is more determining than the system of indices by which the slope of the social trajectory line is being recalled – the zero slope of all social backgrounds and of most 'stable' classes being a particular case of all the conditions which enclose the marks of ascension or of decline. In short, the tendency to persevere in their being that groups owe, amongst other reasons, to the fact that agents which make them up are endowed with durable dispositions, capable of surviving the economic and social conditions of their own production, can be the principle of inadaptability as well as adaptability, of revolt as well as resignation.*

It is necessary to bring to mind, without going into systematic analysis,[5] the universe of possible relational forms between dispositions and conditions to think the anticipated adjustment of the habitus to the objective conditions as a 'particular case of the possible', to use Bachelard's term, and therefore to avoid unconsciously *universalising* the quasi circular model of relations of quasi perfect reproduction which only completely applies in the case where the conditions of production of habitus and that of their functioning are identical and homothetic. In such a particular case, the constitutive dispositions of the habitus which are durably inculcated by objective conditions and by a pedagogical action tendentially adjusted to these conditions tend to engender expectations and practices which are objectively compatible with these conditions and adapted beforehand to their objective demands; in other words, being the product of a determined class of objective regularities (those, for example, which characterise a class condition that science apprehends through such constructed regularities as objective probabilities), these general and transposable dispositions therefore tend to engender all the 'reasonable' practices which are possible within the limits of these regularities, and only these, excluding the 'follies', that is, the behaviours condemned to be negatively sanctioned because they are incompatible with objective demands. In other words, they tend to assure, outside of any rational calculation and any conscious judgment of chances for success, the immediate correspondence between the a priori or ex ante probability which is accorded to an event (with or without the accompanying subjective experiences such as hopes, fears, etc.) and the a posteriori or ex post probability which can be established on the basis of past experience.[6]

But, is it not to come back, by other routes, to the theory of practice that some economists operate, at least implicitly, when they suggest that, for example, investments tend to adapt themselves either to the expected rate of profit or to that actually obtained in the past? To show up the difference and at the same time to specify previous analyses, you only have to consider the Weberian theory of 'objective probabilities', which has the merit of bringing to light one of the most fundamental assumptions, although tacit, of the economy, namely the existence of a 'relation of intelligible causality' between *generic chances* ('typical') 'existing objectively on average' and 'subjective expectations'.[7] By speaking of 'average chances', that is to say, valuable for *anyone*, for an *indeterminate* and *interchangeable* agent, a 'one', as Heiddegger[8] would say, and by recalling that rational action, 'carefully' orientated according to what is 'objectively valuable',[9] is that which 'would have happened if the actors had knowledge of all the circumstances and all the intentions of the participants',[10] that is to say, what is 'valuable in the eyes of the scientist', who is the only one capable of constructing by calculation the system of objective chances to which an action accomplished in perfect knowledge of its causes should adjust, Max Weber clearly showed that the pure model of rational action cannot be considered as an anthropological description of practice. However, if it is too obvious that, without exception, real agents are a long way from having *complete information* of a situation implied by rational action, how does one explain that economic models founded on the hypothesis of correspondence between objective chances and practices account for, rather exactly and in most cases, practices which do not have knowledge of the objective chances as principle?[11] By being satisfied with implicitly postulating correspondence between objective chances and practices – for example, between the profit rate and the propensity to invest – and by omitting to ask the question of the conditions of possibility – therefore of the theoretical and empirical limits – of this correspondence, one leaves the field open to the most contradictory explanatory theories.[12]

'The causality of the probable'[13]

The inherent abstraction of an economic theory which only knows rational 'responses' of an indeterminate and interchangeable agent to 'potential opportunities' (*responses to potential opportunities*) or, more precisely, to average chances (like 'average profit rates' promised by different markets) never appears as clear as when economists treat pre-capitalist economies as being under economic or political domination. This sort of experimental situation where the conditions of agreement between structures and dispositions are not fulfilled, since agents are not the product of the economic conditions to which they have to adapt, shows up as evidence that the adaptation to the demands of the economy is no longer the effect of a conversion of awareness any more than a mechanical adaptation to the constraints of economic necessity: the invention that it supposes is only accessible to those who hold a minimum of economic and cultural capital, that is to say, a minimum of power over mechanisms they have to master. Through the self-regulated mechanisms of the market, which take the shape of the calculable and expected necessity of the natural world, the imported and imposed 'economic cosmos' tacitly demands dispositions from all its economic agents, in particular dispositions with respect to time, such as inclination and aptitude to regulate practices with respect to the future and master economic mechanisms through anticipation and calculation, which are a function of the effectively held mastery of these mechanisms: the practical propensity and, all the more so, the conscious ambition to appropriate the future for oneself through rational calculation depend narrowly on the chances to succeed in such an appropriation which are set within current economic conditions. The competence demanded by the 'choice' of better objective strategies (for example, the choice of financial investment, scholastic establishment or professional career) is very unequally distributed, since it varies almost exactly according to the power on which success with these strategies depends.

The extreme case of the sub-proletariat that their total powerlessness dooms them to alternation between fantasising and resignation brings to light one of the aspects of the relation between the current power and dispositions: the practices of futureless men with neither economy nor strategy, and in particular, the fatalistic abandoning to a natural fecundity, bears witness that below a certain threshold, the strategic disposition itself, which implies a practical reference to a future, sometimes quite distant, cannot form itself, as if the *effective* ambition to master the future was unconsciously proportional to the effective power to master it. And, far from representing a denial, the dreamed ambitions and the millenarian hopes that these people sometimes express bear witness again that, as different from this 'demand without effect', based, as Marx said, on need and desire, the 'effective demand' has its foundation, and at the same time its limits in *power*, that measures the chances of appeasing the desire and satisfying the need. The effective aspirations, capable of really orientating practices, because endowed with a reasonable probability of being followed by effect, have nothing in common with dreamt aspirations, wishes 'without effect, without being real, without object', as Marx said,[14] or with simple projects, conscious and explicit projections, of what is equally possible to happen or not to happen and expressively constituted as ends of actions destined to make them happen: if the worst comes to the worst, that is, as they get rid of all constraints and all limitations, in order to situate themselves, as one says, in the 'ideal', these imaginary desires tend, as in the case study of Shubkin,[15] to reproduce the social structure but *in reverse*, the rarest positions in reality being the most frequent in ideal. On the contrary, *effective vocation* includes, as disposition acquired in certain social conditions, reference to these (social) conditions of realisation in such a way that it tends to adjust itself to objective potentialities.[16]

Economic strategies are not responses to an abstract, omnibus situation, such as a determined state of the labour market or the daily profit rate, but a singular configuration of positive or negative indices, set in the social space, where a specific relation between assets held and the different markets is expressed, that is to say, a determined degree of potential and current power over the instruments of production and reproduction. The chances of mastering instruments of production and reproduction (that the scientific discourse expresses, for example, in the form of the probabilities of access to goods or institutions) are united by a dialectical relation to the aptitude and inclination to dominate these instruments, that is to say, to take hold of the chances of investment and profit, to organise the available means, etc., in short, everything that one might commonly put under the name of 'spirit of enterprise'. Because objective conditions (as opposed to the 'abstract' situation of economists and psychologists) define themselves as a specific relation between mechanisms such as the labour market and the scholastic market and the totality of the constitutive properties of the assets of a particular class of agents, practices that create habitus are adjusted to the objective conditions each time that it is the product of similar conditions as those to which it must respond, that is to say, in every case where the structures and the mechanisms that reproduce them and/or the position of agents relative to these structures have not known any important change. In this case, the concordance of expectations and probabilities, anticipations and realisations is the principle of this type of 'realism', as sense of reality and realities so that, beyond dreams and revolt, each tends to live 'conforming to their condition', according to the Thomist maxim, and to unconsciously make themselves complicit in processes which tend to make the probable become actual.

The normative definition of adapted economic practice that economic theory implicitly assumes by omitting to ask the question of the conditions which make it possible has the effect and probably the function to conceal the adaptation of dispositions to objective conditions such as they have been defined, which can, in the case of economically and culturally disadvantaged classes, be the principle of a maladaptation to a 'situation' and of a resignation to this maladaptation: these are the same dispositions which, by adapting the poorest to the specific condition of which they are the product, contribute to make their adaptation to the generic demands of the economic cosmos improbable or impossible (for example, of calculation or forecast) and which lead them to accept negative sanctions resulting from this non-adaptation, that is to say, their disadvantaged condition. We can see what conceals the abstract notions of economic theory which, by virtue of a fictio juris, converts the immanent law of the economy into a universal norm of proper economic practice: the rational habitus, which is the condition of an immediately and perfectly adapted economic practice is the product of a particular economic condition, that defines the possession of necessary economic and cultural capital in order to effectively take hold of the 'potential occasions' formally offered to everyone, but really accessible to the sole holders of the necessary instruments to own them.[17]

Economic competence is therefore not an aptitude universally and uniformly widespread: the art of estimating and controlling the chances, to see in the present configuration of the situation the future 'present there' (as Husserl said, in order to resist an imaginary future of the project), the aptitude to forestall the future by a sort of practical induction or even to play the possible against the probable with a calculated risk, these are here as so many dispositions which can only be acquired under certain conditions, that is to say, in certain social conditions. As in the case of the spirit of enterprise, economic information is a function of power over the economy: because the propensity to acquire it depends on successful use and the chances of acquiring it also. An economic competence which, similar to that of housewives of the working class, owes its characteristics to the particular conditions of its acquisition and use, and which functions as a system of defence entirely orientated to the minimisation of spending, is only a disparate collection of half-knowledge capable of founding defensive, passive and individual strategies: the practical mastery of the systems of classification, such as product 'brands', price scales, quality categories, etc. joins with precepts, recipes and rationalisations of a sort of economic vulgate, a set of half-truths selected with respect to ethical dispositions (ethos), which confers on them a practical coherence. But, the logic of 'good buys' is as far from 'the logic of business' as 'the art of saving money' is from the power of 'doing without'. Condemned to short-term and short-sighted strategies, the poor consumer can only make different sellers compete with each other at the price of considerable expenditure of time and work (calculations, 'anxieties', moves, etc.) and he has nothing with which to fight other than getting out (exit) or powerless protests (voice) against the strategies of salesmen and, in particular, their effort to systematically muddle the indices which guide the available systems of classification (imitations, similes, mistruths, etc.).

The petit-bourgeois maintain with the capital market a relation altogether homologous to that which working class housewives maintain with the consumer market: their purely defensive strategies give them a competence of the same nature. As a paradigmatic example of cultural mumbo jumbo, their economic speech owes its logic, that of the disparate and decontextualised notions of bric-a-brac, to half-mastered words, down to their phonetic appearance, and to recipes detached from their principle, in its genesis and function. These fragments of knowledge collected without either method or order, from chance conversations, readings or transactions, or collected together rapidly, to deal with an imminent economic decision, will be used to test the good faith of a salesman or to show one is not gullible (like a technical word one might bring up in front of a mechanic) and above all perhaps in order to rationalise an economic decision after the event, whilst in fact it was brought forth by unconscious principles of class ethos. These anarchic counterattacks are also as far as possible from the strategies of big companies who possess the means to predict market fluctuations and to exploit them, in truth to determine them, thanks to the power they hold over the market. Theoretically almighty, since their simultaneous defection, in the way of a vote against, could ruin the producer's business, consumers are in fact reduced to powerlessness through their impossibility of collectively organising their strategies; their individual defections are only effective through statistical aggregation which operates independently of them and on which they have no power. Protest strategies (voice), or even boycott in the style of Nader, remain statistical actions which, being the result of a simple aggregate, an added group of agents passively and mechanically totalised (as votes in an election), are in sharp contrast to real collective actions, such as claims, strikes, demonstrations or revolutions, carried out by groups mobilised by and for the realisation of a common strategy, on the basis of a preliminary orchestration of dispositions and interests produced and guaranteed by a permanently and explicitly mandated body.

Every economic agent is very much a kind of entrepreneur who looks to get the best return from rare resources. But the success of their business depends first on the chances they have to conserve or raise their assets given their volume and structure and, consequently, on the instruments of production and reproduction that they possess and control; and, second, on their economic dispositions (in the broad sense of the word), that is to the say, their propensity and aptitude to take their chances. These two factors are not independent: dispositions with respect to the future (of which economic dispositions are a particular dimension) depend on the objective future of assets – itself a function of the investment strategies of previous generations – that is to say, on the present and potential position of the agent or the group of agents as considered in the structure of the distribution of capital (economic, cultural and social) that is understood as power over the instruments of production and reproduction. It follows that agents tend all the more to look for safety in 'profitable investments', which offer weakly dispersed profits, thus uncertain, but weak and prone to devaluation, as they have less important capital at their disposal; they all the more turn to the opposite risky but fruitful investments from speculation as they possess greater capital, capable of ensuring the necessary resources to meet the full cost of risk and to re-establish themselves in case of failure.

Evidence of this is clear in the case of strategies for scholastic investment.[18] *In the absence of sufficiently up-to-date information in order to know at the right time the 'bets' to make, bets of economic capital sufficiently important to allow for uncertain expectations of return and of social capital sufficiently large to find an alternative in case of failure, the middle and working class families (at least the non-salaried fractions) have every chance of making bad scholastic investments. In an area where, as elsewhere, the profitability of investments depends heavily on the time they are made, the poorest can only come across the good systems – establishments, sections, options, specialities, etc. – with delay, when they are in any case devalued by dint of the fact that they have become available.*[19] *We see moreover what separates the abstract information that a student from the working or middle class can obtain on a body specialising in coveted positions and the familiarity that a child from the upper class can procure from direct company with acquaintances occupying these positions and which allows the adoption of 'rational' strategies without having to think about them as such in the form of an explicit, calculated or cynical life plan (which constitutes a decisive advantage each time that 'sincerity' and 'naïvety' of 'vocation' or 'conversion' forms part of the tacit conditions to occupy the position, as in the case of artistic professions). Furthermore, the social capital associated with belonging to the dominant class (the 'relations'), which allows for the maximisation of economic and symbolic profit from academic titles in the labour market, allows also for the minimisation of losses in the case of failure: then, the different fractions, according to the structure of their capital, will find their compensatory strategies of reproduction either in transmission of economic capital (business takeovers, etc.), as industrial or commercial bosses and even professional people, whilst fractions relatively weak in economic capital but rich in cultural or social capital will turn rather towards artistic professions, show business or, today, 'shelter-careers' in public and private bureaucracies of research or mass cultural production. The safety that the intimate certainty of the ability to count on a series of 'protective networks' provides is the principle of all fearlessness, including intellectual, which the anxious insecurity of safety forbids to the petit-bourgeois. It is not by chance that, at all the crossroads of the scholastic route (and all the turnings of the intellectual career), a 'choice' is offered between the saving strategies attached to maximising safety by ensuring returns, and the speculative strategies aspiring to maximise profit: the most risky areas and careers, thus often the most prestigious, always have a sort of less glorious doublet, forsaken for those who do not have enough capital (economic, cultural and social) in order to take the risk of losing everything whilst wishing to win all, risks that one would only take when sure of not losing everything whilst risking to win all. It is probably in the space bounded by the terms of these alternatives that the feeling of success or failure is formed, each particular trajectory receiving its felt value from its position in the hierarchical system of alternative trajectories, which were rejected or lost: thus, for example, it is on the inside of the system of trajectories, apparently originally mixed up, where the avant-garde painter or philosopher represents the summit, that the most fundamental properties of the professions such as design teacher or philosophy teacher are defined, objectively and subjectively determined by their negative relation to the totality of lost trajectories. The intensity of necessary diversion in order to get to a lower trajectory measures therefore the importance of the work of disinvestment that has to be carried out in order to 'get back from it', as one says commonly, that is to say, in order to overcome the effects of over-investment favoured by the initial lack of differentiation of the trajectories.*[20] *Replaced in the order of succession, the alternative of risk and safety, savings or speculation, re-expresses itself in the opposition between the form par excellence that takes the shape of the monopolistic appropriation in the order of symbolic goods, namely the temporal priority (of which the given distinctive exclusivity in different areas such as avant-gardism and snobbism forms a particular case), and the unbeknown dispossessed possession, which gains only a devalued good, not through time but by dispersal or better still disclosure that happens through time.*

The economic and social world, positions to take, studies to do, goods to consume, properties to buy, women to marry, etc. never hides more, if not in the imaginary experience that supposes the neutralisation of the sense of realities, the form of a universe of possibles equally compossibles for each possible subject. It presents itself as a field immediately structured according to the opposition between what is already appropriated by others, by fact or right, therefore impossible, alienated, and that which is possessed in advance and belongs to the normal universe of what is taken for granted. To have power is to potentially possess exclusive or privileged use of goods or services formally available to anyone: the power gives monopoly of certain possibles, formally registered in the future of every agent.[21] Heritage, and not only economic, is a totality of *pre-emption rights on the future*, on social positions liable to be occupied and, that way, the possible ways of being a man. This is why it is necessary to read the class distribution of access chances to different qualifications in the education system, the projection of differential powers on this system and, in that way, on the material and symbolic profits procured by the titles that it gives, briefly on the different privileges that it transmits, with the insensibly extorted collaboration of the dispossessed classes, which tend to proportion their scholastic investments to promised profits, therefore to pre-empt the verdict of the system.[22]

The rights which give the right are only the explicit, guaranteed and legitimate form of this whole totality of *appropriated chances*, of monopolised possibles, by which present power relations project themselves onto the future, and dictate in return present dispositions. Power, as anticipated appropriation, as appropriated future, is what supports relations between agents beyond continuous creation of occasional interactions. Against this, one might oppose, if it was the place to do so, social formations where the only lasting relations are personally dependent relations, which can only be maintained through time, beyond individual persons, at the price of incessant work, and other formations where the mastery of mechanisms (such as the labour market or the scholastic market), which, by their own functioning, tend to assure the reproduction of relations of domination, confer a right of pre-emption over possibles dispensing with the incessant work which is necessary, in other contexts, in order to permanently appropriate to themselves the future of others.

The slope and the gradient

By making a virtue out of a necessity, class ethos is the propensity to the probable through which the causality of the objective future is brought about in every case of correspondence between dispositions and chances (or the present and potential positions in the structure of the distribution of economic and cultural capital); thus, it would be pointless to try statistically to isolate the effect of ethical dispositions, perfectly redundant in this case, with the conditions of which they are the product and which they tend to reproduce. Briefly, the effects of habitus are never as well hidden as when they appear as the direct effect of structures (or of a determined position in the structures such that it can be spotted through indicators of economic capital or cultural capital) because they are produced by agents who are a 'man-made' structure. Nevertheless, there are cases where the effects of this ever-present ethos allow themselves to be directly seen because the capital effectively possessed *at a given moment* – or the objective future that it ensures – is not enough to completely explain practices or, which amounts to the same, the dispositions that it necessarily engenders to account for past acquisitions that potentially set their future and consequently the propensity to make it happen.

It is such that the practices of the up-and-coming fraction of the petite-bourgeoisie (and, more generally, rising classes and upwardly mobile individuals) do not allow themselves to be completely understood through knowledge of synchronically measured chances or, in other terms, to distinguish themselves systematically from what they ought to be theoretically if they depended only on economic capital and/or cultural capital.

This shows itself particularly well in the case of childbirth, which, strong for lower income, passes by a minimum, corresponding grosso modo to medium income and rises again for higher income. If such is the case, it is the relative child cost, weak for families on lowest income who, not being able to envisage for their children another future than their present one, take on extremely reduced educative investments, weak also for families endowed with high income, since income grows in parallel to investments, passes by a maximum corresponding to medium income, that is to say, that in the middle classes the ambition for social mobility necessitates educational investments relatively disproportionate to their resources.[23] *The relative cost is defined in terms of the relationship between resources that the family has and the monetary or non-monetary investments that they have to set aside in order to reproduce through its offspring its position – dynamically defined – in the social structure, that is to say, in order to have the future to which it is promised, by giving to their children the means to realise the effective ambitions that it creates for them. Thus is explained the form of the relation that one observes between childbirth strategies of different classes or fractions of class and the chance of social mobility objectively given to their members. The working class, for whom the chances of access to the managerial class in two generations are almost zero, has a high birth rate, which goes down slightly when the chances of intergenerational mobility go up. As soon as the probability of access to the managerial class (or which comes down to the same, to the instruments capable of ensuring it, such as the system of Higher Education institutions) attains a certain threshold with foremen and office workers, the fraction in transition between the working class and the middle class,*[24] *the birth rate shows a clear drop; to this intermediate band also belongs artisans, a fraction also in transition but in decline. In the truly named middle classes, for whom the chances of mobility are incomparably much higher (and much more dispersed than income), the birth rate maintains itself at a minimum (oscillating between 1.67 and 1.71); as for the upper classes, the birth rate rises strongly, bearing witness that biological reproduction does not fulfil the same function in the system of reproduction strategies for these categories who only have to maintain their position.*

The upwardly mobile petits-bourgeois define themselves properly by the fact that they determine themselves as a function of the objective chances that they would not have if they had not the *pretension* to have them and as if they did not in this way add *moral resources* to their resources in economic and cultural capital. As this additional force is only able to act *negatively*, as power of limitation and restriction, it is understandable that one can only measure the effects of it in the form of 'negative grandeurs', as Kant would have said, whether it is a question of 'economies', as least expense or of limitation of births, as a restriction on natural fertility, that is to say, in all *moral* cases or, which comes to the same thing, economic, the 'most moral of the moral sciences'. If, in this case, dispositions are not totally defined in relation to a given moment in time between possessed capital and the state of the market, that is to say, the chances objectively associated with possession of a determined capital, if, in other words, certain categories of agents can overestimate their chances, and therefore really increase them, it is because the dispositions tend to reproduce not the position of which they are the product, caught at a certain period of time, but the *angle*, at a particular point, of the individual and collective trajectory. More precisely, dispositions with respect to the future and, as a consequence, strategies of reproduction depend not only on the synchronically defined position of class and the individual in the class but on the slope of the collective trajectory of the group of which the individual forms a part or the group (for example, class fraction, line) and, secondarily, the slope of the particular trajectory of an individual or encompassed group with respect to the encompassing group.

If, on the condition of situating oneself at quite a crude level of statistical aggregation, one sets a petit-bourgeois ethos of abstinence and saving against the bourgeois ethos of ease, it remains that this disposition holds as many specific modalities and even singular ones as there are ways of accessing an average position in the social structure, ways of maintaining or passing through it: members of the same class can have dispositions with respect to the future, thus moral dispositions, which are radically different according to whether they belong to a fraction which is globally rising or declining; and secondarily, according to whether they are themselves, as members of a line first of all and then as individuals, in ascending or descending movement. It is thus that if the petit-bourgeois in their totality tend to show themselves to be more rigorous each time that moral questions are at stake, a whole lot of indices set the repressive rigour of fractions in regression (in particular, small artisans and shopkeepers on the decline) and the ascetic rigorism of rising fractions (one and the other distinct from the ethical conservatism which is found in the large traditional bourgeoisie). Because, as much in the production as in the evaluation of practices, such disposition does not know or recognise definitively any criteria other than the contribution that these practices can bring to social mobility, the rising petite-bourgeoisie, which shows itself to be communally a lot more rigorous than the other classes (in particular with respect to everything that concerns the education of children, their work, their outdoor leisure, their reading, their sexuality, etc.), can, without any contradiction, show itself to be a lot more rigorous than the dominant morality, each time that forbidden practices (like abortion and teenage contraception) are put to the good use of mobility.[25] *This ascetic rigorism, most often associated with a prudent progressivism in politics, differs radically in its modality and in the number of its effects from repressive rigorism, most often in the declining fractions, which, having resentment linked to social descent, seem to have no other end than to obtain for those who only have one past the satisfaction of symbolically condemning those who have a future, that is to chiefly say, young people.*[26] *And one can see the best indication of this distinction in the fact that the members of the rising fractions slide from optimistic asceticism to repressive pessimism, as they get older and disenchanted with the future that their sacrifices justified.*[27] *'The present', La Bruyere said, 'is for the rich, the future is for the virtuous and the clever'. All the existence of the rising petit-bourgeois is the anticipation of a future which can only be lived by procurement, through the intermediary of their children, by which they 'transfer their ambitions', as one says. As a sort of imaginary projection of their past trajectory, the future 'that they dream about for their son' and in which they desperately project themselves, eats their present. Because they are doomed to strategies over several generations that are imposed each time that the delayed access to coveted goods exceeds the limits of one human life, they are the men of a differed present and pleasure, which are taken later, 'when one has the time', 'when one has stopped paying', 'when one has concluded studying', 'when the children are grown up', or 'when one has retired'. That is to say, very often, when it is too late, when, having taken out credit on life, there is no longer time to make use of one's funds and it is necessary, as one says, 'to lower one's sights', or better 'let go of them'. There is no repair for a lost present, above all, when the disproportion between satisfactions and sacrifices eventually crops up and dispossesses from its meaning a past entirely defined through its tension towards the future (with the break of the relation of identification with children, for example). To those parsimonious who have given everything without counting the cost, to those hard on themselves who, by a fullness of egoistic generosity or generous egoism, have completely sacrificed themselves to an alter ego, which they hoped to be, either in the short term in first person, by rising in the social hierarchy, or in the long term through the intermediary of a substitute fashioned in their image, this son for whom 'they have done everything' and who 'owes them everything', only resentment remains, which has always haunted them, in a state of virtuality, in the form of the fear of being duped by a social world which has demanded so much from them. In order to have revenge, they just have to place themselves in their area of expertise, that of morality, to make a virtue out of their necessity, to erect their particular morality as universal morality, so perfectly conforming to the common idea of morality. This means that they do not only have the morality of their interest, as everyone; they have interest in morality: for these denouncers of privilege, morality is the only title that opens the right to all privileges. Moral indignation engenders taking up certain fundamentally ambiguous political stances: the humanistic and a little tearful anarchism which can go on beyond adolescence with some old long-haired bohemians to veer off with age towards fascist nihilism wrapped around in ruminations of scandals and conspiracies.*[28]

This evocation of *systematic variants* of ascetic life-style, which really characterises the middle classes, is enough to show that strategies objectively orientated towards the maintenance and improvement of the position occupied in the social structure constitute a system which can only be apprehended and understood as such provided that one goes back to its unifying and generating principle, class ethos, through the mediation of which all the vision of the economic and social world, all relationship to others and to the body itself, in short everything which makes the proper style of a group, asserts itself in each of the practices, be them the most natural in appearance, the least controlled by conscience, by reason or even by morality. The family planning of the rising petit-bourgeois, as well as their academic strategies, only reveal their meaning and function so long as one places them back in the system of characteristic reproduction strategies of a class which can only succeed in its *formation* of economic and cultural *capital* on the condition that it restricts its consumption and concentrates all its resources on a very small number of offspring, charged with extending the upward trajectory of the group. The petit-bourgeois who, being successful in tearing themselves away from the proletariat, their past, claim access to the bourgeoisie, their future, must, in order to realise the initial necessary accumulation for this mobility, deduct from somewhere the resources which are indispensable to compensate for the absence of capital, this energy of social life. Their habitus is the angle of their social individual or collective trajectory, and has become the gradient by which this rising trajectory tends to last and succeed: as a sort of *nisus perseverandi* where the previous course conserves itself in the form of a disposition with respect to the future, where the *no … longer* extends in a *not yet*, it delimits 'reasonable' ambitions, and consequently, the price that it is necessary to pay to realise this realistic pretension. The rising petite-bourgeoisie remake forever the history of the origins of capitalism: in order to do that, they can only count on, as with puritans, its asceticism. In social exchanges where others can advance real guarantees, of money, of culture or of relations, they can only offer moral guarantees; poor (relatively) in economic, cultural and social capital, they can only 'justify their pretensions', as one says, and by that give themselves the chances to realise them, on condition that they pay through sacrifices, hardship, deprivation, briefly, virtue.

If the fractions richest in economic capital, that is to say, the small and middle-sized traders, artisans or landowners, bear rather more (at least until recently) towards savings whilst the fractions richest in cultural capital (middle managers and employees) mainly resort to schools, one and another have in common investment in their academic and economic strategies through ascetic dispositions, which makes them an ideal clientele for the bank or school: good cultural will and thriftiness, serious and industrious – so many guarantees that the petit-bourgeois gives to these institutions, all whilst putting themselves entirely at their mercy (in contrast to those who hold *real* economic or cultural capital) since it is only by these means that they can obtain profits of a fundamentally negative legacy.[29]

The pretension can also be phrased pre-tension: a rising angle converted into an inclination to perpetuate the past mobility of which it is a product has its counterpart in thriftiness and all the 'petitesse' associated with petit-bourgeois virtues. If pre-tension constrains the petit-bourgeois to *compete* or to enter competitions of antagonistic pretensions and to push it always to live *beyond their means*, at the price of a permanent *tension*, always ready to explode into aggressiveness (rather than aggression), it is also what gives them the necessary force to gather, through all forms of auto-exploitation, asceticism and Malthusianism in particular, the economic and cultural means which are indispensable for mobility.

It is in the form of sociability and correlative satisfactions that the petit-bourgeois makes their most important sacrifices, if not the most obvious. Assured that they owe their position only to their own merit, they are convinced that one has only to count on oneself for one's own salvation: every one for himself and by himself. The concern to concentrate efforts and to reduce costs leads to breaking links, even familial, which creates obstacles to individual mobility: one has neither the means nor the taste to maintain relations with other members of the family who have not known how to 'sort themselves out'.[30] The impoverishment of these vicious circles and the solidarity exercises which contribute to link the least dispossessed (relatively) with the most deprived makes of misery an eternal new beginning. 'Taking off' always supposes a *rupture* of which breaking with past companions of bad luck represents only one aspect. What is demanded of the defector is a turning over the table of values, a conversion of all attitudes. Thus, to substitute a small or single-child family for a large family – the negative causes of which, such as insufficient mastery of contraceptive techniques, are not the only explanation – is to eschew the popular conception of family relations and the functions of domestic unity, is to abandon, besides the satisfactions of a large integrated family, united through a real traditional mode of sociability, with its exchanges, its special occasions, conflicts, etc., the assurances that numerous offspring give, the only protection virtually sure, above all for mothers, against the uncertainties of old age, in a universe haunted by domestic instability and economic and social insecurity. This conversion of attitude with respect to the familial group is inseparable from a conversion of dispositions with respect to the future: to acquire many offspring is to take real guarantees against the future, through a strategy which is in some ways the functional equivalent of the constitution of reserves, it is to raise against it, in advance, protection, it is not to strive to submit to it by calculation, to master it through an investment strategy which organises present practice as a function of expected profits or predictable costs. Family or friendship relations can no longer be for the petit-bourgeois what they are for the proletariat, an insurance against bad luck or calamity, against loneliness or poverty, a network of support and protection that one will receive when in need through a helping hand, a loan or a place. They are not yet what is called elsewhere 'relations', that is to say, social capital indispensable for obtaining the best return on economic and cultural capital.[31] They are only hindrances, that it is necessary to break down at all costs, because gratitude, self-help, solidarity and the material and symbolic satisfactions that they give, in the long and short term, are part of forbidden luxuries.[32]

By limiting their family to a small number of children, if not a single child, on which all hopes and efforts are concentrated, the petit-bourgeois only obeys the system of constraints implied by their ambition: for lack of being able to raise wages, it is necessary for them to restrict expenditure, that is to say, the number of consumers. But, doing this, in addition they tacitly conform to the dominant representation of legitimate fertility, that is to say, subordinated to the imperatives of social reproduction: restricting births is a form (probably the basic form) of *numerus clausus*. The petit-bourgeois are proletarians who make themselves small in order to become bourgeois. By eschewing the prolificacy of the proletariat, who reproduce themselves as such and in great number, the petit-bourgeois 'choose' a restrained and selective reproduction, often limited to a single product, conceived and fashioned as a function of rigorously selective imported class expectations. They tuck themselves into a strictly united family, but narrow and a little oppressive. It is not by chance that the adjective 'small' or any of its synonyms, always a little pejorative, perhaps placed side by side with everything said, thought and done, has or is the petit-bourgeois, in their morality even, their strong point though: strict and rigorous, they have something narrow and constrained, tense and susceptible, cramped and rigid by dint of their formalism and scruples. Small concerns, small needs, the petit-bourgeois are bourgeois who live small. Their bodily *hexis* even, where all their objective relation to the social world is expressed, is of persons who have to make themselves small in order to cross the narrow door which gives access to the bourgeoisie: by dint of being strict and sober, discrete and severe, in their style of dress, but also of speaking – this hypercorrect language through excess of vigilance and care – in their gestures and all their demeanour, they still lack a little stature, depth, breadth and largesse.[33]

The dominant ethical taxonomy, application in the moral field of the system of social ranking of the dominant class, is summed up in a system of qualities and qualifiers which organise themselves around the opposition between positively or 'distinguished' manners (that is to say, the manners of the dominant) and negatively sanctioned manners. Rather indelible tracks of two modes of acquisition which tend to perpetuate themselves in experience – at least, finally, in the form of uncertainty and worry about good manners favoured by an illegitimate mode of acquisition – and which constitute by this fact the symbolic accompaniment of every practice, these two styles are predisposed to supply an ultimate irrevocable criterion to judgement of social distinction. To this principle of division another one can be added: the quality, assessed from the point of view of the dominant class, of the relation that the holders of negatively qualified manners (accent, bodily hexis, etc.) entertain with the qualities that the dominant taxonomy assigns to them. Concretely, the fundamental opposition between ease, dominant quality, and discomfort, dominated quality, is doubled through a secondary opposition between pretension as refused discomfort (in the double sense of the word) (by an 'overestimation of oneself which pushes ambitions, to excessive sights' as the Robert says – a famous French dictionary) and modesty, as acceptable discomfort (through a worthy 'moderation in the assessment of one's own worth'). It is thus that the dominated qualities always receive two expressions: one, frankly negative, is situated in the series of expectations (that it is necessary to lessen); the other, euphemistic, bestows to the dominated qualities of respect that they attract by accepting them as such. Namely a few of these qualifiers which, because of their polysemy, can enter into complex relations of opposition with different adjectives from the other series, each of which underlines one of the aspects of fundamental opposition between the big (or extensive) and the small from which all the specific oppositions are generated.[34]

(BOURGEOIS) *'Distinguished'*	*(PETITS-BOURGEOIS)* *'Pretentious'*	*(PEOPLE)* *'Modest'*
easy, ample (spirit, gesture, etc.), generous, noble, riche, breadth (of ideas, etc.), liberal, free, subtle, natural, easy, casual, assured, open, vast, etc.	narrow, cramped, borrowed, small, petty, chary, parsimonious, strict, formalist, severe, rigid, edgy, restrained, scrupulous, precise, etc.	gauche, heavy, embarrassed, shy, clumsy, 'uncomfortable', poor, 'modest', 'easy going', 'nature', frank (speaking), solid

These two classes of habitus that can themselves be infinitely subdivided – as one thinks, for example, of the 'forced ease' of the upstart petit-bourgeois – as a function of secondary variables, each time designating the characteristics of the conditions of production of habitus, come back to two modes of acquisition in the final analysis, that is to say, two systems of material and symbolic sanctions associated with two classes of conditions of existence considered in terms of their educational effectiveness. Ease (just like 'discomfort', its antonym) designates a manner of being and a particular type of material conditions of existence at one and the same time, more precisely a distinguished disposition and the conditions of existence of which it is the product and which are continually brought to mind through it: the principle and the effect of this distinguished and distinctive disposition is nothing but an experience of the world and of oneself as necessary, as realised coincidence of being and necessity-of-being, which founds and authorises all the intimate or exteriorised forms of certainty about oneself, assurance, casualness, grace, facility, subtleness, freedom, elegance or, in a word, nature.

Everything predisposes the petit-bourgeois to enter into a struggle of pretension and distinction, this form of daily class struggle they necessarily quit defeated, and without recourse, since by engaging with it they have recognised the legitimacy of the game and the value of the issue. This competition is a particular case of all the *competition* relations in which the privileged class attempt to lessen the pretensions (nobiliary, scholastic or others) of those who immediately follow them, among other things by treating their ambitions and aspirations as a sort of subjective delirium, founded on too big an estimation of oneself, and by trying to make them act as pretentious, that is to say, presumptive, disproportioned, excessive, arrogant, ridiculous or, at least, premature. It affirms by that their own distinction with respect to the lower class, opposing their legalism to the monopoly of titles (nobiliary, scholastic or others) on which rests their own privileges. So far as the lower class is concerned, it demands and claims access to privileges until then reserved for the upper class; in other words, the members of the lower class convert into legitimate expectations their pre-tension (hence their propensity to formalism), that is to say, their will to have in advance, before time, *on credit*, the advantages that, at least in a situation of competition, therefore of permanent translation, they will have anyhow. There is no seeing a denial of our previous analyses in the fact that the ascetic petite-bourgeoisie, traditionally devoted to saving, turns, in a competitive society, to credit: it is also the pretension to the bourgeoisie, principle of all their negative virtues, which brings the petite-bourgeoisie to ask for the means to live above their means, at the cost of a tension and permanent contention, and which imprisons them therefore in a new form of asceticism, and so to fulfil by other means, better adjusted to new economic structures, old functions.

Inheritance structures and strategies of reproduction

Thus, outside of the exceptional case where the conditions (economic and others) are fulfilled which are necessary so that rational action is possible, where the agent acts as a function of a calculation of possible profits to be secured by different markets, the practices of a specific class of agents depends not only on the structure of average theoretical chances of profit but on the chances specifically attached to this class, that is, on the relation at a given moment between this objective structure (scientifically calculable) and the structure of the distribution of different types of capital (economic capital, cultural capital, social capital) understood in the relationship considered here as instruments of appropriation of these chances. The practical anticipation, more or less adequate, which is within this 'causality of the probable' is actually habitus, generative matrix of already adapted responses (at the price of a permanent improvisation) to all the objective conditions that are identical or homologous to the conditions of its production: by guiding itself by the indices that it is predisposed to perceive and to decipher and which, in a certain way, only exist for itself, habitus creates practices in this case which pre-empts the objective future. It would probably be pointless, in these conditions, to look for a linear string of cases in the criss-cross of significant relations that leads to a practice objectively adjusted to the probable. It is thus that, when it is apprehended according to schemes of appreciation which come together in parent and pupil categories most directly under scholastic authority, scholastic success (itself determined, at least partly, by the identification of indices which always serve as a basis to cooptation, such as good dispositions with respect to the institution) functions as a reactivating stimulus which redoubles the propensity to invest in school and reinforces the effect of consecration exerted by scholastic sanction. Everything occurs as if the objective future which is potential in the present can only become what it is with the collaboration or even the complicity of a practice itself ordered by this objective future, as if, in other words, the fact of having positive or negative chances to be, to have or to do anything predisposes, while predestining, to act in a way that these chances realise themselves. In fact, the causality of the probable is the result of this sort of dialectic between habitus, whose practical anticipations rest on all past experience, and probable meaning, that is to say, the given that it gives itself by a selective perception and a biased appreciation of the indices of the future to which it has to contribute to make happen (things 'to do', 'to say', etc.): practices are the result of this meeting between a predisposed and appraised agent, and an *assumed world*, that is to say, already sensed and forejudged, the only thing they ever know.

The presence of the past in this sort of false anticipation of the future never comes to light, paradoxically, except when the causality of the probable fails to keep up and when the mismatch between objective and practical chances (with the aspirations that these imply or which accompany them) necessarily invokes the momentum of a past trajectory and the *hysteresis* of old dispositions.[35] For example, in the case of the mobile petite-bourgeoisie, habitus no longer functions as a practical operator of the causality of the probable, but targets a sort of imaginary point, disconnected from the future virtually set within the present in the form of instruments of appropriation of the currently possessed future. Thus, the propensity of families and school children to invest money, hopes and efforts in the scholastic system tends to *reproduce* (in the double sense) the objective relation between the considered class of agents and the scholastic institution which concretely works through practical indices, such as the frequency in the familial universe (extended or restricted family, 'relations' to the neighbourhood or to work), of sixth-formers (high school in the US, lycée in France), students or graduates.[36] And the positive or negative sanctions of the scholastic institution can only bring a secondary reinforcement to the practical certainties of spontaneous statistics, which leads to sensing the access to these qualifications and these institutions to be natural and normal or improbable, un-hoped for or impossible. But, precisely, as one sees it in the case of the son of a teacher where his good academic will inclines him towards an elite training school to continue the paternal trajectory, it is the slope of the trajectory of two or three generational lines and, more specifically, the history of the objective relation to the scholastic institution which, tacitly lived or explicitly communicated through judgments, advice and precepts, orders, at each moment, the practical relation to this institution. Thus, habitus represents the inertia of the group, deposited in each organism in the form of schemes of perceptions, appreciation and action which tend, more surely than all the explicit norms, moreover generally congruent with dispositions, to assure conformity of practices throughout generations. Habitus, that is to say, the organism which the group appropriates and which is appropriated to the group, functions as the material support of collective memory: as the instrument of a group, it tends to reproduce in successors what has been gained by the predecessors, or, quite simply, the predecessors in the successors. Social heredity of acquired characteristics that it secures offers to the group one of the most efficient ways to perpetuate itself as a group and to transcend the limits of biological finiteness in order to safeguard its distinctive way of existing. This sort of group tendency to persevere in its being has no subject, properly speaking, although it can embody itself, at each moment, in any one of its members; it operates at a much deeper level than 'family traditions', whose permanence supposes a consciously managed loyalty, as well as caretakers, and which have, as a result, a strange rigidity towards habitus strategies, capable of creating new ways of fulfilling old functions, when faced with new situations (such as recourse to reproduction instruments, like school, unknown or refused in the past); deeper also than the conscious strategies by which agents intend expressively to act on their future and to fashion it in the image of the past, like testimonial dispositions or even explicit norms, simple *calls to order*, that is to say, to the probable, of which they redouble the effectiveness.

Phenomenally, the very different strategies and practices that agents produce and, through their intervention, groups which appropriate them, always partly fulfil some reproduction functions: whatever might be the functions that the creators or the group officially assign to them, they are objectively orientated towards the conservation or augmentation of inheritance and, correlatively, towards maintaining or improving the position of the group in the social structure. In order to ascribe strategies of reproduction to rational calculation or strategic intention, it would be necessary to include, under this concept, only strategies explicitly constituted with a view to accomplishing this function, that is to say, proper inheritance strategies, and to tacitly accept the official definition of reproduction strategies recognised as *legitimate* at a given moment in time.[37] In fact, the habitus as inherited relation to a heritage is the common root of practices which do not owe their coherence to a conscious project, even if the explicit consciousness of chances and issues can confer an explicit systematicity, in certain respects, on the objective systematicity of the practical 'choices' of habitus:[38] nothing would be more dangerous than trying to account for strategies explicitly orientated towards maintaining or increasing inheritance and, *a fortiori*, towards safeguarding its integrity beyond generations, without taking account of strategies which never seem as such, like those that shape practices around having children, 'choice' of partner or 'choice' of scholastic establishment.

These strategies owe their *practical coherence* to the fact that, objectively orientated towards the accomplishment of the same function, they are the product of a single generative principle which functions as a unifying principle. As structured structures (*opus operatum*) which the same structuring structure (*modus operandi*) endlessly produces, at the price of *retranslations* imposed by the very logic of different *fields*, all practices of the same agent are objectively harmonised between them, without any intentional searching for coherence, and objectively orchestrated, outside of any conscious dialogue, with those of all the members of the same class.[39] Being the product of the application of objective structures of the economic and social cosmos to an organism that its very logic entices to function in a systematic way, habitus continuously brings forth practical metaphors, that is to say, in another language, transfers (of which the transfer of motor habits is only one example) or, better still, *systematic transpositions* imposed by the particular conditions of its practical implementation, the same ascetic ethos of which one might expect to have always expressed in savings, in a specific context, able to show themselves in a particular style of credit usage. The practices of a same agent and, more broadly, the practices of all agents of the same class owe their affinity of style, which means that each one of them is a metaphor for any of the others, to the fact that they are the product of incessant transfers from one field to another of the same schemes of perception, thought and action: a familiar paradigm of this analogue operator that is habitus, the acquired disposition that one calls 'writing', that is to say, a way of plotting characters, always produces the same 'writing', that is to say, the graphic lines which, despite differences of size, material and colour linked to support, paper sheet or black board, or instrument, pen or pencil, despite therefore differences between the motor totalities mobilised, presents an affinity of style, an immediately perceptible family air.

To construct such an object as the system of reproduction strategies, sequences of practices objectively ordered and orientated that every group has to produce in order to reproduce itself as a group,[40] is to give oneself the means to think in their unity phenomena objectively linked that different human sciences apprehend as in a dispersed order and a separate state.[41] Restoring to the science of practices the unity of practices, one can thus contemplate by this concept the totality of negative reproduction strategies which aim to avoid chopping up the correlative inheritance of the excessive multiplication of beneficiaries: in the first place, *childbirth strategies* (or, more exactly, birth control), long-term strategies, since the whole future of the lineage and its inheritance depend on it, which aim to limit the number of children and, by that, the work of social reproduction by reducing the number of those claiming inheritance; in the second place, indirect birth control strategies, like late marriages and bachelorhood, which has the double advantage of preventing biological reproduction and excluding offspring (at least as a fact) from the heritage (this is the function of orientation towards the priesthood of some children in aristocratic and bourgeois families under the Ancien Régime or the celibacy of the youngest in certain peasant traditions).[42] Added to this, all the positive strategies, namely *successor strategies*, whose codified tracks in custom and law only represent the most visible aspect, strategies openly orientated towards their real function – to transmit inheritance, with the least problem, from one generation to the next – which has, amongst other things, to win back those who failed with birth control, like having an excessive number of children, or inevitable accidents of biological reproduction (like an excessive number of daughters). But one also has to take into account, inseparably, *educative strategies*, conscious or unconscious – of which the scholastic strategies of families and scholastic children are a particular case – very long-term investments which are not necessarily seen as such and which cannot be reduced, as in the economy of 'human capital', to their strictly economic dimension, or even monetary, since they aim primarily to produce social agents capable and worthy of receiving the heritage of the group, in other words, to be inherited by the group; the *strategies* that we can call *prophylactic*, destined to maintain the biological inheritance of the group by securing for its members the continuous and temporary care destined to maintain health and avoid sickness; *truly economic strategies* in the short and the long term, like operations of credit, savings and investment, destined to ensure the reproduction of economic inheritance; *social investment strategies*, consciously or unconsciously oriented towards the foundation and upkeep of directly mobile and usable social relations, in the short and long run, that is to say, towards transformation, operated by the alchemy of money, work, time, etc. exchanges, in durable *obligations*, subjectively felt (feelings of recognition, respect, etc.) or institutionally guaranteed (rights); *matrimonial strategies*, a particular case of precedents, which have to ensure the biological reproduction of the group without threatening its social reproduction by mis-marriages and cater to the maintenance of social capital, through alliance with a group at least equivalent in all pertinent social relationships; finally, *ideological strategies* which aim to legitimise privileges by naturalising them. By reducing reproduction strategies to their products grasped in a separated state and as a *fait accompli*, one condemns oneself either to turn the system of practices of an agent or of a class of agents into a rhapsody of data, ruled over by so many positivist laws, or to 'connect instances', in other words, to connect indefinitely from the speech to the instances. In fact, all being the product of the same principle, these strategies are *objectively orchestrated*, which tends to exclude incompatibilities between practices that are necessarily interdependent – since each one of them must practically count on the consequences of the other[43] – and to favour the *functional substitutions* as biologists say. Every attempt to highlight the complete system of relations between the strategies that each one of the classes of determined social formation implements in different practical fields comes up against not only the absence of systematically constructed statistics, but also the fact that statistical aggregation tends to blur the relations which practically establish themselves, in the existence of each individual agent or each elementary agent, between all the successive practices, each new strategy finding its starting point and its limits in the product of previous strategies.[44] One can, nevertheless, as if by successive flashes of light, clarify little by little the different sectors of the network of relations which endow the practice of a class with its coherence and its adaptation to their own conditions of existence.

Thus, statistics on secondary school entrance according to social class and the number of children in the family allows, for example, to grasp the relation which nearly directly establishes itself between family planning strategies and education strategies:[45] *one reads there that the chances of entering secondary school of the children belonging to middle class families (artisans and shop keepers, middle management and employees) which distinguish themselves from the rest of their class by a strong birth-rate (four children or more) are not higher than those of the children of workers belonging to a family of two or three children; one can also see there that the chances of entering a sixth-form college (high school, lycée) (which supposes a higher degree of scholastic ambition) are still more narrowly linked to the size of the family (above all with respect to the employees and artisans or shopkeepers). Contrary to the apparent explanation, which would make the number of children (and the correlative costs) the cause of the drop in the rate of education, it is necessary to see in birth control and scholastic ambition two manifestations of the same ascetic disposition for mobility.*

Just as scholastic strategies have to count on the results of family planning strategies, which are lived in advance through the demands of scholastic investment, marriage strategies are probably not independent from scholastic strategies and, more generally, from the totality of reproduction strategies. It is enough to think of the transformation of strategies that the dominant class traditionally implements in order to get their daughters married and which, concomitant to the transformation of family planning strategies (which it probably contributes to explain), is correlative of a transformation in the objective relations between the ruling class and the education system. With progress in the entry of women into higher education, the mechanisms of self-orientation ('vocation') and selection, which produces very socially homogeneous scholastic groups (faculty or school, discipline), have tended to ensure class (or fraction) endogamy at least as effectively, but by quite another mode, as the interventionism of families and in particular their efforts to organise directly controlled occasions to meet (dances, surprise parties, rallies, etc.). This unexpected effect of schooling has probably not contributed to encourage families to abandon their interventionist policy (or at least very difficult to impose it) in favour of laissez-faire at a time of a complete redefinition of the system of criteria that determined the value of women in the matrimonial market, whether it is a question of economic capital (dowry) or capital of honour (virginity, demeanour, etc.).[46] *And one can ask oneself if it is not necessary to see the effect of another process of functional substitution in the growth in childbirth of the dominant class and even the dominant fractions of this class, whose reproduction rested principally on the transmission of economic capital: contrary to what is observed when reproduction is ensured by the direct transmission of economic inheritance to one of the descendants (to the detriment of the interests of the individuals whose rank – youngest – gender or some other socially recognised indication excludes them from the status of legitimate inheritors), nothing, except the cost of studies, prevents ensuring the 'establishment' of the totality of descendants (this although transferable cultural capital per person probably wanes concurrently with the number of children because, unlike cultural capital, theoretically dividable to infinity, adult time available for transmission is finite), when reproduction can be ensured, at least partially, through the transmission of cultural capital and use of the education system. In these conditions, one understands that the bourgeois can today avoid limiting childbirth which was previously necessary for them (as is the case for the petit-bourgeois today) as one of the fundamental conditions of social reproduction.*

In order to perceive the need to think, as it is, of the system of reproduction strategies, there is probably no better example than that of education investment, which the division of labour between disciplines is dedicated to making the object of partial and abstract concerns. Economists have the apparent merit of explicitly asking the question about the relationship – and its evolution in time – between the rates of guaranteed profits through education investment and economic investment. But, besides the fact that their measure of return from scholastic investment only takes account of investments and monetary profits or those directly convertible into money, like expenses involved in study and the monetary equivalent of the time dedicated to study, they cannot explain the relative parts that different agents or different classes give to economic investment and cultural investment, through lack of systematically taking into account the structure of the differential chances of profit which are promised to them by different markets as a function of the volume and the structure of their assets.[47] *Moreover, by omitting to put scholastic investment strategies back in the totality of education strategies and the system of reproduction strategies, they leave themselves open to leaving out, by a necessary paradox, the most hidden and the socially most important of the education investments, namely, the domestic transmission of cultural capital: naïve interrogations on the relationship between 'aptitude' (ability) to study and investment in study are evidence that one ignores that 'aptitude' or 'gift' is also the product of an investment in time and in cultural capital.*[48] *One understands that, serving to evaluate the profits of scholastic investment, one only goes beyond the consideration of individual monetary incomes in order to wonder, through a typically functionalist logic, about the profitability of educative expenses for 'society' as a whole (social rate of return)*[49] *or about the contribution that education brings to 'national productivity' (the social gain of education measured by its effects on national productivity).*[50] *This definition of the functions of education, which bears little idea of the contribution that the education system brings to the reproduction of the social structure by sanctioning the hereditary transmission of cultural capital, is in fact implicated, right from the beginning, in a definition of 'human capital' which, despite 'humanist' connotations, does not escape from economism and which ignores, amongst other things, that scholastic return on scholastic action depends on cultural capital invested beforehand by the family and that the economic and social return of academic certificates depends on social capital, itself also inherited, which can be put to use.*

But, conversely, the internal study of the education system and the strategies that it creates might distract from the construction of the complete system of relationships through which scholastic strategies are defined if one only observed that the propensity to invest in scholastic work and commitment does not depend exclusively on the volume of cultural capital possessed:[51] *the richest fractions of the middle classes (for example, teachers) have a propensity to invest in the scholastic market (that is to say, a good cultural will as scholastic spirit of enterprise) incomparably higher than the dominant fractions of the dominant class, who are however no less rich in cultural capital.*[52] *As different from the sons of teachers who tend to concentrate all their investments in the scholastic market, the sons of the leaders of industry and business who, having other means and other routes to success, do not depend on scholastic sanctions to the same degree, invest less interest and work in their studies and do not gain the same scholastic return (the same success) from their cultural capital. This means that the propensity for scholastic investment, one of the factors of scholastic success (with cultural capital), depends not only on actual or expected success (i.e. the chances of success promised to the category in its totality given its cultural capital) but also on the degree to which the reproduction of the position of this class of agents depends – in the past as in the future – on scholastic capital as a socially certified and guaranteed form of cultural capital. The 'interest' that an agent or class of agents brings to 'study' depends on their scholastic success and the degree to which scholastic success is, in its particular case, a necessary and sufficient condition of social success. The propensity to invest in the scholastic system, which, with the cultural capital on which it partly depends, determines scholastic success, depends itself therefore on the extent to which social success depends on scholastic success.*[53] *Thus, given on the one hand that the less completely dependent on scholastic capital for its reproduction, the richer in economic capital and on the other hand that the economic and social return from scholastic capital depends on the social and economic capital which can be put to work, scholastic strategies (and more generally the totality of education strategies, even domestic) depend not only on cultural capital possessed, one of the factors determining scholastic success and by that the propensity for scholastic investment, but on the relative weight of cultural capital in the structure of the assets, and therefore cannot be isolated from the totality of conscious or unconscious strategies through which groups aim to maintain or improve their position in the social structure.*

In order to completely explain reproduction strategies, it is thus necessary to take into account not only the global chances of reproduction (such as they can be grasped, for example, through the chances of social mobility, as we have done in the case of family planning strategies) but also the *system of differential chances* of profit that *different markets* offer (labour market, scholastic market) to those possessing a certain volume and structure of assets. It is so, therefore, that a cultural capital that is weak in absolute value can exercise a determined influence on practices when – as with employees, for example – it has a relatively strong weight in the structure of assets. In other words, these strategies depend on the relationship which is established at a determined moment between, on the one hand, the inheritance of different agents and classes of agents considered in its global volume but also its *structure* (that is to say, with regard to the relative respective weight of economic capital, cultural capital and social capital) and, on the other hand, the different instruments of reproduction available, whether official or officious or even secret: it is in effect this relation which defines the chances of differential return that different instruments of reproduction are able to give to the investments of each class or fraction of class. More precisely, the structure of the system of reproduction strategies characteristic of a family unit or of a social class, its *mode of reproduction*, as a particular combination of strategies of reproduction to which effectively it has recourse in order to maintain or raise assets, and its position in the structure, depends on the relative value of profit that different types of investments can ensure given its effective power over the different institutionalised mechanisms (such as the economic market, the matrimonial market and the scholastic market) able to function like instruments of reproduction: the structure of the distribution of power over reproduction instruments is, in a determined state of the dominant definition of what is legitimately transmissible and the legitimate ways of transmitting them, the determining factor of the differential return that different reproduction instruments are able to give to different classes or fractions of class and, by that, the reproducibility of their assets and their social position, therefore of the structure of differential propensities to invest in different markets.

That is to say that one can only completely explain the conscious and unconscious strategies orientated towards the reproduction of assets on the condition of possessing a knowledge (synchronic and diachronic) of the economic, cultural and social inheritance of each class fraction. One can in any case observe that different fractions of the ruling class, who distinguish themselves through the asset structure, that is, the profile of the distribution of different types (and sub-types) of capital that they possess and, correlatively, by the structure of their income, orientate themselves towards reproduction strategies which present inverse structures, either that, as was the case up until a recent time in France, the dominated fractions and the dominant fraction accord inverse weights respectively to economic investments and to cultural and scholastic investments, or, as is the case today, they distinguish themselves at least as much through the sub-types of scholastic capital that they tend to ensure by considerable greater scholastic investments (above all in the dominant fractions) as through the relative weight that they accord to economic investments and scholastic investments.[54]

It follows that every change in the relation between assets (considered in their volume and structure) and the system of reproduction instruments, with the correlative transformation of the system of chances for profit, tends to bring about a *restructuration* of the system of investment strategies; the holders of capital can only maintain their position in the social structure (or in the structure of a determined field, like the artistic or scientific field) at the price of *reconversions* of the types of capital that they hold into other more profitable types and/or more legitimate in a considered state of instruments of reproduction: these reconversions which are objectively imposed by the necessity to avoid devaluation of the inheritance can be subjectively experienced as changes in taste of vocation, that is to say, like *conversions.*[55] In social formations where the state of power relations between classes means that the ruling class must constantly change to persist, the dominant fractions of this class necessarily tend to split themselves up, above all in periods of rapid transformation and crisis in the mode of reproduction in force, according to the 'degrees' (and the forms) of reconversion of their practical and ideological strategies of reproduction, therefore according to the degree to which they are adapted to the new situation. Appearing when the established mode of reproduction no longer works by itself and when one can no longer simply let the reproduction mechanisms act on their own, conservative ideologies, whose function is either to legitimate the old mode of reproduction, by saying what goes without saying as long as it gets by on its own, by therefore transforming *doxa* into *orthodoxy*, or to rationalise, in the double sense of the term, reconversion by hastening the realisation of transformations and the elaboration of the adapted strategies and by legitimising the new strategies in the eyes of the 'fundamentalist', tend to invariably present, in the most different contexts, three *variants*:[56] the avant-garde conservatism of those who, having realised the reconversion of their reproduction strategies, do not hesitate to participate in the dispute over the previous bases of domination of their class; the reactionary conservatism of the class rear-garde which is made to search in a retrograde ideology of compensation for its social and economic regression (as was the case, on the eve of the French Revolution, on the part of the 'noble plebs', whose refusal to stand down led to an arrogant suffering, as Mathiez said);[57] and finally, the enlightened conservatism of those who, occupying an intermediary position (as is the case of the State bureaucracies, for example), attempt to reconcile extremes and enlighten the members of their class whose reactionary or revolutionary blindness threatens the class in its totality.[58] These forms and these degrees of reconversion, and the ideological strategies which are correlative of them, correspond, obviously, to different economic and social conditions, the propensity and aptitude to reconversion, depending on the volume and the structure of the assets possessed: the (relatively) richest agents or groups in a type of capital besides that which served as a base for previous power will be the most inclined and the most apt to undertake a conversion; on the contrary, those fractions most linked to the type of capital threatened (for example, the provincial aristocrats without either wealth or culture, the professors of ancient languages most closely linked to aggregation exercises) will be condemned to a conservatism of despair.[59]

Reconversions represent so many *shifts* in a social space that the latter has nothing in common with the both abstract and realist space of 'social mobility' studies. The same realism which spurs to describe as 'rising mobility' the effects of translation in the structure of class relations (with, for example, the intergenerational passage from teacher to professor of C.E.G) ends up ignoring that the reproduction of the social structure can, in certain conditions, demand a very weak 'professional heredity' (or, if one wishes, a very weak 'rigidity'): it is the case every time that agents can only maintain their *position* in the social structure at the price of a reconversion of their capital, that is to say, of a change of *condition* (with, for example, the passage of the small land owner condition to that of the lower civil servants or the small artisan to commercial employee). Briefly, the theory of social classes and their transformation comes down to a theory of fields, that is to say, a *social topology* capable of distinguishing between *shifts inside of the actual space of a field*, associated with the accumulation (positive or negative) of the type of capital constituting the specific issue of competition which exclusively defines it, and the *shifts between fields*, associated with the reconversion of a determined type of capital into another type, having currency in another field, so that both groups of shifts depend for their significance and value on objective relations between different fields, therefore on the rates of conversion of different types of capital, and on the changes which affect them throughout time, and finally the struggles between classes and class fractions.

Notes

1 This is a translation of the article 'Avenir de classe et causalité du probable', published in *Revue française de sociologie*, 1974, 15(1): 3–42. The editors wish to thank the publishers who have kindly given permission for the use of this article.

2 Ludwig von Mises has the merit of offering a clear expression of the double theory of action, which haunts, in an implicit way, economic theory. By holding all conscious and intentional action to be a 'rational action' (an expression which, as he remarks, constitutes thenceforth a pleonasm), he does not recognise any other action than as a reflex action to stimuli (cf. L. von Mises, 1949, *Human Action: A Treatise on Economics*, New Haven, 18–20).

3 Therefore, concerning Durkheim's attempts to 'explain the genesis of symbolic thought' (instead of 'taking it as a given'), Claude Lévi-Strauss writes:

> Modern sociologists and psychologists solve such problems by calling on the unconscious activity of the mind; but at the time when Durkheim was writing, psychology and modern linguistics had not yet obtained their principal results. This explains why Durkheim fought against what he saw as an irreducible antinomy (which was already a considerable improvement on the ways of thinking at the end of the nineteenth century, such as, for example, Spencer): the blind character of history and the finalism of the consciousness. Between the two we find *obviously the unconscious finality of the mind.*
>
> (C. Lévi-Strauss, in G. Gurvitch and W. E. Moore, eds, *La sociologie au XXe siecle*, Paris: Presses Universitaire de France, 1947, T. II, 527, my emphasis)

The two readings, mechanist and finalist, are equally probable, alternatively or simultaneously, each time that science discovers mysterious regularities (for example, when one thinks about the cycle, a characteristic of traditional agrarian economies, of a full harvest which 'brings about' a growth in the population, which 'brings about' food shortages and the return to equilibrium, and more generally to all the demographic trends). The illusion of the thermostat or, according to another metaphor, the homeostasis, is only a euphemistic form of finalist naïveties in the style of Bernardin de Saint-Pierre.

4 To convince ourselves of the necessity to abandon the alternative of mechanism and finalism, there are no better examples than the scholastic self-exclusion of children of the working class and, even more so, the correspondence between the chances of social climbing and family planning strategies, a case where the hypothesis of rational economic calculation is particularly untenable and where appearances of finality hold sway with a particular force (v. infra).

5 The form that this time lag takes between the dispositions and structures in the case of the translation quoted above, as well as in the particularly interesting case where this process is suddenly stopped, is analysed in another article.

6 Unfortunately, we need not assume intentional misunderstanding to understand that a sociologist who made himself known by working on mathematical analyses of social facts may understand the analysis of the dialectical relations between subjective dispositions and objective probabilities only by giving agents the intention to not make statistics lie:

> Objectively, that is according to statistics, the chances of a worker's son entering university are very low. This statistic is indirectly *perceived, on a subjective ground*, by a teenager coming from a worker's family where practically none of his slightly older friends belonging to the same milieu have reached university level. The teenager *will behave in such a way as to actualise* what he *perceives* as a statistical fact: when one belongs to a poor milieu, one does not go to university. Once this hypothesis is set out, one deduces from it that the statistics with respect to inequalities of scholastic opportunity do not change in time since individuals finally behave *in such a way* that previous statistics remain true.
>
> (R. Boudon, 1973, *l'Inegalite des chances*, Paris: Armand Colin, 55, my emphasis)

If one sees without difficulty why the author of this rather rudimentary summary is only *able* to understand the proposed analysis as 'finalist', it is necessary to keep in mind the persuasiveness of the epistemological couple that makes up apparently antagonistic positions, but which are in fact complementary mechanism and finalism, to understand that the same analysis is scholarly catalogued, a few lines above, as a 'hypothesis of the mechanism of repetition'.

7 Cf. M. Weber, 1965, *Essais sur la théorie de la science*, Paris: Plon, 348.

8 Heidegger explicitly links the concept of 'one' to that of 'average' in a sociologically telltale page: the elementary aristocratism, which is ordinarily concealed by the mask of metaphysics, appears in plain sight (cf. M. Heidegger, 1964, *L'Etre et le temps*, Paris: Gallimard, 158–160).

9 M. Weber, Ibid.: 335–336.

10 M. Weber, 1967, *Economie et Société*, Paris: Plon, T. I, 6.

11 In the psychology literature, one finds some examples of attempts to verify directly this axiom that economics often accepts implicitly (cf. E. Brunswik, 1949, 'Systematic and representative design of psychological experiments', in J. Neymen, ed., *Proceedings of the Berkeley Symposium on Mathematical Statistics and Probability*, Berkeley: University of California Press, 143–202; M. G. Preston and P. Baratta, 1948, 'An experimental study of the action-value of an uncertain income', *American Journal of Psychology*, 61: 183–193; F. Attneave, 1953, 'Psychological probability as a function of experience frequency', *Journal of Experimental Psychology*, 46, 2: 81–86). Indeed, it would require devising the processes of a genuine *experimental*

sociology, capable of assessing the variations of acquired dispositions given the social conditions of acquisition. For instance, one might think of transposing techniques used by psychologists (e.g. H. Helson) to study how the feeling of distance, size and other measures works and how it comes into being: the experimental analysis (in laboratory and in the field) of socially constituted dispositions, such as the sense of 'beauty' and 'ugliness' (applied to things or persons, to more or less 'legitimate' or illegitimate objects, etc.), 'over-value' and 'fair bargain', of 'bright' and 'seriousness', 'distinction' and 'vulgarity', etc., should lead to a system of indices (like accents) to which these *social senses* refer and thus should enable to link their different social forms to the corresponding classes of social conditions of production.

12 Either, for lack of questioning the economic, cultural conditions of economic rational calculus, we endow all the economic agents or only the 'entrepreneurs' with the ability to adequately perceive and assess the objective chances on different markets that would suppose a quasi-scientific information or a quasi-divine 'feel' for favourable occasions. Or, on the contrary, by thinking less of capital market than of labour or consumption markets, we endow the auto-regulated mechanisms of the market with the quasi-absolute power of ruling and regulating wills and preferences, of which, all said and done, science does not have to know, since, lest they be eliminated, agents have no choice but to act according to prices set by the mechanisms of supply and demand (these two incompatible stances could not co-exist without the dualism inherent to the dominant ideology that thinks differently when it thinks of the dominant class or the other classes: the bourgeois, who is readily spiritualist for himself and materialist for others, liberal for himself and rigorist for others, is just as intellectualist for himself and mechanist for others). Or, finally, that we strive to evade the abstraction by taking heed of the distribution of resources and scales of individual preferences, the 'tastes' or 'motives' of consumers or the skill or information of 'entrepreneurs', but by disregarding the economic and social conditions of these dispositions and the specific logic of their functioning. It is thus that so original an attempt as the one of Albert Hirschman who, breaking with mechanism, brings out the two (individual) strategies that consumers can oppose to companies, *exit*, the defection (in favour of a competitor), and *voice*, the protest, does not totally evade intellectualism for want of locating these strategies of extraordinary situations with regard to strategies ordinarily adapted to ordinary situations (and thus bound to be unnoticed) and, particularly, for want of describing the economic and cultural conditions of access to each of them (A. O. Hirschman, 1970, *Exit, Voice and Loyalty*, Cambridge, MA: Harvard University Press).

13 G. Bachelard (1934) *Le Nouvel esprit scientifique*, Paris: Presses Universitaires de France, 117.

14 K. Marx (1968) 'Ebauche d'une critique de l'économie politique', in *OEuvres, Economie, II*, Paris: Gallimard, 117.

15 Schubkin notes that the universe of wished social positions ('professions') takes the form of a pyramid that would rest on its summit, unlike the pyramid of the actual positions, where the positions are all the more numerous as they are less prestigious (V. Schubkin, 1968, 'Le choix d'une profession. Résultats d'une enquête sociologique auprès des jeunes de la région de Novosibirsk', *Revue française de sociologie*, 9, 1: 35–50).

16 Therefore, it is known that the propensity to abandon studies is higher, all things being equal (and especially academic success), the lower the objective chances of access to higher academic levels for a given class; and the effects of this 'causality of the probable' are noticed beyond practices up to subjective representations of the future and statements of expectations. Thus, even at a high level of curriculum and despite the effects of over-selection, we notice that students are all the more modest as to academic ambitions (as they are in the evaluation of their own results) and all the more narrow-minded in their career plans as they belong to classes whose academic chances are lowest.

17 The analysis of the particular conditions that must be fulfilled so that scientific knowledge may be possible, that is, simply put, economics, would have probably also led, by other ways, to condemn this paradigmatic form of objectivist error which consists of bestowing the value of an anthropological description of the generative principle of practices on the theoretical model built by the scientist in order to account for practices.

18 Although, to the best of my knowledge, there is no empirical study of the link between assets and investment strategies, admittedly, as far as school is concerned, agents who are richer in capital (and especially in cultural capital), are more inclined to speculate, as opposed to searching for safety. Thus, despite the lack of a more relevant indicator, one is able to notice that, very large as regards the possession of stocks, the gap between upper managerial classes and other social classes is very small for investments that are 'for keeps' such as bonds or deposit accounts; more precisely, the possession of a stock portfolio, which strongly rises as a function of income (which entertains a robust statistical correlation with educational standard), depends also on the sole educational standard since, at all income levels, the holders of high-school and university diplomas have more chances to hold stocks than others (cf. P. L'Hardy, 1973, 'Les disparités du patrimoine', *Economie et statistique*, 42, February: 3–23). The link between investment strategies and cultural capital raises the question of ethos integration and scientific skill or, so to speak, of the link between the practical command and the symbolic command of such a practice, of which education provides the instruments (we will study this link as to aesthetical consumptions).

19 This time-lag might also lead to maladapted strategies, because they are completed at an inappropriate moment; thus, workers who had their careers bounded due to lack of high-school diplomas often expand their investments so that their children may have such diplomas and these diplomas only; this, at a time where these diplomas do not fulfil anymore the negative and positive functions they once had, when they separated the 'back door', inferior entrance, from the 'front door', open to the sole holders of a nobility title.

20 The schooling institution fosters this confusion by gathering the individuals promised to very diverging careers (fine arts, for example, or literary studies) and by toying with the dispersion of promised careers so as to obtain investments virtually incommensurate to the compensation they will actually receive. Let us add this other factor of discordance between aspirations and objective chances, namely that, in a context of translating chances of access, the educational system places the individuals that are subject to its actions in a temporary condition (that of quasi-student or student) which, by tearing them away from production, and more or less completely (boarding school) from their family, makes them susceptible to subjectively being diverted from their objective fate and which carries the implicit promise of a future far-removed from the condition to which it objectively dooms most of them. Hence, we may put forward the following assumption: the probability that an educational investment does not meet the expected yield, i.e. the probability of an *over-investment*, both economic and psychological, and the correlative frustration, is all the greater as (1) profits enabled by the considered course or career (school, university, discipline) are more *dispersed* and that, the exact anticipation of educational profits of investments in cultural capital and the economical, symbolic profits of educational titles being more difficult, the discrepancy between aspirations that tend to be adjusted on maximum profits and real achievements is very likely to be wider; (2) the scarcity of educational titles in the labour market (where they are necessarily invested *a long while after*) diminished more as to what it was when the holders of these titles began their studies (or received their titles), or, more exactly, as to the investors' (i.e. the educated individuals and their families) representation with regard to the scarcity of expected titles and correlative profits in accordance with dispositions inscribed in a prior state of the market; (3) the investors are poorer in all sorts of capital other than cultural, thus compelled to

expect everything from educational investments (even if their cultural capital is relatively weak) and poorly armed to obtain the best economic and symbolic yields of their titles (e.g. the salaried fractions of the middle class).

21 The sociology of temporal experience, that is, the analysis of economic and social conditions that make the different forms of temporal experience possible, from the forced improvidence of the underclass to the generalised planning of the entrepreneur, constitutes one of the fundamental dimensions of economic sociology. Temporal structures and, especially, dispositions towards the future that are imperceptibly inculcated by the 'soft pressure of economic relations' as Marx says, that is, by the system of economic and symbolic sanctions associated with a given position in the economic structures, are one of the mediations through which the objective structures manage to structure all experience, without following the trails of either mechanistic determination nor adequate realisation.

22 In politics also, the command of instruments tends to rule the propensity to command them: in this regard, provided that one knows that skill is always, in a legal sense, recognised power, one understands that electoral abstention, which despairs political scientists, is nothing but the effect of exclusion. It seems very likely that the chances to entertain an opinion on such an institution, elementary manifestation of the pretension to command it, be it to maintain or transform it, basically depend on the power effectively wielded by such institution. Among all information provided by the secondary analysis of a set of questions concerning education over the past years by different French research institutes, the most important is certainly contained in the variation of non-responses as a function of the social, educational characteristics of the respondents, on the one hand, and the features of the questions asked on the other.

The analysis of the sampling structure of spontaneous respondents to an opinion poll on the crisis of the educational system, ordered by all French medias, discloses, in an even more conspicuous manner, that the *mobilised opinion* (in the logic of political petition) as to education coincides approximately with the population of present and future users, direct or indirect, of universities. Owing to the fact that the interest in the functioning of the educational system depends on the degree to which this system serves the interests of the group or class, the lower the chances of access to the educational system, the lower the chances of access to an explicit, systematic opinion on the educational system (whose production requires anyway a high-level of education). And, when the members of these destitute classes have access to it, they have few chances to perceive the objective functions of this system. In short, the probability for an isolated agent of accessing an explicit, consistent opinion on the educational system, outside any process of proxy or delegation, and to take part in a statistical action destined to influence its functioning, depends on the degree to which this educational system depends on him or her for its reproduction and to which he or she is interested, objectively thus subjectively, in its functioning.

23 P. Bourdieu and A. Darbel (1966) 'La fin d'un malthusianisme?' in Darras, *Le Partage des bénéfices*, Paris: Minuit, 136–154.

24 The categories of clerks and salesmen are rather ill-defined. Therefore, in the category of clerks, there are storekeepers and railway workers, alongside bank employees and civil servants. The category of salesmen is certainly even more heterogeneous, since there are butchers' assistants (whereas bakers' and pork butchers' assistants are classified as skilled workmen) alongside sales representatives and shopkeepers of multiple branches.

25 As the comparison between the petite-bourgeoisie of promotion (clerks, middle management, etc.) and the petite-bourgeoisie of presentation and representation (such as employees of big companies, designers, receptionists, organisers, etc.) shows, dispositions towards the future and thus towards the entire set of practices and opinions, depend also, secondarily, on the age and range of social climbing and its direction in the social space: members of the new petite-bourgeoisie, sellers of symbolic goods

who rise towards the status of a 'full of promise future' that is still ill-defined, ill-located in the social structure and for whom, as the saying goes, 'every hope', even unrealistic, is being 'held out', have less ascetic dispositions than the members of the petite-bourgeoisie of promotion who move towards long-defined status, clearly located in a hierarchy etc., often through an autodidactic effort.

26 Therefore, one notices, for instance, that artisans and shopkeepers manifest a suspicion close to hostility towards artists and are more inclined to claim that teachers are unable to command respect and are more prone to ascribe the academic failures of their children to the fact that 'they do not work hard enough'.

27 The hypothesis stated above seems to *begin* to be evidenced by the fact that, within the fraction of middle management and clerks, the discrepancies between ages are more marked than within other classes each time the questions asked offer to repressive dispositions an occasion to manifest themselves.

28 What is described is a form, among others, of the evolution of political dispositions, the one which entices clerks and middle management to take, while aging, regressive and repressive stances closer to those of little shopkeepers and, especially, of waning little artisans than to the youngest members of their own class, more rigorist than harsh. Of course, one should keep oneself from establishing a transhistorical relation between aging and evolution towards conservatism. The apparent link between changes in the dispositions and political stances and age operates only through the intermediation of changes of social status achieved over time; there are as many forms of evolution of political opinions as there are forms of social aging, that is, social trajectories. The conservative ideology that holds the link between evolution towards conservatism and aging (implicitly associated to a progress towards wisdom and reason) as an anthropological law and that finds in this link the best substantiation to its pessimistic, disillusioned representation of ideologies and revolutionary ideologists ('boys will be boys') appears justified: given that, on the one hand, to make it simpler, the innumerable forms of social aging that present themselves to petits-bourgeois and bourgeois teenagers (the only ones taken into account by the ideology) can be distributed into two broad classes, corresponding roughly to social success or failure, and, on the other hand, these two classes of trajectories lead by different ways to conservative dispositions (very different, of course, in their modalities). One sees that it suffices to ignore the variety of ideologies and social principles of variation of the link between biological and social aging to transform a statistical link sociologically intelligible into a natural law.

29 The ideal bank customer, as she appears through the speeches of managers and, especially, the bureaucratic processes implemented to pick the borrowers (cf. P. Bourdieu, L. Boltanski and J.-C. Chamboredon, 1963, *La Banque et sa clientèle. Eléments pour une sociologie du crédit*, Paris: Centre de sociologie Européenne) does not significantly differ from school's ideal customer, the 'good student' as objectively defined by screening and assessment operations by teachers: the 'good customer' works hard and honestly; her 'personal provision' is low; she asks for a relatively low, long-term credit; she does not have real guarantees, but only personal ones, chiefly her virtues; she knows enough about the system to be the object of rational utilisation, but not enough to rationally defend her interests and take the maximum advantage of the opportunities. To the ideal customer, middle manager, preferably civil servant, informed enough to understand the bureaucratic demands but not too much, that is, to the point of being capable of organised resistance, predictable enough to be sagacious enough without being wealthy enough to dispense with credit, are opposed, on the one hand, the 'annoying customer', rather upper managerial class with high cultural capital (e.g. law professor) who 'can wait' since she is not haunted by the fear of missing *the* occasion or urged to find accommodation, has a high personal provision and does not need too long a payment period, who has real guarantees and has at her disposal the intellectual means for the wisest use of her assets, and, on the other hand,

the 'little motivating customer', rather a member of popular classes, spurred by emergency, without personal provision, who wants a long-term credit, has no real guarantees and few personal ones and is located below the economic rationality threshold. The latter is the one to whom we refuse; the former is the one whom we'd like to refuse, since he or she reaps the maximum profit from the economic advantages offered by the bank and particularly from 'personification'.

'Credit is the economic judgment on the morality of a man', said Marx. Hence the deep ambiguity of credit personification: when the bank is interested in the person, it is interested in the guarantees of solvency attached to the person, as defined by economics, that is, to her or his monetary value, to the potential saving he or she represents given his or her age, job and health and morality. But, at the cost of some ability, the bank can appear to be interested in the total person, with his or her surroundings, features, projects and even anxieties in his or her most intimate dimensions.

30 Conflicts and costs that are the compensation of upward mobility are particularly important in societies where traditions of solidarity are the burden of ascending individuals. Thus, in a study on the domestic economy in Algeria in 1960, we observe that the take-off phase, where the petite-bourgeoisie is located, corresponds to a tightening of solidarity networks and a withdrawal to the elementary entity, the household.

31 Family integration is, so to speak, more and more 'functional' as one climbs the social ladder, since it enables to cumulate the capital of all its members (cf. P. Bourdieu, L. Boltanski and M. de Saint-Martin, Ibid.).

32 Without being absolutely exclusive, the individual ambition of climbing the social ladder and participating in the protection of the collective interests of one's class are far from being easy to reconcile, for practical reasons and also because they get their inspiration from two visions of the social world totally alien to each other. Enterprises of recycling or internal promotion (domestic contests, etc.) would not be as positively sanctioned if, like technical improvement, they did not warrant the support for the institution and the social order of which they are a part.

33 If it is true that, as we tried to show, the petit-bourgeois is a petite bourgeois in actuality and not just in the mind of the sociologist, we see all we'd lose by abandoning the concept of petit-bourgeois in the name of an objectivist definition of objectivity. Here as elsewhere, the indigenous concepts focus on an especially evocative form, the maximum of sociologically relevant features. Besides, the objectifying reduction, as brutal as it may be, has nothing to do with class contempt – which bursts out in so many writings devoted to petits-bourgeois, usual scapegoats of aestheticised prophecy and a favourite target of political anathema (one just has to think of Marx talking about Proudhon…) – because it links the features of the habitus, often spotted by class racism, such as 'pretension' or 'narrow-mindedness', to the objective conditions of which they are the product: those who can afford less sour virtues and less 'inelegant' faces forget that the features they condemn are the inevitable compensation of social climbing, that is, the selective sampling of conforming individuals; as if petits-bourgeois' 'vice' and 'virtue' (which – should it be recalled? – are defined as such only with regard to the dominant morality) should, in their sole case, be ascribed to agents and not to structures, on the pretext that the structures granted them the freedom to 'choose' their alienation.

34 One should refrain oneself from treating this taxonomy carried along by common language like semiologists and ethnomethodologists do, that is, as a reified system of logical relations of opposition and complementarity. Destined to function in practice in the service of practical functions it obeys a *practical logic*. Thus, when the 'bourgeois' (that is, rather the dominating fraction of the dominant class) think of the 'people' as opposed to the 'petite-bourgeoisie', it is not the same 'people' when they think of it as opposed to industrial workers; likewise, it is not the 'people' generated by populist imagination (more widespread in the dominated fraction of the dominant class), as opposed at the same time to the 'bourgeois' and the 'petit-bourgeois', that

is, the good and beautiful 'proletarian', burly, simple, candid, steady and generous, slightly separated by some inversions of sign from the good, humble, clumsy worker of conservative imagination.

35 In this case, the expectations of the habitus are all the more realistic as the past trajectory which manifests itself in them, that is, in the agents' and their group's history, persists more completely in the future trajectory: when the future is as if it is implied in the past – in the case, for example, of the teacher's son, himself peasant's son, who will become a teacher – the dispositions produced by the past position, itself subject to change, accompany the future of the position by forerunning it.

36 The propensity to invest in the educational system depends also in part on the form of the distribution of cultural capital between classes: the effect of demonstration and the stimulating action (competition) that dominant practices exert (the educational practices of the dominant class) cannot be exerted when the distribution of the objective probability of access is too brutally asymmetric; the 'demoralising' effects of a low probability of access are thus strengthened by the effect of exclusion caused by the quasi-monopoly, which entices the outcast to hold the appropriation of a given good or practice as an inherent *feature* of the *out-group*.

37 At every moment, the delineation of what is legitimately transmissible and, inseparably, of the legitimate ways of preserving and transmitting, is the issue of a covert or overt struggle between classes. As the dominated strengthen the subversive criticism, which seeks to reach the ruling class in its principle of perpetuation, tends to restrict the realm of what is legitimately transmissible by unveiling the arbitrariness of the established mode of transmission and the criticism of the ideologies dedicated to justify it (for instance, the ideology of 'birth'). This strengthening of critical vigilance and institutional controls of transmission is one of the factors that contributes to involve a transformation of the strategies of reproduction: the costless, efficient strategies, but overt, such as the transmission of power and privileges by succession in direct line, little by little make way for strategies of covert transmission, which can be unrecognised as such, thus perfectly recognised and legitimate, but at the cost of a greater loss and concealing (like educational investment).

38 The scope of the field of objective strategies of reproduction that are explicitly constituted as successional strategies and whose principles are explicitly phrased and legally warranted is broadening, just like inheritance. A study of the set of all practices aiming at securing inheritance between generations with a minimum loss would certainly tend to show that, provided that it is possible with classical investigation methods, the bigger the assets, the more rationalised the properly successional strategies, from the acquisition of paintings to the different forms of tax evasion. And the same assumption would also be valid, *mutatis mutandis*, for the transmission of cultural capital, more and more explicitly considered as such and rationally organised, the bigger the cultural capital possessed, in relative if not in absolute value. Arguably, to 'be in touch with the real world', the sense of 'what we are not allowed to do', is all the more likely to remain at a state of practical sense, that is, falling short of an explanation, as one is located at the bottom of social hierarchy: it thus wields on practices a domination that has the opacity and also the rigidity of the undisputed, of what goes without saying, of a *doxa* functioning as tacit fate. If the link to objective conditions tends to become more and more free, comfortable, detached as soon as we climb the social ladder, it does not mean that practices become more and more *unrealistic*. In fact, amateurism, casualness and selflessness, when they remain within the boundaries of sensibility, are among the liberties allowed, if not recommended, by the objective definition of the situation. Also, the quasi-rationalised link to objective conditions enabled by explanation and analysis offers other means of adaptation.

39 The habitus is a *constructum* irreducible to the manifestations outside of which it cannot be apprehended; which does not mean that, in accordance with the alternative of realism and nominalism, one should see it as a simple name, more or less arbitrary

and more or less arbitrarily applied to a set of statistical links. (There is a more systematic exposition of the characteristics of the habitus, and particularly of its circumscribed creativity in: P. Bourdieu, 1972, *Esquisse d'une théorie de la pratique*, Paris-Genève: Droz, 174–189.)

40 If, properly speaking, strategies of reproduction can only appear in the classes or the fractions of classes that are logically (if not practically) exposed to a drop-in status because they have something to lose, in particular on the occasion of capital transmission between generations, we notice, in the lower fringes of the petite-bourgeoisie or even in the upper fringes of the working class, strategies through which these persons aim at reproducing what separates them from the condition of the classes doomed to the simple reproduction of their existence (proletariat and underclass): thus one might explain the apparition of the propensity to invest in the educational system within the upper fringes of the proletariat, who are anxious to save their kids from falling again in the underclass (especially one comprised of strangers).

41 The condition of such a construction is the destruction of the traditional divisions of the scientific object that are nothing but the organisational divisions of social science, in turn modelled on the institutional divisions of social practice, but constituted in separate realms of objectivity, ruled by independent laws, those of the sociology of education having nothing to do with those of the sociological economy and, even more so, of economics. Furthermore, only a comparative sociology of the historically observed systems of strategies of reproduction would allow to empirically establish the universe of the possible uses of the different institutional or informal instruments that the ruling class might have at its disposal, at various times, in order to warrant its own reproduction and the functioning laws of historical mechanisms through which it tends to perpetuate its own domination. Systematically describing, that is, as a system, the set of distinctive strategies of reproduction of a period would not be tantamount to regressing to the ideography of factual or anecdotal history; on the contrary, it would amount to providing oneself the means to evade the alternative of ideography or typology, unsatisfying compromise between construction and description, within which so many historical works lock themselves, when they do not eschew the niceties, now condemned, of ideography, and the boldness, little compatible with the image of science, of a genuine theoretical construction, in a positivistic use of quantitative methods.

42 On the social functions of the bachelorhood of the youngest in the tradition of Béarn, see P. Bourdieu (1972) 'Les stratégies matrimoniales dans le système des stratégies de reproduction', *Annales*, 27(4–5): 1105–1127. On the functions of priests' bachelorhood during the time of Ancien Régime, see F. Y. Besnard (1880) *Souvenirs d'un nonagénaire*, Paris, I, 1–2, cited in E. G. Barber (1967) *The Bourgeoisie in 18th Century France*, Princeton: Princeton University Press, 126.

43 Due to the fact that they apply to different points in the life cycle as an irreversible process, the different strategies of reproduction are also *chronologically structured*, each one of them having to count, at every moment, on the achievements of their predecessors or those who are more short-lived among the others: thus, for example, in the tradition of Béarn, the matrimonial strategies depended very closely on childbirth strategies (through the number of claimers to inheritance and their gender, that is, the number of children to be endowed with an estate or compensation), on educational strategies, whose success was the condition of the implementation of strategies aiming at keeping away from inheritance the girls and the youngest (the former by appropriate marriage, the latter by bachelorhood or emigration), on properly economic strategies with a view to maintaining or increasing land property, among other things.... This interdependence would stretch over many generations. A family could have to force itself to make heavy sacrifices for a long while so as to compensate the outgoing expenses (sometimes in terms of land) necessary to 'endow' with land or money a too large family or so as to recover the material and especially symbolic position of a group after a misalliance.

44 The *life style* is at stake, that is, the set of systematic distinctive features that characterise all practices and works of a singular agent or class of agents (class or class fraction) as well as the *style of works of art of a period*: and the history of the life of an individual or a group, where we see the same *modus operandi* finding numerous points of reference and triggers in its own products (be they malfunctions, generative of contradictions and questions), certainly provides the best image of the auto-constitution of a system of works united by a set of meaningful relations.

45 Cf. A. Girard and H. Bastide (1970) 'La stratification sociale de la démocratisation de l'enseignement', in *'Population' et l'enseignement*, Paris: Presses Universitaires de France.

46 The same phenomenon was observed in the US, where the 'social endogamy' that is correlative of the 'development of mass education' associated to an increase in educational selection tends to compensate the effects of 'the rise in the liberty given to young people in the choice of their mate', correlative of 'the wane of traditional family links' (cf. B. K. Eckland, 1970, 'New mating boundaries in education', *Social Biology*, 17, 4: 269–277).

47 Cf. in particular G. S. Becker (1964) *Human Capital*, New York: Columbia University Press.

48 Ibid.: 63–66.

49 Ibid.: 121.

50 Ibid.: 155.

51 Cf. P. Bourdieu (1971) 'Reproduction culturelle et reproduction sociale', *Information sur les sciences sociales*, 10(2): 45–79.

52 The relative independence of the disposition as regards the sole cultural capital and the theoretical chances it would warrant in the absence of an extra investment in 'virtue' stems also from the fact that it tends to reproduce the family's trajectory, as we have seen.

53 It is no question to describe here the comprehensive universe of practical mediations through which the link between the volume and the structure of assets and investment strategies is established in each case. We might only note that, in the case of educational investment, academic success that depends on the cultural capital possessed and on the propensity to invest in school (in turn, a function of the volume of cultural capital and its weight in the pyramidal structure), strengthens by itself the propensity to invest, constituted on the basis of practical indices of the objective relation to the educational institution (such as, for instance, the degree to which the family owes its position towards school or education, through its head – the father – or, to a lesser degree, through any other member). As regards the proper effect of assets structure, it certainly stems from the fact that this consecration effect is all the more efficient as it is exerted on classes of agents relatively deprived of economic capital, and thus of competing interests.

54 There are further studies on French social classes and, especially, on the ruling class, to enable us to specify these analyses. Research on the transformation of the structure of the university field – grandes écoles and universities – that is correlated to the transformation of the mode of appropriation of economic capital profits (analysed in P. Bourdieu, L. Boltanski and M. de Saint-Martin, Ibid.) enables us to specify the analysis of educational strategies of the different fractions of the ruling class and their transformations due to changes in the economic field. The investigations that were undertaken with a view to re-locate the tastes and cultural consumptions of the different fractions of the ruling class in the system of practices constitutive of their distinctive *life style* aim at apprehending the generative principle of the different systems of strategies in its practical functioning. At the end of these partial systematisations, it is possible to construct the system of relations between the patrimonial structures of different classes and class fractions (with the transformations affecting them) and the investment and transmission strategies of economic, cultural and social capital (which

implies that we take heed, besides the different forms of investment in the economy, of less recognised forms of investment, which can be grasped – while waiting for an adequate study – only through dispersed indices such as the rate of marriage contracts, dowries, testaments, painting acquisitions, holidays abroad, participation in associations, etc.).

55 Such is the principle of social phenomena, very different in scale and nature, namely the reconversion of a landed nobility into a state bureaucracy or, at the other extreme, the partial or total reconversion of a scientific discipline into another, or a literary, artistic genre into another (in this case, the discrepancy between the objective and the subjective truths is maximum and it should be, since the reconversion can only succeed, that is, produce its symbolic effect, if it is lived and perceived as conversion).

56 The Prussian nobility is certainly a case in point of these analyses, with all its ideologues and ideologies of blood and soil that began to spread when the traditional basis of class power was jeopardised (cf. H. Rosenberg, 1958, *Bureaucracy and Aristocracy: The Prussian Experience, 1660–1815*, Cambridge: Harvard University Press, especially p. 24; J. R. Gillis, 1971, *The Prussian Bureaucracy in Crisis, 1840–1860: Origins of an Administrative Ethos*, Stanford: Stanford University Press; and above all, R. Berdahl, 1973, 'The Stände and the origins of conservatism in Prussia', *Eighteenth Century Studies*, 6, 3: 298–321).

57 A. Mathiez, 1951, *La Révolution Française*, Paris: A Colin, T. I, 7–8.

58 We will try to describe elsewhere the shape that enlightened conservatism takes nowadays in France by relating the structure of this ideology to the structure of the field of production and circulation within which it constitutes itself and functions (with, among other things, 'neutral places' such as conferences where the different fractions meet) and to the functions of dialogue of the strategies of reconversion that it fulfils for the different fractions.

59 Of course, only a comparative study of the strategies of reconversion could enable us to completely build the system of factors that facilitates or bars reconversions, case by case, according to their range (from the simple glide to a condition close to a leap in another universe), their moment (from the very outset of the phase, the riskiest but also the most profitable, to the rallying of eleventh-hour converts), the secondary changes they imply (from the reconversion on the field, for example, to the reconversion implying emigration), etc. We should have at our disposal analyses that could re-establish the pattern of the ruling class constructed as a *field of positions* at different moments, that is, the objective relations between agents' and groups' positions arrived at different degrees of reconversion: trailblazers, reactionaries and moderate trailblazers. These analyses should also link the structure of the field of ideological stances to the structure of this field of positions.

Part VII

Conclusions

15 Some answers, more questions – a final note from the editors

Asimina Christoforou and Michael Lainé

The current global crisis and its consequences on well-being for generations to come have yet again resoundingly revealed the weaknesses of an economic system founded on principles of utility-maximisation and the 'free' movement of labour, capital and services. These principles, the flag of mainstream economics, could not provide a complete and realistic account of economic behaviour, and thus failed to respond to human needs and problems. The mainstream tradition has lost view of how markets and societies function:

- It religiously looks upon markets to uncover the 'natural laws' that govern economic decision and social exchange and therefore overlooks the role played by both human agency and non-economic structures.
- It applies a set of mathematical conceptions of utility maximisation or statistical techniques of quantification that disregard the multiplicity of subjective and objective principles and systems of evaluation used not only by the object of study – consumers, producers – but also by the subject of study – researchers, scientists, practitioners and policy-makers.
- It restricts theory and policy to a means–ends and cost–benefit analysis and prevents economics from engaging in fruitful dialogue with other social science disciplines that could shed light on the non-economic dimensions of economic behaviour.
- It seeks for a kind of 'rationality' in human decision and expectations and, at the same time, turns a blind eye to the 'reality' of power relations and social inequalities that considerably influence how economic agents and structures behave.

In this book, our objective was to re-think economics and present an alternative view based on the sociological analyses of Pierre Bourdieu. As discussed throughout the chapters and various topics addressed in the book, there is much to gain from exploring the theories of Bourdieu and adopting his framework to build an alternative understanding of human action and economic systems.

For Bourdieu, 'economy' is distinguished from 'economism', that is, from the fallacy that all actions are reduced to a calculative, self-oriented rational choice principle, supported by mainstream economics. He uses the term 'economic' practice in its broader sense, which is determined by economic interests and profits, in their restricted sense, as well as by considerations shaped outside the economic field. Moreover, he asserts that this understanding of practice should incorporate the reality of a social world determined by relations of distinction and domination. His study on the housing market, for example, reveals the difference between a 'house' and a 'home', and how people with differential access to various material and immaterial resources perceive their 'home' and thus their chances of making one for their family.

Of course, these are aspects of economic behaviour that have been discussed in the past by major economists, such as Keynes and his conception of 'animal spirits' (see Lainé's chapter). In our view, Bourdieu's contribution is located in its ability to build on this legacy, which has been forgotten, and suggest new ways of thinking that incorporate social dimensions of economic behaviour. Indeed, Bourdieu takes the argument further by constructing a 'general theory of economic practice' that unifies the social sciences, reconceptualises capital and explains action in terms of field theory. In this way, it sheds light on the interplay between agency and structure, the evolution of power relations and the possibilities for social change. Orthodox and heterodox economists alike have paid little attention to the insights offered by Bourdieu's analysis.

Nonetheless, it would be erroneous, if not arrogant, to claim that this book has managed to cover the richness and depth of Bourdieu's theories. We undertook the more humble, yet no less challenging, task of introducing economists to his way of thinking and we hope to create an incentive for further research. Indeed, a series of volumes would have been required for a proper meta-analysis of Bourdieu's research programme. This has definitely been the case in other areas of social study, like art, culture, journalism, religion, politics, to mention a few, that have engaged in this type of analysis and host hundreds of publications. Before closing, we wish to make note of some of many of the issues that have not been directly addressed in this book, but are very important to our understanding of Bourdieu's work and its potential for future developments.

First of all, our series of theoretical analyses might give the impression that Bourdieu did not conduct empirical research. This is definitely not the case – his long list of publications reveals an abundance of empirical studies, which actually constitute the basis of his theoretical framework that we discuss here. These studies featured a series of methodological techniques that ingeniously and originally combine statistical and contextual analyses, and that were applied in a variety of spatial and historical settings. To illustrate, some of these studies explored the mechanisms that drove human behaviour and social change during the modernisation of rural societies in Algeria and France, or the global expansion of neoliberalism in the late twentieth century. Even if these studies were conducted in the 1960s and 1970s, Bourdieu's epistemological stance is still original and insightful and can be a source of inspiration for social scientists today, especially economists.

Field analysis and the various forms of cultural, social and symbolic capital have a central place in Bourdieu's framework. They are used to unravel forms of domination and symbolic violence and explain processes of social reproduction and transformation. Bourdieu employed these analytical tools in his study of art and cultural production, masculine domination and neoliberalism. The dominance of bankers and financiers and the history of the current crisis was one of the topics discussed in this book. However, other forms of domination could be the topic of study. Here, we would like to suggest concrete avenues for future research in some areas of study for scholars who are willing to test, use and improve Bourdieu's conceptual apparatus. Indicatively, researchers could:

- gauge the cultural capital of entrepreneurs and investors (the multiple correspondence analysis to be found in *Distinction*, through which Bourdieu assessed cultural capital, gives only a graphical representation of categorical data; it is not made for statistical calculus of multiple regressions: how to derive a numerical index from it would be an interesting challenge).
- test whether high cultural capital is correlated to higher risk-taking, as Bourdieu suggested in some articles of the 1970s and 1980s, without ever putting his assumption to a test. This might be of major interest to economists who cannot explain why some individuals are risk-averse while others are inclined to take more risks.
- gauge also symbolic capital in the labour market and financial markets, for example, which to our knowledge has never been done, to answer questions like: how do employers perceive the skill and personality of applicants? Is the symbolic capital of a given company a proxy for its long-term profitability? Could we compare the stock prices of two equivalent firms in terms of economic results and see whether the differences in the evolution of these prices stem from a difference in symbolic capital? The difficulties would be daunting, and the main question would be: can this capital be numerically measured? But it is worth the attempt.
- measure social capital in other empirical contexts and see whether it can explain market strategies and economic investment. For instance, social capital can be studied in relation to global conglomerates, local business networks, research joint ventures and social enterprises and how it supports different ways of doing business in the economic field.
- develop empirical studies on analogical reasoning, since habitus is said to use analogies extensively. It could help to see how the repetitive dispositions of the habitus articulate to its generative dispositions, that is, how we could reconcile the repetition of the same patterns with the generation of novel ones. Supposedly, analogy does the trick: how, precisely? How could the habitus be creative and bounded at the same time? Could analogies be represented by logical calculus? How could its qualitative features function? Keith Holyoak, Douglas Hofstadter, Paul Thagard and Mark Turner, to mention but a few prominent scholars who are versed in this field, have written numerous papers on the issue of analogy. How could we reconcile their works with Bourdieu's?

- examine further the relationship between habitus and reason (virtually never done by Bourdieu: how could the latter overcome the former? For example, in which circumstances? At what costs? To what extent? And so on).
- see whether there are activities *outside* the scope of fields as some critics contended (Lahire 1998, 2001). Is family a field? Why could some activities locate themselves outside? How does this affect Bourdieu's conceptual apparatus? Bourdieu went on repeating that fields did not always exist. For example, the literary field did not exist prior to Flaubert, or the painting field prior to Manet (Bourdieu 1992a). Before the nineteenth century, they slowly emerged and did not exist because they were not sufficiently autonomous. Hence, could they disappear? Are some fields on the verge of disappearing in the twenty-first century?
- investigate new and improved forms of masculine domination, such as the 'super-woman' ideal, as a woman who is completely competent in taking on all challenges in the public sphere, while excelling in child-rearing, decorating, cooking, keeping up with fashion and entertaining friends and family. Is this ideal of a 'super-powerful' woman actually 'dis-empowering?
- unravel the mysteries of virtual networking and social media. These outlets can exclude large segments of the population from access to new information and opportunities for work or leisure, if individuals lack the technical skill and cultural capital as is the case in poor urban/rural areas. At the same time, they can impose new forms of domination over people's perception of the world and their relationship with it.
- study the differential distribution of natural resources that is cause for conflicts around the globe. This involves not only limited coal and oil reserves, but clean water and air, as well as the limited supply of basic foods (wheat, rice) or nutrient-rich foods. Bourdieu's analysis could help us confront questions regarding: why do not countries sign treaties for the preservation of the environment or for the regulation of food trade? How are markets used to exchange 'pollution' or provide a solution to obesity and what are the consequences of this? Are there alternatives proposed by local and global movements?

Another substantial element in Bourdieu's research programme is his conception of reflexivity. We have yet to tackle the 'big questions' in social theory: How do societies change? What role is there for human agency? And, more importantly, how do we resist conforming to structures of inequality and domination? How do we uncover and dismiss the all-powerful? Bourdieu's conception of reflexivity plays a large role in this process as it places agents, particularly scientists, in the position of a constant evaluation of social structures. Even though access to capital resources determine the extent to which we develop skills to 'reflect', Bourdieu recognises that certain groups with less access to capital resources can still have a 'practical knowledge' of social structures that stems from their experience of everyday life: the ways the workplace is organised, the state functions and the family survives.

It is the lack of resources that prevents some groups from claiming social change, and this is where the 'collective intellectual' comes in. Bourdieu reserves a crucial role for scholars, artists and writers, producers of 'cultural capital': they work to reveal the inequalities that symbolic violence conceals and engage in the fight to confront them. They recognise their obligation to serve public welfare in this manner, rather than restricting their activities to counting citations, enriching their CV and getting tenure. There is no science without commitment – be it recognised or not. Networks of individuals that seriously take heed of their role as a collective intellectual can constitute a significantly influential force in pursuing social change and public welfare. But even 'intellectuals' are not exempt from their obligation to 'reflect' on the practices of their disciplines and assess them in terms of promoting social and scientific progress. Still there is a long way to go in explaining how reflexivity is attached to change, given the over-arching effects of power structures on individuals' lives and the difficulties in resolving problems of collective action.

And this is the point in which we appeal to the other social sciences, not only to the economists and sociologists who have been our main focus here. Being economists and sociologists ourselves, our efforts to incorporate the multiple aspects of economic behaviour and develop a fuller account of the human psyche and mind were naturally constrained by the very training we have received (ironically, some of us were even trained in the mainstream tradition and making our own transition). We thus invite political scientists, psychologists and anthropologists and anyone who engages in the study of the economy and society to share their knowledge in answering the major social questions. They need not endorse Bourdieu's capital and field theory. The only requirement is that they share his vision to overcome the segregation of social science research and knowledge, and to exchange their ideas, theories and methods to achieve a better understanding of the economy and society.

Finally, it can also be the case that the reader will be left with more questions than answers. We did not begin the book thinking that we would have all the answers. We would consider it a great success if we at least provided the reader with *one* answer by saying that 'Bourdieu's work offers an alternative; it's worth exploring'. Because if we see things differently and ask the *right questions* then it will be all the more probable that we will find the *right answers* to deal with economic problems and crises and promote policies for social welfare.

Bibliography

Selected works by Pierre Bourdieu

Bourdieu, P. (1958) *Sociologie de l'Algérie*, Paris: PUF.

Bourdieu, P. (1958) trans. A. Ross (1962) *The Algerians*, Boston: Beacon Press.

Bourdieu, P. (1962) 'Célibat et condition paysanne', *Études rurales*, 5–6: 32–135.

Bourdieu, P. (1963) 'La société traditionnelle. Attitude à l'égard du temps et conduite économique', *Sociologie du travail*, 1: 24–44.

Bourdieu, P. (1967) 'Postface', in E. Panofsky (ed.) *Architecture gothique et pensée scolastique*, Paris: Minuit, 135–167.

Bourdieu, P. (1971) 'Genèse et structure du champ religieux', *Revue française de sociologie*, 12(3): 295–334.

Bourdieu, P. (1972a) 'Les stratégies matrimoniales dans le système de reproduction', *Annales*, 4–5: 1105–1127.

Bourdieu, P. (1972b) *Esquisse d'une théorie de la pratique*, Genève: Droz and (2000) Paris: Seuil.

Bourdieu, P. (1972b) trans. R. Nice (1977; 27th edn 2012) *Outline of a Theory of Practice*, Cambridge: Cambridge University Press.

Bourdieu, P. (1974) 'Avenir de classe et causalité du probable', *Revue française de sociologie*, 15(1): 3–42.

Bourdieu, P. (1975a) 'La lecture de Marx ou quelques remarques critiques à propos de "Quelques remarques critiques à propos de *Lire Le Capital*" ', *Actes de la recherche en sciences sociales*, 5/6: 65–79.

Bourdieu, P. (1975b) 'Déclaration d'intention', *Actes de la recherche en sciences sociales*, 5/6: 3.

Bourdieu, P. (1976) 'Les modes de domination', *Actes de la recherche en sciences sociales*, 2/3: 122–132.

Bourdieu, P. (1977a) *Algérie 60. Structures économiques et structures temporelles*, Paris: Minuit.

Bourdieu, P. (1977b) 'La production de la croyance', *Actes de la recherche en sciences sociales*, 13: 3–43.

Bourdieu, P. (1977c) 'Le paradoxe du sociologue', Arras, *Centre culturel de Noroit*, 222, 223.

Bourdieu, P. (1977d) 'Questions de politique', *Actes de la recherche en sciences sociales*, 16: 55–89.

Bourdieu, P. (1977e) 'Sur le pouvoir symbolique', *Annales*, 32(3): 405–411.

Bourdieu, P. (1977e) trans. C. Wringe (1977) 'Symbolic power', in D. Gleeson (ed.)

Identity and Structure: Issues in the Sociology of Education, Driffield: Nafferton Books, 112–117.
Bourdieu, P. (1977e) trans. R. Nice (1979) 'Symbolic power', *Critique of Anthropology*, 4: 77–85.
Bourdieu, P. (1977e) trans. M. Adamson (1991) 'On symbolic power', in P. Bourdieu, *Language and Symbolic Power*, Cambridge: Polity Press, 163–170.
Bourdieu, P. (1977f) 'Une classe objet', *Actes de la recherche en sciences sociales*, 17/18: 2–5.
Bourdieu, P. (1979) *La Distinction. Critique sociale du jugement*, Paris: Minuit.
Bourdieu, P. (1979) trans. R. Nice (1984) *Distinction. A Social Critique of the Judgment of Taste*, Cambridge, MA: Harvard University Press and (1986) London: Routledge.
Bourdieu, P. (1980a) 'Le capital social, notes provisoires', *Actes de la recherche en sciences sociales*, 31: 2–3.
Bourdieu, P. (1980b) *Questions de sociologie*, Paris: Minuit.
Bourdieu, P. (1980b) trans. R. Nice (1993) *Sociology in Question*, London and Thousand Oaks, CA: Sage.
Bourdieu, P. (1980c) 'Décrire et prescrire: les conditions de possibilité et les limites de l'efficacité politique', *Actes de la recherche en sciences sociales*, 30: 69–74.
Bourdieu, P. (1980d) 'Une science qui dérange' (Interview with P. Thuillier), *La Recherche*, 112: 738–743.
Bourdieu, P. (1980e) 'Où sont les terroristes?', *Esprit*, 11–12: 253–258.
Bourdieu, P. (1980f) 'L'Identité et la représentation: Éléments pour une réflexion critique sur l'idée de région', *Actes de la recherche en sciences sociales*, 35: 63–72.
Bourdieu, P. (1980g) *Le Sens pratique*, Paris: Minuit.
Bourdieu, P. (1980g) trans. R. Nice (1990) *The Logic of Practice*, Cambridge: Polity Press and (1992) Stanford: Stanford University Press.
Bourdieu, P. (1981) 'Structures, strategies, and the habitus', in C. C. Lemert (ed.) *French Sociology. Rupture and Renewal since 1968*, New York: Columbia University Press, 86–96.
Bourdieu, P. (1982a) *Ce que parler veut dire. L'économie des échanges linguistiques*, Paris: Fayard.
Bourdieu, P. (1982a) trans. G. Raymond and M. Adamson (1991) *Language and Symbolic Power*, Cambridge, MA: Harvard University Press.
Bourdieu, P. (1982b) *Leçon sur la leçon*, Paris: Minuit.
Bourdieu, P. (1982b) trans. M. Adamson (1990) 'A lecture on the lecture', in *In Other Words*, Oxford: Polity Press, 177–198.
Bourdieu, P. (1982c) 'Dévoiler les ressorts du pouvoir' (Interview with D. Eribon), *Libération*, 18 October.
Bourdieu, P. (1983) 'Entretien avec J. Heilbron et B. Maso', *Sociologisch tijdschrift*, Amsterdam, X, 2.
Bourdieu, P. (1984a) *Homo Academicus*, Paris: Minuit.
Bourdieu, P. (1984a) trans. P. Collier (1988) *Homo Academicus*, Stanford: Stanford University Press.
Bourdieu, P. (1984b) 'La délégation et le fétichisme politique', *Actes de la recherche en sciences sociales*, 52/53: 49–55.
Bourdieu, P. (1984c) 'Espace social et genèse des "classes"', *Actes de la recherche en sciences sociales*, 52/53: 3–12.
Bourdieu, P. (1984c) trans. R. Nice (1985) 'The social space and the genesis of groups', *Theory and Society*, 14(6): 723–744.

Bourdieu, P. (1984d) 'Réponses aux économistes', *Economies et sociétés*, 18(10): 23–32.

Bourdieu, P. (1984e) 'Le plaisir de savoir', *Le Monde*, 27 June.

Bourdieu, P. (1984f) 'Université: les rois sont nus' (Interview with D. Éribon), *Le Nouvel Observateur*, 2–8 November.

Bourdieu, P. (1985a) 'Der Kampf um die symbolische Ordnung', *Ästhetik und Kommunikation*, 16(61/62): 42–163.

Bourdieu, P. (1985b) 'De la règle aux stratégies', *Terrains*, 4.

Bourdieu, P. (1986a) 'The forms of capital', in J. G. Richardson (ed.) *Handbook of Theory and Research for the Sociology of Education*, New York: Greenwood, 241–258.

Bourdieu, P. (1986b) 'L'illusion biographique', *Actes de la recherche en sciences sociales*, 62(62–63): 69–72.

Bourdieu, P. (1986b) trans. Y. Winkin and W. Leeds-Hurwitz (1987) 'The biographical illusion', in R. J. Parmentier and G. Urban (eds) *Working Papers and Proceedings of the Centre for Psychosocial Studies*, Chicago, IL., 14: 1–7.

Bourdieu, P. (1986c) 'À quand un lycée Bernard Tapie?', *Libération*, 4 December.

Bourdieu, P. (1987a) *Choses dites*, Paris: Minuit.

Bourdieu, P. (1987a) trans. L. J. D. Wacquant with M. Lawson (1990) *In Other Words. Essays Towards a Reflexive Sociology*, Stanford: Stanford University Press and (1990) Oxford: Polity Press.

Bourdieu, P. (1987b) 'Espace social et pouvoir symbolique', in *Choses dites*, Paris: Minuit, 147–166.

Bourdieu, P. (1987b) trans. L. J. D. Wacquant (1989) 'Social space and symbolic power', *Sociological Theory*, 7(1): 14–25.

Bourdieu, P. (1987c) 'What makes a social class? On the theoretical and practical existence of groups', *Berkeley Journal of Sociology*, 32: 1–18.

Bourdieu, P. (1988) *L'Ontologie politique de Martin Heidegger*, Paris: Minuit.

Bourdieu, P. (1988) trans. P. Collier (1991) *Political Ontology of Martin Heidegger*, Stanford: Stanford University Press.

Bourdieu, P. (1989a) 'Reproduction interdite. La dimension symbolique de la dimension économique', *Etudes rurales*, 113–114: 15–36.

Bourdieu, P. (1989b) *La Noblesse d'État. Grandes écoles et esprit de corps*, Paris: Minuit.

Bourdieu, P. (1989b) trans. L. Clough (1996) *The State Nobility: Elite Schools and the Field of Power*, Cambridge: Polity Press and (1998) Stanford: Stanford University Press.

Bourdieu, P. (1989c) 'L'histoire se lève à l'Est. Pour une politique de la vérité. Ni Staline, ni Thatcher', *Liber*, 2.

Bourdieu, P. (1990) 'Que peut-on attendre maintenant de l'éducation?' (Interview with T. Horio, H. Kato and J.-F. Sabouret and translated by Y. Delsaut and M.-C. de Rivière in 2009), *Sekaï*, May, 15–36.

Bourdieu, P. (1992a) *Les Règles de l'art. Genèse et structure du champ littéraire*, Paris: Seuil.

Bourdieu, P. (1992a) trans. S. Emanuel (1996) *The Rules of Art: Genesis and Structure of the Literary Field*, Cambridge: Polity Press and (1996) Stanford: Stanford University Press.

Bourdieu, P. (1992b) 'La saine colère d'un sociologue' (Interview with L. Roméo), *Politis*, 19 March.

Bourdieu, P. (1992c) 'Questions de mots. Une vision plus modeste du rôle des journalistes', in Reporters sans frontières, *Les Mensonges du Golfe*, Paris: Arléa.

Bourdieu, P. (1993a) 'Les murs mentaux', *Liber*, January.
Bourdieu, P. (1993b) 'Esprits d'État: genèse et structure du champ bureaucratique', *Actes de la recherche en sciences sociales*, 96(96–97): 49–62.
Bourdieu, P. (1993b) trans. L. J. D. Wacquant and S. Farage (1994) 'Rethinking the State: genesis and structure of the bureaucratic field', *Sociological Theory*, 12(1): 1–18.
Bourdieu, P. (1994a) *Raisons pratiques. Sur la théorie de l'action*, Paris: Seuil.
Bourdieu, P. (1994a) trans. R. Johnson *et al.* (1998) *Practical Reason: On the Theory of Action*, Stanford: Stanford University Press and (1998) Cambridge: Polity Press.
Bourdieu, P. (1994b) 'L'économie des biens symboliques', *Cahiers de recherche*, 13.
Bourdieu, P. (1996a) *Sur la télévision*, Paris: Liber/Raisons d'agir.
Bourdieu, P. (1996a) trans. P. P. Ferguson (1998) *On Television*, New York: The New Press.
Bourdieu, P. (1996b) 'On the family as a realised category', *Theory, Culture and Society*, 13(3): 19–26.
Bourdieu, P. (1997a) *Méditations pascaliennes*, Paris: Seuil.
Bourdieu, P. (1997a) trans. R. Nice (2000) *Pascalian Meditations*, Cambridge: Polity Press and (2000) Stanford: Stanford University Press.
Bourdieu, P. (1997b) 'Dévoiler et divulguer le refoulé', in J. Joseph (ed.) *Algérie-France-Islam*, Paris: L'Harmattan, 21–27.
Bourdieu, P. (1997c) 'Gegen die blinde Logik der Ökonomie' (Interview with M. Steinrücke), *Sozialismus*, 6: 1–7. Also as 'Retour sur les grèves de décembre 1995' in P. Bourdieu (2002) *Interventions politiques 1961-2001. Science sociale et action politique*, Marseille: Agone, 335–340.
Bourdieu, P. (1997d) 'Le champ économique', *Actes de la recherche en sciences sociales*, 23(119): 48–66.
Bourdieu, P. (1997e) 'Zur Genese der Begriffe Habitus und Feld', in P. Bourdieu (ed.) *Der Tote packt den Lebenden, Schriften zu Politik und Kultur*, Hamburg: VSA, 59–78.
Bourdieu, P. (1998a) *Contre-feux. Propos pour servir à la résistance contre l'invasion néo-libérale*, Paris: Raisons d'agir.
Bourdieu, P. (1998a) trans. R. Nice (1998) *Acts of Resistance: Against the New Myths of our Times*, Cambridge: Polity Press.
Bourdieu, P. (1998b) *La Domination masculine*, Paris: Seuil.
Bourdieu, P. (1998b) trans. R. Nice (2001) *Masculine Domination*, Cambridge: Polity Press and (2001) Stanford: Stanford University Press.
Bourdieu, P. (1998c) 'Sur les ruses de la raison imperialiste', *Actes de la recherche en sciences sociales*, 121–122: 109–125.
Bourdieu, P. (1998d) 'Die Sozialwissenschaften und die Philosophie', in K. Kufeld (ed.) *Zukunft Gestalten. Reden und Beiträge zum Ernst-Bloch-Preis 1997*, Tübingen: Talheimer.
Bourdieu, P. (1998e) 'The essence of neoliberalism', *Le Monde Diplomatique*, December, http://mondediplo.com/1998/12/08bourdieu.
Bourdieu, P. (1999) 'Une révolution conservatrice dans l'édition', *Actes de la recherche en sciences sociales*, 126/127: 3–28.
Bourdieu, P. (2000a) 'Making the economic habitus. Algerian worker revisited' (trans. R. Nice and L. J. D. Wacquant), *Ethnography*, 1(1): 17–47.
Bourdieu, P. (2000b) *Les Structures sociales de l'économie*, Paris: Seuil.
Bourdieu, P. (2000b) trans. C. Turner (2005) *The Social Structures of the Economy*, Cambridge: Polity Press.
Bourdieu, P. (2000c) *Propos sur le champ politique*, Lyon: Presses Universitaires de Lyon.

Bourdieu, P. (2001a) *Contre-feux 2. Pour un mouvement social européen*, Paris: Raisons d'agir.
Bourdieu, P. (2001b) *Langage et pouvoir symbolique*, Paris: Seuil.
Bourdieu, P. (2001c) *Science de la science et réflexivité*, Paris: Raison d'agir.
Bourdieu, P. (2001c) trans. R. Nice (2004) *Science of Science and Reflexivity*, Chicago: Chicago University Press.
Bourdieu, P. (2002a) *Interventions politiques 1961–2001. Science sociale et action politique*, selected and introduced by F. Poupeau and T. Discepolo, Marseille: Agone.
Bourdieu, P. (2002a) trans. D. Fernbach (2008) *Political Interventions: Social Science and Political Action*, Brooklyn and London: Verso Books.
Bourdieu, P. (2002b) *Le Bal des célibataires: crise de la société paysanne en Béarn*, Paris: Seuil.
Bourdieu, P. (2002b) trans. R. Nice (2008) *Bachelors' Ball: The Crisis of Peasant Society in Béarn*, Chicago: University of Chicago Press.
Bourdieu, P. (2004) *Esquisse pour une auto-analyse*, Paris: Raison d'agir.
Bourdieu, P. (2004) trans. R. Nice (2008) *Sketch for a Self-analysis*, Chicago: University of Chicago Press.
Bourdieu, P. (2005a) 'Principles of an economic anthropology', in N. J. Smelser and R. Swedberg (eds) *The Handbook of Economic Sociology*, Princeton: Princeton University Press, 75–89.
Bourdieu, P. (2005b) 'Secouez un peu vos structures!', in J. Dubois, P. Durand and Y. Winkin (eds) *Le Symbolique et le social. La réception internationale de la pensée de Pierre Bourdieu*, Liège: Éditions de l'Université de Liège, 325–342.
Bourdieu, P. (2007) 'Postface. La noblesse: capital social et capital symbolique', in D. Lancien and M. de Saint-Martin (eds) *Anciennes et nouvelles aristocratie de 1880 à nos jours*, Paris: MSH, 385–397.
Bourdieu, P. (2008) *Esquisses algériennes*, Paris: Seuil (edited and presented by Tasadit Yacine).
Bourdieu, P. (2012) *Sur l'État. Cours au Collège de France, 1989–1992*, Paris: Raison d'agir – Seuil.
Bourdieu, P. (2013) *Manet. Une révolution symbolique: Cours au Collège de France (1998–2000)*, Paris: Seuil – Raison d'agir.
Bourdieu, P. (ed.) (1993) *La Misère du monde*, Paris: Seuil.
Bourdieu, P. (ed.) (1993) trans. P. P. Ferguson (1999) *The Weight of the World: Social Suffering in Contemporary Society*, Stanford: Stanford University Press.
Bourdieu, P. and Boltanski, L. (1976) 'La production de l'idéologie dominante', *Actes de la recherche en sciences sociales*, 2(2–3): 3–73.
Bourdieu, P. and Chartier, R. (2010) *Le Sociologue et l'historien*, Paris: Agone/Raisons d'agir.
Bourdieu, P. and Darbel, A. (1966) 'La fin d'un malthusianisme?' in Darras (ed.) *Le Partage des benefices expansion et inégalités en France*, Paris: Minuit, 136–154.
Bourdieu, P. and de Saint-Martin, M. (1976) 'Anatomie du goût', *Actes de la recherche en sciences sociales*, 5: 2–81.
Bourdieu, P. and de Saint-Martin, M. (1978) 'Le patronat', *Actes de la recherche en sciences sociales*, 20/21: 3–82.
Bourdieu, P. and de Saint-Martin, M. (1987) 'Agrégation et ségrégation. Le champ des grandes écoles et le champ du pouvoir', *Actes de la recherche en sciences sociales*, 69: 2–50.

Bourdieu, P. and Delsaut, Y. (1975) 'Le couturier et sa griffe. Contribution à une théorie de la magie', *Actes de la recherche en sciences sociales*, 1: 7–36.

Bourdieu, P. and Eagleton, T. (1992) 'In conversation: doxa and common life', *New Left Review*, I(191): 111–122.

Bourdieu, P. and Nice, R. (1980) 'The production of belief: contribution to an economy of symbolic goods', *Media, Culture, and Society*, 2: 261–293.

Bourdieu, P. and Passeron, J.-C. (1964) *Les Héritiers. Les étudiants et la culture*, Paris: Minuit.

Bourdieu, P. and Passeron, J.-C. (1964) trans. R. Nice (1979) *The Inheritors: French Students and their Relation to Culture, with a new Epilogue*, Chicago: University of Chicago Press.

Bourdieu, P. and Passeron, J.-C. (1970) *La Reproduction. Éléments pour une théorie du système d'enseignement*, Paris: Minuit.

Bourdieu, P. and Passeron, J.-C. (1970) trans. R. Nice (1977) *Reproduction in Education, Society and Culture*, London: Sage.

Bourdieu, P. and Sayad, A. (1964) *Le Déracinement, la crise de l'agriculture traditionnelle en Algérie*, Paris: Minuit.

Bourdieu, P. and Wacquant, L. J. D. (1992) *Réponses. Pour une anthropologie réflexive*, Paris: Seuil.

Bourdieu, P. and Wacquant, L. J. D. (1992) trans. L. J. D. Wacquant (1992) *An Invitation to Reflexive Sociology*, Chicago: University of Chicago Press and (1992) Oxford: Polity Press.

Bourdieu, P., Boltanski, L., Castel, R. and Chamboredon, J.-C. (1965) *Un art moyen. Essais sur les usages sociaux de la photographie*, Paris: Minuit.

Bourdieu, P., Boltanski, L., Castel, R. and Chamboredon, J.-C. (1965) trans. S. Whiteside (1990) *Photography: A Middle-Brow Art*, Stanford: Stanford University Press.

Bourdieu, P., Chamboredon, J.-C. and Passeron, J.-C. (1968) *Le Métier de sociologue. Préalables épistémologiques*, Paris: E.H.E.S.S. and Mouton.

Bourdieu, P., Chamboredon, J.-C. and Passeron, J.-C. (1968) trans. R. Nice (1991) *Craft of Sociology: Epistemological preliminaries*, Berlin and New York: Walter de Gruyter.

Bourdieu, P., Darbel, A. and Schnapper, D. (1966) *L'Amour de l'art. Les musées d'art européens et leur public*, Paris: Minuit.

Bourdieu, P., Darbel, A. and Schnapper, D. (1966) trans. C. Beattie and N. Merriman (1990) *The Love of Art. European Art Museums and their Public*, Cambridge: Polity Press and Stanford: Stanford University Press.

Bourdieu, P., Darbel, A., Rivet, J.-P. and Seibel, C. (1963) *Travail et travailleurs en Algérie*, Paris and La Haye: Mouton.

Bourdieu, P., Eliard, M. and Passeron, J.-C. (1964) 'Les étudiants et leurs études', *Cahiers du Centre de Sociologie Européene*, 1, Paris and La Haye: Mouton.

General bibliography

Adams, B., Jardine, L., Maloney, M., Rosenthal, N. and Shone, R. (1997) *Sensation: Young British Artists from the Saatchi Collection*, London: Thames and Hudson.

Adkins, L. (2003) 'Reflexivity: freedom or habit of gender?', *Theory, Culture and Society*, 20(6): 21–42.

Aglietta, M. (1976) *Régulation et crises du capitalisme*, Paris: Calmann-Lévy.

Aglietta, M. (1976) trans. D. Fernbach (2000) *A Theory of Capitalist Regulation: The U.S. Experience*, London and New York: Verso.

Aglietta, M. and Orléan, A. (1998) *La Monnaie souveraine*, Paris: Odile Jacob.
Aglietta, M. and Rebérioux, A. (2004) *Dérives du capitalisme financier*, Paris: Albin Michel.
Aglietta, M. and Rebérioux, A. (2005) *Corporate Governance Adrift. A Critique of Shareholder Value*, Cheltenham: Edward Elgar.
Akerlof, G. A. and Yellen, J. L. (1990) 'The fair-wage hypothesis and unemployment', *The Quarterly Journal of Economics*, 105(2): 255–283.
Akerlof, G. and Shiller, R. (2009) *Animal Spirits*, Princeton: Princeton University Press.
Alexander, J. C. (1995) *Fin de Siècle Social Theory: Relativism, Reductionism, and the Problem of Reason*, London: Verso Books.
Alexander, J. C. (1995) trans. N. Zaccaï-Reyners and J. Lejeune (2000) *La Réduction. Critique de Bourdieu*, Paris: Cerf (translation of 'The reality of reduction: the failed synthesis of Pierre Bourdieu', in *Fin de Siècle Social Theory: Relativism, Reductionism, and the Problem of Reason*, London: Verso Books, 128–217).
Althusser, L. (1976) *Positions*, Paris: Éditions sociales.
Amable, B. (2003) *The Diversity of Modern Capitalism*, Oxford: Oxford University Press.
Amable, B. (2005) *Les Cinq capitalismes. Diversité des systèmes économiques et sociaux dans la mondialisation*, Paris: Seuil.
Amselle, J.-L. (2011) *L'Occident décroché: enquête sur les postcolonialismes*, Paris: Pluriel.
Athané, F. (2011) *Pour une histoire naturelle du don*, Paris: PUF.
Bandelj, N. (2002) 'Embedded economies: social relations as determinants of foreign direct investment in Central and Eastern Europe', *Social Forces*, 81(2): 411–444.
Bateman, B. W. (1987) 'Keynes's changing conception of probability', *Economics and Philosophy*, 3(1): 97–119.
Bateman, B. W. (1991) 'Das Maynard Keynes problem', *Cambridge Journal of Economics*, 15(1): 101–111.
Beaud, S. and Pialoux, M. (1999) *Retour sur la condition ouvrière*, Paris: Fayard.
Bebbington, A. J. (2007) 'Social capital and development studies II: can Bourdieu travel to policy?', *Progress in Development Studies*, 7(2): 155–162.
Bebbington, A. J., Woolcock, M., Guggenheim, S. and Olson, E. A. (2006) *The Search for Empowerment: Social Capital as Idea and Practice at the World Bank*, Bloomfield, CT: Kumarian Press.
Becker, G. B. (1992) 'The economic way of looking at life', *Nobel Prize Lecture*.
Becker, G. B. (1996) *Accounting for Tastes*, Cambridge, MA: Harvard University Press.
Beckert, J. (2009) 'The social order of markets', *Theory and Society*, 38(3): 245–269.
Beckert, J. (2010) 'How do fields change? The interrelations of institutions, network, and cognition in the dynamics of markets', *Organisation Studies*, 31(5): 605–627.
Bénatouïl, T. (1999) 'Critique et pragmatique en sociologie. Quelques principes de lecture', *Annales. Histoire, sciences sociales*, 54(2): 281–317.
Benzécri, J.-P. (1973) *Analyse des données*, tome 2, L'analyse des correspondances, Paris: Dunod.
Bhaskar, R. (2008) *A Realist Theory of Science*, London: Verso Books.
Binmore, K. (1990) *Essays on the Foundation of Game Theory*, Oxford: Blackwell.
Boltanski, L. (2008) *Rendre la réalité inacceptable*, Paris: Démopolis.
Boltanski, L. and Bourdieu, P. (1975a) 'Le titre et le poste. Rapports entre le système de production et le système de reproduction', *Actes de la recherche en sciences sociales*, 2: 95–107.

Boltanski, L. and Bourdieu, P. (1975b) 'Le fétichisme de la langue', *Actes de la recherche en sciences sociales*, 4: 2–32.

Boltanski, L. and Chiapello, É. (1999) *Le Nouvel Esprit du capitalisme*, Paris: Gallimard.

Bouveresse, J. (1999) *Prodiges et vertiges de l'analogie*, Paris: Raisons d'agir.

Boyer, R. (2000) 'Is a finance-led growth regime a viable alternative to Fordism? A preliminary analysis', *Economy and Society*, 29(1): 111–145.

Boyer, R. (2005) 'From shareholder value to CEO power: the paradox of the 1990s', *Competition and Change*, 9(1): 7–47.

Boyer, R. (2007) 'Assessing the impact of fair value upon financial crisis', *Socio-economic Review*, 5(4): 779–807.

Boyer, R. (2008) 'Pierre Bourdieu, a theoretician of change? The view from *Régulation* Theory', in A. Ebner and N. Beck (eds) *The Institutions of the Market: Organisations, Social Systems, and Governance*, Oxford: Oxford University Press, 348–397.

Boyer, R. (2011) *Les Financiers détruiront-ils le capitalisme?*, Paris: Economica.

Boyer, R. and Saillard, Y. (eds) (1995) *La Théorie de la régulation: l'état des savoirs*, Paris: La Découverte.

Boyer, R. and Saillard, Y. (eds) (1995) trans. C. Shread (2001) *Régulation Theory: The State of the Art*, London: Routledge.

Boyer, R., Isogai, A. and Uemora, H. (eds) (2011) *Diversity and Transformations of Asian Capitalisms: A de facto Regional Integration*, London and New York: Routledge.

Brinton, M. (1988) 'The socio-institutional bases of gender stratification: Japan as an illustrative case', *American Journal of Sociology*, 94(2): 300–334.

Burger, J., Ostrom, E., Norgaard, R. B., Policansky, D. and Goldstein, B. D. (2001) *Protecting the Commons: A Framework for Resource Management in the Americas*, Washington D.C.: Island Press.

Burt, R. (1995) 'Le capital social, les trous structuraux et l'entrepreneur', *Revue française de sociologie*, 36: 599–628.

Burt, R. (2005) *Brokerage and Closure: An Introduction to Social Capital*, Oxford: Oxford University Press.

Caillé, A. (1994) *Don, intérêt et désintéressement. Bourdieu, Mauss, Platon et quelques autres*, Paris: La Découverte-MAUSS.

Calhoun, C. (2013) 'For the social history of the present: Bourdieu as historical sociologist', in P. S. Gorski (ed.) *Bourdieu and Historical Analysis*, Durham and London: Duke University Press, 36–66.

Camerer, C. and Loewenstein, G. (2004) 'Behavioural economics: past, present, future', in C. Camerer, G. Loewenstein and M. Rabin (eds) *Advances in Behavioural Economics*, Princeton: Princeton University Press, 3–51.

Carabelli, A. (1988) *On Keynes's Method*. London: Macmillan.

Castel, R. (2007) *La Discrimination négative. Citoyens ou indigènes*, Paris: Seuil.

Champagne, P. (1993) 'Un avenir incertain', in P. Bourdieu (ed.) *La Misère du monde*, Paris: Seuil, 533–549.

Champagne, P. (2002) *Un héritage refusé. La crise de la reproduction sociale de la paysannerie française (1950–2000)*, Paris: Seuil.

Champagne, P. and Christin, O. (2004) *Mouvements d'une pensée. Pierre Bourdieu*, Paris: Bordas.

Christofferson, M. (2009) *Les Intellectuels contre la gauche. L'idéologie antitotalitaire en France (1968–1981)*, Marseille: Agone.

Christoforou, A. (2014) 'Social capital, inequality and power from a Bourdieusian

perspective' in A. Christoforou and J. B. Davis (eds) *Social Capital and Economics: Social Values, Power, and Social Identity*, London: Routledge, forthcoming.
Colander, D. and Coats, A. W. (1993) *The Spread of Economic Ideas*, Cambridge: Cambridge University Press.
Coleman, J. S. (1988) 'Social capital in the creation of human capital', *American Journal of Sociology*, 94(Supplement): S95–S120.
Collectif P.E.C.R.E.S. (2011) *Recherche précarisée, recherche atomisée. Production et transmission des savoirs à l'heure de la précarisation*, Paris: Raisons d'agir.
Colliot-Thélène, C. (2011) *La Démocratie sans demos*, Paris: PUF.
Corcuff, P. (2003) *Bourdieu autrement, fragilités d'un sociologue de combat*, Paris: Textuel.
Coulangeon, P. and Duval, J. (eds) (2013) *Trente ans après 'La Distinction'*, Paris: La Découverte.
Crossley, N. (2001) 'The phenomenological habitus and its construction', *Theory and Society*, 30(1): 81–120.
Dallery, T., Eloire, F. and Melmiès, J. (2009) 'La fixation des prix en situation d'incertitude et de concurrence: Keynes et White à la même table', *Revue française de socio-économie*, 4: 177–198.
Dardot, P. and Laval, C. (2010) *La Nouvelle raison du monde*, Paris: La Découverte.
Davidson, P. (1991) 'Is probability theory relevant for uncertainty? A post-Keynesian perspective', *Journal of Economic Perspectives*, 5: 129–143.
Davidson, P. (1996) 'Reality and economic theory', *Journal of Post Keynesian Economics*, 18(4): 479–508.
Davis, J. B. (1991) 'Keynes's critiques of Moore: philosophical foundations of Keynes's economics', *Cambridge Journal of Economics*, 15(1): 61–77.
Davis, J. B. (1994) *Keynes's Philosophical Development*, Cambridge: Cambridge University Press.
Delsaut, Y. and Rivière, M.-C. (2009) *Bibliographie des travaux de Pierre Bourdieu*, Paris: Le Temps des Cerises.
Dequech, D. (2003) 'Cognitive and cultural embeddedness: combining institutional economics and economic sociology', *Journal of Economic Issues*, 37(2): 461–470.
Dequech, D. (2006) 'The new institutional economics and the theory of behaviour under uncertainty', *Journal of Economic Behaviour and Organisation*, 59(1): 109–131.
Descartes, R. (1649; new edn 1999), *Les Passions de l'âme*, Paris: Flammarion.
Descombes, V. (1999) 'L'action', in D. Kambouchner (ed.) *Notions de philosophie*, Paris: Gallimard, 103–174.
Dewey, J. (1910) *How We Think*, Boston: Courier Dover Publications.
Dewey, J. (1930) *Human Nature and Conduct*, New York: The Modern Library.
Dobbin, F. (2004) 'Introduction: the sociology of the economy', in F. Dobbin (ed.) *The Sociology of the Economy*, New York: Russell Sage Foundation, 1–26.
Dostaler, G. (2007) *Keynes and his Struggles*, Cheltenham and London: Edward Elgar.
Durkheim, É. (1990) *Leçons de sociologie*, Paris: PUF.
Earl, P. E. (2001) 'Introduction', in P. E. Earl (ed.) *The Legacy of Herbert Simon in Economic Analysis*, Cheltenham and London: Edward Elgar, xiii–xxv.
Einhorn, H. and Hogarth, R. (1987) 'Decision making under ambiguity', in R. Hogarth and M. Reder (eds) *Rational Choice: The Contrast between Economics and Psychology*, Chicago: University of Chicago Press, 41–66.
Eloire, F. (2010) 'Une approche sociologique de la concurrence sur un marché: le cas des restaurateurs lillois', *Revue française de sociologie*, 51(3): 481–517.

Eloire, F. (2011) 'Capital social et concurrence de statut', *Revue européenne des sciences sociales*, 49(2): 7–41.

Eloire, F., Pénalva, E. and Lazega, E. (2011) 'Application de l'analyse des réseaux complets à l'échelle interorganisationnelle: apports et limites', *Terrains & Travaux*, 19: 77–98.

Engels, F. (1878; new edn 1950) *Anti-Dühring*, Paris: Éditions sociales.

Engels, F. and Marx, K. (1845/1846; new edn 2005) *L'Idéologie allemande*, Paris: Éditions sociales.

Engels, F. and Marx, K. (1864) *Lettres sur 'Le Capital'*, Paris: Éditions sociales.

Eribon, D. (2010) *Retour à Reims*, Paris: Flammarion.

Ertürk, I., Froud, J., Johal, S., Leaver, A. and Williams, K. (eds) (2008) *Financialization at Work: Key Texts and Commentary*, London: Routledge.

Fabiani, J.-L. (2010) *Qu'est-ce qu'un philosophe français? La vie sociale des concepts, 1880–1980*, Paris: EHESS.

Farmer, R. (2009) 'Confidence, crashes and the animal spirits', *NBER Working Papers*, 14846.

Farmer, R. (2010) 'Animal spirits, persistent unemployment and the belief function', *NBER Working Papers*, 16522.

Favereau, O. (2001a) 'L'économie du sociologue ou: penser (l'orthodoxie) à partir de Pierre Bourdieu', in B. Lahire (ed.) *Le Travail sociologique de Pierre Bourdieu: dettes et critiques*, Paris: La Découverte, 255–314.

Favereau, O. (2001b) 'Penser (l'orthodoxie) à partir de Bourdieu ou l'économie du sociologue', Ronéotypé Université Paris X et F.O.R.U.M. upresa-CNRS 7028, May.

Ferry, L. and Renaut, A. (1985) *La Pensée 68. Essai sur l'anti-humanisme contemporain*, Paris: Gallimard.

Fine, B. (2010) *Theories of Social Capital – Researchers Behaving Badly*, London: Pluto Press.

Fligstein, N. (1993) *The Transformation of Corporate Control*, Cambridge, MA: Harvard University Press.

Fligstein, N. (2001a) *The Architecture of Markets. An Economic Sociology of Twenty-First Century Capitalist Societies*, Princeton: Princeton University Press.

Fligstein, N. (2001b) 'Social skill and the theory of fields', *Sociological Theory*, 19(2): 105–125.

Fligstein, N. (2005) 'The political and economic sociology of international economic arrangements', in N. J. Smelser and R. Swedberg (eds) *Handbook of Economic Sociology*, Princeton: Princeton University Press, 183–204.

Fligstein, N. and Dauter, L. (2007) 'The sociology of markets', *Annual Review of Sociology*, 33: 105–128.

Fligstein, N. and McAdam, D. (2011) 'Toward a general theory of strategic action fields', *Sociological Theory*, 29(1): 1–26.

Fligstein, N. and McAdam, D. (2012) *A Theory of Fields*, Oxford: Oxford University Press.

Florian, M. and Hillebrandt, F. (2006) *Pierre Bourdieu: Neue Perspektiven für die Soziologie der Wirtschaft*, Wiesbaden: VS Verlag.

Fourcade-Gourinchas, M. (2002) 'Les économistes et leurs discours: traditions nationales et science universelle', *Sciences de la société*, 55.

Fourquet, F. (1980) *Les Comptes de la puissance*, Paris: Encres.

Fox, C. and Poldrack, R. (2009) 'Prospect theory and the brain', in P. Glimcher (ed.) *Neuroeconomics: Decision Making and the Brain*, Amsterdam: Elsevier, 145–173.

Freeman, L. (2004) *The Development of Social Network Analysis: A Study in the Sociology of Science*, North Charleston, SC: BookSurge.
Friedman, M. (1953) *Essays in Positive Economics*, Chicago: Chicago University Press.
Fuhse, J. and Mützel, S. (2010) *Relationale Soziologie: Zur kulturellen Wende der Netzwerkforschung*, Wiesbaden: VS Verlag.
Gadrey, J., Djellal, F., Gallouj, C., Jany-Catrice, F., Mériot, S.-A. and Ribault, T. (2002) *Hôtellerie-restauration: héberger et restaurer l'emploi, les cas français, américain et japonais*, Paris: La Documentation Française.
Galbraith, J. K. (1994) *A Short History of Financial Euphoria*, London: Penguin.
Gallagher, A. (ed.) (2012) *Damien Hirst*. London: Tate.
Garcia, M.-F. (1986) 'La construction sociale d'un marché parfait: le marché au cadran de Fontaines-en-Sologne', *Actes de la recherche en sciences sociales*, 65: 2–13.
Garcia-Parpet, M.-F. (2009) *Le Marché de l'excellence*, Paris: Seuil.
Gärdenfors, P. and Sahlin, P. (1982) 'Unreliable probabilities, risk taking and decision making', *Synthese*, 53(3): 361–386.
Gerrard, B. (1992) 'From a *Treatise on Probability* to the *General Theory*: continuity or change in Keynes's thought?', in J. V. Hillard and B. Gerrard (eds) *The Philosophy and Economics of J. M. Keynes*, Cheltenham and London: Edward Elgar, 80–95.
Gerrard, B. (1994) 'Beyond rational expectations: a constructive interpretation of Keynes's analysis of behaviour under uncertainty', *Economic Journal*, 104: 327–337.
Gigerenzer, G. (2001) 'The adaptive toolbox', in R. Selten and G. Gigerenzer (eds) *Bounded Rationality: The Adaptive Toolbox*, Cambridge: MIT Press, 37–50.
Gilboa, I. (1987) 'Expected utility with purely subjective non-additive probabilities', *Journal of Mathematical Economics*, 16(1): 65–88.
Gilboa, I., Postlewaite, A. and Schmeidler, D. (2008) 'Probability and uncertainty in economic modeling', *Journal of Economic Perspectives*, 22(3): 173–188.
Girard, A. (1964) 'Le choix du conjoint. Une enquête psycho-sociologique en France', Cahier no. 44 de *l'I.N.E.D.*, Paris: PUF.
Gobille, B. (2008) 'Introduction. Mai-juin 68: crise du consentement et ruptures d'allégeance', in B. Pudal, B. Gobille, F. Matonti and D. Damamme (eds) *Mai-Juin 68*, Paris: Atelier/Éd. Ouvrières, 15–31.
Godechot, O. and Mariot, N. (2004) 'Les deux formes du capital social. Structure relationnelle des jurys de thèses et recrutement en science politique', *Revue française de sociologie*, 45(2): 243–282.
Granovetter, M. (1985) 'Economic action and social structure: the problem of embeddedness', *American Journal of Sociology*, 91(3): 481–510.
Granovetter, M. (1995) *Getting a Job: A Study of Contacts and Careers*, Chicago and London: University of Chicago Press.
Granovetter, M. and Swedberg, R. (2011) *The Sociology of Economic Life*, 3rd edn, Boulder, CO: Westview Press.
Grenfell, M. (2012) *Pierre Bourdieu: Key Concepts*, Durham: Acumen.
Grenfell, M. and Hardy, C. (2003) 'Field manoeuvres: Bourdieu and the Young British Artists', *Space and Culture*, 6(1): 19–34.
Grignon, C. and Passeron, J.-C. (1989) *Le Savant et le populaire. Misérabilisme et populisme en sociologie et en littérature*, Paris: Hautes Études/Gallimard/Seuil.
Guilhot, N. (2001) 'Cyborg pancrator: international relations theory from decisionism to rational choice', *Journal of the History of Behavioural Science*, 47(3): 279–301.
Hacking, I. (1975) *The Emergence of Probabilities*, Cambridge: Cambridge University Press.

Hacking, I. (2001) *An Introduction to Probability and Inductive Logic*, Cambridge: Cambridge University Press.
Hall, P. A. and Soskice, D. (eds) (2001) *Varieties of Capitalism: The Institutional Foundations of Comparative Advantage*, Oxford: Oxford University Press.
Hanappi, D. (2011) 'Economic action, fields and uncertainty', *Journal of Economic Issues*, 45(4): 785–804.
Harvey, J. (1998) 'Heuristic judgment theory', *Journal of Economic Issues*, 32(1): 47–64.
Heilbron, J. (2006) *Naissance de la sociologie*, Marseille: Agone.
Jeanpierre, L. (2012) 'Le populisme du savoir', *Critique*, 776–777: 150–164.
Kahneman, D. (2003) 'Maps of bounded rationality: psychology for behavioural economics', *The American Economic Review*, 93(5): 1449–1475.
Kahneman, D. (2011) *Thinking, Fast and Slow*, New York: Farrar, Straus and Giroux.
Kahneman, D. and Tversky, A. (1982) 'Subjective probability: a judgment of representativeness', in D. Kahneman, P. Slovic and A. Tversky (eds) *Judgment under Uncertainty: Heuristics and Biases*, Cambridge: Cambridge University Press, 32–47.
Kahneman, D. and Tversky, A. (1992) 'Advances in prospect theory: cumulative representation of uncertainty', *Journal of Risk and Uncertainty*, 5(4): 297–323.
Karpik, L. (2007) *L'Économie des singularités*, Paris: Gallimard.
Keucheyan, R. (2012) *Guerre de mouvement et guerre de position*, Paris: La Fabrique.
Keynes, J. M. (1937) 'The general theory of employment', *Quarterly Journal of Economics*, 51(2): 203–223.
Keynes, J. M. (1973) *A Treatise on Probability*, London: Macmillan.
Keynes, J. M. (1978) *Collected Writings, X, Essays in Biography*, London: Macmillan.
Keynes, J. M. (1987a) *Collected Writings, XIII, Defense and Development*, London: Macmillan.
Keynes, J. M. (1987b) *Collected Writings, XIV, Defense and Development*, London: Macmillan.
Keynes, J. M. (1998) *La Théorie générale de l'emploi, de l'intérêt et de la monnaie*, Paris: Payot.
King, A. (2000) 'Thinking with Bourdieu against Bourdieu: a 'practical' critique of the habitus', *Sociological Theory*, 18(3): 417–433.
Laferté, G. (2002) *Folklore savant et folklore commercial: reconstruire la qualité des vins de Bourgogne. Une sociologie économique de l'image régionale dans l'entre-deux-guerres*, Thèse EHESS, December.
Lahire, B. (1998) *L'Homme pluriel*, Paris: Nathan.
Lahire, B. (2001) *La Sociologie de Pierre Bourdieu: dettes et critiques*, Paris: La Découverte.
Latour, B. (1991) *Nous n'avons jamais été modernes. Essai d'anthropologie symétrique*, Paris: La Découverte.
Latour, B. (2006) *Changer de société, refaire de la sociologie*, Paris: La Découverte.
Laval, C., Vergne, F., Clément, P. and Dreux, G. (2011) *La Nouvelle École capitaliste*, Paris: La Découverte.
Lavoie, M. (1992) *Foundations of Post-Keynesian Economic Analysis*, Cheltenham and London: Edward Elgar.
Lawson, T. (1988) 'Probability and uncertainty in economic analysis', *Journal of Post Keynesian Economics*, 11(1): 38–65.
Lawson, T. (2004) 'Keynes and convention', *Review of Social Economy*, 51(2): 174–200.
Lawson, T. (2006) 'The nature of heterodox economics', *Cambridge Journal of Economics*, 30(4): 483–505.

Lazega, E. (1998; new edn 2007) *Réseaux sociaux et structures relationnelles*, Que sais-je?, no. 3399, Paris: PUF.

Le Héron, E. (2006) 'La controverse Keynes-Tinbergen de 1939 sur l'économétrie', *Conférence du PHARE*, Université Paris 1.

Lebaron, F. (2000) *La croyance économique. Les économistes entre science et politique*, Paris: Liber/Seuil.

Lebaron, F. (2001) 'Toward a new critique of economic discourse', *Theory, Culture and Society*, 18(5): 123–129.

Lebaron, F. (2002) 'Les fondements symboliques de l'ordre économique', *Habilitation à diriger des recherches*, Université de Paris 8-Saint-Denis.

Lebaron, F. (2003) 'Economic models against economism', Special Issue on The Sociology of Symbolic Power: A Special Issue in Memory of Pierre Bourdieu, *Theory and Society*, 32(5/6): 551–565.

Lebaron, F. (2008) 'Central bankers in the contemporary field of power: a "social space" approach', *The Sociological Review*, 56(S1): 121–144.

Lebaron, F. (2010) 'How Bourdieu "quantified" Bourdieu: the geometric modelling of data', in K. Robson and C. Sanders (eds) *Quantifying Theory: Pierre Bourdieu*, New York: Springer Science+Business Media B.V. 2009, 11–30.

Lebaron, F. (2014) 'Symbolic capital', in A. C. Michalos (ed.) *Encyclopedia of Quality of Life and Well-Being Research*, New York: Springer, forthcoming.

Lenoir, R. (2004) 'Espace social et classes sociales', in L. Pinto, G. Sapiro and P. Champagne (eds) *Pierre Bourdieu, sociologue*, Paris: Fayard, 133–160.

Léonard, M. (2011) *L'Émancipation des travailleurs. Une histoire de la première internationale*, Paris: La Fabrique.

Leroux, B. and Rouanet, H. (2010) *Multiple Correspondence Analysis*, *Quantitative Applications in the Social Sciences*, London and Thousand Oaks, CA: Sage.

Lesourne, J. (1991) *Économie de l'ordre et du désordre*, Paris: Economica.

Lévi-Strauss, C. (1947; new edn 2002) *Les Structures élémentaires de la parenté*, Berlin and New York: Walter de Gruyter.

Lévi-Strauss, C. (1958) *Anthropologie structurale*, Paris: Plon.

Lin, N. (1999) 'Building a network theory of social capital', *Connections*, 22(1): 28–51.

Lin, N. (2001) *Social Capital: A Theory of Social Structure and Action*, Cambridge: Cambridge University Press.

Locke, R. and Jacoby, W. (1997) 'The dilemmas of diffusion: social embeddedness and the problems of institutional change in Eastern Germany', *Politics and Society*, 25(1): 34–65.

Loewenstein, G. and O'Donoghue, T. (2004) 'Animal spirits: affective and deliberative processes in economic behaviour', *CAE Working Paper*, #04–14.

Lojkine, J. (ed.) (2003) *Les Sociologies critiques du capitalisme. En hommage à Pierre Bourdieu*, Paris: PUF.

Lyotard, J.-F. (1979) *La Condition post-moderne: rapport sur le savoir*, Paris: Minuit.

MacFadden, D. (2000) 'Economic choices', *Nobel Prize Lecture*.

MacKenzie, D. and Millo, Y. (2003) 'Constructing a market, performing theory: the historical sociology of a financial derivatives exchange', *American Journal of Sociology*, 109(1): 107–145.

Mansuri, G. and Rao, V. (2003) 'Community-based and -driven development: a critical review', *The World Bank Research Observer*, 19(1): 1–39.

Marchionatti, R. (1999) 'On Keynes's animal spirits', *Kyklos*, 52(3): 415–439.

Martin, J. (2003) 'What is field theory?', *American Journal of Sociology*, 109(1): 1–49.

Martin-Criado, J. (2008) *Les Deux Algéries de Pierre Bourdieu*, Bellecombe-en-Bauges: Croquant.
Marx, K. (1843; new edn 1998) *Contribution à la critique de la philosophie du droit de Hegel*, Paris: Allia.
Marx, K. (1844a; new edn 1965) *Manuscrits de 1844, Œuvres*, t. 2, Paris: NRF.
Marx, K. (1844b; new edn 1968) *Ébauche d'une critique de l'économie politique, Œuvres*, t. 2, Paris: NRF.
Marx, K. (1845; new edn 1987) *Thèses sur Feuerbach*, Paris: PUF.
Marx, K. (1847; new edn 1961) *Misère de la philosophie*, Paris: Éditions sociales.
Marx, K. (1849; new edn 1965) *Travail salarié et capital, Œuvres*, t. 1, Paris: NRF.
Marx, K. (1852; new edn 1969) *Le Dix-huit Brumaire de Louis Bonaparte*, Paris: Éditions sociales.
Marx, K. (1857; new edn 1965) *Introduction générale à la critique de l'économie politique, Œuvres. Économie I*, Paris: Gallimard.
Marx, K. (1857/1858; new edn 1968) *Principes d'une critique de l'économie politique, Œuvres*, t. 2, Paris: NRF.
Marx, K. (1864/1875; new edn 1968) *Le Capital* (livre III), *Œuvres*, t. 2, Paris: NRF.
Marx, K. (1865; new edn 1965) *Salaire, prix et profit, Œuvres*, t. 1, Paris: NRF.
Marx, K. (1867a; new edn 1965) *Le Capital* (livre I), *Œuvres*, t. 1, Paris: NRF.
Marx, K. (1867b; new edn 1990) *Capital, Vol. I*, London: Penguin Books.
Marx, K. (1869/1879; new edn 1968) *Le Capital* (livre II), *Œuvres*, t. 2, Paris: NRF.
Marx, K. and Engels, F. (1848a; new edn 1965) *Manifeste du Parti communiste, Œuvres*, t. 1, Paris: NRF.
Marx, K. and Engels, F. (1848b; new edn 2002) *The Communist Manifesto*, London: Penguin Books.
Matonti, F. and Poupeau, F. (2004) 'Le capital militant. Essai de définition', *Actes de la recherche en sciences sociales*, 155: 4–11.
Mauger, G. (2012) 'Bourdieu et Marx', in F. Lebaron and G. Mauger (eds) *Lectures de Bourdieu*, Paris: Ellipses, 25–40.
Mauss, M. (1990) *The Gift*, London: Routledge.
McAdam, D. and Scott, R. (2005) 'Organisations and movements', in G. Davis, D. McAdam, R. Scott and N. Mayer (eds) *Social Movements and Organisation Theory*, Cambridge: Cambridge University Press, 4–40.
Menzies, P. and Price, H. (1993) 'Causation as a secondary quality', *British Journal for the Philosophy of Science*, 44(2): 187–203.
Meyer, J. W. and Rowan, B. (1977) 'Institutionalised organisations: formal structure as myth and ceremony', *American Journal of Sociology*, 83(2): 340–363.
Michéa, J.-C. (2007) *L'Empire du moindre mal. Essai sur la civilisation libérale*, Paris: Flammarion/Climats.
Mirowski, P. (1991) 'The when, the how, and the why of mathematical expression in the history of economic analysis', *Journal of Economic Perspectives*, 5(1): 145–157.
Mirowski, P. (2001) *Machine Dreams: Economics Become a Cyborg Science*, New York: Cambridge University Press.
Mischi, J. (2010) *Servir la classe ouvrière. Sociabilités militantes au PCF*, Rennes: PUR.
Mishkin, F. (2009) *Economics of Banking, Money and Financial Markets*, Boston: Addison Wesley.
Moggridge, D. E. (1992) 'Correspondence: the source of animal spirits', *Journal of Economic Perspectives*, 6(3): 207–212.

Montagne, S. (2006) *Les Fonds de pension: entre protection sociale et spéculation*, Paris: Odile Jacob.
Muchielli, L. (1998) *La Découverte du social. Naissance de la sociologie en France (1870–1914)*, Paris: La Découverte.
Muir, G. (2010) *Lucky Kunst: The Rise and Fall of Young British Art*, London: Aurum.
North, D. (1999) 'Orders of the day', *Reason*, 31(6): 58–59.
O'Donnell, R. (1990a) 'Keynes on mathematics: philosophical foundations and economic applications', *Cambridge Journal of Economics*, 14(1): 29–47.
O'Donnell, R. (1990b) 'The epistemology of J. M. Keynes', *British Journal for the Philosophy of Science*, 41(3): 333–350.
O'Donnell, R. (2003) 'The thick and the thin of controversy: a critique of Bateman on Keynes', in J. Runde and S. Mizuhara (eds) *The Philosophy of Keynes's Economics*, London: Routledge, 82–96.
Orléan, A. (1999) *Le Pouvoir de la finance*, Paris: Odile Jacob.
Orléan, A. (2011) *L'Empire de la valeur. Refonder l'économie*, Paris: Seuil.
Ostrom, E. (1990) *Governing the Commons: The Evolution of Institutions for Collective Action*, New York: Cambridge University Press.
Owen, G. and Dunbar, P. (2007) 'Did Damien Hirst really sell diamond skull for £50m?', *Daily Mail*, 9 September.
Paolucci, G. (2010) *Bourdieu dopo Bourdieu*, Torino: Utet.
Paolucci, G. (2011) *Introduzione a Bourdieu*, Bari-Roma: Laterza.
Passeron, J.-C. (2003) 'Mort d'un ami, disparition d'un penseur', in P. Encrevé and R.-M. Lagrave (eds) *Travailler avec Bourdieu*, Paris: Flammarion, 17–90.
Pestaña, J. L. M. (2011) 'Sobre la actualidad del *Oficio de sociólogo*', http://moreno-pestana.blogspot.com.es/2011/12/sobre-la-actualidad-del-oficio-de.html, retrieved 29 January 2014.
Pestaña, J. L. M. (2012) 'Pierre Bourdieu et Jean-Claude Passeron', in F. Lebaron and G. Mauger (eds) *Lectures de Bourdieu*, Paris: Ellipses, 353–372.
Pinto, L. (2002) *Pierre Bourdieu et la théorie du monde social*, Paris: Seuil.
Polanyi, K. (1944; new edn 2001) *The Great Transformation: The Political and Economic Origins of Our Time*, Boston: Beacon.
Polanyi, K., Arensberg, C. and Pearson, H. (1957) *Trade and Market in the Early Empires*, New York: Free Press.
Ponthieux, S. (2006) *Le Capital social*, Paris: La Découverte Repères.
Popper, K. (1989) *A World of Propensities*, Arkansas: University of Arkansas for Medical Science.
Portes, A. and Sensenbrenner, J. (1993) 'Embeddedness and immigration: notes on social determinants of economic action', *American Journal of Sociology*, 98(6): 1320–1350.
Pouch, T. (2001) *Les Économistes et le marxisme en France. Apogée et déclin d'un discours critique (1950–2000)*, Paris: Presses Universitaires de Rennes.
Poupeau, F. (2003) *Une sociologie d'État. L'école et ses experts en France*, Paris: Raisons d'agir.
Poupeau, F. (2008) *Carnets boliviens (1999–2007)*, Paris: Aux lieux d'être.
Powell, W. W. and DiMaggio, P. (eds) (1991) *The New Institutionalism in Organisational Analysis*, Chicago: University of Chicago Press.
Prigogine, I. (1997) *The End of Certainty*, New York: The Free Press.
Pudal, B. (2009) *Un monde défait. Les communistes français de 1956 à nos jours*, Bellecombe-en-Bauges: Croquant.

Putnam, R. D. (1993a) 'The prosperous community: social capital and public life', *The American Prospect*, 4(13): 35–42.
Putnam, R. D. (1993b) *Making Democracy Work: Civic Traditions in Modern Italy*, Princeton: Princeton University Press.
Quelennec, G. (2012) 'Pierre Bourdieu, à propos de Marx, Durkheim et Weber', http://pierrebourdieuunhommage.blogspot.fr/2011/12/en-ligne-pierre-bourdieu-propos-de-marx.html, retrieved 21 August 2012.
Quiggin, J. (1982) 'A theory of anticipated utility', *Journal of Economic Behaviour and Organisation*, 3(2–3): 323–343.
Rabin, M. (1998) 'Psychology and economics', *Journal of Economic Literature*, 36(1): 11–46.
Raijman, R. and Tienda, M. (2003) 'Ethnic foundations of economic transactions: Mexican and Korean immigrant entrepreneurs', *Ethnic and Racial Studies*, 26(5): 783–801.
Ramsey, F. (2003) *Logique, philosophie et probabilités*, Paris: Vrin.
Rancière, J. (1998) *Aux bords du politique*, Paris: La Fabrique.
Raynaud, P. (1980) 'Le sociologue contre le droit', *Esprit*, 3: 82–93.
Renahy, N. (2010) *Les Gars du coin. Enquête sur une jeunesse rurale*, Paris: La Découverte.
Revel, J. (2010) *Foucault, une pensée du discontinu*, Paris: Fayard.
Rimbert, P. and Crespo, S. (2004) 'Devenir syndicaliste ouvrier. "Journal" d'un délégué CGT de la métallurgie', *Actes de la recherche en sciences sociales*, 155: 34–75.
Rothbard, M. (1992) 'Keynes, the man', in M. Skousen (ed.) *Dissent on Keynes: A Critical Appraisal Keynesian Economics*, New York: Praeger, 171–198.
Royster, D. (2003) *Race and the Invisible Hand*, Berkeley: University California Press.
Sapiro, G. (2012) 'Du théoricien du social à l'intellectuel global: la réception internationale de l'œuvre de Pierre Bourdieu et ses effets en retour', in F. Lebaron and G. Mauger (eds) *Lectures de Bourdieu*, Paris: Ellipses, 373–389.
Sartre, J.-P. (1943) *L'Être et le néant*, Paris: Gallimard.
Savage, L. (1954) *The Foundations of Statistics*, New York: John Wiley and Sons.
Schmeidler, D. (1989) 'Subjective probability and expected utility without additivity', *Econometrica*, 57(3): 571–587.
Selten, R. (2001) 'What is bounded rationality?', in R. Selten and G. Gigerenzer (eds) *Bounded Rationality: The Adaptive Toolbox*, Cambridge: MIT Press, 13–36.
Shackle, G. L. (1972) *Epistemics and Economics*, Cambridge: Cambridge University Press.
Shackle, G. L. (1988) *Time, Business and Thought*, London: Routledge.
Simon, H. (1979) 'Rational decision making in business organisations', *American Economic Review*, 69(4): 493–513.
Simon, H. (1982) *Models of Man*, Cambridge: MIT Press.
Simon, H. A. and Stedry, A. C. (1969) 'Psychology and economics', in G. Lindzey and E. Aronson (eds) *The Handbook of Social Psychology*, vol. 5, Reading, MA: Addison-Wesley, 269–314.
Skidelsky, R. (2004) *Keynes: Economist, Statesman, Philosopher*, London: Macmillan.
Skinner, B. F. (1953) *Science and Human Behaviour*, New York: Macmillan.
Somers, M. and Block, F. (2005) 'Beware Trojan horses bearing social capital: how privatisation turned solidarity into a bowling team', in G. Steinmetz (ed.) *The Politics of Method in the Human Sciences: Positivism and its Epistemiological Others*, Durham, NC: Duke University Press, 233–274.

Spence, M. (1973) 'Job market signaling', *The Quarterly Journal of Economics*, 87(3): 355–374.

Spinoza, B. de (1994) *L'Éthique*, Paris: Folio.

Spire, A. (2011) 'La domestication de l'impôt par les classes dominantes', *Actes de la recherche en sciences sociales*, 190: 58–71.

Steiner, P. (2000) 'Marx et la sociologie économique', *Cahiers internationaux de sociologie*, 108: 57–77.

Steiner, P. (2005) *L'École durkheimienne et l'économie*, Genève: Droz.

Stiglitz, J. (1987) 'The causes and the consequences of the dependence of quality on price', *Journal of Economic Literature*, 25: 1–48.

Strange, S. (1994) *States and Markets*, London: Pinter.

Svendsen, G. L. H. and Svendsen, G. T. (2003) 'On the wealth of nations: Bourdieuconomics and social capital', Special Issue on The Sociology of Symbolic Power: A Special Issue in Memory of Pierre Bourdieu, *Theory and Society*, 32(5/6): 607–631.

Svendsen, G. T. and Svendsen, G. L. H. (2009) *Handbook of Social Capital: The Troika of Sociology, Political Science and Economics*, Cheltenham and London: Edward Elgar Publishing.

Swartz, D. L. and Zolberg, V. L. (2005) *After Bourdieu: Influence, Critique, Elaboration*, Dordrecht, The Netherlands: Kluwer Academic Publishers.

Temmar, M., Angermuller, J. and Lebaron, F. (eds) (2013) *Les Discours sur l'économie*, Paris: PUF.

Thaler, R. (2004) 'How behavioural economics differs from traditional economics', *The Concise Encyclopedia of Economics*, www.econlib.org/library/enc/behavioraleconomics.html.

Uzzi, B. (1996) 'The sources and consequences of embeddedness for the economic performance of organisations: the network effect', *American Sociological Review*, 61(4): 674–698.

Uzzi, B. (1997) 'Social structure and competition in interfirm networks: the paradox of embeddedness', *Administrative Science Quarterly*, 42(1): 35–67.

Vandenberghe, F. (1999) 'The real is relational: an epistemological analysis of Pierre Bourdieu's generative structuralism', *Sociological Theory*, 17(1): 32–67.

Veblen, T. (1898) 'The instinct of workmanship and the irksome of labour', *American Journal of Sociology*, 4(2): 187–201.

Von Neumann, J. and Morgenstern, O. (1944) *Theory of Games and Economic Behaviour*, Princeton: Princeton University Press.

Wacquant, L. J. D. (1989) 'Towards a reflexive sociology: a workshop with Pierre Bourdieu', *Sociological Theory*, 7(1): 26–63.

Wacquant, L. J. D. (1993) 'From ideology to symbolic violence: culture, class and consciousness in Marx and Bourdieu', *International Journal of Contemporary Sociology*, 30(2): 125–142.

Wacquant, L. J. D. (1993) trans. (2002) 'De l'idéologie à la violence symbolique: culture, classe et conscience chez Marx et Bourdieu', in J. Lojkine (ed.) *Les Sociologies critiques du capitalisme*, Paris: PUF, 25–40.

Wacquant, L. J. D. (1996) 'Notes tardives sur le "marxisme" de Bourdieu', *Actuel Marx*, 20: 83–90.

Wacquant, L. J. D. (1996) trans. (2001) 'Further notes on Bourdieu's "Marxism"', *International Journal of Contemporary Sociology*, 38(1): 103–109.

Wacquant, L. J. D. (2004) 'Following Pierre Bourdieu into the field', *Ethnography*, 5(4): 387–414.

Wacquant, L. J. D. (2006) 'Pierre Bourdieu', in R. Stones (ed.) *Key Contemporary Thinkers*, London and New York: Macmillan, 261–277.

Walras, L. (1988) *Éléments d'économie politique pure*, Paris: Economica.

Wasserman, S. and Faust, K. (1994) *Social Network Analysis: Methods and Applications, Structural Analysis in the Social Sciences*, Cambridge: Cambridge University Press.

Watson, J. B. (1924) *Behaviourism*, New York: People's Institute.

White, H. (2002) *From Network to Market*, Princeton: Princeton University Press.

Widick, R. (2005) 'Flesh and the free market', in D. L. Swartz and V. L. Zolberg (eds) *After Bourdieu: Influence, Critique, Elaboration*, Dordrecht, The Netherlands: Kluwer Academic Publishers, 193–237.

Yaari, M. (1987) 'The dual theory of choice under risk', *Econometrica*, 55(1): 95–115.

Zelizer, V. (1979) 'Human values and the market: the case of life insurance and death in 19th century America', *American Journal of Sociology*, 84(3): 591–610.

Index

Page numbers in *italics* denote tables, those in **bold** denote figures.